T H U ...

B O ...

WITH AN INTRODUCTION
AND COMMENTARY BY

K. J. DOVER

Professor of Greek
in the University of
St. Andrews

OXFORD
OXFORD UNIVERSITY PRESS

Oxford University Press, Walton Street, Oxford OX2 6DP

Oxford New York Toronto
Delhi Bombay Calcutta Madras Karachi
Petaling Jaya Singapore Hong Kong Tokyo
Nairobi Dar es Salaam Cape Town
Melbourne Auckland

and associated companies in
Berlin Ibadan

Oxford is a trade mark of Oxford University Press

Published in the United States
by Oxford University Press, New York

© Oxford University Press 1965

First published 1965
Reprinted 1971, 1980, 1985, 1989

ISBN 0 19 831832 4

Printed in Great Britain by
Antony Rowe Ltd,
Chippenham

PREFACE

THE purpose of this book is to help senior pupils in schools and students in universities to read, understand, and enjoy Book VI of Thucydides.

The Greek text and apparatus criticus are the Oxford Classical Text reproduced without change. In the Commentary I have discussed textual problems only where I believe this text to be questionable or demonstrably wrong.

The Introduction offers the reader, as concisely as possible, the information which he should have before he embarks on Book VI.

The Commentary is designed (i) to help the reader to translate the text fully and correctly, with the assistance of standard lexica and grammars; (ii) to draw his attention to those features of language, style, and technique which are characteristic of Thucydides; (iii) to make explicit what Thucydides takes for granted; (iv) to offer grounds on which we may decide whether his historical statements are true or false; and (v) to comment on historically interesting aspects of the events which he describes.

References to other Greek texts have been reduced to a minimum, reference to modern books, articles, and editions is wholly excluded, views which I believe wrong are passed over in silence, and I seldom indicate that more than one answer to a question has been offered unless I feel some doubt about the rightness of the answer which I have adopted. For discussion of the arguments on both sides of the questions treated summarily and dogmatically in this volume the reader may refer to the commentary on Book VI which I am contributing to the completion of the *Historical Commentary on Thucydides* which the late Professor A. W. Gomme left unfinished.

I have tried to put into practice two beliefs about the study and teaching of Greek. First, although I have no sympathy or respect for the currently fashionable view that Classical scholars should spend more time in entertaining the public and less in trying to discover what the Greek authors actually said, I do not believe that the learner should be asked to pass judgement on variant or suspect readings except where the difference of reading really matters; there, he should. Secondly, although I do not believe that any worth-while contribution to Greek studies is ever likely to be made by anyone who does not know the Greek language well, I also do not believe that the learner, however young and inexperienced, should be compelled to confine his attention to matters of grammar and forbidden to dabble in such intrinsically interesting problems as the stratification of Thucydides' work or the sources of the material in his digressions.

Anyone who believes that Thucydides was omniscient, dispassionate, and infinitely wise, and that there is nothing to be said on the other side of any question on which Thucydides has made a pronouncement, may find some of my comments irreverent and cynical. I offer no apology.

I am glad to acknowledge a great debt to two friends, neither of whom should be blamed for the consequences of my occasional refusal to take their advice. Professor Andrewes, my collaborator in the completion of Gomme's *Commentary*, patiently rescued me from superficiality on many occasions and taught me that I did not know half as well as I thought I did what kind of questions one should ask in the study of Thucydides. Mr. J. A. L. Hamilton scrutinized every word of the first draft of this volume; from his experience as a teacher he made me see what a young student of Thucydides needs to be told, and his criticisms on points of substance made me change much with which I had been satisfied too soon.

K. J. D.

University of St. Andrews
May 1964

CONTENTS

ABBREVIATIONS

(i) In the apparatus criticus:

See Introduction III (A) for the *sigla codicum*.

Π^7	Oxyrynchus Papyrus 453.
A^I, B^I, etc.	Correction by the first hand.
a, b, etc.	Correction by a later hand.
[A], [B], etc.	Reading illegible.
$\langle G \rangle$	Reading of G illegible but inferred from descendants.
codd.	Consensus of the manuscripts ABCEFGM. (See Introduction III *ad fin.* on the presence of G in this group and absence of H from it.)
recc.	One or more of the manuscripts descended from one or other of ABCEFGM.
m. I	First hand.
γρ.	Variant prefaced by γρ(άφεται).

(ii) In the Introduction and Commentary:

GHI	M. N. Tod, *Greek Historical Inscriptions*, vol. i (Oxford, ed. 2, (1946).
IG	*Inscriptiones Graecae.*
LSJ	Liddell and Scott, *A Greek–English Lexicon,* revised by Sir Henry Stuart Jones and R. McKenzie (Oxford, 1940).
SEG	*Supplementum Epigraphicum Graecum.*
Σ^M	The scholia in the manuscript M.

Names of Greek authors and their works are abbreviated as in LSJ, except:

Diod.	('D.S.' in LSJ)	Diodoros.
Dion. Hal.	('D.H.' in LSJ)	Dionysios of Halikarnassos.

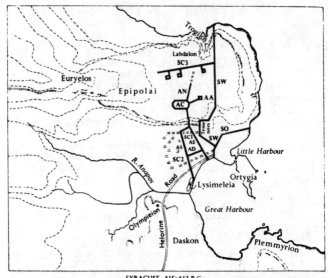

SYRACUSE 415-413 B.C.

------ Contours at intervals of 25 metres   ‿‿‿‿‿ Precipitous ground   ⏶ ⏶ ⏵ Marsh

Note:- The lower reaches of the river were probably not as straight as shown above.

AA Athenian advanced fortification (vi 102)	SC1 First Syracusan Counterwall (vi 99)
AC Athenian Circle (vi 98)	SC2 Second Syracusan Counterwall (vi 101)
AD Athenian Crosswall (vii 60)	SC3 Third Syracusan Counterwall (vii 4,6)
AN Athenian Northern Wall (vi 99)	SO City Wall of Syracuse
AS Athenian Southern Walls (vi 103, vii 2)	SW Syracusan Wall, winter 415/4 (vi 75)

INTRODUCTION

I. THUCYDIDES

1. *Life*

NEARLY all that we know about the life of Thucydides he
tells us himself. He was an Athenian (i. 1. 1) and the son of
a certain Oloros (iv. 104. 4); he owned the working rights of
some gold mines on the Aegean coast of Thrace, and he was
influential with the Thracians in that area (iv. 105. 1). He
began work on a history of the Peloponnesian War when it
broke out in 431 (i. 1. 1). He was elected one of the ten
Athenian generals for 424/3, and during that winter commanded a small force of ships at Thasos (iv. 104. 4), at a time
when the quick and energetic Spartan commander Brasidas
was operating with a Peloponnesian force on the mainland.
Thucydides failed to save Amphipolis for Athens, though he
was just in time to occupy the neighbouring town of Eion
and hold it against Brasidas (iv. 105. 1, 106. 3 f.). Because of
his failure at Amphipolis, he became an exile (v. 26. 5); that
is to say, like other Athenian generals in similar circumstances, he went into exile to avoid what he believed would
be a worse fate if he returned to Athens, and was condemned to death in his absence. He was in exile for twenty
years (v. 26. 5); he returned, therefore, in 404, after the war
had been lost and all the exiles were recalled in accordance
with the terms of peace imposed by Sparta. Some part, at
least, of his twenty years of exile was spent on the Peloponnesian side (v. 26. 5); we do not know where, or whether he
also spent some time in regions which were not involved in
the war. Although he makes some passing references to the
end of the war and its total duration (ii. 65. 2, v. 26. 1), he
did not complete his history; Book VIII breaks off abruptly

in the middle of the events of the autumn of 411, and the story of the war was completed by later historians.

The *Life of Thucydides* which precedes the text of Thucydides in some manuscripts is the work of a commentator of late Roman times, but incorporates the observations of earlier scholars. It adds a little factual information to what has been stated above: that Thucydides' mother was named Hegesipyle (§ 2), that his grave existed at Athens (§§ 16, 31), and that the inscription on the grave showed that he belonged to the deme Halimous (§ 16). The rest is speculation, but much of it is intelligent and probably correct. Given his parents' names, it is certainly likely that he was related to Kimon (§§ 2–17), the great rival of Perikles in the 460's, for Kimon's father Miltiades had married the daughter, Hegesipyle by name, of a Thracian prince called Oloros (Hdt. vi. 40); moreover, when Kimon was dead the opposition to Perikles in the 440's was led by a kinsman of Kimon who bore the name Thucydides (son of Melesias). Again, the *Life* (§ 46) is probably right in saying that it was Kleon who brought the charge against Thucydides for his failure at Amphipolis. In 424/3 Kleon was at the height of his influence, and there are reasons for thinking that he personally prosecuted another general whose achievements had fallen short of expectations; and Thucydides shows a pronounced malice against Kleon (iii. 36. 6, iv. 27 f.).

The notion, still to be found in works of reference, that Thucydides was born in 471 originated in the first century A.D. and was based on the common 'working hypothesis' that a man is born forty years before the decisive action or the most important event of his life—in Thucydides' case, the outbreak of the war and his decision to write a history of it. When he died, we do not know. It is arguable that what he says of Archelaos of Macedon in ii. 100. 2—'Archelaos did more to equip Macedon for war than all the eight kings before him'—was written after the death of Archelaos in 399; and it is obvious that Lysias in §§ 48–52 of his *Epitaphios*, composed in 392, is using Book I of Thucydides; but there is no further evidence. The *Life* (§§ 31–33) tells us that some scholars believed that Thucydides died in Thrace and that his grave at Athens was a cenotaph.

Note. The second, and briefer, *Life* found in some manuscripts adds nothing of importance about the historian and confuses him with Perikles' adversary, Thucydides the son of Melesias.

2. *Character of Thucydides' Work*

Book I is devoted to the causes and antecedents of the war; the narrative of the war itself begins with Book II. Thucydides organizes his material annalistically, taking each year of the war in turn; his year runs from spring to spring, and is divided into two halves, 'summer' (θέρος) and 'winter' (χειμών). He deals with all the events of each half-year, whether or not they were related to one another, before passing on to the next half-year.

In discussing the difficulty of his task (i. 22. 1 f.) he makes a distinction between what was said (ὅσα μὲν λόγῳ εἶπον ἕκαστοι) and what was done (τὰ δ' ἔργα τῶν πραχθέντων), and he clearly attaches great importance to the former. It is natural that he should, since in the Greek world, and especially in democratic states, final decisions were taken by assemblies under the immediate impact of persuasive oratory, and the speeches made to troops before a battle had an effect for good or ill on their morale and therefore on the outcome of the battle. Thucydides thus presents us with the speeches delivered by politicians, generals, or ambassadors on various critical occasions. The language and style of these speeches are uniform and idiosyncratic, and therefore his own; and there are a few occasions on which we wonder whether the speaker was so casually, yet accurately, far-sighted as he is represented as being. Yet the hypothesis that the Thucydidean speeches are pure fiction, bearing no relation, except by accident, to what was actually said is irreconcilable with the principle which he enunciates in i. 22. 1: 'It was difficult for me to recall precisely what was said in the speeches which I heard myself, and difficult for my informants from elsewhere; but I have represented each speaker as presenting, on a given issue, the case which I thought him most likely to have presented, while keeping as close as I could to the argument, as a whole, of what was actually said.' There is no reason to suppose that Thucydides was equally well informed about all the occasions on which important speeches were made; and it is not safe to assume that he was equally tenacious of the principle of i. 22. 1 at all stages of his work. What is quite certain is that a Thucydidean speech is a skilful and psychologically realistic representation of a man trying to persuade his hearers and, when necessary, to deceive them; statements which occur in the course of speeches should not be accepted as true unless they are supported by other evidence.

One of the most striking features of the speeches is the excessive use of argument from generalizations to particular cases. This type of argument is conspicuous also in the forensic speeches of Thucydides' older contemporary, the orator Antiphon, and it was no doubt characteristic of late-fifth-century Athens. It is fully in accord with what Thucydides says (i. 22. 4) of the purpose of history: that it should be 'useful to those who want to know exactly what happened and what is likely, given human nature, to happen in the future in identical or similar form'. Thucydides' fulfilment of this purpose is fortunately not obtrusive, for he possessed a capacity for being interested in his material for its own sake and a talent for powerful and vivid writing. He rarely speculates or criticizes, and his own generalizations, though sometimes exaggerated or one-sided, are never banal and always reflect a determination to penetrate beyond the surface of things. Throughout his narrative he cultivates an objectivity which perhaps did not come easily to him; it makes his occasional moral judgements and expressions of strong emotion all the more impressive. Like all historians, he was necessarily selective, and it is here that the influence of his own standpoint and his conception of the purpose of history is clearest. The thoughts, feelings, and motives which he regarded as deciding the issue of a debate or a battle were important to him; topography, military technique, logistics, finance, and administration were less important, and when we put to him the questions which historical imagination and curiosity prompt in the modern reader we often find him vague, inadequate, or simply silent. Sometimes this is because he was writing for Greeks, and did not tell them what they knew already—how a trireme was organized, for example—but this excuse cannot be made to cover all the obscurities and inadequacies in his account of the sequence of events at Syracuse in 415–413.

Neither Thucydides nor any other historian gives us, or can give us, directly and immediately, 'the facts' of what the Greeks did and thought and felt in the Peloponnesian War. He gives us his picture of the facts, and our business as students of the Greek world is not to treat him as the Recording Angel but to get to know him, as intimately as possible, as the painter of a picture. We are not wholly deprived of independent lines of approach to the reality beyond the painter.

3. *Language and Style*

The characteristics of Thucydides' language and style, by contrast with the norms of Attic prose, are:

1. He uses -ρσ-, -σσ-, and ἤν < εἰ + ἄν, not -ρρ-, -ττ-, and ἐάν. These features he shares with Ionic, Xenophon, and some early Attic prose, but they do not appear in Attic inscriptions.

2. He always uses ξύν, not σύν, both as an independent word and in compounds. Both forms are found in fifth-century Attic inscriptions.

3. A profusion of abstract nouns (the formative -σις is especially favoured). This may owe something to the influence of early philosophical writers. Examples are: 16. 5 οἶδα δὲ τοὺς τοιούτους, καὶ ὅσοι ἔν τινος λαμπρότητι πρόεσχον . . . προσποίησίν τε ξυγγενείας τισί . . . καταλιπόντας, καὶ ἧς ἂν ὦσι πατρίδος, ταύτῃ αὔχησιν; 17. 2 ῥᾳδίας ἔχουσι τῶν πολιτῶν τὰς μεταβολὰς καὶ ἐπιδοχάς. αὔχησις and ἐπιδοχή are not attested elsewhere in Attic prose.

4. Considerable use of adjectives in -τος, e.g. 77. 2 ταύτῃ μόνον ἁλωτοί ἐσμεν, 'in this way alone can we be overcome'; 105. 2 εὐπροφάσιστον . . . τὴν αἰτίαν . . . ἐποίησαν, 'made the charge plausible'.

5. Prepositional compound verbs are formed very readily, and many of them recur seldom or never in extant Classical prose, e.g. 13. 1 ἀντιπαρακελεύομαι, 21. 2 ἐπιμεταπέμπεσθαι, 34. 7 προεπιχειροῦντας.

6. Many other compound verbs, e.g. 17. 2 πολυανδροῦσι = 'have big populations'; 18. 2 φυλοκρινοῖεν, 'draw distinctions of race'; 34. 5 τῷ ταχυναυτοῦντι, a technical term which recurs in the late fourth century.

7. Qualification of nouns by adverbs or phrases, e.g. 80. 5 τὴν αὐτίκα ἀκινδύνως δουλείαν, 'immediate subjection without risk'; 76. 4 περί . . . σφίσιν ἀλλὰ μὴ ἐκείνῳ καταδουλώσεως, 'on the issue of enslavement by the Athenians and not by the Persian King'.

8. Substantives formed by the neuter article with an adjective may be qualified, e.g. 11. 6 τὸ σφέτερον ἀπρεπές, 'their own dishonour'; 16. 2 τῷ ἐμῷ διαπρεπεῖ τῆς Ὀλυμπίαζε θεωρίας, 'the splendour of my attendance at the Olympic Games'.

9. Substantives formed with the neuter article often require for adequate translation an English abstract noun, e.g. 12. 2 τὸ ἑαυτοῦ, 'his own interest'; 34. 5 τὰ τῶν πόλεων, 'the attitude of the cities'. Sometimes correct translation is impossible without careful reference to the context, e.g. 28. 2 τὰ μυστικά, 'the offences against the mysteries'.

10. The reference of demonstratives is often obscure unless attention is paid to the argument, e.g. 11. 3 ἐκείνως, 'if Syracuse ruled Sicily'; 23. 1 τῶν μὲν κρατεῖν τὰ δὲ καὶ διασῶσαι, 'to conquer our objectives and bring our own forces safely home'; 30. 2 τὰ μέν . . . τοὺς δέ, 'their objective . . . their menfolk'.

11. The unemphatic anaphoric pronoun αὐτόν often comes close after the first word of a clause (cf. καί μιν, ὁ δέ σφι, &c., in Herodotos), e.g. 44. 3 ὡς αὐτοὺς ἔσω οὐκ ἐδέχοντο, 'as they did not welcome them into the city'; 56. 2 καὶ αὐτοῖς τὰ μὲν ἄλλα . . . ἐπέπρακτο, 'and they had seen to everything else'.

12. The neuter plural αὐτά is sometimes used, like English 'it' or 'all that', with very vague reference, e.g. 10. 2 οὕτω γάρ . . . ἔπραξαν αὐτά, 'that is the effect of their actions'; 10. 5 χρὴ σκοπεῖν τινὰ αὐτά, 'one must consider'.

13. The pronoun σφεῖς is normally used in subordinate clauses or word-groups to refer to the subject of the main clause, e.g. 6. 2 τὴν . . . ξυμμαχίαν ἀναμιμνήσκοντες τοὺς Ἀθηναίους ἐδέοντο σφίσι ναῦς πέμψαντας ἐπαμῦναι, 'reminding the Athenians of the alliance . . . they' (the Segestans) 'asked (sc. the Athenians) to send a fleet and help them' (the Segestans).

The reflexive σφᾶς αὐτούς = ἑαυτούς; the possessive adjective of both σφεῖς and σφᾶς αὐτούς is σφέτερος, and in the latter sense it may be reinforced (like ἡμέτερος and ὑμέτερος) by αὐτῶν.

14. The infinitive alone is sometimes used in cases where a fourth-century author would use an infinitive with ὥστε or even a final or final relative clause, e.g. 80. 2 τοῖς μὲν οὐκ ἠμύνατε σωθῆναι, 'you have not protected them so that they were kept safe'.

15. In the co-ordination of clauses:

(a) The co-ordinating particle in the first clause is often placed later than we would logically expect, e.g. 77. 1 παραδείγματα τῶν τ᾽ ἐκεῖ Ἑλλήνων . . . καὶ νῦν ἐφ᾽ ἡμᾶς ταὐτὰ

παρόντα σοφίσματα, 'examples furnished by the Greeks of
the Aegean and now the same tricks being used here against
us'. Many such examples have been emended by editors,
wrongly.

(b) In a μέν / δέ co-ordination the element introduced by δέ
is sometimes a different type of clause from the μέν element,
e.g. 72. 4 ἐπιδώσειν γὰρ ἀμφότερα αὐτά, τὴν μὲν μετὰ κινδύνων
μελετωμένην, τὴν δ᾿ εὐψυχίαν . . . θαρσαλεωτέραν ἔσεσθαι, 'both
of them' (discipline and courage) 'would improve, the one'
(discipline) 'by being practised in the presence of danger,
while their courage . . . would gain in confidence'; one might
have expected γιγνομένην in place of ἔσεσθαι.

16. Subordinate clauses which refer to the contents of
statements, thoughts, or feelings commonly lack introduc-
tory words corresponding to the English 'to decide', 'wondering', or 'saying', e.g. 9. 1 ἡ μὲν ἐκκλησία . . . ἥδε ξυνελέγη,
καθ᾿ ὅτι χρή . . . ἐκπλεῖν, 'this assembly has been convened *to
decide on* the details of the expedition'; 30. 2 μετ᾿ ἐλπίδος τε
. . . καὶ ὀλοφυρμῶν, τὰ μὲν ὡς κτήσοιντο, τοὺς δ᾿ εἴ ποτε
ὄψοιντο, 'with expectation and lamentation, *for they believed*
that they would conquer their objectives but *wondered* if
they would ever see their menfolk again'.

17. Thucydides dislikes uniformity of vocabulary or structure, and his avoidance of it is sometimes strained, e.g. 17. 3
ἢ ἐκ τοῦ λέγων πείθειν . . . ἢ στασιάζων, 75. 4 ἐκ μὲν Συρακουσῶν
Ἑρμοκράτους καὶ ἄλλων . . . ἀπὸ δὲ τῶν Ἀθηναίων Εὐφήμου
μεθ᾿ ἑτέρων.

18. Economy of expression sometimes requires us to
understand one form of a verb from another, e.g. 79. 1 ὅταν
ὑπ᾿ ἄλλων καὶ μὴ αὐτοί . . . τοὺς πέλας ἀδικῶσιν, 'when *they
are wronged* by others and are not themselves wronging their
neighbours'; 88. 5 τοὺς μὲν προσηνάγκαζον, τοὺς δὲ καὶ ὑπὸ
τῶν Συρακοσίων . . . ἀπεκωλύοντο, 'they brought some over
by force, but were prevented *from doing this* to others by
the Syracusans'.

19. The nominative case is sometimes used in conformity

with sense but in defiance of grammatical structure, e.g.
24. 3 τοῖς δ' ἐν τῇ ἡλικίᾳ (sc. ἔρως ἐνέπεσεν ἐκπλεῦσαι) τῆς τε
ἀπούσης πόθῳ ὄψεως . . . καὶ εὐέλπιδες ὄντες σωθήσεσθαι, 'and
(sc. desire for the expedition fell upon) those of military age
through a desire to see what was far away and because they
were confident that they would come through safely'.

Where Thucydides differs linguistically from Plato and
the fourth-century orators his affinities are sometimes with
Ionic prose, especially with the fragments of the fifth-
century philosophers, and with the orator Antiphon (who
died in 411). In some respects, however, he stands alone, and
it is reasonable to suppose that he made syntactical experi-
ments, in the interests of economy of expression and variety
of form, which did not commend themselves to later authors;
Dionysios of Halikarnassos, to whom all the Classical prose
literature now lost was available, regarded him as highly
idiosyncratic and sometimes perversely obscure.

The inadequacy of our evidence for the language of
Thucydides' contemporaries—so little written in prose by
Athenians before 400 survives—leaves us uncertain how far
words which we find in him and in poetry, but not in fourth-
century prose, really were at the time recognizably 'poetic',
how far he coined words, or how far he differed from his
contemporaries in doing so. One point which can be made,
however, is that he was largely immune to the very great
influence which the rhetorician Gorgias exercised on prose
literature in the last quarter of the fifth century and the beginning of the fourth. Gorgias made great use of assonance,
and the symmetry of his sentences was simple and obvious;
Thucydides' assonances are conspicuous and memorable
precisely because they are rare, and his love of variation
ensures an asymmetry of form which often actually con-
ceals an underlying symmetrical and antithetical sequence
of thought. It must have been easy to listen to Gorgias as to
an incantation, a kind of verbal music; Thucydides, on the

other hand, gives us the impression that he does not want us to be distracted by the form of what he says from attending to its content. Since he often tries to say too much in too few words, the reading of him demands an unusual degree of concentration.

4. *Books VI and VII*

The division of Thucydides' work into eight books is one of two (possibly three) alternative divisions which were current in the ancient world, and there is no reason to believe that it corresponds to any division which Thucydides himself envisaged. It is unlikely that he intended any kind of break between Book VI and Book VII, still less between Book VII and the first chapter of Book VIII. Between Book V and Book VI a natural break is imposed by the subject-matter itself, but the opening words of Book VI, 'during the same winter . . .', presuppose our acquaintance with the last part of Book V.

Since Thucydides began to work on a history of the war when it broke out, and yet wrote some of this history in its present form (cf. § 1 *supra*) after the end of the war and left the work incomplete, we cannot help wondering whether he wrote it as we have it, from the first chapter of Book I straight through to the last chapter of Book VIII, after the whole war was over, or linked together portions written at widely different dates and revised them with varying degrees of completeness. Curiosity on this score is increased by the fact that Book VIII differs so markedly from the remainder in the treatment and presentation of its material that it is commonly agreed to be 'unrevised', and by the presence in the earlier books of statements which were falsified later in the war, e.g. the mention in ii. 23. 3 of a territory 'which is inhabited by the Oropians, subjects of Athens', although the Oropians ceased to be subjects of Athens early in 411. The solutions offered to problems of this kind are seldom cogent and always disputed, but that does not mean that the difficulties which they are intended to solve are imaginary. The realistic hypothesis is that Thucydides did compose accounts of some portions of the war before its end and that he revised these accounts in many particulars; if we could ask his ghost which parts of his work had received their final revision, he would answer, I suspect, that no part of it would have received a *final* revision, no matter how long he had lived.

No view of the date of composition of Books VI and VII commands universal assent, but the most important considerations are:

(i) vi. 15. 3 f. refer plainly (in the present editor's view) to the end of the war. The favourable judgement which Thucydides there passes on Alkibiades as strategist accords exactly with the judgement implied in ii. 65. 6 f.—a passage in which he surveys the entire course of the war from the death of Perikles down to the final defeat of Athens—but is out of keeping with the narrative of Books VI and VII as a whole, where many readers feel that Alkibiades does not come up to the expectations which the high praise of him in vi. 15. 4 has engendered. Assessment of this discrepancy, however, is not simple.

(ii) The digression in vii. 27–28 on the effect of the Spartan occupation of Dekeleia is ill suited to its immediate context, obscure in argument, and repetitious in expression. Here at least we can feel some confidence in saying that further revision would have changed the whole passage for the better and probably moved it to Book VIII.

(iii) Nothing is said in Book VII about the worsening relations between Athens and Persia, which take us by surprise in viii. 5. 4 f.—a striking omission in an author who in the earlier books adheres to the principle of 'tidying up' all the events of one half-year before going on to the next.

(iv) The words 'the only large-scale night battle in this war' in vii. 44. 1 could possibly be held to imply 'so far' but more naturally imply that the war was over when they were written; cf. 'the greatest achievement in this war' (vii. 87. 5).

(v) Certain references (vi. 62. 2 and vii. 58. 2) to Himera, which was totally destroyed in 409, and to the temporary Athenian occupation of Aigina (vii. 57. 2) and Pylos (vii. 57. 8), admit of more than one interpretation and cannot be treated as decisive.

It is a reasonable hypothesis that the first draft of Books VI and VII was composed fairly soon after 413, perhaps as early as 411, and was continuously, but never systematically, revised and augmented during the following eight or nine years.

II. ATHENS AND SYRACUSE

1. *Down to 431*

The Peloponnesian War was the climax of an antagonism between the two states which emerged from the Persian War with the highest prestige and the greatest power: Sparta, which had headed the whole alliance of the Greek states against Xerxes and retained the leadership of an alliance including the greater part of the Peloponnese, and Athens, which had become the leader of the insular and coastal states of the Aegean immediately after the Persian War and turned these states from allies into subjects.

In the West, the Greeks of Sicily defeated a Carthaginian invasion in the same year as the Greeks of Greece defeated Xerxes. In Sicily, however, there was only one pre-eminent state: Syracuse, which under the tyrant Gelon earned the credit for the defeat of the Carthaginians and under his brother and successor Hieron won a resounding naval victory over the Etruscans. The tyranny ended in 466/5, and Syracuse became a democracy; which it still was fifty years later, at the time of the Athenian attack.

During the thirty years before the outbreak of the Peloponnesian War Athens was not indifferent to the West.

We know that she made an alliance with Segesta in 458/7, with Halikyai in the 430's, and renewed alliances with Leontinoi and Rhegion in 433/2 (when these last two alliances were first made, we do not know); she founded Thurioi, in South Italy, in 446/5, and we have a few other disconnected items of information, of varying reliability, on minor Athenian interventions in the West. What is obscure is the extent to which the alliances represented serious and consistent policy and the end towards which they were directed. When Thucydides describes (ii. 7) the preparations for war made by Sparta and Athens in the spring of 431, he does not suggest that Athens troubled to communicate in any way with any state in the West. The Spartans, on the other hand, asked 'their supporters' in Italy and Sicily for money and ships; but it does not appear from his narrative of subsequent years that these supporters —they included Syracuse, Gela and Selinus, as is clear from iii. 86. 2—responded to the request. Racial sympathies and antipathies, to which we find frequent reference in Thucydides, played a part in determining the alignment of states in East and West alike. Most of the states over which Sparta exercised the strongest control were, like Sparta herself, Dorian, while the majority of the states in the Athenian empire were, like Athens, Ionian. Similarly, Syracuse and her closest friends, Selinus and Gela, were Dorian, while Leontinoi and her most consistent friends were Ionian.

2. 427–422

Leontinoi invoked her alliance with Athens in 427; she was now at war with Syracuse; Naxos, Katane, Kamarina, and Rhegion were on her side, Selinus, Gela, and Lokroi on the side of Syracuse. The Athenians responded by sending twenty ships, which they reinforced with another forty at the beginning of 425. These reinforcements did not arrive in the West until the autumn, and they took part in no major operations, for the effect of their arrival was to make the

Sicilian states compose their differences. Envoys from all the states met at Gela in the spring of 424; Thucydides represents Hermokrates of Syracuse, of whom we hear so much in Books VI and VII, as the forceful proponent of Sicilian unity in the face of Athenian interference. The Athenians' disappointment was reflected in their punishment of their generals.

The unity achieved at Gela did not last long. Internal conflict broke out in Leontinoi, and the upper class (Thucydides v. 4. 3 calls them οἱ δυνατοί) invoked the help of Syracuse; in consequence, the lower class was expelled and dispersed, and the upper class became citizens of Syracuse. Some of them, however, soon left Syracuse and made common cause with the remnant of the lower class, continuing in a state of war against Syracuse from a base in what had been the territory of Leontinoi. In this situation, Athens in the summer of 422 sent a roving embassy, which included the persuasive Phaiax, to enlist help in the West for Leontinoi against Syracuse. This embassy met with a favourable response in Kamarina and Akragas, but not elsewhere.

3. 415

Thucydides mentions no dealings of any kind between Athens and any state in the West in the period 421–417. Then, in the winter of 416/15, Segesta sought Athenian help against Selinus and at the same time revived the claims of the survivors of Leontinoi. Thucydides clearly implies (1. 1 ∼ 6. 1 f.) that this plea did not create, but merely reinforced, an Athenian ambition to secure control of Sicily. There were good reasons why such an ambition should emerge in 416. The first phase of the Peloponnesian War, ending with the Peace of Nikias in 421, had demonstrated that the damage which Sparta and Athens could inflict on each other was limited and indecisive; Sparta could not detach from Athens a significant portion of the Empire which was controlled by Athenian sea-power, and Athens could not gain control of continental Greece by a significant defeat of the Peloponnesian land forces. Maritime operations, however, were expensive, and by 421 the financial reserves with which Athens began the war had run perilously low. In the years after 421 Athens built up her reserves, and tried to organize an alliance of anti-Spartan states in the Peloponnese. In the former she was successful, but in the latter her hopes collapsed with the Spartan victory at Mantinea in 418. It was therefore natural that she should now contemplate making full use of her maritime power to extend her Empire, which would bring about a great increase in tribute and consequently an increase in her reserve of money. She could then build more ships, man them with more sailors recruited from the Greek world, and use them to transport more mercenaries recruited from the non-Greek world; and with these forces she could, if necessary, renew the war against Sparta, establish more fortified bases in the Peloponnese, and knock out Sparta's allies by more sustained and destructive seaborne raids against their territories. This was the prospect entertained by Alkibiades; the argument against it propounded by Nikias was that it was strategically and economically sounder to recover those parts of the Aegean which had been in revolt from Athenian rule for many years than to grasp at a more spectacular prize which could possibly be won but would be very hard to keep.

It has been fashionable from time to time to argue that Athens' real motive for attacking Sicily in 415 was to benefit Athenian trade by acquiring a market from which competitors could be excluded. This hypothesis necessarily implies that Thucydides is guilty either of fundamental error or of thoroughgoing distortion or inadequacy in presenting the arguments and motives of Alkibiades and the Athenians generally. It is not, however, an hypothesis recommended by any positive evidence; it seems to rest on a misunderstanding of the relation between the state, the trader, and the manufacturer in the ancient world, and to ignore the strategic situation and the close interrelation between tribute, financial reserves, and naval operations. Moreover, it must be remembered that no expedition could be sent out from Athens until it had been debated and decided on by the Assembly; and a reason which seemed adequate to the Assembly is, by that very fact, an adequate reason.

4. *The Sicilian Expedition*

Much went wrong with the expedition. The response of states in the West which were believed to be firm friends of Athens was disappointing, and before the end of the summer the three generals in command of the expedition were reduced to two by the recall of Alkibiades to face a charge of parodying the mysteries; he escaped at Thurioi on his way back to Athens, and made his way eventually to Sparta. The Athenians landed in the Great Harbour of Syracuse in the late autumn of 415, and defeated the Syracusan infantry, but were prevented by strong cavalry harassing from following up their victory. They therefore withdrew to Katane for the winter. In the spring of 414 they landed north of Syracuse and gained control of the plateau which overlooks the city. They then pressed on with the building of a siege-wall which would completely cut off Syracuse, and defeated two Syracusan attempts to interfere with this work; but on the second of these occasions the Athenian general Lamachos was killed, and Nikias was thus left in sole command. Meanwhile, Alkibiades at Sparta had persuaded the Spartans of the need to help Syracuse both by sending a Spartan commander to take charge of the Syracusan military organization and by establishing a permanent fortified base in Attica to harass Athens directly.

Gylippos, the Spartan commander appointed, set off with a small force of Peloponnesian ships about midsummer in 414. He was very nearly too late. The Syracusans had despaired of preventing Nikias from completing his circumvallation, and had opened tentative negotiations for peace; the arrival of one Corinthian ship with news of the approach of Gylippos heartened them, and from that moment the tide of the campaign ran in their favour. The Athenian siege operations were decisively spoilt by a counterwall, reinforcements came steadily into Syracuse from other parts of Sicily, and the Syracusan fleet gained daily in confidence and skill. Athens, at Nikias' request, sent very powerful reinforcements in the summer of 413, too late to save the campaign. The Syracusans defeated an Athenian attempt to capture the counterwall, and followed this up by a naval victory in the Great Harbour. They then blocked the harbour mouth; in a fierce attempt to escape the Athenian fleet was shattered, and the rest of the Athenian forces, retreating overland, were shortly afterwards destroyed.

5. *Other Sources*

Our principal sources, other than Thucydides, for the events of 415–413 are:

(i) Diodoros ('Diodorus Siculus'), xii. 82–xiii. 33. Diodoros was a contemporary of Augustus; his value for us lies in the fact that he drew on two much earlier historians whose works, now lost and known to us only from citations and references in other authors, were widely read and influential in the ancient world: Ephoros of Kyme (*c.* 405–340) and Timaios of Tauromenion (*c.* 350–260). Timaios, in turn, utilized another lost historian, Philistos of Syracuse (*c.* 430–355), who, as a boy, had been in Syracuse during the Athenian siege.

(ii) Plutarch's *Nicias* (especially chapters 12–30) and *Alcibiades* (especially chapters 17–23). Plutarch was a contemporary of the Flavians and Trajan; he too utilized (and sometimes mentions explicitly) Philistos and Timaios.

Thus whenever we find in Diodoros or Plutarch incidents in the siege of Syracuse which are not mentioned by Thucydides we cannot dismiss them without more ado as later embroidery; they may be derived ultimately from Philistos.

(iii) Relevant anecdotes and scraps of information are offered by a variety of later writers, and should never be dismissed without investigation. It is important to remember that most of the work of the numerous historians of the fourth century B.C., and much of the oratory of that period, is now lost but was available to writers of Hellenistic and Roman times.

(iv) The Athenian Andokides was implicated, as a young man, in the mutilation of the herms, and, indirectly, in the profanation of the mysteries. A substantial part (§§ 11–69) of his speech *De Mysteriis* (delivered in 399) is devoted to the events of the summer of 415.

(v) Some valuable information can be gleaned from the fragmentary Athenian official inscriptions of the period, notably: (*a*) the decrees which authorized the Sicilian expedition and made detailed provision for it (*GHI* 77, very fragmentary); (*b*) the record of payments made to generals and officials by the Treasurers of Athena (ibid. 75); (*c*) records of the sale of the property confiscated from the men condemned for mutilation of the herms or profanation of the mysteries (*SEG* xiii. 12–22, cf. *GHI* 79).

III. HISTORY OF THE TEXT

The text of Book VI of Thucydides is constituted from the following sources:

(A) *Direct Tradition*, i.e. manuscripts which purport to be copies of copies of copies . . . and so on . . . of what Thucydides himself wrote. Papyri, i.e. fragments of copies made between the third century B.C. and the sixth century A.D., make a negligible contribution to Book VI, though they are important for some of the other books. There are over seventy medieval manuscripts, copies made between the tenth and sixteenth centuries A.D.; the great majority ('recc.', i.e. *recentiores*, in the apparatus criticus) are either known or reasonably believed to be descendants of the seven 'primary' manuscripts ('codd.', i.e. *codices*, in the apparatus). The primary manuscripts are:

10th century: 'C' = Laurentianus LXIX 2 (Florence)
11th century: 'M' = Britannicus Add. 11727 (London)
              'E' = Palatinus 252 (Heidelberg)
              'F' = Monacensis 430 (Munich)
              'B' = Vaticanus graecus 126 (Vatican)
11th or 12th
  century: 'A' = Parisinus suppl. gr. 255 (Paris)
14th century: 'H' = Parisinus graecus 1734 (Paris)

(B) *Indirect Tradition.* (i) Citations from Thucydides by other authors, especially (*a*) Dionysios of Halikarnassos, a literary critic, contemporary with Augustus, and (*b*) lexicographers of late antiquity or the early Middle Ages; it is sometimes clear that the text available to such an author was different from what we have in the extant manuscripts.

(ii) Scholia, i.e. the explanatory comments which are found in the margins of manuscripts. These scholia are ultimately descended from ancient commentaries on Thucydides, but medieval scholars added much of their own and omitted or condensed some of the ancient material. The scholia sometimes mention readings which were in manuscripts known to them but lost to us; sometimes, again, a scholion is clearly inapplicable to the reading of the manuscripts in which it is found and we can reconstruct the reading to which it was meant to apply.

(iii) Translations: Lorenzo Valla's translation of Thucydides into Latin (1452) is closer to the text of H than to that of any other extant manuscript, but evidently drew on some other manuscripts, now lost, in addition.

(C) *Conjectural Emendation.* In cases where neither the direct nor the indirect tradition provides us with a reading which makes satisfactory sense, we have to use reason and knowledge and conjecture what Thucydides wrote. Conjectural emendation is not a purely modern phenomenon; ancient and medieval scholars were willing to correct what they believed (often rightly) to be nonsense.

The interrelation of the primary manuscripts in Book VI is as follows:

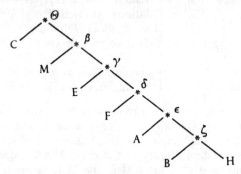

The asterisks and Greek letters represent the minimum number of hypothetical manuscripts the existence of which has to be assumed to account for the essentials of the relationship between the seven texts concerned. *Θ* is by definition the 'archetype', i.e. the latest common ancestor of all the extant manuscripts, wherever and whenever that existed.

Stemmata (i.e. manuscript family trees) of this kind look too simple to be the whole truth, and it is necessary to introduce into this stemma the following complications:

(i) A source (*Φ*) independent of *Θ* was used by the copyist of an intermediate stage between *β* and M; he drew from it a few variant readings which are to be found in M, and, more important, a mass of scholia which are quite different from those which were in *Θ* and often relate to readings different from *Θ*'s. This material was added to C and F by fourteenth-century copyists.

(ii) E occasionally has a reading which makes sense in a passage where all the other manuscripts agree in error; this and other peculiarities of E are most easily accounted for by the hypothesis that the copyist of a stage between γ and E drew on another manuscript which was related to C but contained material from a source (Ψ) independent of Θ.

(iii) At vi. 92. 5 the character of B and H changes drastically, and it is clear that from there onwards their common ancestor ζ was a composite manuscript, including both the readings which it inherited from ϵ and those which it obtained from a most valuable source (Ω) independent of Θ. H also has some interesting readings as variants or corrections in earlier parts of Book VI, and it is natural to suppose that these came direct from Ω to H.

The *recentiores* cannot all be dismissed as having nothing to contribute to the text, since we sometimes find in one or more of them an excellent reading which does not seem to be a medieval conjecture and is probably derived from Ω. It seems strange that Ω should have left us no direct descendants; the natural explanation is that it was a very old and badly mutilated manuscript, unsuitable for complete transcription but valued as a source of variant readings.

(*Note*: In the present edition the text and apparatus criticus are printed exactly as in the Oxford Classical Text of 1942. Since then, the study of the history of the text of Thucydides has continued; the account given above summarizes the results obtained by 1964, but it will be seen that in the apparatus criticus H is not mentioned—it is classed among 'recc.'—and G, a thirteenth-century manuscript of composite origin, is treated as a primary manuscript.)

ΙΣΤΟΡΙΩΝ Ζ

Τοῦ δ᾽ αὐτοῦ χειμῶνος ᾿Αθηναῖοι ἐβούλοντο αὖθις μείζονι 1
παρασκευῇ τῆς μετὰ Λάχητος καὶ Εὐρυμέδοντος ἐπὶ Σικελίαν
πλεύσαντες καταστρέψασθαι, εἰ δύναιντο, ἄπειροι οἱ πολλοὶ
ὄντες τοῦ μεγέθους τῆς νήσου καὶ τῶν ἐνοικούντων τοῦ
5 πλήθους καὶ ῾Ελλήνων καὶ βαρβάρων, καὶ ὅτι οὐ πολλῷ
τινὶ ὑποδεέστερον πόλεμον ἀνῃροῦντο ἢ τὸν πρὸς Πελοποννησίους. Σικελίας γὰρ περίπλους μέν ἐστιν ὁλκάδι οὐ 2
πολλῷ τινὶ ἔλασσον ἢ ὀκτὼ ἡμερῶν, καὶ τοσαύτη οὖσα ἐν
εἰκοσισταδίῳ μάλιστα μέτρῳ τῆς θαλάσσης διείργεται τὸ μὴ
10 ἤπειρος εἶναι· ᾠκίσθη δὲ ὧδε τὸ ἀρχαῖον, καὶ τοσάδε ἔθνη 2
ἔσχε τὰ ξύμπαντα. παλαίτατοι μὲν λέγονται ἐν μέρει τινὶ
τῆς χώρας Κύκλωπες καὶ Λαιστρυγόνες οἰκῆσαι, ὧν ἐγὼ
οὔτε γένος ἔχω εἰπεῖν οὔτε ὁπόθεν ἐσῆλθον ἢ ὅποι ἀπε-
χώρησαν· ἀρκείτω δὲ ὡς ποιηταῖς τε εἴρηται καὶ ὡς ἕκαστός
15 πῃ γιγνώσκει περὶ αὐτῶν. Σικανοὶ δὲ μετ᾽ αὐτοὺς πρῶτοι 2
φαίνονται ἐνοικισάμενοι, ὡς μὲν αὐτοί φασι, καὶ πρότεροι
διὰ τὸ αὐτόχθονες εἶναι, ὡς δὲ ἡ ἀλήθεια εὑρίσκεται, Ἴβηρες
ὄντες καὶ ἀπὸ τοῦ Σικανοῦ ποταμοῦ τοῦ ἐν Ἰβηρίᾳ ὑπὸ Λιγύων
ἀναστάντες. καὶ ἀπ᾽ αὐτῶν Σικανία τότε ἡ νῆσος ἐκαλεῖτο,
20 πρότερον Τρινακρία καλουμένη· οἰκοῦσι δὲ ἔτι καὶ νῦν τὰ
πρὸς ἑσπέραν τὴν Σικελίαν. Ἰλίου δὲ ἁλισκομένου τῶν 3

4 τὸ πλῆθος A B E F M   9 εἴκοσι σταδίων c f G : εἴκοσι σταδίοις
A B   μέτρῳ om. Schol. Patm.   10 εἶναι recc., legerunt Demetrius
Phalereus alii : οὖσα codd.   ὧδε Aldina : ἧ(ι)δε vel ἧδε codd.
13 ἀνεχώρησαν M : ἂν ἐχώρησαν E

Τρώων τινὲς διαφυγόντες Ἀχαιοὺς πλοίοις ἀφικνοῦνται πρὸς
τὴν Σικελίαν, καὶ ὅμοροι τοῖς Σικανοῖς οἰκήσαντες ξύμπαντες
μὲν Ἔλυμοι ἐκλήθησαν, πόλεις δ' αὐτῶν Ἔρυξ τε καὶ Ἔγεστα.
προσξυνῴκησαν δὲ αὐτοῖς καὶ Φωκέων τινὲς τῶν ἀπὸ Τροίας
τότε χειμῶνι ἐς Λιβύην πρῶτον, ἔπειτα ἐς Σικελίαν ἀπ' 5
4 αὐτῆς κατενεχθέντες. Σικελοὶ δ' ἐξ Ἰταλίας (ἐνταῦθα γὰρ
ᾤκουν) διέβησαν ἐς Σικελίαν, φεύγοντες Ὀπικούς, ὡς μὲν
εἰκὸς καὶ λέγεται, ἐπὶ σχεδιῶν, τηρήσαντες τὸν πορθμὸν
κατιόντος τοῦ ἀνέμου, τάχα ἂν δὲ καὶ ἄλλως πως ἐσπλεύ-
σαντες. εἰσὶ δὲ καὶ νῦν ἔτι ἐν τῇ Ἰταλίᾳ Σικελοί, καὶ ἡ 10
χώρα ἀπὸ Ἰταλοῦ βασιλέως τινὸς Σικελῶν, τοὔνομα τοῦτο
5 ἔχοντος, οὕτως Ἰταλία ἐπωνομάσθη. ἐλθόντες δὲ ἐς τὴν
Σικελίαν στρατὸς πολὺς τούς τε Σικανοὺς κρατοῦντες μάχῃ
ἀνέστειλαν πρὸς τὰ μεσημβρινὰ καὶ ἑσπέρια αὐτῆς καὶ ἀντὶ
Σικανίας Σικελίαν τὴν νῆσον ἐποίησαν καλεῖσθαι, καὶ τὰ 15
κράτιστα τῆς γῆς ᾤκησαν ἔχοντες, ἐπεὶ διέβησαν, ἔτη ἐγγὺς
τριακόσια πρὶν Ἕλληνας ἐς Σικελίαν ἐλθεῖν· ἔτι δὲ καὶ νῦν
6 τὰ μέσα καὶ τὰ πρὸς βορρᾶν τῆς νήσου ἔχουσιν. ᾤκουν δὲ
καὶ Φοίνικες περὶ πᾶσαν μὲν τὴν Σικελίαν ἄκρας τε ἐπὶ τῇ
θαλάσσῃ ἀπολαβόντες καὶ τὰ ἐπικείμενα νησίδια ἐμπορίας 20
ἕνεκεν τῆς πρὸς τοὺς Σικελούς· ἐπειδὴ δὲ οἱ Ἕλληνες
πολλοὶ κατὰ θάλασσαν ἐπεσέπλεον, ἐκλιπόντες τὰ πλείω
Μοτύην καὶ Σολόεντα καὶ Πάνορμον ἐγγὺς τῶν Ἐλύμων
ξυνοικήσαντες ἐνέμοντο, ξυμμαχίᾳ τε πίσυνοι τῇ τῶν Ἐλύμων, καὶ ὅτι ἐντεῦθεν ἐλάχιστον πλοῦν Καρχηδὼν Σικελίας 25
ἀπέχει. βάρβαροι μὲν οὖν τοσοίδε Σικελίαν καὶ οὕτως
ᾤκησαν.

3 Ἑλλήνων δὲ πρῶτοι Χαλκιδῆς ἐξ Εὐβοίας πλεύσαντες
μετὰ Θουκλέους οἰκιστοῦ Νάξον ᾤκισαν, καὶ Ἀπόλλωνος
Ἀρχηγέτου βωμὸν ὅστις νῦν ἔξω τῆς πόλεώς ἐστιν ἱδρύ- 30
σαντο, ἐφ' ᾧ, ὅταν ἐκ Σικελίας θεωροὶ πλέωσι, πρῶτον

3 πόλεις c G : πόλις cett.   7 Ὀπικας A¹ B F   11 Σικελοῦ
CG   14 ἀνέστειλαν Bekker : ἀπέστειλαν codd.   24 συνοικίσαντες
CE   28 πρῶτοι recc. : ρῶτον codd.

θύουσιν. Συρακούσας δὲ τοῦ ἐχομένου ἔτους Ἀρχίας τῶν 2
Ἡρακλειδῶν ἐκ Κορίνθου ᾤκισε, Σικελοὺς ἐξελάσας πρῶτον
ἐκ τῆς νήσου ἐν ᾗ νῦν οὐκέτι περικλυζομένῃ ἡ πόλις ἡ ἐντός
ἐστιν· ὕστερον δὲ χρόνῳ καὶ ἡ ἔξω προστειχισθεῖσα πολυ-
5 άνθρωπος ἐγένετο. Θουκλῆς δὲ καὶ οἱ Χαλκιδῆς ἐκ Νάξου 3
ὁρμηθέντες ἔτει πέμπτῳ μετὰ Συρακούσας οἰκισθείσας Λεοντίνους τε πολέμῳ τοὺς Σικελοὺς ἐξελάσαντες οἰκίζουσι, καὶ
μετ' αὐτοὺς Κατάνην· οἰκιστὴν δὲ αὐτοὶ Καταναῖοι ἐποιήσαντο Εὔαρχον. κατὰ δὲ τὸν αὐτὸν χρόνον καὶ Λάμις ἐκ 4
10 Μεγάρων ἀποικίαν ἄγων ἐς Σικελίαν ἀφίκετο, καὶ ὑπὲρ
Παντακύου τε ποταμοῦ Τρώτιλόν τι ὄνομα χωρίον οἰκίσας,
καὶ ὕστερον αὐτόθεν τοῖς Χαλκιδεῦσιν ἐς Λεοντίνους ὀλίγον
χρόνον ξυμπολιτεύσας καὶ ὑπὸ αὐτῶν ἐκπεσὼν καὶ Θάψον
οἰκίσας αὐτὸς μὲν ἀποθνῄσκει, οἱ δ' ἄλλοι ἐκ τῆς Θάψου
15 ἀναστάντες Ὑβλωνος βασιλέως Σικελοῦ προδόντος τὴν
χώραν καὶ καθηγησαμένου Μεγαρέας ᾤκισαν τοὺς Ὑβλαίους
κληθέντας. καὶ ἔτη οἰκήσαντες πέντε καὶ τεσσαράκοντα καὶ 2
διακόσια ὑπὸ Γέλωνος τυράννου Συρακοσίων ἀνέστησαν ἐκ
τῆς πόλεως καὶ χώρας. πρὶν δὲ ἀναστῆναι, ἔτεσιν ὕστερον
20 ἑκατὸν ἢ αὐτοὺς οἰκίσαι, Πάμιλλον πέμψαντες Σελινοῦντα
κτίζουσι, καὶ ἐκ Μεγάρων τῆς μητροπόλεως οὔσης αὐτοῖς
ἐπελθὼν ξυγκατῴκισεν. Γέλαν δὲ Ἀντίφημος ἐκ Ῥόδου 3
καὶ Ἔντιμος ἐκ Κρήτης ἐποίκους ἀγαγόντες κοινῇ ἔκτισαν,
ἔτει πέμπτῳ καὶ τεσσαρακοστῷ μετὰ Συρακουσῶν οἴκισιν.
25 καὶ τῇ μὲν πόλει ἀπὸ τοῦ Γέλα ποταμοῦ τοὔνομα ἐγένετο,
τὸ δὲ χωρίον οὗ νῦν ἡ πόλις ἐστὶ καὶ ὃ πρῶτον ἐτειχίσθη
Λίνδιοι καλεῖται· νόμιμα δὲ Δωρικὰ ἐτέθη αὐτοῖς. ἔτεσι δὲ 4
ἐγγύτατα ὀκτὼ καὶ ἑκατὸν μετὰ τὴν σφετέραν οἴκισιν Γελῷοι
Ἀκράγαντα ᾤκισαν, τὴν μὲν πόλιν ἀπὸ τοῦ Ἀκράγαντος
30 ποταμοῦ ὀνομάσαντες, οἰκιστὰς δὲ ποιήσαντες Ἀριστόνουν καὶ

1 ἐρχομένου ΑΒΕFM   2 ᾤκησε ΑΒΕFM   15 παραδόντος Classen   20 οἰκῆται ΑΒΕFM   μεταπέμψαντες Marchant   24 οἴκησιν ΑΒΕΜ   27 καλοῦνται Β?   28 οἴκισιν
F: οἴκησιν cett.   29 ᾤκισαν C: ᾤκησαν cett.

5 Πυστίλον, νόμιμα δὲ τὰ Γελῴων δόντες. Ζάγκλη δὲ τὴν μὲν
ἀρχὴν ἀπὸ Κύμης τῆς ἐν Ὀπικίᾳ Χαλκιδικῆς πόλεως λῃστῶν
ἀφικομένων ᾠκίσθη, ὕστερον δὲ καὶ ἀπὸ Χαλκίδος καὶ τῆς
ἄλλης Εὐβοίας πλῆθος ἐλθὸν ξυγκατενείμαντο τὴν γῆν· καὶ
οἰκισταὶ Περιήρης καὶ Κραταιμένης ἐγένοντο αὐτῆς, ὁ μὲν ἀπὸ 5
Κύμης, ὁ δὲ ἀπὸ Χαλκίδος. ὄνομα δὲ τὸ μὲν πρῶτον Ζάγκλη
ἦν ὑπὸ τῶν Σικελῶν κληθεῖσα, ὅτι δρεπανοειδὲς τὴν ἰδέαν τὸ
χωρίον ἐστί (τὸ δὲ δρέπανον οἱ Σικελοὶ ζάγκλον καλοῦσιν),
ὕστερον δ᾽ αὐτοὶ μὲν ὑπὸ Σαμίων καὶ ἄλλων Ἰώνων ἐκ-
6 πίπτουσιν, οἳ Μήδους φεύγοντες προσέβαλον Σικελίᾳ, τοὺς 10
δὲ Σαμίους Ἀναξίλας Ῥηγίνων τύραννος οὐ πολλῷ ὕστερον
ἐκβαλὼν καὶ τὴν πόλιν αὐτὸς ξυμμείκτων ἀνθρώπων οἰκίσας
Μεσσήνην ἀπὸ τῆς ἑαυτοῦ τὸ ἀρχαῖον πατρίδος ἀντωνόμασεν.
5 καὶ Ἱμέρα ἀπὸ Ζάγκλης ᾠκίσθη ὑπὸ Εὐκλείδου καὶ Σίμου καὶ
Σάκωνος, καὶ Χαλκιδῆς μὲν οἱ πλεῖστοι ἦλθον ἐς τὴν ἀποικίαν, 15
ξυνῴκισαν δὲ αὐτοῖς καὶ ἐκ Συρακουσῶν φυγάδες στάσει
νικηθέντες, οἱ Μυλητίδαι καλούμενοι· καὶ φωνὴ μὲν μεταξὺ
τῆς τε Χαλκιδέων καὶ Δωρίδος ἐκράθη, νόμιμα δὲ τὰ Χαλ-
2 κιδικὰ ἐκράτησεν. Ἄκραι δὲ καὶ Κασμέναι ὑπὸ Συρακοσίων
ᾠκίσθησαν, Ἄκραι μὲν ἑβδομήκοντα ἔτεσι μετὰ Συρακούσας, 20
3 Κασμέναι δ᾽ ἐγγὺς εἴκοσι μετὰ Ἄκρας. καὶ Καμάρινα τὸ
πρῶτον ὑπὸ Συρακοσίων ᾠκίσθη, ἔτεσιν ἐγγύτατα πέντε καὶ
τριάκοντα καὶ ἑκατὸν μετὰ Συρακουσῶν κτίσιν· οἰκισταὶ δὲ
ἐγένοντο αὐτῆς Δάσκων καὶ Μενέκωλος. ἀναστάτων δὲ
Καμαριναίων γενομένων πολέμῳ ὑπὸ Συρακοσίων δι᾽ ἀπό- 25
στασιν, χρόνῳ Ἱπποκράτης ὕστερον Γέλας τύραννος, λύτρα
ἀνδρῶν Συρακοσίων αἰχμαλώτων λαβὼν τὴν γῆν τὴν Καμαριναίων, αὐτὸς οἰκιστὴς γενόμενος κατῴκισε Καμάριναν. καὶ
αὖθις ὑπὸ Γέλωνος ἀνάστατος γενομένη τὸ τρίτον κατῳκίσθη
ὑπὸ Γελῴων. 30
6 Τοσαῦτα ἔθνη Ἑλλήνων καὶ βαρβάρων Σικελίαν ᾤκει,

12 αὐτὸς Dobree: αὐτοῖς codd. 13 ἀντωνόμασεν] αὐτὸ ὠνό-
μασε(ν) ABEFM 16 ξυνῴκησαν CEFGM 30 Γελῴων
Dodwell: Γέλωνος codd.

καὶ ἐπὶ τοσήνδε οὖσαν αὐτὴν οἱ Ἀθηναῖοι στρατεύειν
ὥρμηντο, ἐφιέμενοι μὲν τῇ ἀληθεστάτῃ προφάσει τῆς πάσης
ἄρξαι, βοηθεῖν δὲ ἅμα εὐπρεπῶς βουλόμενοι τοῖς ἑαυτῶν
ξυγγενέσι καὶ τοῖς προσγεγενημένοις ξυμμάχοις. μάλιστα 2
5 δ' αὐτοὺς ἐξώρμησαν Ἐγεσταίων [τε] πρέσβεις παρόντες καὶ
προθυμότερον ἐπικαλούμενοι. ὅμοροι γὰρ ὄντες τοῖς Σελινουντίοις ἐς πόλεμον καθέστασαν περί τε γαμικῶν τινῶν καὶ
περὶ γῆς ἀμφισβητήτου, καὶ οἱ Σελινούντιοι Συρακοσίους
ἐπαγόμενοι ξυμμάχους κατεῖργον αὐτοὺς τῷ πολέμῳ καὶ
10 κατὰ γῆν καὶ κατὰ θάλασσαν· ὥστε τὴν γενομένην ἐπὶ
Λάχητος καὶ τοῦ προτέρου πολέμου Λεοντίνων οἱ Ἐγεσταῖοι
ξυμμαχίαν ἀναμιμνῄσκοντες τοὺς Ἀθηναίους ἐδέοντο σφίσι
ναῦς πέμψαντας ἐπαμῦναι, λέγοντες ἄλλα τε πολλὰ καὶ
κεφάλαιον, εἰ Συρακόσιοι Λεοντίνους τε ἀναστήσαντες ἀτι-
15 μώρητοι γενήσονται καὶ τοὺς λοιποὺς ἔτι ξυμμάχους αὐτῶν
διαφθείροντες αὐτοὶ τὴν ἅπασαν δύναμιν τῆς Σικελίας σχή-
σουσι, κίνδυνον εἶναι μή ποτε μεγάλῃ παρασκευῇ Δωριῆς τε
Δωριεῦσι κατὰ τὸ ξυγγενὲς καὶ ἅμα ἄποικοι τοῖς ἐκπέμψασι
Πελοποννησίοις βοηθήσαντες καὶ τὴν ἐκείνων δύναμιν ξυγ-
20 καθέλωσιν· σῶφρον δ' εἶναι μετὰ τῶν ὑπολοίπων ἔτι ξυμμάχων ἀντέχειν τοῖς Συρακοσίοις, ἄλλως τε καὶ χρήματα
σφῶν παρεξόντων ἐς τὸν πόλεμον ἱκανά. ὧν ἀκούοντες οἱ 3
Ἀθηναῖοι ἐν ταῖς ἐκκλησίαις τῶν τε Ἐγεσταίων πολλάκις λεγόντων καὶ τῶν ξυναγορευόντων αὐτοῖς ἐψηφίσαντο
25 πρέσβεις πέμψαι πρῶτον ἐς τὴν Ἔγεσταν περί τε τῶν
χρημάτων σκεψομένους εἰ ὑπάρχει, ὥσπερ φασίν, ἐν τῷ
κοινῷ καὶ ἐν τοῖς ἱεροῖς, καὶ τὰ τοῦ πολέμου ἅμα πρὸς τοὺς
Σελινουντίους ἐν ὅτῳ ἐστὶν εἰσομένους.

Καὶ οἱ μὲν πρέοβεις τῶν Ἀθηναίων ἀπεστάλησαν ἐς τὴν 7
30 Σικελίαν· Λακεδαιμόνιοι δὲ τοῦ αὐτοῦ χειμῶνος καὶ οἱ ξύμμαχοι πλὴν Κορινθίων στρατεύσαντες ἐς τὴν Ἀργείαν τῆς

3 ἄρξαι Stahl : ἄρξειν codd.   4 προγεγενημένοις Ε G M   5 τε
om. recc.   9 ἐπαγαγόμενοι Krüger   13 πέμψαντας recc. :
πέμψαντες codd.   16 διαφθείραντες F. Portus   25 πέμψαι recc. :
πέμψαντες codd.

τε γῆς ἔτεμον οὐ πολλὴν καὶ σῖτον ἀνεκομίσαντό τινα ζεύγη
κομίσαντες, καὶ ἐς Ὀρνεὰς κατοικίσαντες τοὺς Ἀργείων
φυγάδας καὶ τῆς ἄλλης στρατιᾶς παρακαταλιπόντες αὐτοῖς
ὀλίγους, καὶ σπεισάμενοί τινα χρόνον ὥστε μὴ ἀδικεῖν
Ὀρνεάτας καὶ Ἀργείους τὴν ἀλλήλων, ἀπεχώρησαν τῷ 5
2 στρατῷ ἐπ᾽ οἴκου. ἐλθόντων δὲ Ἀθηναίων οὐ πολλῷ ὕστερον ναυσὶ τριάκοντα καὶ ἑξακοσίοις ὁπλίταις, οἱ Ἀργεῖοι
μετὰ τῶν Ἀθηναίων πανστρατιᾷ ἐξελθόντες τοὺς μὲν ἐν
Ὀρνεαῖς μίαν ἡμέραν ἐπολιόρκουν· ὑπὸ δὲ νύκτα αὐλισα-
μένου τοῦ στρατεύματος ἄπωθεν ἐκδιδράσκουσιν οἱ ἐκ τῶν 10
Ὀρνεῶν. καὶ τῇ ὑστεραίᾳ οἱ Ἀργεῖοι ὡς ᾔσθοντο, κατα-
σκάψαντες τὰς Ὀρνεὰς ἀνεχώρησαν καὶ οἱ Ἀθηναῖοι ὕστερον
ταῖς ναυσὶν ἐπ᾽ οἴκου.

3   Καὶ ἐς Μεθώνην τὴν ὅμορον Μακεδονίᾳ ἱππέας κατὰ
θάλασσαν κομίσαντες Ἀθηναῖοι σφῶν τε αὐτῶν καὶ Μακε- 15
δόνων τοὺς παρὰ σφίσι φυγάδας ἐκακούργουν τὴν Περδίκκου.
4 Λακεδαιμόνιοι δὲ πέμψαντες παρὰ Χαλκιδέας τοὺς ἐπὶ Θρᾴ-
κης, ἄγοντας πρὸς Ἀθηναίους δεχημέρους σπονδάς, ξυμπολεμεῖν ἐκέλευον Περδίκκᾳ· οἱ δ᾽ οὐκ ἤθελον. καὶ ὁ χειμὼν
ἐτελεύτα, καὶ ἕκτον καὶ δέκατον ἔτος ἐτελεύτα τῷ πολέμῳ 20
τῷδε ὃν Θουκυδίδης ξυνέγραψεν.

8   Τοῦ δ᾽ ἐπιγιγνομένου θέρους ἅμα ἦρι οἱ τῶν Ἀθηναίων
πρέσβεις ἧκον ἐκ τῆς Σικελίας καὶ οἱ Ἐγεσταῖοι μετ᾽ αὐτῶν
ἄγοντες ἑξήκοντα τάλαντα ἀσήμου ἀργυρίου ὡς ἐς ἑξήκοντα
2 ναῦς μηνὸς μισθόν, ἃς ἔμελλον δεήσεσθαι πέμπειν. καὶ οἱ 25
Ἀθηναῖοι ἐκκλησίαν ποιήσαντες καὶ ἀκούσαντες τῶν τε
Ἐγεσταίων καὶ τῶν σφετέρων πρέσβεων τά τε ἄλλα ἐπ-
αγωγὰ καὶ οὐκ ἀληθῆ καὶ περὶ τῶν χρημάτων ὡς εἴη ἑτοῖμα
ἔν τε τοῖς ἱεροῖς πολλὰ καὶ ἐν τῷ κοινῷ, ἐψηφίσαντο ναῦς
ἑξήκοντα πέμπειν ἐς Σικελίαν καὶ στρατηγοὺς αὐτοκράτορας 30
Ἀλκιβιάδην τε τὸν Κλεινίου καὶ Νικίαν τὸν Νικηράτου καὶ

---

1 ἀνεκόμισαν C   8 ἐξελθόντες Aem. Portus (egressi Valla) : ἐξελ-
θόντων codd.   μὲν om. A B E F M   29 τῷ κοινῷ recc. : τοῖς κοινοῖς
codd.

Λάμαχον τὸν Ξενοφάνους, βοηθοὺς μὲν Ἐγεσταίοις πρὸς
Σελινουντίους, ξυγκατοικίσαι δὲ καὶ Λεοντίνους, ἤν τι περιγίγνηται αὐτοῖς τοῦ πολέμου, καὶ τᾶλλα τὰ ἐν τῇ Σικελίᾳ
πρᾶξαι ὅπῃ ἂν γιγνώσκωσιν ἄριστα Ἀθηναίοις. μετὰ δὲ 3
5 τοῦτο ἡμέρᾳ πέμπτῃ ἐκκλησία αὖθις ἐγίγνετο, καθ' ὅτι χρὴ
τὴν παρασκευὴν ταῖς ναυσὶ τάχιστα γίγνεσθαι, καὶ τοῖς
στρατηγοῖς, εἴ του προσδέοιντο, ψηφισθῆναι ἐς τὸν ἔκπλουν.
καὶ ὁ Νικίας ἀκούσιος μὲν ᾑρημένος ἄρχειν, νομίζων δὲ τὴν 4
πόλιν οὐκ ὀρθῶς βεβουλεῦσθαι, ἀλλὰ προφάσει βραχείᾳ καὶ
10 εὐπρεπεῖ τῆς Σικελίας ἁπάσης, μεγάλου ἔργου, ἐφίεσθαι,
παρελθὼν ἀποτρέψαι ἐβούλετο, καὶ παρῄνει τοῖς Ἀθηναίοις
τοιάδε.

'Ἡ μὲν ἐκκλησία περὶ παρασκευῆς τῆς ἡμετέρας ἤδε 9
ξυνελέγη, καθ' ὅτι χρὴ ἐς Σικελίαν ἐκπλεῖν· ἐμοὶ μέντοι
15 δοκεῖ καὶ περὶ αὐτοῦ τούτου ἔτι χρῆναι σκέψασθαι, εἰ ἄμεινόν
ἐστιν ἐκπέμπειν τὰς ναῦς, καὶ μὴ οὕτω βραχείᾳ βουλῇ περὶ
μεγάλων πραγμάτων ἀνδράσιν ἀλλοφύλοις πειθομένους πόλεμον οὐ προσήκοντα ἄρασθαι. καίτοι ἔγωγε καὶ τιμῶμαι ἐκ 2
τοῦ τοιούτου καὶ ἧσσον ἑτέρων περὶ τῷ ἐμαυτοῦ σώματι
20 ὀρρωδῶ, νομίζων ὁμοίως ἀγαθὸν πολίτην εἶναι ὃς ἂν καὶ τοῦ
σώματός τι καὶ τῆς οὐσίας προνοῆται· μάλιστα γὰρ ἂν ὁ
τοιοῦτος καὶ τὰ τῆς πόλεως δι' ἑαυτὸν βούλοιτο ὀρθοῦσθαι.
ὅμως δὲ οὔτε ἐν τῷ πρότερον χρόνῳ διὰ τὸ προτιμᾶσθαι
εἶπον παρὰ γνώμην οὔτε νῦν, ἀλλὰ ᾗ ἂν γιγνώσκω βέλτιστα,
25 ἐρῶ. καὶ πρὸς μὲν τοὺς τρόπους τοὺς ὑμετέρους ἀσθενὴς 3
ἄν μου ὁ λόγος εἴη, εἰ τά τε ὑπάρχοντα σῴζειν παραινοίην
καὶ μὴ τοῖς ἑτοίμοις περὶ τῶν ἀφανῶν καὶ μελλόντων κιν-
δυνεύειν· ὡς δὲ οὔτε ἐν καιρῷ σπεύδετε οὔτε ῥᾴδιά ἐστι
κατασχεῖν ἐφ' ἃ ὥρμησθε, ταῦτα διδάξω.

30 'Φημὶ γὰρ ὑμᾶς πολεμίους πολλοὺς ἐνθάδε ὑπολιπόντας 10
καὶ ἑτέρους ἐπιθυμεῖν ἐκεῖσε πλεύσαντας δεῦρο ἐπαγαγέσθαι.

18 αἴρεσθαι C G : αἴρασθαι E   21 προνοῆται] πρόηται recc.
Stobaeus   30 ὑμᾶς Aldina : ἡμᾶς codd.   31 δεῦρο recc. (huc
Valla) : δεύτερον codd.

2 καὶ οἴεσθε ἴσως τὰς γενομένας ὑμῖν σπονδὰς ἔχειν τι βέ-
βαιον, αἳ ἡσυχαζόντων μὲν ὑμῶν ὀνόματι σπονδαὶ ἔσονται
(οὕτω γὰρ ἐνθένδε τε ἄνδρες ἔπραξαν αὐτὰ καὶ ἐκ τῶν ἐναντίων), σφαλέντων δέ που ἀξιόχρεῳ δυνάμει ταχεῖαν τὴν ἐπιχείρησιν ἡμῖν οἱ ἐχθροὶ ποιήσονται, οἷς πρῶτον μὲν διὰ 5
ξυμφορῶν ἡ ξύμβασις καὶ ἐκ τοῦ αἰσχίονος ἢ ἡμῖν κατ'
ἀνάγκην ἐγένετο, ἔπειτα ἐν αὐτῇ ταύτῃ πολλὰ τὰ ἀμφισβη-
3 τούμενα ἔχομεν. εἰσὶ δ' οἳ οὐδὲ ταύτην πω τὴν ὁμολογίαν
ἐδέξαντο, καὶ οὐχ οἱ ἀσθενέστατοι· ἀλλ' οἱ μὲν ἄντικρυς
πολεμοῦσιν, οἱ δὲ καὶ διὰ τὸ Λακεδαιμονίους ἔτι ἡσυχάζειν 10
4 δεχημέροις σπονδαῖς καὶ αὐτοὶ κατέχονται. τάχα δ' ἂν
ἴσως, εἰ δίχα ἡμῶν τὴν δύναμιν λάβοιεν, ὅπερ νῦν σπεύ-
δομεν, καὶ πάνυ ἂν ξυνεπιθοῖντο μετὰ Σικελιωτῶν, οὓς πρὸ
πολλῶν ἂν ἐτιμήσαντο ξυμμάχους γενέσθαι ἐν τῷ πρὶν
5 χρόνῳ. ὥστε χρὴ σκοπεῖν τινὰ αὐτὰ καὶ μὴ μετεώρῳ τε 15
⟨τῇ⟩ πόλει ἀξιοῦν κινδυνεύειν καὶ ἀρχῆς ἄλλης ὀρέγεσθαι
πρὶν ἣν ἔχομεν βεβαιωσώμεθα, εἰ Χαλκιδῆς γε οἱ ἐπὶ
Θράκης ἔτη τοσαῦτα ἀφεστῶτες ἀφ' ἡμῶν ἔτι ἀχείρωτοί
εἰσι καὶ ἄλλοι τινὲς κατὰ τὰς ἠπείρους ἐνδοιαστῶς ἀκρο-
ῶνται. ἡμεῖς δὲ Ἐγεσταίοις δὴ οὖσι ξυμμάχοις ὡς ἀδικου- 20
μένοις ὀξέως βοηθοῦμεν· ὑφ' ὧν δ' αὐτοὶ πάλαι ἀφεστώτων
11 ἀδικούμεθα, ἔτι μέλλομεν ἀμύνεσθαι. καίτοι τοὺς μὲν κατερ-
γασάμενοι κἂν κατάσχοιμεν· τῶν δ' εἰ καὶ κρατήσαιμεν, διὰ
πολλοῦ γε καὶ πολλῶν ὄντων χαλεπῶς ἂν ἄρχειν δυναίμεθα.
ἀνόητον δ' ἐπὶ τοιούτους ἰέναι ὧν κρατήσας τε μὴ κατασχή- 25
σει τις καὶ μὴ κατορθώσας μὴ ἐν τῷ ὁμοίῳ καὶ πρὶν ἐπιχει-
2 ρῆσαι ἔσται. Σικελιῶται δ' ἄν μοι δοκοῦσιν, ὥς γε νῦν
ἔχουσι, καὶ ἔτι ἂν ἧσσον δεινοὶ ἡμῖν γενέσθαι, εἰ ἄρξειαν
αὐτῶν Συρακόσιοι· ὅπερ οἱ Ἐγεσταῖοι μάλιστα ἡμᾶς ἐκφο-
3 βοῦσιν. νῦν μὲν γὰρ κἂν ἔλθοιεν ἴσως Λακεδαιμονίων 30
ἕκαστοι χάριτι, ἐκείνως δ' οὐκ εἰκὸς ἀρχὴν ἐπὶ ἀρχὴν στρα-

---

4 δέ recc.: om. codd.   11 ἂν δ' ABEFM   16 τῇ addidit
Jones   17 βεβαιωσώμεθα C: βεβαιωσόμεθα cett.   18 ἀφ' om. CGM
20 ξυμμάχοις G M¹: ξύμμαχοι cett.   21 αὐτοὶ Reiske: αὐτῶν codd.

τεῦσαι· ᾧ γὰρ ἂν τρόπῳ τὴν ἡμετέραν μετὰ Πελοποννησίων
ἀφέλωνται, εἰκὸς ὑπὸ τῶν αὐτῶν καὶ τὴν σφετέραν διὰ τοῦ
αὐτοῦ καθαιρεθῆναι. ἡμᾶς δ' ἂν οἱ ἐκεῖ Ἕλληνες μάλιστα 4
μὲν ἐκπεπληγμένοι εἶεν εἰ μὴ ἀφικοίμεθα, ἔπειτα δὲ καὶ εἰ
5 δείξαντες τὴν δύναμιν δι' ὀλίγου ἀπέλθοιμεν· τὰ γὰρ διὰ
πλείστου πάντες ἴσμεν θαυμαζόμενα καὶ τὰ πεῖραν ἥκιστα
τῆς δόξης δόντα. εἰ δὲ σφαλείημέν τι, τάχιστ' ἂν ὑπεριδόντες μετὰ τῶν ἐνθάδε ἐπιθοῖντο. ὅπερ νῦν ὑμεῖς ὦ 5
Ἀθηναῖοι ἐς Λακεδαιμονίους καὶ τοὺς ξυμμάχους πεπόνθατε·
10 διὰ τὸ παρὰ γνώμην αὐτῶν πρὸς ἃ ἐφοβεῖσθε τὸ πρῶτον
περιγενῆσθαι, καταφρονήσαντες ἤδη καὶ Σικελίας ἐφίεσθε.
χρὴ δὲ μὴ πρὸς τὰς τύχας τῶν ἐναντίων ἐπαίρεσθαι, ἀλλὰ 6
τὰς διανοίας κρατήσαντας θαρσεῖν, μηδὲ Λακεδαιμονίους
ἄλλο τι ἡγήσασθαι ἢ διὰ τὸ αἰσχρὸν σκοπεῖν ὅτῳ τρόπῳ
15 ἔτι καὶ νῦν, ἢν δύνωνται, σφήλαντες ἡμᾶς τὸ σφέτερον
ἀπρεπὲς εὖ θήσονται, ὅσῳ καὶ περὶ πλείστου καὶ διὰ πλείστου δόξαν ἀρετῆς μελετῶσιν. ὥστε οὐ περὶ τῶν ἐν Σικελίᾳ 7
Ἐγεσταίων ἡμῖν, ἀνδρῶν βαρβάρων, ὁ ἀγών, εἰ σωφρονοῦ-
μεν, ἀλλ' ὅπως πόλιν δι' ὀλιγαρχίας ἐπιβουλεύουσαν ὀξέως
20 φυλαξόμεθα.

‘Καὶ μεμνῆσθαι χρὴ ἡμᾶς ὅτι νεωστὶ ἀπὸ νόσου μεγάλης 12
καὶ πολέμου βραχύ τι λελωφήκαμεν, ὥστε καὶ χρήμασι καὶ
τοῖς σώμασιν ηὐξῆσθαι· καὶ ταῦτα ὑπὲρ ἡμῶν δίκαιον ἐνθάδε
εἶναι ἀναλοῦν, καὶ μὴ ὑπὲρ ἀνδρῶν φυγάδων τῶνδε ἐπικου-
25 ρίας δεομένων, οἷς τό τε ψεύσασθαι καλῶς χρήσιμον καὶ
τῷ τοῦ πέλας κινδύνῳ, αὐτοὺς λόγους μόνον παρασχομένους,
ἢ κατορθώσαντας χάριν μὴ ἀξίαν εἰδέναι ἢ πταίσαντάς που
τοὺς φίλους ξυναπολέσαι. εἴ τέ τις ἄρχειν ἄσμενος αἱρε- 2
θεὶς παραινεῖ ὑμῖν ἐκπλεῖν, τὸ ἑαυτοῦ μόνον σκοπῶν, ἄλλως

5–8 τὰ γὰρ . . . δόντα post ἐπιθοῖντο in codd. leguntur, transp.
Rauchenstein   11 ante καταφρονήσαντες add. καὶ G[1]   ἐφίεσθε recc.:
ἐφίεσθαι codd.   19 ὀλιγαρχίας] ὀλίγου Badham   20 φυλαξόμεθα
CE : φυλαξώμεθα cett.   24 εἶναι om. C [M]   26 αὐτῶν ABF
suprascr. G   28 ξυναπολέσαι Reiske : ξυναπολέσθαι codd.

τε καὶ νεώτερος ὢν ἔτι ἐς τὸ ἄρχειν, ὅπως θαυμασθῇ μὲν
ἀπὸ τῆς ἱπποτροφίας, διὰ δὲ πολυτέλειαν καὶ ὠφεληθῇ τι ἐκ
τῆς ἀρχῆς, μηδὲ τούτῳ ἐμπαράσχητε τῷ τῆς πόλεως κινδύνῳ
ἰδίᾳ ἐλλαμπρύνεσθαι, νομίσατε δὲ τοὺς τοιούτους τὰ μὲν
δημόσια ἀδικεῖν, τὰ δὲ ἴδια ἀναλοῦν, καὶ τὸ πρᾶγμα μέγα εἶναι 5
καὶ μὴ οἷον νεωτέρῳ βουλεύσασθαί τε καὶ ὀξέως μεταχειρίσαι.

13 'Οὓς ἐγὼ ὁρῶν νῦν ἐνθάδε τῷ αὐτῷ ἀνδρὶ παρακελευστοὺς
καθημένους φοβοῦμαι, καὶ τοῖς πρεσβυτέροις ἀντιπαρακελεύομαι μὴ καταισχυνθῆναι, εἴ τῴ τις παρακάθηται τῶνδε,
ὅπως μὴ δόξει, ἐὰν μὴ ψηφίζηται πολεμεῖν, μαλακὸς εἶναι, 10
μηδ᾽, ὅπερ ἂν αὐτοὶ πάθοιεν, δυσέρωτας εἶναι τῶν ἀπόντων,
γνόντας ὅτι ἐπιθυμίᾳ μὲν ἐλάχιστα κατορθοῦνται, προνοίᾳ
δὲ πλεῖστα, ἀλλ᾽ ὑπὲρ τῆς πατρίδος ὡς μέγιστον δὴ τῶν
πρὶν κίνδυνον ἀναρριπτούσης ἀντιχειροτονεῖν, καὶ ψηφί-
ζεσθαι τοὺς μὲν Σικελιώτας οἷσπερ νῦν ὅροις χρωμένους 15
πρὸς ἡμᾶς, οὐ μεμπτοῖς, τῷ τε Ἰονίῳ κόλπῳ παρὰ γῆν ἤν
τις πλέῃ, καὶ τῷ Σικελικῷ διὰ πελάγους, τὰ αὑτῶν νεμο-
2 μένους καθ᾽ αὑτοὺς καὶ ξυμφέρεσθαι· τοῖς δ᾽ Ἐγεσταίοις ἰδίᾳ
εἰπεῖν, ἐπειδὴ ἄνευ Ἀθηναίων καὶ ξυνῆψαν πρὸς Σελινουντίους τὸ πρῶτον πόλεμον, μετὰ σφῶν αὐτῶν καὶ καταλύεσθαι· 20
καὶ τὸ λοιπὸν ξυμμάχους μὴ ποιεῖσθαι ὥσπερ εἰώθαμεν, οἷς
κακῶς μὲν πράξασιν ἀμυνοῦμεν, ὠφελίας δ᾽ αὐτοὶ δεηθέντες
οὐ τευξόμεθα.

14 'Καὶ σύ, ὦ πρύτανι, ταῦτα, εἴπερ ἡγεῖ σοι προσήκειν κή-
δεσθαί τε τῆς πόλεως καὶ βούλει γενέσθαι πολίτης ἀγαθός, 25
ἐπιψήφιζε καὶ γνώμας προτίθει αὖθις Ἀθηναίοις, νομίσας,
εἰ ὀρρωδεῖς τὸ ἀναψηφίσαι, τὸ μὲν λύειν τοὺς νόμους μὴ
μετὰ τοσῶνδ᾽ ἂν μαρτύρων αἰτίαν σχεῖν, τῆς δὲ πόλεως
⟨κακῶς⟩ βουλευσαμένης ἰατρὸς ἂν γενέσθαι, καὶ τὸ καλῶς
ἄρξαι τοῦτ᾽ εἶναι, ὃς ἂν τὴν πατρίδα ὠφελήσῃ ὡς πλεῖστα 30
ἢ ἑκὼν εἶναι μηδὲν βλάψῃ.᾽

1 ἔτι ὢν A B E F (corr. F¹): ἔτι om. C   6 νεωτέρους Pluygers
10 δόξει C : δόξῃ cett.   12 κατορθοῦνται Göller   16 ἡμᾶς B : ὑμᾶς cett.
20 τὸ recc. : τὸν codd.   29 κακῶς recc. et, ut videtur, Schol. : om. codd.

Ὁ μὲν Νικίας τοιαῦτα εἶπε, τῶν δὲ Ἀθηναίων παριόντες 15
οἱ μὲν πλεῖστοι στρατεύειν παρήνουν καὶ τὰ ἐψηφισμένα μὴ
λύειν, οἱ δέ τινες καὶ ἀντέλεγον. ἐνῆγε δὲ προθυμότατα 2
τὴν στρατείαν Ἀλκιβιάδης ὁ Κλεινίου, βουλόμενος τῷ τε
5 Νικίᾳ ἐναντιοῦσθαι, ὧν καὶ ἐς τἆλλα διάφορος τὰ πολιτικὸ
καὶ ὅτι αὐτοῦ διαβόλως ἐμνήσθη, καὶ μάλιστα στρατηγῆσαί
τε ἐπιθυμῶν καὶ ἐλπίζων Σικελίαν τε δι' αὐτοῦ καὶ Καρχηδόνα λήψεσθαι καὶ τὰ ἴδια ἅμα εὐτυχήσας χρήμασί τε καὶ
δόξῃ ὠφελήσειν. ὢν γὰρ ἐν ἀξιώματι ὑπὸ τῶν ἀστῶν, ταῖς 3
10 ἐπιθυμίαις μείζοσιν ἢ κατὰ τὴν ὑπάρχουσαν οὐσίαν ἐχρῆτο
ἔς τε τὰς ἱπποτροφίας καὶ τὰς ἄλλας δαπάνας· ὅπερ καὶ
καθεῖλεν ὕστερον τὴν τῶν Ἀθηναίων πόλιν οὐχ ἥκιστα.
φοβηθέντες γὰρ αὐτοῦ οἱ πολλοὶ τὸ μέγεθος τῆς τε κατὰ τὸ 4
ἑαυτοῦ σῶμα παρανομίας ἐς τὴν δίαιταν καὶ τῆς διανοίας ὧν
15 καθ' ἓν ἕκαστον ἐν ὅτῳ γίγνοιτο ἔπρασσεν, ὡς τυραννίδος
ἐπιθυμοῦντι πολέμιοι καθέστασαν, καὶ δημοσίᾳ κράτιστα
διαθέντι τὰ τοῦ πολέμου ἰδίᾳ ἕκαστοι τοῖς ἐπιτηδεύμασιν
αὐτοῦ ἀχθεσθέντες, καὶ ἄλλοις ἐπιτρέψαντες, οὐ διὰ μακροῦ
ἔσφηλαν τὴν πόλιν. τότε δ' οὖν παρελθὼν τοῖς Ἀθηναίοις 5
20 παρῄνει τοιάδε.

'Καὶ προσήκει μοι μᾶλλον ἑτέρων, ὦ Ἀθηναῖοι, ἄρχειν 16
(ἀνάγκη γὰρ ἐντεῦθεν ἄρξασθαι, ἐπειδή μου Νικίας καθ-
ήψατο), καὶ ἄξιος ἅμα νομίζω εἶναι. ὧν γὰρ πέρι ἐπιβόη-
τός εἰμι, τοῖς μὲν προγόνοις μου καὶ ἐμοὶ δόξαν φέρει ταῦτα,
25 τῇ δὲ πατρίδι καὶ ὠφελίαν. οἱ γὰρ Ἕλληνες καὶ ὑπὲρ 2
δύναμιν μείζω ἡμῶν τὴν πόλιν ἐνόμισαν τῷ ἐμῷ διαπρεπεῖ
τῆς Ὀλυμπίαζε θεωρίας, πρότερον ἐλπίζοντες αὐτὴν κατα-
πεπολεμῆσθαι, διότι ἅρματα μὲν ἑπτὰ καθῆκα, ὅσα οὐδείς
πω ἰδιώτης πρότερον, ἐνίκησα δὲ καὶ δεύτερος καὶ τέταρτος
30 ἐγενόμην καὶ τἆλλα ἀξίως τῆς νίκης παρεσκευασάμην. νόμῳ
μὲν γὰρ τιμὴ τὰ τοιαῦτα, ἐκ δὲ τοῦ δρωμένου καὶ δύναμις
ἅμα ὑπονοεῖται. καὶ ὅσα αὖ ἐν τῇ πόλει χορηγίαις ἢ ἄλλῳ 3

---

5 τὰ πολιτικὰ secl. Weidner : πολεμικὰ C G   13 αὐτοῦ om. C
17 διαθέντι recc. : διαθέντα codd.

τῷ λαμπρύνομαι, τοῖς μὲν ἀστοῖς φθονεῖται φύσει, πρὸς
δὲ τοὺς ξένους καὶ αὕτη ἰσχὺς φαίνεται. καὶ οὐκ ἄχρηστος
ἥδ' ἡ ἄνοια, ὃς ἂν τοῖς ἰδίοις τέλεσι μὴ ἑαυτὸν μόνον ἀλλὰ
4 καὶ τὴν πόλιν ὠφελῇ. οὐδέ γε ἄδικον ἐφ' ἑαυτῷ μέγα
φρονοῦντα μὴ ἴσον εἶναι, ἐπεὶ καὶ ὁ κακῶς πράσσων πρὸς 5
οὐδένα τῆς ξυμφορᾶς ἰσομοιρεῖ· ἀλλ' ὥσπερ δυστυχοῦντες
οὐ προσαγορευόμεθα, ἐν τῷ ὁμοίῳ τις ἀνεχέσθω καὶ ὑπὸ
τῶν εὐπραγούντων ὑπερφρονούμενος, ἢ τὰ ἴσα νέμων τὰ
5 ὁμοῖα ἀνταξιούτω. οἶδα δὲ τοὺς τοιούτους, καὶ ὅσοι ἔν
τινος λαμπρότητι προέσχον, ἐν μὲν τῷ καθ' αὑτοὺς βίῳ 10
λυπηροὺς ὄντας, τοῖς ὁμοίοις μὲν μάλιστα, ἔπειτα δὲ καὶ
τοῖς ἄλλοις ξυνόντας, τῶν δὲ ἔπειτα ἀνθρώπων προσποίησίν
τε ξυγγενείας τισὶ καὶ μὴ οὖσαν καταλιπόντας, καὶ ἧς ἂν
ὦσι πατρίδος, ταύτῃ αὔχησιν ὡς οὐ περὶ ἀλλοτρίων οὐδ'
ἁμαρτόντων, ἀλλ' ὡς περὶ σφετέρων τε καὶ καλὰ πραξάντων. 15
6 ὧν ἐγὼ ὀρεγόμενος καὶ διὰ ταῦτα τὰ ἴδια ἐπιβοώμενος τὰ
δημόσια σκοπεῖτε εἴ του χεῖρον μεταχειρίζω. Πελοποννήσου γὰρ τὰ δυνατώτατα ξυστήσας ἄνευ μεγάλου ὑμῖν
κινδύνου καὶ δαπάνης Λακεδαιμονίους ἐς μίαν ἡμέραν
κατέστησα ἐν Μαντινείᾳ περὶ τῶν ἁπάντων ἀγωνίσασθαι· 20
ἐξ οὗ καὶ περιγενόμενοι τῇ μάχῃ οὐδέπω καὶ νῦν βεβαίως
θαρσοῦσιν.

17   'Καὶ ταῦτα ἡ ἐμὴ νεότης καὶ ἄνοια παρὰ φύσιν δοκοῦσα
εἶναι ἐς τὴν Πελοποννησίων δύναμιν λόγοις τε πρέπουσιν
ὡμίλησε καὶ ὀργῇ πίστιν παρασχομένη ἔπεισεν. καὶ νῦν μὴ 25
πεφόβησθε αὐτήν, ἀλλ' ἕως ἐγώ τε ἔτι ἀκμάζω μετ' αὐτῆς καὶ
ὁ Νικίας εὐτυχὴς δοκεῖ εἶναι, ἀποχρήσασθε τῇ ἑκατέρου ἡμῶν
2 ὠφελίᾳ. καὶ τὸν ἐς τὴν Σικελίαν πλοῦν μὴ μεταγιγνώσκετε
ὡς ἐπὶ μεγάλην δύναμιν ἐσόμενον. ὄχλοις τε γὰρ ξυμμείκτοις
πολυανδροῦσιν αἱ πόλεις καὶ ῥᾳδίας ἔχουσι τῶν πολιτῶν τὰς 30

---

1 ἀστοῖς] αὐτοῖς A B F. F M   3 ἥδ' ἡ ἄνοια M Schol : ἡ διάνοια
cett.   17 χείρω C G   26 πεφόβησθε Reiske : πεφοβῆσθαι
codd. 'ex -εισθαι c)   27 ἀποχρήσασθε f : ἀποχρήσασθαι M : ἀποχρή-
σεσθαι C : ἀποχρήσεσθε cett.   30 πολιτῶν E : πολιτειῶν cett.

μεταβολὰς καὶ ἐπιδοχάς. καὶ οὐδεὶς δι' αὐτὸ ὡς περὶ οἰκείας 3
πατρίδος οὔτε τὰ περὶ τὸ σῶμα ὅπλοις ἐξήρτυται οὔτε τὰ ἐν
τῇ χώρᾳ νομίμοις κατασκευαῖς· ὅτι δὲ ἕκαστος ἢ ἐκ τοῦ
λέγων πείθειν οἴεται ἢ στασιάζων ἀπὸ τοῦ κοινοῦ λαβὼν
5 ἄλλην γῆν, μὴ κατορθώσας, οἰκήσειν, ταῦτα ἑτοιμάζεται.
καὶ οὐκ εἰκὸς τὸν τοιοῦτον ὅμιλον οὔτε λόγου μιᾷ γνώμῃ 4
ἀκροᾶσθαι οὔτε ἐς τὰ ἔργα κοινῶς τρέπεσθαι· ταχὺ δ' ἂν ὡς
ἕκαστοι, εἴ τι καθ' ἡδονὴν λέγοιτο, προσχωροῖεν, ἄλλως τε
καὶ εἰ στασιάζουσιν, ὥσπερ πυνθανόμεθα. καὶ μὴν οὐδ' 5
10 ὁπλῖται οὔτ' ἐκείνοις ὅσοιπερ κομποῦνται, οὔτε οἱ ἄλλοι
Ἕλληνες διεφάνησαν τοσοῦτοι ὄντες ὅσους ἕκαστοι σφᾶς
αὐτοὺς ἠρίθμουν, ἀλλὰ μέγιστον δὴ αὐτοὺς ἐψευσμένη ἡ
Ἑλλὰς μόλις ἐν τῷδε τῷ πολέμῳ ἱκανῶς ὡπλίσθη. τά τε 6
οὖν ἐκεῖ, ἐξ ὧν ἐγὼ ἀκοῇ αἰσθάνομαι, τοιαῦτα καὶ ἔτι
15 εὐπορώτερα ἔσται (βαρβάρους [τε] γὰρ πολλοὺς ἕξομεν οἳ
Συρακοσίων μίσει ξυνεπιθήσονται αὐτοῖς) καὶ τὰ ἐνθάδε οὐκ
ἐπικωλύσει, ἢν ὑμεῖς ὀρθῶς βουλεύησθε. οἱ γὰρ πατέρες 7
ἡμῶν τοὺς αὐτοὺς τούτους οὕσπερ νῦν φασὶ πολεμίους ὑπολεί-
ποντας ἂν ἡμᾶς πλεῖν καὶ προσέτι τὸν Μῆδον ἐχθρὸν ἔχοντες
20 τὴν ἀρχὴν ἐκτήσαντο, οὐκ ἄλλῳ τινὶ ἢ τῇ περιουσίᾳ τοῦ
ναυτικοῦ ἰσχύοντες. καὶ νῦν οὔτε ἀνέλπιστοί πω μᾶλλον 8
Πελοποννήσιοι ἐς ἡμᾶς ἐγένοντο, εἴ τε καὶ πάνυ ἔρρωνται,
τὸ μὲν ἐς τὴν γῆν ἡμῶν ἐσβάλλειν, κἂν μὴ ἐκπλεύσωμεν,
ἱκανοί εἰσι, τῷ δὲ ναυτικῷ οὐκ ἂν δύναιντο βλάπτειν·
25 ὑπόλοιπον γὰρ ἡμῖν ἐστιν ἀντίπαλον ναυτικόν. ὥστε τί 18
ἂν λέγοντες εἰκὸς ἢ αὐτοὶ ἀποκνοῖμεν ἢ πρὸς τοὺς ἐκεῖ
ξυμμάχους σκηπτόμενοι μὴ βοηθοῖμεν; οἷς χρεών, ἐπειδή
γε καὶ ξυνωμόσαμεν, ἐπαμύνειν, καὶ μὴ ἀντιτιθέναι ὅτι οὐδὲ
ἐκεῖνοι ἡμῖν. οὐ γὰρ ἵνα δεῦρο ἀντιβοηθῶσι προσεθέμεθα
30 αὐτούς, ἀλλ' ἵνα τοῖς ἐκεῖ ἐχθροῖς ἡμῶν λυπηροὶ ὄντες
δεῦρο κωλύωσιν αὐτοὺς ἐπιέναι. τήν τε ἀρχὴν οὕτως ἐκτη- 2

σάμεθα καὶ ἡμεῖς καὶ ὅσοι δὴ ἄλλοι ἦρξαν, παραγιγνόμενοι
προθύμως τοῖς αἰεὶ ἢ βαρβάροις ἢ Ἕλλησιν ἐπικαλουμένοις,
ἐπεὶ εἴ γε ἡσυχάζοιεν πάντες ἢ φυλοκρινοῖεν οἷς χρεὼν
βοηθεῖν, βραχὺ ἄν τι προσκτώμενοι αὐτῇ περὶ αὐτῆς ἂν
ταύτης μᾶλλον κινδυνεύοιμεν. τὸν γὰρ προύχοντα οὐ μόνον 5
ἐπιόντα τις ἀμύνεται, ἀλλὰ καὶ ὅπως μὴ ἔπεισι προκατα-
3 λαμβάνει. καὶ οὐκ ἔστιν ἡμῖν ταμιεύεσθαι ἐς ὅσον βουλόμεθα ἄρχειν, ἀλλ᾽ ἀνάγκη, ἐπειδήπερ ἐν τῷδε καθέσταμεν,
τοῖς μὲν ἐπιβουλεύειν, τοὺς δὲ μὴ ἀνιέναι, διὰ τὸ ἀρχθῆναι
ἂν ὑφ᾽ ἑτέρων αὐτοῖς κίνδυνον εἶναι, εἰ μὴ αὐτοὶ ἄλλων 10
ἄρχοιμεν. καὶ οὐκ ἐκ τοῦ αὐτοῦ ἐπισκεπτέον ὑμῖν τοῖς
ἄλλοις τὸ ἥσυχον, εἰ μὴ καὶ τὰ ἐπιτηδεύματα ἐς τὸ ὁμοῖον
μεταλήψεσθε.

4   ‘Λογισάμενοι οὖν τάδε μᾶλλον αὐξήσειν, ἐπ᾽ ἐκεῖνα ἢν
ἴωμεν, ποιώμεθα τὸν πλοῦν, ἵνα Πελοποννησίων τε στορέ- 15
σωμεν τὸ φρόνημα, εἰ δόξομεν ὑπεριδόντες τὴν ἐν τῷ παρόντι
ἡσυχίαν καὶ ἐπὶ Σικελίαν πλεῦσαι· καὶ ἅμα ἢ τῆς Ἑλλάδος
τῶν ἐκεῖ προσγενομένων πάσῃ τῷ εἰκότι ἄρξομεν, ἢ κακώ-
σομέν γε Συρακοσίους, ἐν ᾧ καὶ αὐτοὶ καὶ οἱ ξύμμαχοι
5 ὠφελησόμεθα. τὸ δὲ ἀσφαλές, καὶ μένειν, ἤν τι προχωρῇ, 20
καὶ ἀπελθεῖν, αἱ νῆες παρέξουσιν· ναυκράτορες γὰρ ἐσόμεθα
6 καὶ ξυμπάντων Σικελιωτῶν. καὶ μὴ ὑμᾶς ἡ Νικίου τῶν
λόγων ἀπραγμοσύνη καὶ διάστασις τοῖς νέοις ἐς τοὺς πρεσβυ-
τέρους ἀποτρέψῃ, τῷ δὲ εἰωθότι κόσμῳ, ὥσπερ καὶ οἱ πατέρες
ἡμῶν ἅμα νέοι γεραιτέροις βουλεύοντες ἐς τάδε ἦραν αὐτά, 25
καὶ νῦν τῷ αὐτῷ τρόπῳ πειρᾶσθε προαγαγεῖν τὴν πόλιν,
καὶ νομίσατε νεότητα μὲν καὶ γῆρας ἄνευ ἀλλήλων μηδὲν
δύνασθαι, ὁμοῦ δὲ τό τε φαῦλον καὶ τὸ μέσον καὶ τὸ πάνυ
ἀκριβὲς ἂν ξυγκραθὲν μάλιστ᾽ ἂν ἰσχύειν, καὶ τὴν πόλιν,
ἐὰν μὲν ἡσυχάζῃ, τρίψεσθαί τε αὐτὴν περὶ αὐτὴν ὥσπερ καὶ 30
ἄλλο τι, καὶ πάντων τὴν ἐπιστήμην ἐγγηράσεσθαι, ἀγωνι-

6 ὅπως μὴ recc. : μὴ ὅπως codd.   20 προχωρῇ recc. : προσχωρῇ
codd.   21 ναυκράτορες Valckenaer : αὐτοκράτορες codd.   24 ἀποτρέψῃ Poppo : ἀποστρέψῃ codd.

ζομένην δὲ αἰεὶ προσλήψεσθαί τε τὴν ἐμπειρίαν καὶ τὸ
ἀμύνεσθαι οὐ λόγῳ ἀλλ' ἔργῳ μᾶλλον ξύνηθες ἕξειν.
παράπαν τε γιγνώσκω πόλιν μὴ ἀπράγμονα τάχιστ' ἄν μοι 7
δοκεῖν ἀπραγμοσύνης μεταβολῇ διαφθαρῆναι, καὶ τῶν ἀνθρώ-
5 πων ἀσφαλέστατα τούτους οἰκεῖν οἳ ἂν τοῖς παροῦσιν ἤθεσι
καὶ νόμοις, ἢν καὶ χείρω ᾖ, ἥκιστα διαφόρως πολιτεύωσιν.'
   Τοιαῦτα μὲν ὁ Ἀλκιβιάδης εἶπεν· οἱ δ' Ἀθηναῖοι 19
ἀκούσαντες ἐκείνου τε καὶ τῶν Ἐγεσταίων καὶ Λεοντίνων
φυγάδων, οἳ παρελθόντες ἐδέοντό τε καὶ τῶν ὁρκίων ὑπο-
10 μιμνήσκοντες ἱκέτευον βοηθῆσαι σφίσι, πολλῷ μᾶλλον ἢ
πρότερον ὥρμηντο στρατεύειν. καὶ ὁ Νικίας γνοὺς ὅτι ἀπὸ 2
μὲν τῶν αὐτῶν λόγων οὐκ ἂν ἔτι ἀποτρέψειε, παρασκευῆς
δὲ πλήθει, εἰ πολλὴν ἐπιτάξειε, τάχ' ἂν μεταστήσειεν αὐτούς,
παρελθὼν αὐτοῖς αὖθις ἔλεγε τοιάδε.
15   ''Ἐπειδὴ πάντως ὁρῶ ὑμᾶς, ὦ Ἀθηναῖοι, ὡρμημένους 20
στρατεύειν, ξυνενέγκοι μὲν ταῦτα ὡς βουλόμεθα, ἐπὶ δὲ τῷ
παρόντι ἃ γιγνώσκω σημανῶ. ἐπὶ γὰρ πόλεις, ὡς ἐγὼ 2
ἀκοῇ αἰσθάνομαι, μέλλομεν ἰέναι μεγάλας καὶ οὔθ' ὑπηκόους
ἀλλήλων οὔτε δεομένας μεταβολῆς, ᾗ ἂν ἐκ βιαίου τις
20 δουλείας ἄσμενος ἐς ῥᾴω μετάστασιν χωροίη, οὐδ' ἂν τὴν
ἀρχὴν τὴν ἡμετέραν εἰκότως ἀντ' ἐλευθερίας προσδεξαμένας,
τό τε πλῆθος ὡς ἐν μιᾷ νήσῳ πολλὰς τὰς Ἑλληνίδας. πλὴν 3
γὰρ Νάξου καὶ Κατάνης, ἃς ἐλπίζω ἡμῖν κατὰ τὸ Λεοντίνων
ξυγγενὲς προσέσεσθαι, ἄλλαι εἰσὶν ἑπτά, καὶ παρεσκευασμέναι
25 τοῖς πᾶσιν ὁμοιοτρόπως μάλιστα τῇ ἡμετέρᾳ δυνάμει, καὶ οὐχ
ἥκιστα ἐπὶ ἃς μᾶλλον πλέομεν, Σελινοῦς καὶ Συράκουσαι.
πολλοὶ μὲν γὰρ ὁπλῖται ἔνεισι καὶ τοξόται καὶ ἀκοντισταί, 4
πολλαὶ δὲ τριήρεις καὶ ὄχλος ὁ πληρώσων αὐτάς. χρήματά τ' ἔχουσι τὰ μὲν ἴδια, τὰ δὲ καὶ ἐν τοῖς ἱεροῖς ἐστὶ
30 Σελινουντίοις, Συρακοσίοις δὲ καὶ ἀπὸ βαρβάρων τινῶν
ἀπαρχὴ ἐσφέρεται· ᾧ δὲ μάλιστα ἡμῶν προύχουσιν, ἵππους

21 προσδεξομένας C E M   27 μὲν om. C G   31 ἀπαρχὴ ἐσφέρεται
recc.: ἀπαρχῆς (ἀπ' ἀρχῆς G) φέρεται codd.

τε πολλοὺς κέκτηνται καὶ σίτῳ οἰκείῳ καὶ οὐκ ἐπακτῷ
χρῶνται.

21   'Πρὸς οὖν τοιαύτην δύναμιν οὐ ναυτικῆς καὶ φαύλου
στρατιᾶς μόνον δεῖ, ἀλλὰ καὶ πεζὸν πολὺν ξυμπλεῖν, εἴπερ
βουλόμεθα ἄξιον τῆς διανοίας δρᾶν καὶ μὴ ὑπὸ ἱππέων πολλῶν 5
εἴργεσθαι τῆς γῆς, ἄλλως τε καὶ εἰ ξυστῶσιν αἱ πόλεις
φοβηθεῖσαι καὶ μὴ ἀντιπαράσχωσιν ἡμῖν φίλοι τινὲς γενό-
2 μενοι ἄλλοι ἢ Ἐγεσταῖοι ᾧ ἀμυνούμεθα ἱππικόν (αἰσχρὸν
δὲ βιασθέντας ἀπελθεῖν ἢ ὕστερον ἐπιμεταπέμπεσθαι, τὸ
πρῶτον ἀσκέπτως βουλευσαμένους)· αὐτόθεν δὲ παρασκευῇ 10
ἀξιόχρεῳ ἐπιέναι, γνόντας ὅτι πολύ τε ἀπὸ τῆς ἡμετέρας
αὐτῶν μέλλομεν πλεῖν καὶ οὐκ ἐν τῷ ὁμοίῳ στρατευσόμενοι
καὶ ὅτε ἐν τοῖς τῇδε ὑπηκόοις ξύμμαχοι ἤλθετε ἐπί τινα,
ὅθεν ῥᾴδιαι αἱ κομιδαὶ ἐκ τῆς φιλίας ὧν προσέδει, ἀλλ' ἐς
ἀλλοτρίαν πᾶσαν ἀπαρτήσοντες, ἐξ ἧς μηνῶν οὐδὲ τεσσάρων 15
22 τῶν χειμερινῶν ἄγγελον ῥᾴδιον ἐλθεῖν. ὁπλίτας τε οὖν
πολλούς μοι δοκεῖ χρῆναι ἡμᾶς ἄγειν καὶ ἡμῶν αὐτῶν καὶ
τῶν ξυμμάχων, τῶν τε ὑπηκόων καὶ ἤν τινα ἐκ Πελοποννήσου
δυνώμεθα ἢ πεῖσαι ἢ μισθῷ προσαγαγέσθαι, καὶ τοξότας
πολλοὺς καὶ σφενδονήτας, ὅπως πρὸς τὸ ἐκείνων ἱππικὸν 20
ἀντέχωσι, ναυσί τε καὶ πολὺ περιεῖναι, ἵνα καὶ τὰ ἐπιτήδεια
ῥᾷον ἐσκομιζώμεθα, τὸν δὲ καὶ αὐτόθεν σῖτον ἐν ὁλκάσι,
πυροὺς καὶ πεφρυγμένας κριθάς, ἄγειν, καὶ σιτοποιοὺς ἐκ
τῶν μυλώνων πρὸς μέρος ἠναγκασμένους ἐμμίσθους, ἵνα,
ἤν που ὑπὸ ἀπλοίας ἀπολαμβανώμεθα, ἔχῃ ἡ στρατιὰ τὰ 25
ἐπιτήδεια (πολλὴ γὰρ οὖσα οὐ πάσης ἔσται πόλεως ὑποδέ-
ξασθαι), τά τε ἄλλα ὅσον δυνατὸν ἑτοιμάσασθαι, καὶ μὴ ἐπὶ
ἑτέροις γίγνεσθαι, μάλιστα δὲ χρήματα αὐτόθεν ὡς πλεῖστα
ἔχειν. τὰ δὲ παρ' Ἐγεσταίων, ἃ λέγεται ἐκεῖ ἑτοῖμα,
23 νομίσατε καὶ λόγῳ ἂν μάλιστα ἑτοῖμα εἶναι. ἢν γὰρ αὐτοὶ 30
ἔλθωμεν ἐνθένδε μὴ ἀντίπαλον μόνον παρασκευασάμενοι,

πλήν γε πρὸς τὸ μάχιμον αὐτῶν, τὸ ὁπλιτικόν, ἀλλὰ καὶ
ὑπερβάλλοντες τοῖς πᾶσι, μόλις οὕτως οἷοί τε ἐσόμεθα τῶν
μὲν κρατεῖν, τὰ δὲ καὶ διασῶσαι. πόλιν τε νομίσαι χρὴ ἐν 2
ἀλλοφύλοις καὶ πολεμίοις οἰκιοῦντας ἰέναι, οὓς πρέπει τῇ
5 πρώτῃ ἡμέρᾳ ᾗ ἂν κατάσχωσιν εὐθὺς κρατεῖν τῆς γῆς, ἢ
εἰδέναι ὅτι, ἢν σφάλλωνται, πάντα πολέμια ἕξουσιν. ὅπερ 3
ἐγὼ φοβούμενος, καὶ εἰδὼς πολλὰ μὲν ἡμᾶς δέον εὖ βουλεύ-
σασθαι, ἔτι δὲ πλείω εὐτυχῆσαι (χαλεπὸν δὲ ἀνθρώπους
ὄντας), ὅτι ἐλάχιστα τῇ τύχῃ παραδοὺς ἐμαυτὸν βούλομαι
10 ἐκπλεῖν, παρασκευῇ δὲ ἀπὸ τῶν εἰκότων ἀσφαλὴς ἐκπλεῦσαι.
ταῦτα γὰρ τῇ τε ξυμπάσῃ πόλει βεβαιότατα ἡγοῦμαι καὶ
ἡμῖν τοῖς στρατευσομένοις σωτήρια. εἰ δέ τῳ ἄλλως δοκεῖ,
παρίημι αὐτῷ τὴν ἀρχήν.᾽

Ὁ μὲν Νικίας τοσαῦτα εἶπε νομίζων τοὺς Ἀθηναίους τῷ 24
15 πλήθει τῶν πραγμάτων ἢ ἀποτρέψειν ἤ, εἰ ἀναγκάζοιτο
στρατεύεσθαι, μάλιστ᾽ ⟨ἂν⟩ οὕτως ἀσφαλῶς ἐκπλεῦσαι· οἱ 2
δὲ τὸ μὲν ἐπιθυμοῦν τοῦ πλοῦ οὐκ ἐξῃρέθησαν ὑπὸ τοῦ
ὀχλώδους τῆς παρασκευῆς, πολὺ δὲ μᾶλλον ὥρμηντο, καὶ
τοὐναντίον περιέστη αὐτῷ· εὖ τε γὰρ παραινέσαι ἔδοξε καὶ
20 ἀσφάλεια νῦν δὴ καὶ πολλὴ ἔσεσθαι. καὶ ἔρως ἐνέπεσε 3
τοῖς πᾶσιν ὁμοίως ἐκπλεῦσαι· τοῖς μὲν γὰρ πρεσβυτέροις
ὡς ἢ καταστρεψομένοις ἐφ᾽ ἃ ἔπλεον ἢ οὐδὲν ἂν σφαλεῖσαν
μεγάλην δύναμιν, τοῖς δ᾽ ἐν τῇ ἡλικίᾳ τῆς τε ἀπούσης πόθῳ
ὄψεως καὶ θεωρίας, καὶ εὐέλπιδες ὄντες σωθήσεσθαι· ὁ δὲ
25 πολὺς ὅμιλος καὶ στρατιώτης ἔν τε τῷ παρόντι ἀργύριον
οἴσειν καὶ προσκτήσεσθαι δύναμιν ὅθεν ἀίδιον μισθοφορὰν
ὑπάρξειν. ὥστε διὰ τὴν ἄγαν τῶν πλεόνων ἐπιθυμίαν, εἴ 4
τῳ ἄρα καὶ μὴ ἤρεσκε, δεδιὼς μὴ ἀντιχειροτονῶν κακόνους
δόξειεν εἶναι τῇ πόλει ἡσυχίαν ἦγεν. καὶ τέλος παρελθὼν 25
30 τις τῶν Ἀθηναίων καὶ παρακαλέσας τὸν Νικίαν οὐκ ἔφη

4 οἰκιοῦντας a f : οἰκειοῦντας codd.   7 εὖ om. A B F   10 παρασκευῇ A B C M   12 στρατευομένοις E G   16 ἂν add.
Bekker   20 δὴ] δὲ A B E F   26 προσκτήσεσθαι G : προσκτήσασθαι
codd.

χρῆναι προφασίζεσθαι οὐδὲ διαμέλλειν, ἀλλ᾽ ἐναντίον ἁπάντων ἤδη λέγειν ἥντινα αὐτῷ παρασκευὴν ᾽Αθηναῖοι ψηφί-
2 σωνται.　ὁ δὲ ἄκων μὲν εἶπεν ὅτι καὶ μετὰ τῶν ξυναρχόντων
καθ᾽ ἡσυχίαν μᾶλλον βουλεύσοιτο, ὅσα μέντοι ἤδη δοκεῖν
αὐτῷ, τριήρεσι μὲν οὐκ ἔλασσον ἢ ἑκατὸν πλευστέα εἶναι 5
(αὐτῶν δ᾽ ᾽Αθηναίων ἔσεσθαι ὁπλιταγωγοὺς ὅσαι ἂν δοκῶσι,
καὶ ἄλλας ἐκ τῶν ξυμμάχων μεταπεμπτέας εἶναι), ὁπλίταις
δὲ τοῖς ξύμπασιν ᾽Αθηναίων καὶ τῶν ξυμμάχων πεντακισχιλίων μὲν οὐκ ἐλάσσοσιν, ἢν δέ τι δύνωνται, καὶ
πλέοσιν· τὴν δὲ ἄλλην παρασκευὴν ὡς κατὰ λόγον, καὶ 10
τοξοτῶν τῶν αὐτόθεν καὶ ἐκ Κρήτης καὶ σφενδονητῶν, καὶ ἤν
26 τι ἄλλο πρέπον δοκῇ εἶναι, ἑτοιμασάμενοι ἄξειν.　ἀκούσαντες
δ᾽ οἱ ᾽Αθηναῖοι ἐψηφίσαντο εὐθὺς αὐτοκράτορας εἶναι καὶ
περὶ στρατιᾶς πλήθους καὶ περὶ τοῦ παντὸς πλοῦ τοὺς στρατηγοὺς πράσσειν ᾗ ἂν αὐτοῖς δοκῇ ἄριστα εἶναι [᾽Αθηναίοις]. 15
2 καὶ μετὰ ταῦτα ἡ παρασκευὴ ἐγίγνετο, καὶ ἔς τε τοὺς
ξυμμάχους ἔπεμπον καὶ αὐτόθεν καταλόγους ἐποιοῦντο.　ἄρτι
δ᾽ ἀνειλήφει ἡ πόλις ἑαυτὴν ἀπὸ τῆς νόσου καὶ τοῦ ξυνεχοῦς
πολέμου ἔς τε ἡλικίας πλῆθος ἐπιγεγενημένης καὶ ἐς χρημάτων ἄθροισιν διὰ τὴν ἐκεχειρίαν, ὥστε ῥᾷον πάντα 20
ἐπορίζετο.　καὶ οἱ μὲν ἐν παρασκευῇ ἦσαν.

27　　᾽Εν δὲ τούτῳ, ὅσοι ῾Ερμαῖ ἦσαν λίθινοι ἐν τῇ πόλει τῇ
᾽Αθηναίων (εἰσὶ δὲ κατὰ τὸ ἐπιχώριον, ἡ τετράγωνος ἐργασία,
πολλοὶ καὶ ἐν ἰδίοις προθύροις καὶ ἐν ἱεροῖς), μιᾷ νυκτὶ οἱ
2 πλεῖστοι περιεκόπησαν τὰ πρόσωπα.　καὶ τοὺς δράσαντας 25
ᾔδει οὐδείς, ἀλλὰ μεγάλοις μηνύτροις δημοσίᾳ οὗτοί τε ἐζη-
τοῦντο καὶ προσέτι ἐψηφίσαντο, καὶ εἴ τις ἄλλο τι οἶδεν
ἀσέβημα γεγενημένον, μηνύειν ἀδεῶς τὸν βουλόμενον καὶ
3 ἀστῶν καὶ ξένων καὶ δούλων.　καὶ τὸ πρᾶγμα μειζόνως
ἐλάμβανον· τοῦ τε γὰρ ἔκπλου οἰωνὸς ἐδόκει εἶναι καὶ ἐπὶ 30
ξυνωμοσίᾳ ἅμα νεωτέρων πραγμάτων καὶ δήμου καταλύσεως

2 ψηφίσονται ABEFM　　14 post πλοῦ habent τοῦ codd.: om.
rell.　15 ᾽Αθηναίοις seclusit Jones (monente Herwerdeno)　23 ἡ
... ἐργασία non legit Schol. Patm.

γεγενῆσθαι. μηνύεται οὖν ἀπὸ μετοίκων τέ τινων καὶ ἀκο- 28
λούθων περὶ μὲν τῶν Ἑρμῶν οὐδέν, ἄλλων δὲ ἀγαλμάτων
περικοπαί τινες πρότερον ὑπὸ νεωτέρων μετὰ παιδιᾶς καὶ
οἴνου γεγενημέναι, καὶ τὰ μυστήρια ἅμα ὡς ποιεῖται ἐν
5 οἰκίαις ἐφ' ὕβρει· ὧν καὶ τὸν Ἀλκιβιάδην ἐπῃτιῶντο. καὶ 2
αὐτὰ ὑπολαμβάνοντες οἱ μάλιστα τῷ Ἀλκιβιάδῃ ἀχθόμενοι
ἐμποδὼν ὄντι σφίσι μὴ αὐτοῖς τοῦ δήμου βεβαίως προεστάναι,
καὶ νομίσαντες, εἰ αὐτὸν ἐξελάσειαν, πρῶτοι ἂν εἶναι, ἐμεγά-
λυνον καὶ ἐβόων ὡς ἐπὶ δήμου καταλύσει τά τε μυστικὰ καὶ
10 ἡ τῶν Ἑρμῶν περικοπὴ γένοιτο καὶ οὐδὲν εἴη αὐτῶν ὅτι οὐ
μετ' ἐκείνου ἐπράχθη, ἐπιλέγοντες τεκμήρια τὴν ἄλλην αὐτοῦ
ἐς τὰ ἐπιτηδεύματα οὐ δημοτικὴν παρανομίαν. ὁ δ' ἔν τε 29
τῷ παρόντι πρὸς τὰ μηνύματα ἀπελογεῖτο καὶ ἑτοῖμος ἦν
πρὶν ἐκπλεῖν κρίνεσθαι, εἴ τι τούτων εἰργασμένος ἦν (ἤδη
15 γὰρ καὶ τὰ τῆς παρασκευῆς ἐπεπόριστο), καὶ εἰ μὲν τούτων
τι εἴργαστο, δίκην δοῦναι, εἰ δ' ἀπολυθείη, ἄρχειν. καὶ 2
ἐπεμαρτύρετο μὴ ἀπόντος πέρι αὐτοῦ διαβολὰς ἀποδέχεσθαι,
ἀλλ' ἤδη ἀποκτείνειν, εἰ ἀδικεῖ, καὶ ὅτι σωφρονέστερον εἴη
μὴ μετὰ τοιαύτης αἰτίας, πρὶν διαγνῶσι, πέμπειν αὐτὸν ἐπὶ
20 τοσούτῳ στρατεύματι. οἱ δ' ἐχθροὶ δεδιότες τό τε στράτευμα 3
μὴ εὔνουν ἔχῃ, ἢν ἤδη ἀγωνίζηται, ὅ τε δῆμος μὴ μαλα-
κίζηται θεραπεύων ὅτι δι' ἐκεῖνον οἵ τ' Ἀργεῖοι ξυνεστράτευον
καὶ τῶν Μαντινέων τινές, ἀπέτρεπον καὶ ἀπέσπευδον, ἄλλους
ῥήτορας ἐνιέντες οἳ ἔλεγον νῦν μὲν πλεῖν αὐτὸν καὶ μὴ
25 κατασχεῖν τὴν ἀναγωγήν, ἐλθόντα δὲ κρίνεσθαι ἐν ἡμέραις
ῥηταῖς, βουλόμενοι ἐκ μείζονος διαβολῆς, ἣν ἔμελλον ῥᾷον
αὐτοῦ ἀπόντος ποριεῖν, μετάπεμπτον κομισθέντα αὐτὸν ἀγωνίσασθαι. καὶ ἔδοξε πλεῖν τὸν Ἀλκιβιάδην.

Μετὰ δὲ ταῦτα θέρους μεσοῦντος ἤδη ἡ ἀναγωγὴ ἐγίγνετο 30
30 ἐς τὴν Σικελίαν. τῶν μὲν οὖν ξυμμάχων τοῖς πλείστοις καὶ
ταῖς σιταγωγοῖς ὁλκάσι καὶ τοῖς πλοίοις καὶ ὅση ἄλλη παρασκευὴ ξυνείπετο πρότερον εἴρητο ἐς Κέρκυραν ξυλλέγεσθαι

ὡς ἐκεῖθεν ἀθρόοις ἐπὶ ἄκραν Ἰαπυγίαν τὸν Ἰόνιον δια-
βαλοῦσιν· αὐτοὶ δ' Ἀθηναῖοι καὶ εἴ τινες τῶν ξυμμάχων
παρῆσαν, ἐς τὸν Πειραιᾶ καταβάντες ἐν ἡμέρᾳ ῥητῇ ἅμα ἕῳ
2 ἐπλήρουν τὰς ναῦς ὡς ἀναξόμενοι. ξυγκατέβη δὲ καὶ ὁ ἄλλος
ὅμιλος ἅπας ὡς εἰπεῖν ὁ ἐν τῇ πόλει καὶ ἀστῶν καὶ ξένων, 5
οἱ μὲν ἐπιχώριοι τοὺς σφετέρους αὐτῶν ἕκαστοι προπέμποντες,
οἱ μὲν ἑταίρους, οἱ δὲ ξυγγενεῖς, οἱ δὲ υἱεῖς, καὶ μετ' ἐλπίδος
τε ἅμα ἰόντες καὶ ὀλοφυρμῶν, τὰ μὲν ὡς κτήσοιντο, τοὺς δ'
εἴ ποτε ὄψοιντο, ἐνθυμούμενοι ὅσον πλοῦν ἐκ τῆς σφετέρας
31 ἀπεστέλλοντο. καὶ ἐν τῷ παρόντι καιρῷ, ὡς ἤδη ἔμελλον 10
μετὰ κινδύνων ἀλλήλους ἀπολιπεῖν, μᾶλλον αὐτοὺς ἐσῄει τὰ
δεινὰ ἢ ὅτε ἐψηφίζοντο πλεῖν· ὅμως δὲ τῇ παρούσῃ ῥώμῃ,
διὰ τὸ πλῆθος ἑκάστων ὧν ἑώρων, τῇ ὄψει ἀνεθάρσουν. οἱ
δὲ ξένοι καὶ ὁ ἄλλος ὄχλος κατὰ θέαν ἧκεν ὡς ἐπ' ἀξιόχρεων
καὶ ἄπιστον διάνοιαν. παρασκευὴ γὰρ αὕτη πρώτη ἐκπλεύ- 15
σασα μιᾶς πόλεως δυνάμει Ἑλληνικῇ πολυτελεστάτη δὴ καὶ
2 εὐπρεπεστάτη τῶν ἐς ἐκεῖνον τὸν χρόνον ἐγένετο. ἀριθμῷ
δὲ νεῶν καὶ ὁπλιτῶν καὶ ἡ ἐς Ἐπίδαυρον μετὰ Περικλέους
καὶ ἡ αὐτὴ ἐς Ποτείδαιαν μετὰ Ἅγνωνος οὐκ ἐλάσσων ἦν·
τετράκις γὰρ χίλιοι ὁπλῖται αὐτῶν Ἀθηναίων καὶ τριακόσιοι 20
ἱππῆς καὶ τριήρεις ἑκατόν, καὶ Λεσβίων καὶ Χίων πεντήκοντα,
3 καὶ ξύμμαχοι ἔτι πολλοὶ ξυνέπλευσαν. ἀλλὰ ἐπί τε βραχεῖ
πλῷ ὡρμήθησαν καὶ παρασκευῇ φαύλῃ, οὗτος δὲ ὁ στόλος
ὡς χρόνιός τε ἐσόμενος καὶ κατ' ἀμφότερα, οὗ ἂν δέῃ, καὶ
ναυσὶ καὶ πεζῷ ἅμα ἐξαρτυθείς, τὸ μὲν ναυτικὸν μεγάλαις 25
δαπάναις τῶν τε τριηράρχων καὶ τῆς πόλεως ἐκπονηθέν, τοῦ
μὲν δημοσίου δραχμὴν τῆς ἡμέρας τῷ ναύτῃ ἑκάστῳ διδόντος
καὶ ναῦς παρασχόντος κενὰς ἑξήκοντα μὲν ταχείας, τεσσαράκοντα δὲ ὁπλιταγωγοὺς καὶ ὑπηρεσίας ταύταις τὰς κρατί-
σ̣τας, τῶν ⟨δὲ⟩ τριηράρχων ἐπιφοράς τε πρὸς τῷ ἐκ δημοσίου 30
μισθῷ διδόντων τοῖς θρανίταις τῶν ναυτῶν καὶ ταῖς ὑπηρεσίαις
καὶ τἆλλα σημείοις καὶ κατασκευαῖς πολυτελέσι χρησαμένων,

16 Ἑλληνικῆς Haacke   30 δὲ add. Schol. Patm.

καὶ ἐς τὰ μακρότατα προθυμηθέντος ἑνὸς ἑκάστου ὅπως αὐτῷ
τινὶ εὐπρεπείᾳ τε ἡ ναῦς μάλιστα προέξει καὶ τῷ ταχυναυτεῖν,
τὸ δὲ πεζὸν καταλόγοις τε χρηστοῖς ἐκκριθὲν καὶ ὅπλων καὶ
τῶν περὶ τὸ σῶμα σκευῶν μεγάλῃ σπουδῇ πρὸς ἀλλήλους
5 ἁμιλληθέν. ξυνέβη δὲ πρός τε σφᾶς αὐτοὺς ἅμα ἔριν 4
γενέσθαι, ᾧ τις ἕκαστος προσετάχθη, καὶ ἐς τοὺς ἄλλους
Ἕλληνας ἐπίδειξιν μᾶλλον εἰκασθῆναι τῆς δυνάμεως καὶ
ἐξουσίας ἢ ἐπὶ πολεμίους παρασκευήν. εἰ γάρ τις ἐλογίσατο 5
τήν τε τῆς πόλεως ἀνάλωσιν δημοσίαν καὶ τῶν στρατευο-
10 μένων τὴν ἰδίαν, τῆς μὲν πόλεως ὅσα τε ἤδη προετετελέκει
καὶ ἃ ἔχοντας τοὺς στρατηγοὺς ἀπέστελλε, τῶν δὲ ἰδιωτῶν
ἅ τε περὶ τὸ σῶμά τις καὶ τριήραρχος ἐς τὴν ναῦν ἀνηλώκει
καὶ ὅσα ἔτι ἔμελλεν ἀναλώσειν, χωρὶς δ' ἃ εἰκὸς ἦν καὶ ἄνευ
τοῦ ἐκ τοῦ δημοσίου μισθοῦ πάντα τινὰ παρασκευάσασθαι
15 ἐφόδιον ὡς ἐπὶ χρόνιον στρατείαν, καὶ ὅσα ἐπὶ μεταβολῇ
τις ἢ στρατιώτης ἢ ἔμπορος ἔχων ἔπλει, πολλὰ ἂν τάλαντα
ηὑρέθη ἐκ τῆς πόλεως τὰ πάντα ἐξαγόμενα.   καὶ ὁ στόλος 6
οὐχ ἧσσον τόλμης τε θάμβει καὶ ὄψεως λαμπρότητι περιβόητος ἐγένετο ἢ στρατιᾶς πρὸς οὓς ἐπῇσαν ὑπερβολῇ, καὶ
20 ὅτι μέγιστος ἤδη διάπλους ἀπὸ τῆς οἰκείας καὶ ἐπὶ μεγίστῃ
ἐλπίδι τῶν μελλόντων πρὸς τὰ ὑπάρχοντα ἐπεχειρήθη.

Ἐπειδὴ δὲ αἱ νῆες πλήρεις ἦσαν καὶ ἐσέκειτο πάντα ἤδη 32
ὅσα ἔχοντες ἔμελλον ἀνάξεσθαι, τῇ μὲν σάλπιγγι σιωπὴ
ὑπεσημάνθη, εὐχὰς δὲ τὰς νομιζομένας πρὸ τῆς ἀναγωγῆς
25 οὐ κατὰ ναῦν ἑκάστην, ξύμπαντες δὲ ὑπὸ κήρυκος ἐποιοῦντο,
κρατῆράς τε κεράσαντες παρ' ἅπαν τὸ στράτευμα καὶ ἐκπώ-
μασι χρυσοῖς τε καὶ ἀργυροῖς οἵ τε ἐπιβάται καὶ οἱ ἄρχοντες
σπένδοντες.   ξυνεπηύχοντο δὲ καὶ ὁ ἄλλος ὅμιλος ὁ ἐκ τῆς 2
γῆς τῶν τε πολιτῶν καὶ εἴ τις ἄλλος εὔνους παρῆν σφίσιν.
30 παιανίσαντες δὲ καὶ τελεώσαντες τὰς σπονδὰς ἀνήγοντο,
καὶ ἐπὶ κέρως τὸ πρῶτον ἐκπλεύσαντες ἅμιλλαν ἤδη μέχρι

10 προτετελέκει (sic) M : προσετετελέκει cett.   14 alterum τοῦ
om. C G   15 στρατείαν f : στρατιάν codd.   30 παιανίσαντες f :
παιωνίσαντες codd.   τελ]ε[ώσαντες incipit Π⁷

Αἰγίνης ἐποιοῦντο. καὶ οἱ μὲν ἐς τὴν Κέρκυραν, ἔνθαπερ
καὶ τὸ ἄλλο στράτευμα τῶν ξυμμάχων ξυνελέγετο, ἠπείγοντο
ἀφικέσθαι.

3 Ἐς δὲ τὰς Συρακούσας ἠγγέλλετο μὲν πολλαχόθεν τὰ
περὶ τοῦ ἐπίπλου, οὐ μέντοι ἐπιστεύετο ἐπὶ πολὺν χρόνον 5
οὐδέν, ἀλλὰ καὶ γενομένης ἐκκλησίας ἐλέχθησαν τοιοίδε
λόγοι ἀπό τε ἄλλων, τῶν μὲν πιστευόντων τὰ περὶ τῆς
στρατείας τῆς τῶν Ἀθηναίων, τῶν δὲ τὰ ἐναντία λεγόντων,
καὶ Ἑρμοκράτης ὁ Ἕρμωνος παρελθὼν αὐτοῖς, ὡς σαφῶς
οἰόμενος εἰδέναι τὰ περὶ αὐτῶν, ἔλεγε καὶ παρῄνει τοιάδε.   10

33 'Ἄπιστα μὲν ἴσως, ὥσπερ καὶ ἄλλοι τινές, δόξω ὑμῖν·
περὶ τοῦ ἐπίπλου τῆς ἀληθείας λέγειν, καὶ γιγνώσκω ὅτι οἱ
τὰ μὴ πιστὰ δοκοῦντα εἶναι ἢ λέγοντες ἢ ἀπαγγέλλοντες
οὐ μόνον οὐ πείθουσιν, ἀλλὰ καὶ ἄφρονες δοκοῦσιν εἶναι·
ὅμως δὲ οὐ καταφοβηθεὶς ἐπισχήσω κινδυνευούσης τῆς 15
πόλεως, πείθων γε ἐμαυτὸν σαφέστερόν τι ἑτέρου εἰδὼς
2 λέγειν. Ἀθηναῖοι γὰρ ἐφ' ὑμᾶς, ὃ πάνυ θαυμάζετε, πολλῇ
στρατιᾷ ὥρμηνται καὶ ναυτικῇ καὶ πεζῇ, πρόφασιν μὲν
Ἐγεσταίων ξυμμαχίᾳ καὶ Λεοντίνων κατοικίσει, τὸ δὲ ἀληθὲς
Σικελίας ἐπιθυμίᾳ, μάλιστα δὲ τῆς ἡμετέρας πόλεως, ἡγού- 20
3 μενοι, εἰ ταύτην σχοῖεν, ῥαδίως καὶ τἄλλα ἕξειν. ὡς οὖν ἐν
τάχει παρεσομένων, ὁρᾶτε ἀπὸ τῶν ὑπαρχόντων ὅτῳ τρόπῳ
κάλλιστα ἀμυνεῖσθε αὐτούς, καὶ μήτε καταφρονήσαντες
ἄφαρκτοι ληφθήσεσθε μήτε ἀπιστήσαντες τοῦ ξύμπαντος
4 ἀμελήσετε. εἰ δέ τῳ καὶ πιστά, τὴν τόλμαν αὐτῶν καὶ 25
δύναμιν μὴ ἐκπλαγῇ. οὔτε γὰρ βλάπτειν ἡμᾶς πλείω οἷοί
τ' ἔσονται ἢ πάσχειν, οὔθ' ὅτι μεγάλῳ στόλῳ ἐπέρχονται,
ἀνωφελεῖς, ἀλλὰ πρός τε τοὺς ἄλλους Σικελιώτας πολὺ
ἄμεινον (μᾶλλον γὰρ ἐθελήσουσιν ἐκπλαγέντες ἡμῖν ξυμμαχεῖν), καὶ ἢν ἄρα ἢ κατεργασώμεθα αὐτοὺς ἢ ἀπράκτους 30
ὧν ἐφίενται ἀπώσωμεν (οὐ γὰρ δὴ μὴ τύχωσί γε ὧν προσδέ-

5 χρόνο]ν desinit Π⁷   8 στρατιᾶς A B E F M   Ἀθηνῶν A B E F M
18 πεζῇ recc.: πεζικῇ codd.   19 κατοικήσει A B E F M   28 ἀνω-
φελὲς Faber (inutile Valla)

χονται φοβοῦμαι), κάλλιστον δὴ ἔργον ἡμῖν ξυμβήσεται, καὶ
οὐκ ἀνέλπιστον ἔμοιγε. ὀλίγοι γὰρ δὴ στόλοι μεγάλοι ἢ 5
Ἑλλήνων ἢ βαρβάρων πολὺ ἀπὸ τῆς ἑαυτῶν ἀπάραντες
κατώρθωσαν. οὔτε γὰρ πλείους τῶν ἐνοικούντων καὶ ἀστυ-
5 γειτόνων ἔρχονται (πάντα γὰρ ὑπὸ δέους ξυνίσταται), ἤν τε
δι' ἀπορίαν τῶν ἐπιτηδείων ἐν ἀλλοτρίᾳ γῇ σφαλῶσι, τοῖς
ἐπιβουλευθεῖσιν ὄνομα, κἂν περὶ σφίσιν αὐτοῖς τὰ πλείω
πταίσωσιν, ὅμως καταλείπουσιν. ὅπερ καὶ Ἀθηναῖοι αὐτοὶ 6
οὗτοι, τοῦ Μήδου παρὰ λόγον πολλὰ σφαλέντος, ἐπὶ τῷ
10 ὀνόματι ὡς ἐπ' Ἀθήνας ᾔει ηὐξήθησαν, καὶ ἡμῖν οὐκ ἀνέλπιστον τὸ τοιοῦτο ξυμβῆναι.

'Θαρσοῦντες οὖν τά τε αὐτοῦ παρασκευαζώμεθα καὶ ἐς τοὺς 34
Σικελοὺς πέμποντες τοὺς μὲν μᾶλλον βεβαιωσώμεθα, τοῖς
δὲ φιλίαν καὶ ξυμμαχίαν πειρώμεθα ποιεῖσθαι, ἔς τε τὴν
15 ἄλλην Σικελίαν πέμπωμεν πρέσβεις δηλοῦντες ὡς κοινὸς ὁ
κίνδυνος, καὶ ἐς τὴν Ἰταλίαν, ὅπως ἢ ξυμμαχίαν ποιώμεθα
ἡμῖν ἢ μὴ δέχωνται Ἀθηναίους. δοκεῖ δέ μοι καὶ ἐς Καρ- 2
χηδόνα ἄμεινον εἶναι πέμψαι· οὐ γὰρ ἀνέλπιστον αὐτοῖς,
ἀλλ' αἰεὶ διὰ φόβου εἰσὶ μή ποτε Ἀθηναῖοι αὐτοῖς ἐπὶ τὴν
20 πόλιν ἔλθωσιν, ὥστε τάχ' ἂν ἴσως νομίσαντες, εἰ τάδε
προήσονται, κἂν σφεῖς ἐν πόνῳ εἶναι, ἐθελήσειαν ἡμῖν ἤτοι
κρύφα γε ἢ φανερῶς ἢ ἐξ ἑνός γέ του τρόπου ἀμῦναι.
δυνατοὶ δὲ εἰσὶ μάλιστα τῶν νῦν, βουληθέντες· χρυσὸν γὰρ
καὶ ἄργυρον πλεῖστον κέκτηνται, ὅθεν ὅ τε πόλεμος καὶ
25 τἆλλα εὐπορεῖ. πέμπωμεν δὲ καὶ ἐς τὴν Λακεδαίμονα καὶ ἐς 3
Κόρινθον δεόμενοι δεῦρο κατὰ τάχος βοηθεῖν καὶ τὸν ἐκεῖ
πόλεμον κινεῖν. ὃ δὲ μάλιστα ἐγώ τε νομίζω ἐπίκαιρον 4
ὑμεῖς τε διὰ τὸ ξύνηθες ἥσυχον ἥκιστ' ἂν ὀξέως πείθοισθε,
ὅμως εἰρήσεται. Σικελιῶται γὰρ εἰ ἐθέλοιμεν ξύμπαντες,
30 εἰ δὲ μή, ὅτι πλεῖστοι μεθ' ἡμῶν, καθελκύσαντες ἅπαν τὸ
ὑπάρχον ναυτικὸν μετὰ δυοῖν μηνοῖν τροφῆς ἀπαντῆσαι

---

1 ἔργον f (G) suprascr. M¹: ἔργων cett.   8 πταίωσιν ABFM
16 ξυμμαχίδα Coraes

Ἀθηναίοις ἐς Τάραντα καὶ ἄκραν Ἰαπυγίαν, καὶ δῆλον ποιῆσαι
αὐτοῖς ὅτι οὐ περὶ τῆς Σικελίας πρότερον ἔσται ὁ ἀγὼν ἢ
τοῦ ἐκείνους περαιωθῆναι τὸν Ἰόνιον, μάλιστ' ἂν αὐτοὺς
ἐκπλήξαιμεν καὶ ἐς λογισμὸν καταστήσαιμεν ὅτι ὁρμώμεθα
μὲν ἐκ φιλίας χώρας φύλακες (ὑποδέχεται γὰρ ἡμᾶς Τάρας), 5
τὸ δὲ πέλαγος αὐτοῖς πολὺ περαιοῦσθαι μετὰ πάσης τῆς
παρασκευῆς, χαλεπὸν δὲ διὰ πλοῦ μῆκος ἐν τάξει μεῖναι,
καὶ ἡμῖν ἂν εὐεπίθετος εἴη, βραδεῖά τε καὶ κατ' ὀλίγον
5 προσπίπτουσα. εἰ δ' αὖ τῷ ταχυναυτοῦντι ἀθροωτέρῳ
κουφίσαντες προσβάλοιεν, εἰ μὲν κώπαις χρήσαιντο, ἐπι- 10
θοίμεθ' ἂν κεκμηκόσιν, εἰ δὲ μὴ δοκοίη, ἔστι καὶ ὑποχωρῆσαι
ἡμῖν ἐς Τάραντα· οἱ δὲ μετ' ὀλίγων ἐφοδίων ὡς ἐπὶ ναυμαχίᾳ
περαιωθέντες ἀποροῖεν ἂν κατὰ χωρία ἐρῆμα, καὶ ἢ μένοντες
πολιορκοῖντο ἂν ἢ πειρώμενοι παραπλεῖν τήν τε ἄλλην παρασκευὴν ἀπολείποιεν ἂν καὶ τὰ τῶν πόλεων οὐκ ἂν βέβαια 15
6 ἔχοντες, εἰ ὑποδέξοιντο, ἀθυμοῖεν. ὥστ' ἔγωγε τούτῳ τῷ
λογισμῷ ἡγοῦμαι ἀποκλῃομένους αὐτοὺς οὐδ' ἂν ἀπᾶραι ἀπὸ
Κερκύρας, ἀλλ' ἢ διαβουλευσαμένους καὶ κατασκοπαῖς χρωμένους, ὁπόσοι τ' ἐσμὲν καὶ ἐν ᾧ χωρίῳ, ἐξωσθῆναι ἂν τῇ
ὥρᾳ ἐς χειμῶνα, ἢ καταπλαγέντας τῷ ἀδοκήτῳ καταλῦσαι 20
ἂν τὸν πλοῦν, ἄλλως τε καὶ τοῦ ἐμπειροτάτου τῶν στρατηγῶν,
ὡς ἐγὼ ἀκούω, ἄκοντος ἡγουμένου καὶ ἀσμένου ἂν πρόφασιν
7 λαβόντος, εἴ τι ἀξιόχρεων ἀφ' ἡμῶν ὀφθείη. ἀγγελλοίμεθα
δ' ἂν εὖ οἶδ' ὅτι ἐπὶ τὸ πλέον· τῶν δ' ἀνθρώπων πρὸς τὰ
λεγόμενα καὶ αἱ γνῶμαι ἵστανται, καὶ τοὺς προεπιχειροῦντας 25
ἢ τοῖς γε ἐπιχειροῦσι προδηλοῦντας ὅτι ἀμυνοῦνται μᾶλλον
8 πεφόβηνται, ἰσοκινδύνους ἡγούμενοι. ὅπερ ἂν νῦν Ἀθηναῖοι
πάθοιεν. ἐπέρχονται γὰρ ἡμῖν ὡς οὐκ ἀμυνουμένοις, δικαίως
κατεγνωκότες ὅτι αὐτοὺς οὐ μετὰ Λακεδαιμονίων ἐφθείρομεν·
εἰ δ' ἴδοιεν παρὰ γνώμην τολμήσαντας, τῷ ἀδοκήτῳ μᾶλλον 30
ἂν καταπλαγεῖεν ἢ τῇ ἀπὸ τοῦ ἀληθοῦς δυνάμει.

2 τῆς Σικελίας recc. : τῇ Σικελίᾳ codd.   8 βραχεῖα A B E F M
κατ' ὀλίγον recc. : κατὰ λόγον codd.   15 ἀπολίποιεν A B E F M
26 ἀμύνονται A B F M   28 ἀμυνομένοις C G

'Πείθεσθε οὖν μάλιστα μὲν ταῦτα τολμήσαντες, εἰ δὲ μή, 9
ὅτι τάχιστα τᾶλλα ἐς τὸν πόλεμον ἑτοιμάζειν, καὶ παραστῆναι παντὶ τὸ μὲν καταφρονεῖν τοὺς ἐπιόντας ἐν τῶν
ἔργων τῇ ἀλκῇ δείκνυσθαι, τὸ δ' ἤδη τὰς μετὰ φόβου παρα-
5 σκευὰς ἀσφαλεστάτας νομίσαντας ὡς ἐπὶ κινδύνου πράσσειν
χρησιμώτατον ἂν ξυμβῆναι. οἱ δὲ ἄνδρες καὶ ἐπέρχονται
καὶ ἐν πλῷ εὖ οἶδ' ὅτι ἤδη εἰσὶ καὶ ὅσον οὔπω πάρεισιν.'

Καὶ ὁ μὲν Ἑρμοκράτης τοσαῦτα εἶπεν· τῶν δὲ Συρακοσίων 35
ὁ δῆμος ἐν πολλῇ πρὸς ἀλλήλους ἔριδι ἦσαν, οἱ μὲν ὡς
10 οὐδενὶ ἂν τρόπῳ ἔλθοιεν οἱ Ἀθηναῖοι οὐδ' ἀληθῆ ἐστὶν ἃ
λέγει, τοῖς δέ, εἰ καὶ ἔλθοιεν, τί ἂν δράσειαν αὐτοὺς ὅτι οὐκ
ἂν μεῖζον ἀντιπάθοιεν. ἄλλοι δὲ καὶ πάνυ καταφρονοῦντες
ἐς γέλωτα ἔτρεπον τὸ πρᾶγμα. ὀλίγον δ' ἦν τὸ πιστεῦον
τῷ Ἑρμοκράτει καὶ φοβούμενον τὸ μέλλον. παρελθὼν δ' 2
15 αὐτοῖς Ἀθηναγόρας, ὃς δήμου τε προστάτης ἦν καὶ ἐν τῷ
παρόντι πιθανώτατος τοῖς πολλοῖς, ἔλεγε τοιάδε.

'Τοὺς μὲν Ἀθηναίους ὅστις μὴ βούλεται οὕτω κακῶς 36
φρονῆσαι καὶ ὑποχειρίους ἡμῖν γενέσθαι ἐνθάδε ἐλθόντας, ἢ
δειλός ἐστιν ἢ τῇ πόλει οὐκ εὔνους· τοὺς δὲ ἀγγέλλοντας
20 τὰ τοιαῦτα καὶ περιφόβους ὑμᾶς ποιοῦντας τῆς μὲν τόλμης
οὐ θαυμάζω, τῆς δὲ ἀξυνεσίας, εἰ μὴ οἴονται ἔνδηλοι εἶναι.
οἱ γὰρ δεδιότες ἰδίᾳ τι βούλονται τὴν πόλιν ἐς ἔκπληξιν 2
καθιστάναι, ὅπως τῷ κοινῷ φόβῳ τὸν σφέτερον ἐπηλυγά-
ζωνται. καὶ νῦν αὗται αἱ ἀγγελίαι τοῦτο δύνανται· οὐκ
25 ἀπὸ ταὐτομάτου, ἐκ δὲ ἀνδρῶν οἵπερ αἰεὶ τάδε κινοῦσι ξύγ-
κεινται. ὑμεῖς δὲ ἢν εὖ βουλεύησθε, οὐκ ἐξ ὧν οὗτοι 3
ἀγγέλλουσι σκοποῦντες λογιεῖσθε τὰ εἰκότα, ἀλλ' ἐξ ὧν ἂν
ἄνθρωποι δεινοὶ καὶ πολλῶν ἔμπειροι, ὥσπερ ἐγὼ Ἀθηναίους
ἀξιῶ, δράσειαν. οὐ γὰρ αὐτοὺς εἰκὸς Πελοποννησίους τε 4
30 ὑπολιπόντας καὶ τὸν ἐκεῖ πόλεμον μήπω βεβαίως καταλελυμένους ἐπ' ἄλλον πόλεμον οὐκ ἐλάσσω ἑκόντας ἐλθεῖν, ἐπεὶ

4 τῇ ἀλκῇ τῶν ἔργων C G   10 οὐδ' E F: οἱ δ' B: οἱ δ' cett.
11 λέγει, τοῖς] λέγεται, οἱ Madvig   23 τὸν, ut videtur, legit
Schol.: τὸ codd.

ἔγωγε ἀγαπᾶν οἴομαι αὐτοὺς ὅτι οὐχ ἡμεῖς ἐπ᾽ ἐκείνους
37 ἐρχόμεθα, πόλεις τοσαῦται καὶ οὕτω μεγάλαι. εἰ δὲ δή,
ὥσπερ λέγονται, ἔλθοιεν, ἱκανωτέραν ἡγοῦμαι Σικελίαν
Πελοποννήσου διαπολεμῆσαι ὅσῳ κατὰ πάντα ἄμεινον ἐξήρτυται, τὴν δὲ ἡμετέραν πόλιν αὐτὴν τῆς νῦν στρατιᾶς, ὥς 5
φασιν, ἐπιούσης, καὶ εἰ δὶς τοσαύτη ἔλθοι, πολὺ κρείσσω
εἶναι, οἷς γ᾽ ἐπίσταμαι οὔθ᾽ ἵππους ἀκολουθήσοντας, οὐδ᾽
αὐτόθεν πορισθησομένους εἰ μὴ ὀλίγους τινὰς παρ᾽ Ἐγεσταίων, οὔθ᾽ ὁπλίτας ἰσοπλήθεις τοῖς ἡμετέροις ἐπὶ νεῶν γε
ἐλθόντας (μέγα γὰρ τὸ καὶ αὐταῖς ταῖς ναυσὶ κούφαις τοσοῦ- 10
τον πλοῦν δεῦρο κομισθῆναι), τήν τε ἄλλην παρασκευὴν
ὅσην δεῖ ἐπὶ πόλιν τοσήνδε πορισθῆναι, οὐκ ὀλίγην οὖσαν.
2 ὥστε, παρὰ τοσοῦτον γιγνώσκω, μόλις ἄν μοι δοκοῦσιν, εἰ
πόλιν ἑτέραν τοσαύτην ὅσαι Συράκουσαί εἰσιν ἔλθοιεν ἔχοντες καὶ ὅμορον οἰκίσαντες τὸν πόλεμον ποιοῖντο, οὐκ ἂν 15
παντάπασι διαφθαρῆναι, ἦ πού γε δὴ ἐν πάσῃ πολεμίᾳ
Σικελίᾳ (ξυστήσεται γάρ) στρατοπέδῳ τε ἐκ νεῶν ἱδρυθέντι
καὶ ἐκ σκηνιδίων καὶ ἀναγκαίας παρασκευῆς οὐκ ἐπὶ πολὺ
ὑπὸ τῶν ἡμετέρων ἱππέων ἐξιόντες. τό τε ξύμπαν οὐδ᾽ ἂν
κρατῆσαι αὐτοὺς τῆς γῆς ἡγοῦμαι· τοσούτῳ τὴν ἡμετέραν 20
παρασκευὴν κρείσσω νομίζω.

38 ʿ Ἀλλὰ ταῦτα, ὥσπερ ἐγὼ λέγω, οἵ τε Ἀθηναῖοι γιγνώσκοντες τὰ σφέτερα αὐτῶν εὖ οἶδ᾽ ὅτι σῴζουσι, καὶ ἐνθένδε
2 ἄνδρες οὔτε ὄντα οὔτε ἂν γενόμενα λογοποιοῦσιν, οὓς ἐγὼ
οὐ νῦν πρῶτον, ἀλλ᾽ αἰεὶ ἐπίσταμαι ἤτοι λόγοις γε τοιοῖσδε 25
καὶ ἔτι τούτων κακουργοτέροις ἢ ἔργοις βουλομένους κατα-
πλήξαντας τὸ ὑμέτερον πλῆθος αὐτοὺς τῆς πόλεως ἄρχειν.
καὶ δέδοικα μέντοι μήποτε πολλὰ πειρῶντες καὶ κατορθώσω-
σιν· ἡμεῖς δὲ κακοί, πρὶν ἐν τῷ παθεῖν ὦμεν, προφυλάξα-
3 σθαί τε καὶ αἰσθόμενοι ἐπεξελθεῖν. τοιγάρτοι δι᾽ αὐτὰ ἡ 30
πόλις ἡμῶν ὀλιγάκις μὲν ἡσυχάζει, στάσεις δὲ πολλὰς καὶ

9 οὔθ᾽ Haacke : οὐδ᾽ codd.   15 ὅμοροι recc.   οἰκίσαντες
Marchant : οἰκήσαντες codd.   19 τε Haase : δὲ codd.

ἀγῶνας οὐ πρὸς τοὺς πολεμίους πλέονας ἢ πρὸς αὐτὴν
ἀναιρεῖται, τυραννίδας δὲ ἔστιν ὅτε καὶ δυναστείας ἀδίκους.
ὧν ἐγὼ πειράσομαι, ἤν γε ὑμεῖς ἐθέλητε ἕπεσθαι, μήποτε 4
ἐφ' ἡμῶν τι περιιδεῖν γενέσθαι, ὑμᾶς μὲν τοὺς πολλοὺς
5 πείθων, τοὺς δὲ τὰ τοιαῦτα μηχανωμένους κολάζων, μὴ
μόνον αὐτοφώρους (χαλεπὸν γὰρ ἐπιτυγχάνειν), ἀλλὰ καὶ ὧν
βούλονται μέν, δύνανται δ' οὔ (τὸν γὰρ ἐχθρὸν οὐχ ὧν δρᾷ
μόνον, ἀλλὰ καὶ τῆς διανοίας προαμύνεσθαι χρή, εἴπερ καὶ
μὴ προφυλαξάμενός τις προπείσεται), τοὺς δ' αὖ ὀλίγους τὰ
10 μὲν ἐλέγχων, τὰ δὲ φυλάσσων, τὰ δὲ καὶ διδάσκων· μάλιστα
γὰρ δοκῶ ἄν μοι οὕτως ἀποτρέπειν τῆς κακουργίας. καὶ 5
δῆτα, ὃ πολλάκις ἐσκεψάμην, τί καὶ βούλεσθε, ὦ νεώτεροι;
πότερον ἄρχειν ἤδη; ἀλλ' οὐκ ἔννομον· ὁ δὲ νόμος ἐκ τοῦ
μὴ δύνασθαι ὑμᾶς μᾶλλον ἢ δυναμένους ἐτέθη ἀτιμάζειν.
15 ἀλλὰ δὴ μὴ μετὰ πολλῶν ἰσονομεῖσθαι; καὶ πῶς δίκαιον
τοὺς αὐτοὺς μὴ τῶν αὐτῶν ἀξιοῦσθαι; φήσει τις δημοκρατίαν 39
οὔτε ξυνετὸν οὔτ' ἴσον εἶναι, τοὺς δ' ἔχοντας τὰ χρήματα
καὶ ἄρχειν ἄριστα βελτίστους. ἐγὼ δέ φημι πρῶτα μὲν
δῆμον ξύμπαν ὠνομάσθαι, ὀλιγαρχίαν δὲ μέρος, ἔπειτα φύ-
20 λακας μὲν ἀρίστους εἶναι χρημάτων τοὺς πλουσίους, βουλεῦσαι δ' ἂν βέλτιστα τοὺς ξυνετούς, κρῖναι δ' ἂν ἀκούσαντας
ἄριστα τοὺς πολλούς, καὶ ταῦτα ὁμοίως καὶ κατὰ μέρη καὶ
ξύμπαντα ἐν δημοκρατίᾳ ἰσομοιρεῖν. ὀλιγαρχία δὲ τῶν μὲν 2
κινδύνων τοῖς πολλοῖς μεταδίδωσι, τῶν δ' ὠφελίμων οὐ
25 πλεονεκτεῖ μόνον, ἀλλὰ καὶ ξύμπαντ' ἀφελομένη ἔχει· ἃ
ὑμῶν οἵ τε δυνάμενοι καὶ οἱ νέοι προθυμοῦνται, ἀδύνατα ἐν
μεγάλῃ πόλει κατασχεῖν.

'Ἀλλ' ἔτι καὶ νῦν, ὦ πάντων ἀξυνετώτατοι, εἰ μὴ μαν-
θάνετε κακὰ σπεύδοντες, ἢ ἀμαθέστατοί ἐστε ὧν ἐγὼ οἶδα
30 Ἑλλήνων, ἢ ἀδικώτατοι, εἰ εἰδότες τολμᾶτε. ἀλλ' ἤτοι 40
μαθόντες γε ἢ μεταγνόντες τὸ τῆς πόλεως ξύμπασι κοινὸν

18 βελτίους C   22 post κατὰ add. τὰ E F G M   25 ξύμπαντ'
Herwerden : ξύμπαν codd.   29 ἢ ἀμαθέστατοί ἐστε secl. Madvig

αὔξετε, ἡγησάμενοι τοῦτο μὲν ἂν καὶ ἴσον καὶ πλέον οἱ ἀγαθοὶ
ὑμῶν [ἤπερ τὸ τῆς πόλεως πλῆθος] μετασχεῖν, εἰ δ' ἄλλα
βουλήσεσθε, καὶ τοῦ παντὸς κινδυνεῦσαι στερηθῆναι· καὶ
τῶν τοιῶνδε ἀγγελιῶν ὡς πρὸς αἰσθανομένους καὶ μὴ ἐπι-
2 τρέψοντας ἀπαλλάγητε. ἡ γὰρ πόλις ἥδε, καὶ εἰ ἔρχονται 5
Ἀθηναῖοι, ἀμυνεῖται αὐτοὺς ἀξίως αὑτῆς, καὶ στρατηγοί
εἰσιν ἡμῖν οἳ σκέψονται αὐτά· καὶ εἰ μή τι αὐτῶν ἀληθές
ἐστιν, ὥσπερ οὐκ οἴομαι, οὐ πρὸς τὰς ὑμετέρας ἀγγελίας
καταπλαγεῖσα καὶ ἑλομένη ὑμᾶς ἄρχοντας αὐθαίρετον δουλείαν ἐπιβαλεῖται, αὐτὴ δ' ἐφ' αὑτῆς σκοποῦσα τούς τε 10
λόγους ἀφ' ὑμῶν ὡς ἔργα δυναμένους κρινεῖ καὶ τὴν ὑπάρχουσαν ἐλευθερίαν οὐχὶ ἐκ τοῦ ἀκούειν ἀφαιρεθήσεται, ἐκ δὲ
τοῦ ἔργῳ φυλασσομένη μὴ ἐπιτρέπειν πειράσεται σῴζειν.'
41 Τοιαῦτα δὲ Ἀθηναγόρας εἶπεν. τῶν δὲ στρατηγῶν εἷς
ἀναστὰς ἄλλον μὲν οὐδένα ἔτι εἴασε παρελθεῖν, αὐτὸς δὲ 15
2 πρὸς τὰ παρόντα ἔλεξε τοιάδε. ' διαβολὰς μὲν οὐ σῶφρον
οὔτε λέγειν τινὰς ἐς ἀλλήλους οὔτε τοὺς ἀκούοντας ἀποδέχεσθαι, πρὸς δὲ τὰ ἐσαγγελλόμενα μᾶλλον ὁρᾶν, ὅπως εἷς
τε ἕκαστος καὶ ἡ ξύμπασα πόλις καλῶς τοὺς ἐπιόντας παρα-
3 σκευασόμεθα ἀμύνεσθαι. καὶ ἢν ἄρα μηδὲν δεήσῃ, οὐδεμία 20
βλάβη τοῦ τε τὸ κοινὸν κοσμηθῆναι καὶ ἵπποις καὶ ὅπλοις
4 καὶ τοῖς ἄλλοις οἷς ὁ πόλεμος ἀγάλλεται (τὴν δ' ἐπιμέλειαν
καὶ ἐξέτασιν αὐτῶν ἡμεῖς ἕξομεν), καὶ τῶν πρὸς τὰς πόλεις
διαπομπῶν ἅμα ἔς τε κατασκοπὴν καὶ ἤν τι ἄλλο φαίνηται
ἐπιτήδειον. τὰ δὲ καὶ ἐπιμεμελήμεθα ἤδη, καὶ ὅτι ἂν αἰ- 25
σθώμεθα ἐς ὑμᾶς οἴσομεν.' καὶ οἱ μὲν Συρακόσιοι τοσαῦτα
εἰπόντος τοῦ στρατηγοῦ διελύθησαν ἐκ τοῦ ξυλλόγου.
42 Οἱ δ' Ἀθηναῖοι ἤδη ἐν τῇ Κερκύρᾳ αὐτοί τε καὶ οἱ ξύμμαχοι ἅπαντες ἦσαν. καὶ πρῶτον μὲν ἐπεξέτασιν τοῦ

2 ἤπερ . . . πλῆθος secl. Krüger   4 πρὸς αἰσθανομένους] προ-
αισθομένους g (ex προαισθανομένους) M   αἰσθανομένους] αἰσθομένους
ABEF   ἐπιστρέψοντας ABEFM   6 αὑτῆς f : αὐτῆς codd.
11 δυναμένους] βουλομένους C   14 prius δὲ C : μὲν cett.   19 παρα-
σκευασώμεθα G M   21 γε Abresch

στρατεύματος καὶ ξύνταξιν, ὥσπερ ἔμελλον ὁρμιεῖσθαί τε
καὶ στρατοπεδεύεσθαι, οἱ στρατηγοὶ ἐποιήσαντο, καὶ τρία
μέρη νείμαντες ἐν ἑκάστῳ ἐκλήρωσαν, ἵνα μήτε ἅμα πλέοντες ἀπορῶσιν ὕδατος καὶ λιμένων καὶ τῶν ἐπιτηδείων ἐν
5 ταῖς καταγωγαῖς, πρός τε τἆλλα εὐκοσμότεροι καὶ ῥᾴους
ἄρχειν ὦσι, κατὰ τέλη στρατηγῷ προστεταγμένοι· ἔπειτα δὲ 2
προύπεμψαν καὶ ἐς τὴν Ἰταλίαν καὶ Σικελίαν τρεῖς ναῦς
εἰσομένας αἵτινες σφᾶς τῶν πόλεων δέξονται. καὶ εἴρητο
αὐταῖς προαπαντᾶν, ὅπως ἐπιστάμενοι καταπλέωσιν. μετὰ 43
10 δὲ ταῦτα τοσῇδε ἤδη τῇ παρασκευῇ Ἀθηναῖοι ἄραντες ἐκ
τῆς Κερκύρας ἐς τὴν Σικελίαν ἐπεραιοῦντο, τριήρεσι μὲν
ταῖς πάσαις τέσσαρσι καὶ τριάκοντα καὶ ἑκατόν, καὶ δυοῖν
Ῥοδίοιν πεντηκοντόροιν (τούτων Ἀττικαὶ μὲν ἦσαν ἑκατόν,
ὧν αἱ μὲν ἑξήκοντα ταχεῖαι, αἱ δ᾽ ἄλλαι στρατιώτιδες, τὸ δὲ
15 ἄλλο ναυτικὸν Χίων καὶ τῶν ἄλλων ξυμμάχων), ὁπλίταις δὲ
τοῖς ξύμπασιν ἑκατὸν καὶ πεντακισχιλίοις (καὶ τούτων Ἀθηναίων μὲν αὐτῶν ἦσαν πεντακόσιοι μὲν καὶ χίλιοι ἐκ καταλόγου, ἑπτακόσιοι δὲ θῆτες ἐπιβάται τῶν νεῶν, ξύμμαχοι δὲ
οἱ ἄλλοι ξυνεστράτευον, οἱ μὲν τῶν ὑπηκόων, οἱ δ᾽ Ἀργείων
20 πεντακόσιοι καὶ Μαντινέων καὶ μισθοφόρων πεντήκοντα καὶ
διακόσιοι), τοξόταις δὲ τοῖς πᾶσιν ὀγδοήκοντα καὶ τετρακο-
σίοις (καὶ τούτων Κρῆτες οἱ ὀγδοήκοντα ἦσαν) καὶ σφενδονή-
ταις Ῥοδίων ἑπτακοσίοις, καὶ Μεγαρεῦσι ψιλοῖς φυγάσιν
εἴκοσι καὶ ἑκατόν, καὶ ἱππαγωγῷ μιᾷ τριάκοντα ἀγούσῃ
25 ἱππέας.

Τοσαύτη ἡ πρώτη παρασκευὴ πρὸς τὸν πόλεμον διέπλει. 44
τούτοις δὲ τὰ ἐπιτήδεια ἄγουσαι ὁλκάδες μὲν τριάκοντα σιτα-
γωγοί, καὶ τοὺς σιτοποιοὺς ἔχουσαι καὶ λιθολόγους καὶ
τέκτονας καὶ ὅσα ἐς τειχισμὸν ἐργαλεῖα, πλοῖα δὲ ἑκατόν,
30 ἃ ἐξ ἀνάγκης μετὰ τῶν ὁλκάδων ξυνέπλει· πολλὰ δὲ καὶ
ἄλλα πλοῖα καὶ ὁλκάδες ἑκούσιοι ξυνηκολούθουν τῇ στρατιᾷ

2 στρατοπεδεύσεσθαι Krüger   3 ἐν f : ἐν codd.   ἅμα πλέοντες
Hudson (si pariter navigarent Valla) : ἀναπλέοντες codd.   20 post
alterum καὶ add. ἄλλων Classen

ἐμπορίας ἕνεκα· ἃ τότε πάντα ἐκ τῆς Κερκύρας ξυνδιέβαλλε
2 τὸν Ἰόνιον κόλπον. καὶ προσβαλοῦσα ἡ πᾶσα παρασκευὴ
πρός τε ἄκραν Ἰαπυγίαν καὶ πρὸς Τάραντα καὶ ὡς ἕκαστοι
ηὐπόρησαν, παρεκομίζοντο τὴν Ἰταλίαν, τῶν μὲν πόλεων οὐ
δεχομένων αὐτοὺς ἀγορᾷ οὐδὲ ἄστει, ὕδατι δὲ καὶ ὅρμῳ, 5
Τάραντος δὲ καὶ Λοκρῶν οὐδὲ τούτοις, ἕως ἀφίκοντο ἐς
3 Ῥήγιον τῆς Ἰταλίας ἀκρωτήριον. καὶ ἐνταῦθα ἤδη ἠθροί-
ζοντο, καὶ ἔξω τῆς πόλεως, ὡς αὐτοὺς ἔσω οὐκ ἐδέχοντο,
στρατόπεδόν τε κατεσκευάσαντο ἐν τῷ τῆς Ἀρτέμιδος ἱερῷ,
οὗ αὐτοῖς καὶ ἀγορὰν παρεῖχον, καὶ τὰς ναῦς ἀνελκύσαντες 10
ἡσύχασαν. καὶ πρός [τε] τοὺς Ῥηγίνους λόγους ἐποιήσαντο,
ἀξιοῦντες Χαλκιδέας ὄντας Χαλκιδεῦσιν οὖσι Λεοντίνοις
βοηθεῖν· οἱ δὲ οὐδὲ μεθ' ἑτέρων ἔφασαν ἔσεσθαι, ἀλλ' ὅτι
4 ἂν καὶ τοῖς ἄλλοις Ἰταλιώταις ξυνδοκῇ, τοῦτο ποιήσειν. οἱ
δὲ πρὸς τὰ ἐν τῇ Σικελίᾳ πράγματα ἐσκόπουν ὅτῳ ρρόπῳ 15
ἄριστα προσοίσονται· καὶ τὰς προπλους ναῦς ἐκ τῆς Ἐγέστης
ἅμα προσέμενον, βουλόμενοι εἰδέναι περὶ τῶν χρημάτων εἰ
ἔστιν ἃ ἔλεγον ἐν ταῖς Ἀθήναις οἱ ἄγγελοι.

45   Τοῖς δὲ Συρακοσίοις ἐν τούτῳ πολλαχόθεν τε ἤδη καὶ ἀπὸ
τῶν κατασκόπων σαφῆ ἠγγέλλετο ὅτι ἐν Ῥηγίῳ αἱ νῆές εἰσι, 20
καὶ ὡς ἐπὶ τούτοις παρεσκευάζοντο πάσῃ τῇ γνώμῃ καὶ
οὐκέτι ἠπίστουν. καὶ ἔς τε τοὺς Σικελοὺς περιέπεμπον,
ἔνθα μὲν φύλακας, πρὸς δὲ τοὺς πρέσβεις, καὶ ἐς τὰ περι-
πόλια τὰ ἐν τῇ χώρᾳ φρουρὰς ἐσεκόμιζον, τά τε ἐν τῇ
πόλει ὅπλων ἐξετάσει καὶ ἵππων ἐσκόπουν εἰ ἐντελῆ ἐστί, 25
καὶ τἆλλα ὡς ἐπὶ ταχεῖ πολέμῳ καὶ ὅσον οὐ παρόντι
καθίσταντο.

46   Αἱ δ' ἐκ τῆς Ἐγέστης τρεῖς νῆες αἱ πρόπλοι παραγίγνονται
τοῖς Ἀθηναίοις ἐς τὸ Ῥήγιον, ἀγγέλλουσαι ὅτι τἆλλα μὲν
οὐκ ἔστι χρήματα ἃ ὑπέσχοντο, τριάκοντα δὲ τάλαντα μόνα 30
2 φαίνεται. καὶ οἱ στρατηγοὶ εὐθὺς ἐν ἀθυμίᾳ ἦσαν, ὅτι
αὐτοῖς τοῦτό τε πρῶτον ἀντεκεκρούκει καὶ οἱ Ῥηγῖνοι οὐκ

ἐθελήσαντες ξυστρατεύειν, οὓς πρῶτον ἤρξαντο πείθειν καὶ
εἰκὸς ἦν μάλιστα, Λεοντίνων τε ξυγγενεῖς ὄντας καὶ σφίσιν
αἰεὶ ἐπιτηδείους. καὶ τῷ μὲν Νικίᾳ προσδεχομένῳ ἦν τὰ
παρὰ τῶν Ἐγεσταίων, τοῖν δὲ ἑτέροιν καὶ ἀλογώτερα. οἱ 3
5 δὲ Ἐγεσταῖοι τοιόνδε τι ἐξετεχνήσαντο τότε ὅτε οἱ πρῶτοι
πρέσβεις τῶν Ἀθηναίων ἦλθον αὐτοῖς ἐς τὴν κατασκοπὴν
τῶν χρημάτων. ἔς τε τὸ ἐν Ἔρυκι ἱερὸν τῆς Ἀφροδίτης
ἀγαγόντες αὐτοὺς ἐπέδειξαν τὰ ἀναθήματα, φιάλας τε καὶ
οἰνοχόας καὶ θυμιατήρια καὶ ἄλλην κατασκευὴν οὐκ ὀλίγην,
10 ἃ ὄντα ἀργυρᾶ πολλῷ πλείω τὴν ὄψιν ἀπ᾽ ὀλίγης δυνάμεως χρημάτων παρείχετο· καὶ ἰδίᾳ ξενίσεις ποιούμενοι τῶν
τριηριτῶν τά τε ἐξ αὐτῆς Ἐγέστης ἐκπώματα καὶ χρυσᾶ
καὶ ἀργυρᾶ ξυλλέξαντες καὶ τὰ ἐκ τῶν ἐγγὺς πόλεων καὶ
Φοινικικῶν καὶ Ἑλληνίδων αἰτησάμενοι ἐσέφερον ἐς τὰς
15 ἑστιάσεις ὡς οἰκεῖα ἕκαστοι. καὶ πάντων ὡς ἐπὶ τὸ πολὺ 4
τοῖς αὐτοῖς χρωμένων καὶ πανταχοῦ πολλῶν φαινομένων
μεγάλην τὴν ἔκπληξιν τοῖς ἐκ τῶν τριήρων Ἀθηναίοις
παρεῖχε, καὶ ἀφικόμενοι ἐς τὰς Ἀθήνας διεθρόησαν ὡς
χρήματα πολλὰ ἴδοιεν. καὶ οἱ μὲν αὐτοί τε ἀπατηθέντες 5
20 καὶ τοὺς ἄλλους τότε πείσαντες, ἐπειδὴ διῆλθεν ὁ λόγος ὅτι
οὐκ εἴη ἐν τῇ Ἐγέστῃ τὰ χρήματα, πολλὴν τὴν αἰτίαν εἶχον
ὑπὸ τῶν στρατιωτῶν· οἱ δὲ στρατηγοὶ πρὸς τὰ παρόντα
ἐβουλεύοντο.

Καὶ Νικίου μὲν ἦν γνώμη πλεῖν ἐπὶ Σελινοῦντα πάσῃ τῇ 47
25 στρατιᾷ, ἐφ᾽ ὅπερ μάλιστα ἐπέμφθησαν, καὶ ἢν μὲν παρέ-
χωσι χρήματα παντὶ τῷ στρατεύματι Ἐγεσταῖοι, πρὸς ταῦτα
βουλεύεσθαι, εἰ δὲ μή, ταῖς ἑξήκοντα ναυσίν, ὅσασπερ ᾐτή-
σαντο, ἀξιοῦν διδόναι αὐτοὺς τροφήν, καὶ παραμείναντας
Σελινουντίους ἢ βίᾳ ἢ ξυμβάσει διαλλάξαι αὐτοῖς, καὶ οὕτω
30 παραπλεύσαντας τὰς ἄλλας πόλεις καὶ ἐπιδείξαντας μὲν τὴν
δύναμιν τῆς Ἀθηναίων πόλεως, δηλώσαντας δὲ τὴν ἐς τοὺς
φίλους καὶ ξυμμάχους προθυμίαν, ἀποπλεῖν οἴκαδε, ἢν μή τι

10 ἐπάργυρα Meineke : ὑπάργυρα Naber   29 αὐτοῖς C : αὐτοὺς cett.

δι' ὀλίγου καὶ ἀπὸ τοῦ ἀδοκήτου ἢ Λεοντίνους οἷοί τε ὦσιν
ὠφελῆσαι ἢ τῶν ἄλλων τινὰ πόλεων προσαγαγέσθαι, καὶ τῇ
πόλει δαπανῶντας τὰ οἰκεῖα μὴ κινδυνεύειν.

48 Ἀλκιβιάδης δὲ οὐκ ἔφη χρῆναι τοσαύτῃ δυνάμει ἐκπλεύ-
σαντας αἰσχρῶς καὶ ἀπράκτους ἀπελθεῖν, ἀλλ' ἔς τε τὰς 5
πόλεις ἐπικηρυκεύεσθαι πλὴν Σελινοῦντος καὶ Συρακουσῶν
τὰς ἄλλας, καὶ πειρᾶσθαι καὶ τοὺς Σικελοὺς τοὺς μὲν ἀφ-
ιστάναι ἀπὸ τῶν Συρακοσίων, τοὺς δὲ φίλους ποιεῖσθαι, ἵνα
σῖτον καὶ στρατιὰν ἔχωσι, πρῶτον δὲ πείθειν Μεσσηνίους
(ἐν πόρῳ γὰρ μάλιστα καὶ προσβολῇ εἶναι αὐτοὺς τῆς 10
Σικελίας, καὶ λιμένα καὶ ἐφόρμησιν τῇ στρατιᾷ ἱκανωτάτην
ἔσεσθαι)· προσαγαγομένους δὲ τὰς πόλεις, εἰδότας μεθ' ὧν
τις πολεμήσει, οὕτως ἤδη Συρακούσαις καὶ Σελινοῦντι
ἐπιχειρεῖν, ἢν μὴ οἱ μὲν Ἐγεσταίοις ξυμβαίνωσιν, οἱ δὲ
Λεοντίνους ἐῶσι κατοικίζειν. 15

49 Λάμαχος δὲ ἄντικρυς ἔφη χρῆναι πλεῖν ἐπὶ Συρακούσας
καὶ πρὸς τῇ πόλει ὡς τάχιστα τὴν μάχην ποιεῖσθαι, ἕως ἔτι
2 ἀπαράσκευοί τε εἰσὶ καὶ μάλιστα ἐκπεπληγμένοι. τὸ γὰρ
πρῶτον πᾶν στράτευμα δεινότατον εἶναι· ἢν δὲ χρονίσῃ πρὶν
ἐς ὄψιν ἐλθεῖν, τῇ γνώμῃ ἀναθαρσοῦντας ἀνθρώπους καὶ τῇ 20
ὄψει καταφρονεῖν μᾶλλον. αἰφνίδιοι δὲ ἢν προσπέσωσιν,
ἕως ἔτι περιδεεῖς προσδέχονται, μάλιστ' ἂν σφεῖς περιγενέσθαι καὶ κατὰ πάντα ἂν αὐτοὺς ἐκφοβῆσαι, τῇ τε ὄψει
(πλεῖστοι γὰρ ἂν νῦν φανῆναι) καὶ τῇ προσδοκίᾳ ὧν πείσονται,
3 μάλιστα δ' ἂν τῷ αὐτίκα κινδύνῳ τῆς μάχης. εἰκὸς δὲ εἶναι 25
καὶ ἐν τοῖς ἀγροῖς πολλοὺς ἀποληφθῆναι ἔξω διὰ τὸ ἀπιστεῖν
σφᾶς μὴ ἥξειν, καὶ ἐσκομιζομένων αὐτῶν τὴν στρατιὰν οὐκ
ἀπορήσειν χρημάτων, ἢν πρὸς τῇ πόλει κρατοῦσα καθέζηται.
4 τούς τε ἄλλους Σικελιώτας οὕτως ἤδη μᾶλλον καὶ ἐκείνοις οὐ
ξυμμαχήσειν καὶ σφίσι προσιέναι καὶ οὐ διαμελλήσειν περι- 30
σκοποῦντας ὁπότεροι κρατήσουσιν. ναύσταθμον δὲ ἐπανα-

χωρήσαντας καὶ ἐφορμηθέντας Μέγαρα ἔφη χρῆναι ποιεῖσθαι,
ἃ ἦν ἐρῆμα, ἀπέχοντα Συρακουσῶν οὔτε πλοῦν πολὺν οὔτε
ὁδόν.

Λάμαχος μὲν ταῦτα εἰπὼν ὅμως προσέθετο καὶ αὐτὸς τῇ 50
5 Ἀλκιβιάδου γνώμῃ. μετὰ δὲ τοῦτο Ἀλκιβιάδης τῇ αὐτοῦ
νηὶ διαπλεύσας ἐς Μεσσήνην καὶ λόγους ποιησάμενος περὶ
ξυμμαχίας πρὸς αὐτούς, ὡς οὐκ ἔπειθεν, ἀλλ' ἀπεκρίναντο
πόλει μὲν ἂν οὐ δέξασθαι, ἀγορὰν δ' ἔξω παρέξειν, ἀπέπλει
ἐς τὸ Ῥήγιον. καὶ εὐθὺς ξυμπληρώσαντες ἑξήκοντα ναῦς ἐκ 2
10 πασῶν οἱ στρατηγοὶ καὶ τὰ ἐπιτήδεια λαβόντες παρέπλεον
ἐς Νάξον, τὴν ἄλλην στρατιὰν ἐν Ῥηγίῳ καταλιπόντες
καὶ ἕνα σφῶν αὐτῶν. Ναξίων δὲ δεξαμένων τῇ πόλει 3
παρέπλεον ἐς Κατάνην. καὶ ὡς αὐτοὺς οἱ Καταναῖοι οὐκ
ἐδέχοντο (ἐνῆσαν γὰρ αὐτόθι ἄνδρες τὰ Συρακοσίων βουλό-
15 μενοι), ἐκομίσθησαν ἐπὶ τὸν Τηρίαν ποταμόν, καὶ αὐλισάμενοι 4
τῇ ὑστεραίᾳ ἐπὶ Συρακούσας ἔπλεον ἐπὶ κέρως ἔχοντες τὰς
ἄλλας ναῦς· δέκα δὲ τῶν νεῶν προύπεμψαν ἐς τὸν μέγαν
λιμένα πλεῦσαί τε καὶ κατασκέψασθαι εἴ τι ναυτικόν ἐστι
καθειλκυσμένον, καὶ κηρῦξαι ἀπὸ τῶν νεῶν προσπλεύσαντας
20 ὅτι Ἀθηναῖοι ἥκουσι Λεοντίνους ἐς τὴν ἑαυτῶν κατοικιοῦντες
κατὰ ξυμμαχίαν καὶ ξυγγένειαν· τοὺς οὖν ὄντας ἐν Συρακούσαις Λεοντίνων ὡς παρὰ φίλους καὶ εὐεργέτας Ἀθηναίους
ἀδεῶς ἀπιέναι. ἐπεὶ δ' ἐκηρύχθη καὶ κατεσκέψαντο τήν τε 5
πόλιν καὶ τοὺς λιμένας καὶ τὰ περὶ τὴν χώραν ἐξ ἧς αὐτοῖς
25 ὁρμωμένοις πολεμητέα ἦν, ἀπέπλευσαν πάλιν ἐς Κατάνην.
καὶ ἐκκλησίας γενομένης τὴν μὲν στρατιὰν οὐκ ἐδέχοντο οἱ 51
Καταναῖοι, τοὺς δὲ στρατηγοὺς ἐσελθόντας ἐκέλευον, εἴ τι
βούλονται, εἰπεῖν. καὶ λέγοντος τοῦ Ἀλκιβιάδου, καὶ τῶν
ἐν τῇ πόλει πρὸς τὴν ἐκκλησίαν τετραμμένων, οἱ στρατιῶται
30 πυλίδα τινὰ ἐνῳκοδομημένην κακῶς ἔλαθον διελόντες, καὶ
ἐσελθόντες ἠγόραζον ἐς τὴν πόλιν. τῶν δὲ Καταναίων οἱ 2
μὲν τὰ τῶν Συρακοσίων φρονοῦντες, ὡς εἶδον τὸ στράτευμα

4 καὶ M: om. cett.   22 Ἀθηναίους recc. : Ἀθηναίων codd.
30 ἐνῳκοδομημένην suprascr. M¹ : ἐνῳκοδομημένων codd.

ἔνδον, εὐθὺς περιδεεῖς γενόμενοι ὑπεξῆλθον οὐ πολλοί τινες,
οἱ δὲ ἄλλοι ἐψηφίσαντό τε ξυμμαχίαν τοῖς Ἀθηναίοις καὶ
3 τὸ ἄλλο στράτευμα ἐκέλευον ἐκ Ῥηγίου κομίζειν. μετὰ δὲ
τοῦτο διαπλεύσαντες οἱ Ἀθηναῖοι ἐς τὸ Ῥήγιον, πάσῃ ἤδη
τῇ στρατιᾷ ἄραντες ἐς τὴν Κατάνην, ἐπειδὴ ἀφίκοντο, 5
κατεσκευάζοντο τὸ στρατόπεδον.

52 Ἐσηγγέλλετο δὲ αὐτοῖς ἔκ τε Καμαρίνης ὡς, εἰ ἔλθοιεν,
προσχωροῖεν ἄν, καὶ ὅτι Συρακόσιοι πληροῦσι ναυτικόν.
ἁπάσῃ οὖν τῇ στρατιᾷ παρέπλευσαν πρῶτον μὲν ἐπὶ Συρα-
κούσας· καὶ ὡς οὐδὲν ηὗρον ναυτικὸν πληρούμενον, παρε- 10
κομίζοντο αὖθις ἐπὶ Καμαρίνης, καὶ σχόντες ἐς τὸν αἰγιαλὸν
ἐπεκηρυκεύοντο. οἱ δ' οὐκ ἐδέχοντο, λέγοντες σφίσι τὰ
ὅρκια εἶναι μιᾷ νηὶ καταπλεόντων Ἀθηναίων δέχεσθαι, ἢν
2 μὴ αὐτοὶ πλείους μεταπέμπωσιν. ἄπρακτοι δὲ γενόμενοι
ἀπέπλεον· καὶ ἀποβάντες κατά τι τῆς Συρακοσίας καὶ 15
ἁρπαγὴν ποιησάμενοι, καὶ τῶν Συρακοσίων ἱππέων βοηθησάντων καὶ τῶν ψιλῶν τινὰς ἐσκεδασμένους διαφθειράντων,
53 ἀπεκομίσθησαν ἐς Κατάνην. καὶ καταλαμβάνουσι τὴν Σαλαμινίαν ναῦν ἐκ τῶν Ἀθηνῶν ἥκουσαν ἐπί τε Ἀλκιβιάδην ὡς
κελεύσοντας ἀποπλεῖν ἐς ἀπολογίαν ὧν ἡ πόλις ἐνεκάλει, 20
καὶ ἐπ' ἄλλους τινὰς τῶν στρατιωτῶν τῶν μετ' αὐτοῦ μεμηνυμένων περὶ τῶν μυστηρίων ὡς ἀσεβούντων, τῶν δὲ καὶ περὶ
2 τῶν Ἑρμῶν. οἱ γὰρ Ἀθηναῖοι, ἐπειδὴ ἡ στρατιὰ ἀπέπλευσεν,
οὐδὲν ἧσσον ζήτησιν ἐποιοῦντο τῶν περὶ τὰ μυστήρια καὶ
τῶν περὶ τοὺς Ἑρμᾶς δρασθέντων, καὶ οὐ δοκιμάζοντες τοὺς 25
μηνυτάς, ἀλλὰ πάντα ὑπόπτως ἀποδεχόμενοι, διὰ πονηρῶν
ἀνθρώπων πίστιν πάνυ χρηστοὺς τῶν πολιτῶν ξυλλαμβά-
νοντες κατέδουν, χρησιμώτερον ἡγούμενοι εἶναι βασανίσαι
τὸ πρᾶγμα καὶ εὑρεῖν ἢ διὰ μηνυτοῦ πονηρίαν τινὰ καὶ
χρηστὸν δοκοῦντα εἶναι αἰτιαθέντα ἀνέλεγκτον διαφυγεῖν. 30
3 ἐπιστάμενος γὰρ ὁ δῆμος ἀκοῇ τὴν Πεισιστράτου καὶ τῶν

4 διαπλεύσαντες B: πλεύσαντες cett.   20 κελεύσαντας ABFM
suprascr. G

παίδων τυραννίδα χαλεπὴν τελευτῶσαν γενομένην καὶ
προσέτι οὐδ᾽ ὑφ᾽ ἑαυτῶν καὶ ῾Αρμοδίου καταλυθεῖσαν, ἀλλ᾽
ὑπὸ τῶν Λακεδαιμονίων, ἐφοβεῖτο αἰεὶ καὶ πάντα ὑπόπτως
ἐλάμβανεν.

5 Τὸ γὰρ ᾿Αριστογείτονος καὶ ῾Αρμοδίου τόλμημα δι᾽ ἐρω- 54
τικὴν ξυντυχίαν ἐπεχειρήθη, ἣν ἐγὼ ἐπὶ πλέον διηγησάμενος
ἀποφανῶ οὔτε τοὺς ἄλλους οὔτε αὐτοὺς ᾿Αθηναίους περὶ τῶν
σφετέρων τυράννων οὐδὲ περὶ τοῦ γενομένου ἀκριβὲς οὐδὲν
λέγοντας. Πεισιστράτου γὰρ γηραιοῦ τελευτήσαντος ἐν τῇ 2
10 τυραννίδι οὐχ ῞Ιππαρχος, ὥσπερ οἱ πολλοὶ οἴονται, ἀλλ᾽
῾Ιππίας πρεσβύτατος ὢν ἔσχε τὴν ἀρχήν. γενομένου δὲ
῾Αρμοδίου ὥρᾳ ἡλικίας λαμπροῦ ᾿Αριστογείτων ἀνὴρ τῶν
ἀστῶν, μέσος πολίτης, ἐραστὴς ὢν εἶχεν αὐτόν. πειραθεὶς 3
δὲ ὁ ῾Αρμόδιος ὑπὸ ῾Ιππάρχου τοῦ Πεισιστράτου καὶ οὐ
15 πεισθεὶς καταγορεύει τῷ ᾿Αριστογείτονι. ὁ δὲ ἐρωτικῶς
περιαλγήσας καὶ φοβηθεὶς τὴν ῾Ιππάρχου δύναμιν μὴ βίᾳ
προσαγάγηται αὐτόν, ἐπιβουλεύει εὐθὺς ὡς ἀπὸ τῆς ὑπαρχούσης ἀξιώσεως κατάλυσιν τῇ τυραννίδι. καὶ ἐν τούτῳ 4
ὁ ῞Ιππαρχος ὡς αὖθις πειράσας οὐδὲν μᾶλλον ἔπειθε τὸν
20 ῾Αρμόδιον, βίαιον μὲν οὐδὲν ἐβούλετο δρᾶν, ἐν τρόπῳ δέ
τινι ἀφανεῖ ὡς οὐ διὰ τοῦτο δὴ παρεσκευάζετο προπηλακιῶν
αὐτόν. οὐδὲ γὰρ τὴν ἄλλην ἀρχὴν ἐπαχθὴς ἦν ἐς τοὺς 5
πολλούς, ἀλλ᾽ ἀνεπιφθόνως κατεστήσατο· καὶ ἐπετήδευσαν
ἐπὶ πλεῖστον δὴ τύραννοι οὗτοι ἀρετὴν καὶ ξύνεσιν, καὶ
25 ᾿Αθηναίους εἰκοστὴν μόνον πρασσόμενοι τῶν γιγνομένων
τήν τε πόλιν αὐτῶν καλῶς διεκόσμησαν καὶ τοὺς πολέμους
διέφερον καὶ ἐς τὰ ἱερὰ ἔθυον. τὰ δὲ ἄλλα αὐτὴ ἡ πόλις 6
τοῖς πρὶν κειμένοις νόμοις ἐχρῆτο, πλὴν καθ᾽ ὅσον αἰεί τινα
ἐπεμέλοντο σφῶν αὐτῶν ἐν ταῖς ἀρχαῖς εἶναι. καὶ ἄλλοι τε
30 αὐτῶν ἦρξαν τὴν ἐνιαύσιον ᾿Αθηναίοις ἀρχὴν καὶ Πεισίστρατος ὁ ῾Ιππίου τοῦ τυραννεύσαντος υἱός, τοῦ πάππου

3 τῶν om. ABEFM   20 τρόπῳ Levesque : τούτῳ Μ : τόπῳ
cett.   27 αὕτη ABEFM   30 ἐνιαυσίαν ABEFM

ἔχων τοὔνομα, ὃς τῶν δώδεκα θεῶν βωμὸν τὸν ἐν τῇ ἀγορᾷ
7 ἄρχων ἀνέθηκε καὶ τὸν τοῦ Ἀπόλλωνος ἐν Πυθίου. καὶ τῷ
μὲν ἐν τῇ ἀγορᾷ προσοικοδομήσας ὕστερον ὁ δῆμος Ἀθηναίων
μεῖζον μῆκος τοῦ βωμοῦ ἠφάνισε τοὐπίγραμμα· τοῦ δ᾽ ἐν
Πυθίου ἔτι καὶ νῦν δῆλόν ἐστιν ἀμυδροῖς γράμμασι λέγον 5
τάδε·

μνῆμα τόδ᾽ ἧς ἀρχῆς Πεισίστρατος Ἱππίου υἱός
θῆκεν Ἀπόλλωνος Πυθίου ἐν τεμένει.

55 ὅτι δὲ πρεσβύτατος ὢν Ἱππίας ἦρξεν, εἰδὼς μὲν καὶ ἀκοῇ
ἀκριβέστερον ἄλλων ἰσχυρίζομαι, γνοίη δ᾽ ἄν τις καὶ αὐτῷ 10
τούτῳ· παῖδες γὰρ αὐτῷ μόνῳ φαίνονται τῶν γνησίων
ἀδελφῶν γενόμενοι, ὡς ὅ τε βωμὸς σημαίνει καὶ ἡ στήλη
περὶ τῆς τῶν τυράννων ἀδικίας ἡ ἐν τῇ Ἀθηναίων ἀκροπόλει
σταθεῖσα, ἐν ᾗ Θεσσαλοῦ μὲν οὐδ᾽ Ἱππάρχου οὐδεὶς παῖς
γέγραπται, Ἱππίου δὲ πέντε, οἳ αὐτῷ ἐκ Μυρρίνης τῆς 15
Καλλίου τοῦ Ὑπεροχίδου θυγατρὸς ἐγένοντο· εἰκὸς γὰρ ἦν
2 τὸν πρεσβύτατον πρῶτον γῆμαι. καὶ ἐν τῇ αὐτῇ στήλῃ
πρῶτος γέγραπται μετὰ τὸν πατέρα, οὐδὲ τοῦτο ἀπεοικότως
3 διὰ τὸ πρεσβεύειν τε ἀπ᾽ αὐτοῦ καὶ τυραννεῦσαι. οὐ μὴν
οὐδ᾽ ἂν κατασχεῖν μοι δοκεῖ ποτὲ Ἱππίας τὸ παραχρῆμα 20
ῥᾳδίως τὴν τυραννίδα, εἰ Ἵππαρχος μὲν ἐν τῇ ἀρχῇ ὢν
ἀπέθανεν, αὐτὸς δὲ αὐθημερὸν καθίστατο· ἀλλὰ καὶ διὰ τὸ
πρότερον ξύνηθες τοῖς μὲν πολίταις φοβερόν, ἐς δὲ τοὺς
ἐπικούρους ἀκριβές, πολλῷ τῷ περιόντι τοῦ ἀσφαλοῦς κατε-
κράτησε, καὶ οὐχ ὡς ἀδελφὸς νεώτερος ὢν ἠπόρησεν, ἐν 25
4 ᾧ οὐ πρότερον ξυνεχῶς ὡμιλήκει τῇ ἀρχῇ. Ἱππάρχῳ δὲ
ξυνέβη τοῦ πάθους τῇ δυστυχίᾳ ὀνομασθέντα καὶ τὴν δόξαν
τῆς τυραννίδος ἐς τὰ ἔπειτα προσλαβεῖν.

56 Τὸν δ᾽ οὖν Ἁρμόδιον ἀπαρνηθέντα τὴν πείρασιν, ὥσπερ
διενοεῖτο, προυπηλάκισεν· ἀδελφὴν γὰρ αὐτοῦ κόρην ἐπαγ- 30
γείλαντες ἥκειν κανοῦν οἴσουσαν ἐν πομπῇ τινί, ἀπήλασαν

---

11 μόνῳ recc. : μόνον codd.   16 Ὑπεροχίδου C : Ὑπερεχίδου cett.
17 αὐτῇ Poppo (in ipso . . . lapide Valla) : πρώτῃ codd.   22 καὶ
om. C

λέγοντες οὐδὲ ἐπαγγεῖλαι τὴν ἀρχὴν διὰ τὸ μὴ ἀξίαν εἶναι.
χαλεπῶς δὲ ἐνεγκόντος τοῦ Ἁρμοδίου πολλῷ δὴ μᾶλλον δι᾽ 2
ἐκεῖνον καὶ ὁ Ἀριστογείτων παρωξύνετο. καὶ αὐτοῖς τὰ
μὲν ἄλλα πρὸς τοὺς ξυνεπιθησομένους τῷ ἔργῳ ἐπέπρακτο,
5 περιέμενον δὲ Παναθήναια τὰ μεγάλα, ἐν ᾗ μόνον ἡμέρᾳ οὐχ
ὕποπτον ἐγίγνετο ἐν ὅπλοις τῶν πολιτῶν τοὺς τὴν πομπὴν
πέμψοντας ἀθρόους γενέσθαι· καὶ ἔδει ἄρξαι μὲν αὐτούς,
ξυνεπαμύνειν δὲ εὐθὺς τὰ πρὸς τοὺς δορυφόρους ἐκείνους.
ἦσαν δὲ οὐ πολλοὶ οἱ ξυνομωμοκότες ἀσφαλείας ἕνεκα· 3
10 ἤλπιζον γὰρ καὶ τοὺς μὴ προειδότας, εἰ καὶ ὁποσοιοῦν τολ-
μήσειαν, ἐκ τοῦ παραχρῆμα ἔχοντάς γε ὅπλα ἐθελήσειν σφᾶς
αὐτοὺς ξυνελευθεροῦν. καὶ ὡς ἐπῆλθεν ἡ ἑορτή, Ἱππίας 57
μὲν ἔξω ἐν τῷ Κεραμεικῷ καλουμένῳ μετὰ τῶν δορυφόρων
διεκόσμει ὡς ἕκαστα ἐχρῆν τῆς πομπῆς προϊέναι, ὁ δὲ
15 Ἁρμόδιος καὶ ὁ Ἀριστογείτων ἔχοντες ἤδη τὰ ἐγχειρίδια ἐς
τὸ ἔργον προῇσαν. καὶ ὡς εἶδόν τινα τῶν ξυνωμοτῶν σφίσι 2
διαλεγόμενον οἰκείως τῷ Ἱππίᾳ (ἦν δὲ πᾶσιν εὐπρόσοδος ὁ
Ἱππίας), ἔδεισαν καὶ ἐνόμισαν μεμηνῦσθαί τε καὶ ὅσον οὐκ
ἤδη ξυλληφθήσεσθαι. τὸν λυπήσαντα οὖν σφᾶς καὶ δι᾽ 3
20 ὅνπερ πάντα ἐκινδύνευον ἐβούλοντο πρότερον, εἰ δύναιντο,
προτιμωρήσασθαι, καὶ ὥσπερ εἶχον ὥρμησαν ἔσω τῶν πυλῶν,
καὶ περιέτυχον τῷ Ἱππάρχῳ παρὰ τὸ Λεωκόρειον καλούμενον,
καὶ εὐθὺς ἀπερισκέπτως προσπεσόντες καὶ ὡς ἂν μάλιστα δι᾽
ὀργῆς ὁ μὲν ἐρωτικῆς, ὁ δὲ ὑβρισμένος, ἔτυπτον καὶ ἀπο-
25 κτείνουσιν αὐτόν. καὶ ὁ μὲν τοὺς δορυφόρους τὸ αὐτίκα 4
διαφεύγει ὁ Ἀριστογείτων, ξυνδραμόντος τοῦ ὄχλου, καὶ
ὕστερον ληφθεὶς οὐ ῥᾳδίως διετέθη· Ἁρμόδιος δὲ αὐτοῦ
παραχρῆμα ἀπόλλυται. ἀγγελθέντος δὲ Ἱππίᾳ ἐς τὸν 58
Κεραμεικόν, οὐκ ἐπὶ τὸ γενόμενον, ἀλλ᾽ ἐπὶ τοὺς πομπέας
30 τοὺς ὁπλίτας, πρότερον ἢ αἰσθέσθαι αὐτοὺς ἄπωθεν ὄντας,
εὐθὺς ἐχώρησε, καὶ ἀδήλως τῇ ὄψει πλασάμενος πρὸς τὴν

---

7 πέμψοντας f: πέμψαντας codd.   9 ἕνεκα recc.: οὕνεκα codd.
16 ξυνομωμοκότων recc.   21 προτιμωρήσασθαι Μ: προτιμωρήσεσθαι
cett.   22 παρὰ] περὶ recc.   23 prius καὶ recc.: om. codd.

ξυμφορὰν ἐκέλευσεν αὐτούς, δείξας τι χωρίον, ἀπελθεῖν ἐς
2 αὐτὸ ἄνευ τῶν ὅπλων. καὶ οἱ μὲν ἀνεχώρησαν οἰόμενοί τι
ἐρεῖν αὐτόν, ὁ δὲ τοῖς ἐπικούροις φράσας τὰ ὅπλα ὑπολαβεῖν
ἐξελέγετο εὐθὺς οὓς ἐπῃτιᾶτο καὶ εἴ τις ηὑρέθη ἐγχειρίδιον
ἔχων· μετὰ γὰρ ἀσπίδος καὶ δόρατος εἰώθεσαν τὰς πομπὰς 5
ποιεῖν.

59 Τοιούτῳ μὲν τρόπῳ δι' ἐρωτικὴν λύπην ἥ τε ἀρχὴ τῆς
ἐπιβουλῆς καὶ ἡ ἀλόγιστος τόλμα ἐκ τοῦ παραχρῆμα περι-
2 δεοῦς Ἁρμοδίῳ καὶ Ἀριστογείτονι ἐγένετο. τοῖς δ' Ἀθηναίοις χαλεπωτέρα μετὰ τοῦτο ἡ τυραννὶς κατέστη, καὶ ὁ 10
Ἱππίας διὰ φόβου ἤδη μᾶλλον ὢν τῶν τε πολιτῶν πολλοὺς
ἔκτεινε καὶ πρὸς τὰ ἔξω ἅμα διεσκοπεῖτο, εἴ ποθεν ἀσφάλειάν
3 τινα ὁρῴη μεταβολῆς γενομένης ὑπάρχουσάν οἱ. Ἱππόκλου
γοῦν τοῦ Λαμψακηνοῦ τυράννου Αἰαντίδῃ τῷ παιδὶ θυγατέρα
ἑαυτοῦ μετὰ ταῦτα Ἀρχεδίκην Ἀθηναῖος ὢν Λαμψακηνῷ 15
ἔδωκεν, αἰσθανόμενος αὐτοὺς μέγα παρὰ βασιλεῖ Δαρείῳ
δύνασθαι. καὶ αὐτῆς σῆμα ἐν Λαμψάκῳ ἐστὶν ἐπίγραμμα
ἔχον τόδε·

ἀνδρὸς ἀριστεύσαντος ἐν Ἑλλάδι τῶν ἐφ' ἑαυτοῦ
Ἱππίου Ἀρχεδίκην ἥδε κέκευθε κόνις, 20
ἣ πατρός τε καὶ ἀνδρὸς ἀδελφῶν τ' οὖσα τυράννων
παίδων τ' οὐκ ἤρθη νοῦν ἐς ἀτασθαλίην.

4 τυραννεύσας δὲ ἔτη τρία Ἱππίας ἔτι Ἀθηναίων καὶ παυθεὶς
ἐν τῷ τετάρτῳ ὑπὸ Λακεδαιμονίων καὶ Ἀλκμεωνιδῶν τῶν
φευγόντων, ἐχώρει ὑπόσπονδος ἔς τε Σίγειον καὶ παρ' Αἰαν- 25
τίδην ἐς Λάμψακον, ἐκεῖθεν δὲ ὡς βασιλέα. Δαρεῖον, ὅθεν
καὶ ὁρμώμενος ἐς Μαραθῶνα ὕστερον ἔτει εἰκοστῷ ἤδη γέρων
ὢν μετὰ Μήδων ἐστράτευσεν.

60 Ὧν ἐνθυμούμενος ὁ δῆμος ὁ τῶν Ἀθηναίων, καὶ μιμνησκό-
μενος ὅσα ἀκοῇ περὶ αὐτῶν ἠπίστατο, χαλεπὸς ἦν τότε καὶ 30
ὑπόπτης ἐς τοὺς περὶ τῶν μυστικῶν τὴν αἰτίαν λαβόντας,
καὶ πάντα αὐτοῖς ἐδόκει ἐπὶ ξυνωμοσίᾳ ὀλιγαρχικῇ καὶ

2 ἀπεχώρησαν Poppo   5, 6 μετὰ ... ποιεῖν secl. Herwerden

τυραννικῇ πεπρᾶχθαι. καὶ ὡς αὐτῶν διὰ τὸ τοιοῦτον 2
ὀργιζομένων πολλοί τε καὶ ἀξιόλογοι ἄνθρωποι ἤδη ἐν τῷ
δεσμωτηρίῳ ἦσαν καὶ οὐκ ἐν παύλῃ ἐφαίνετο, ἀλλὰ καθ'
ἡμέραν ἐπεδίδοσαν μᾶλλον ἐς τὸ ἀγριώτερόν τε καὶ πλείους
5 ἔτι ξυλλαμβάνειν, ἐνταῦθα ἀναπείθεται εἷς τῶν δεδεμένων,
ὅσπερ ἐδόκει αἰτιώτατος εἶναι, ὑπὸ τῶν ξυνδεσμωτῶν τινος
εἴτε ἄρα καὶ τὰ ὄντα μηνῦσαι εἴτε καὶ οὔ· ἐπ' ἀμφότερα γὰρ
εἰκάζεται, τὸ δὲ σαφὲς οὐδεὶς οὔτε τότε οὔτε ὕστερον ἔχει
εἰπεῖν περὶ τῶν δρασάντων τὸ ἔργον. λέγων δὲ ἔπεισεν 3
10 αὐτὸν ὡς χρή, εἰ μὴ καὶ δέδρακεν, αὑτόν τε ἄδειαν ποιησάμενον σῶσαι καὶ τὴν πόλιν τῆς παρούσης ὑποψίας παῦσαι·
βεβαιοτέραν γὰρ αὐτῷ σωτηρίαν εἶναι ὁμολογήσαντι μετ'
ἀδείας ἢ ἀρνηθέντι διὰ δίκης ἐλθεῖν. καὶ ὁ μὲν αὐτός τε 4
καθ' ἑαυτοῦ καὶ κατ' ἄλλων μηνύει τὸ τῶν Ἑρμῶν· ὁ δὲ
15 δῆμος ὁ τῶν Ἀθηναίων ἄσμενος λαβών, ὡς ᾤετο, τὸ σαφὲς
καὶ δεινὸν ποιούμενοι πρότερον εἰ τοὺς ἐπιβουλεύοντας
σφῶν τῷ πλήθει μὴ εἴσονται, τὸν μὲν μηνυτὴν εὐθὺς καὶ
τοὺς ἄλλους μετ' αὐτοῦ ὅσων μὴ κατηγορήκει ἔλυσαν, τοὺς
δὲ καταιτιαθέντας κρίσεις ποιήσαντες τοὺς μὲν ἀπέκτειναν,
20 ὅσοι ξυνελήφθησαν, τῶν δὲ διαφυγόντων θάνατον κατα-
γνόντες ἐπανεῖπον ἀργύριον τῷ ἀποκτείναντι. κἂν τούτῳ οἱ 5
μὲν παθόντες ἄδηλον ἦν εἰ ἀδίκως ἐτετιμώρηντο, ἡ μέντοι
ἄλλη πόλις ἐν τῷ παρόντι περιφανῶς ὠφέλητο. περὶ δὲ 61
τοῦ Ἀλκιβιάδου ἐναγόντων τῶν ἐχθρῶν, οἵπερ καὶ πρὶν
25 ἐκπλεῖν αὐτὸν ἐπέθεντο, χαλεπῶς οἱ Ἀθηναῖοι ἐλάμβανον·
καὶ ἐπειδὴ τὸ τῶν Ἑρμῶν ᾤοντο σαφὲς ἔχειν, πολὺ δὴ
μᾶλλον καὶ τὰ μυστικά, ὧν ἐπαίτιος ἦν, μετὰ τοῦ αὐτοῦ
λόγου καὶ τῆς ξυνωμοσίας ἐπὶ τῷ δήμῳ ἀπ' ἐκείνου ἐδόκει
πραχθῆναι. καὶ γάρ τις καὶ στρατιὰ Λακεδαιμονίων οὐ 2
30 πολλὴ ἔτυχε κατὰ τὸν καιρὸν τοῦτον ἐν ᾧ περὶ ταῦτα ἐθορυ-
βοῦντο μέχρι Ἰσθμοῦ παρελθοῦσα, πρὸς Βοιωτούς τι πράσ-

---

10 αὑτὸν c: αὐτὸν codd.   14 ἑαυτοῦ fg: ἑαυτὸν codd.
31 πράσσοντας ABEFM

σοντες. ἐδόκει οὖν ἐκείνου πράξαντος καὶ οὐ Βοιωτῶν ἕνεκα
ἀπὸ ξυνθήματος ἥκειν, καὶ εἰ μὴ ἔφθασαν δὴ αὐτοὶ κατὰ τὸ
μήνυμα ξυλλαβόντες τοὺς ἄνδρας, προδοθῆναι ἂν ἡ πόλις.
καί τινα μίαν νύκτα καὶ κατέδαρθον ἐν Θησείῳ τῷ ἐν πόλει
3 ἐν ὅπλοις. οἵ τε ξένοι τοῦ Ἀλκιβιάδου οἱ ἐν Ἄργει κατὰ 5
τὸν αὐτὸν χρόνον ὑπωπτεύθησαν τῷ δήμῳ ἐπιτίθεσθαι, καὶ
τοὺς ὁμήρους τῶν Ἀργείων τοὺς ἐν ταῖς νήσοις κειμένους οἱ
Ἀθηναῖοι τότε παρέδοσαν τῷ Ἀργείων δήμῳ διὰ ταῦτα
4 διαχρήσασθαι. πανταχόθεν τε περιειστήκει ὑποψία ἐς τὸν
Ἀλκιβιάδην. ὥστε βουλόμενοι αὐτὸν ἐς κρίσιν ἀγαγόντες 10
ἀποκτεῖναι, πέμπουσιν οὕτω τὴν Σαλαμινίαν ναῦν ἐς τὴν
Σικελίαν ἐπί τε ἐκεῖνον καὶ ὧν πέρι ἄλλων ἐμεμήνυτο.
5 εἴρητο δὲ προειπεῖν αὐτῷ ἀπολογησομένῳ ἀκολουθεῖν, ξυλλαμβάνειν δὲ μή, θεραπεύοντες τό τε πρὸς τοὺς ἐν τῇ Σικελίᾳ
στρατιώτας τε σφετέρους καὶ πολεμίους μὴ θορυβεῖν καὶ οὐχ 15
ἥκιστα τοὺς Μαντινέας καὶ Ἀργείους βουλόμενοι παραμεῖναι,
6 δι' ἐκείνου νομίζοντες πεισθῆναι σφίσι ξυστρατεύειν. καὶ ὁ
μὲν ἔχων τὴν ἑαυτοῦ ναῦν καὶ οἱ ξυνδιαβεβλημένοι ἀπέπλεον
μετὰ τῆς Σαλαμινίας ἐκ τῆς Σικελίας ὡς ἐς τὰς Ἀθήνας·
καὶ ἐπειδὴ ἐγένοντο ἐν Θουρίοις, οὐκέτι ξυνείποντο, ἀλλ' 20
ἀπελθόντες ἀπὸ τῆς νεὼς οὐ φανεροὶ ἦσαν, δείσαντες τὸ ἐπὶ
7 διαβολῇ ἐς δίκην καταπλεῦσαι. οἱ δ' ἐκ τῆς Σαλαμινίας
τέως μὲν ἐζήτουν τὸν Ἀλκιβιάδην καὶ τοὺς μετ' αὐτοῦ· ὡς
δ' οὐδαμοῦ φανεροὶ ἦσαν, ᾤχοντο ἀποπλέοντες. ὁ δὲ
Ἀλκιβιάδης ἤδη φυγὰς ὢν οὐ πολὺ ὕστερον ἐπὶ πλοίου 25
ἐπεραιώθη ἐς Πελοπόννησον ἐκ τῆς Θουρίας· οἱ δ' Ἀθηναῖοι
ἐρήμῃ δίκῃ θάνατον κατέγνωσαν αὐτοῦ τε καὶ τῶν μετ'
ἐκείνου.

62 Μετὰ δὲ ταῦτα οἱ λοιποὶ τῶν Ἀθηναίων στρατηγοὶ ἐν τῇ
Σικελίᾳ, δύο μέρη ποιήσαντες τοῦ στρατεύματος καὶ λαχὼν 30
ἑκάτερος, ἔπλεον ξύμπαντι ἐπὶ Σελινοῦντος καὶ Ἐγέστης,

9 διαχρήσασθαι M : χρήσεσθαι B : διαχρήσεσθαι cett.   13 ἀπο-
λογησαμένῳ A B E F M   17 σφίσι Lindau : σφᾶς codd.   31 ξύμπαντι recc. : ξὺν παντὶ vel ξύνπαντι codd.

βουλόμενοι μὲν εἰδέναι τὰ χρήματα εἰ δώσουσιν οἱ Ἐγεσταῖοι,
κατασκέψασθαι δὲ καὶ τῶν Σελινουντίων τὰ πράγματα καὶ
τὰ διάφορα μαθεῖν τὰ πρὸς Ἐγεσταίους. παραπλέοντες δ' 2
ἐν ἀριστερᾷ τὴν Σικελίαν, τὸ μέρος τὸ πρὸς τὸν Τυρσηνικὸν
5 κόλπον, ἔσχον ἐς Ἱμέραν, ἥπερ μόνη ἐν τούτῳ τῷ μέρει τῆς
Σικελίας Ἑλλὰς πόλις ἐστίν· καὶ ὡς οὐκ ἐδέχοντο αὐτούς,
παρεκομίζοντο. καὶ ἐν τῷ παράπλῳ αἱροῦσιν Ὕκκαρα, 3
πόλισμα Σικανικὸν μέν, Ἐγεσταίοις δὲ πολέμιον· ἦν δὲ
παραθαλασσίδιον. καὶ ἀνδραποδίσαντες τὴν πόλιν παρέδοσαν
10 Ἐγεσταίοις (παρεγένοντο γὰρ αὐτῶν ἱππῆς), αὐτοὶ δὲ πάλιν
τῷ μὲν πεζῷ ἐχώρουν διὰ τῶν Σικελῶν ἕως ἀφίκοντο ἐς
Κατάνην, αἱ δὲ νῆες περιέπλευσαν τὰ ἀνδράποδα ἄγουσαι.
Νικίας δὲ εὐθὺς ἐξ Ὑκκάρων ἐπὶ Ἐγέστης παραπλεύσας, 4
καὶ τἆλλα χρηματίσας καὶ λαβὼν τάλαντα τριάκοντα παρῆν
15 ἐς τὸ στράτευμα· καὶ τἀνδράποδα ἀπέδοσαν, καὶ ἐγένοντο ἐξ
αὐτῶν εἴκοσι καὶ ἑκατὸν τάλαντα. καὶ ἐς τοὺς τῶν Σικελῶν 5
ξυμμάχους περιέπλευσαν, στρατιὰν κελεύοντες πέμπειν· τῇ
τε ἡμισείᾳ τῆς ἑαυτῶν ἦλθον ἐπὶ Ὕβλαν τὴν Γελεᾶτιν
πολεμίαν οὖσαν, καὶ οὐχ εἷλον. καὶ τὸ θέρος ἐτελεύτα.

20 Τοῦ δ' ἐπιγιγνομένου χειμῶνος εὐθὺς τὴν ἔφοδον οἱ 63
Ἀθηναῖοι ἐπὶ Συρακούσας παρεσκευάζοντο, οἱ δὲ Συρακόσιοι
καὶ αὐτοὶ ὡς ἐπ' ἐκείνους ἰόντες. ἐπειδὴ γὰρ αὐτοῖς πρὸς 2
τὸν πρῶτον φόβον καὶ τὴν προσδοκίαν οἱ Ἀθηναῖοι οὐκ
εὐθὺς ἐπέκειντο, κατά τε τὴν ἡμέραν ἑκάστην προϊοῦσαν
25 ἀνεθάρσουν μᾶλλον καὶ ἐπειδὴ πλέοντές τε τὰ ἐπ' ἐκεῖνα τῆς
Σικελίας πολὺ ἀπὸ σφῶν ἐφαίνοντο καὶ πρὸς τὴν Ὕβλαν
ἐλθόντες καὶ πειράσαντες οὐχ εἷλον βίᾳ, ἔτι πλέον κατε-
φρόνησαν καὶ ἠξίουν τοὺς στρατηγούς, οἷον δὴ ὄχλος φιλεῖ
θαρσήσας ποιεῖν, ἄγειν σφᾶς ἐπὶ Κατάνην, ἐπειδὴ οὐκ
30 ἐκεῖνοι ἐφ' ἑαυτοὺς ἔρχονται. καὶ ἱππῆς προσελαύνοντες 3
αἰεὶ κατάσκοποι τῶν Συρακοσίων πρὸς τὸ στράτευμα τῶν
Ἀθηναίων ἐφύβριζον ἄλλα τε καὶ εἰ ξυνοικήσοντες σφίσιν

25 τε τὰ Reiske : τά τε codd.   30 καὶ recc. : om. codd.

αὐτοὶ μᾶλλον ἥκοιεν ἐν τῇ ἀλλοτρίᾳ ἢ Λεοντίνους ἐς τὴν
64 οἰκείαν κατοικιοῦντες. ἃ γιγνώσκοντες οἱ στρατηγοὶ τῶν
Ἀθηναίων καὶ βουλόμενοι αὐτοὺς ἄγειν πανδημεὶ ἐκ τῆς πόλεως
ὅτι πλεῖστον, αὐτοὶ δὲ ταῖς ναυσὶν ἐν τοσούτῳ ὑπὸ νύκτα
παραπλεύσαντες στρατόπεδον καταλαμβάνειν ἐν ἐπιτηδείῳ 5
καθ᾽ ἡσυχίαν, εἰδότες οὐκ ἂν ὁμοίως δυνηθέντες καὶ εἰ ἐκ
τῶν νεῶν πρὸς παρεσκευασμένους ἐκβιβάζοιεν ἢ κατὰ γῆν
ἰόντες γνωσθεῖεν (τοὺς γὰρ ἂν ψιλοὺς τοὺς σφῶν καὶ τὸν
ὄχλον τῶν Συρακοσίων τοὺς ἱππέας πολλοὺς ὄντας, σφίσι
δ᾽ οὐ παρόντων ἱππέων, βλάπτειν ἂν μεγάλα, οὕτω δὲ 10
λήψεσθαι χωρίον ὅθεν ὑπὸ τῶν ἱππέων οὐ βλάψονται ἄξια
λόγου· ἐδίδασκον δ᾽ αὐτοὺς περὶ τοῦ πρὸς τῷ Ὀλυμπιείῳ
χωρίου, ὅπερ καὶ κατέλαβον, Συρακοσίων φυγάδες, οἳ ξυνείποντο), τοιόνδε τι οὖν πρὸς ἃ ἐβούλοντο οἱ στρατηγοὶ
2 μηχανῶνται. πέμπουσιν ἄνδρα σφίσι μὲν πιστόν, τοῖς δὲ 15
τῶν Συρακοσίων στρατηγοῖς τῇ δοκήσει οὐχ ἧσσον ἐπι-
τήδειον· ἦν δὲ Καταναῖος ὁ ἀνήρ, καὶ ἀπ᾽ ἀνδρῶν ἐκ τῆς
Κατάνης ἥκειν ἔφη ὧν ἐκεῖνοι τὰ ὀνόματα ἐγίγνωσκον καὶ
ἠπίσταντο ἐν τῇ πόλει ἔτι ὑπολοίπους ὄντας τῶν σφίσιν
3 εὔνων. ἔλεγε δὲ τοὺς Ἀθηναίους αὐλίζεσθαι ἀπὸ τῶν ὅπλων 20
ἐν τῇ πόλει, καὶ εἰ βούλονται ἐκεῖνοι πανδημεὶ ἐν ἡμέρᾳ ῥητῇ
ἅμα ἕῳ ἐπὶ τὸ στράτευμα ἐλθεῖν, αὐτοὶ μὲν ἀποκλήσειν· τοὺς
παρὰ σφίσι καὶ τὰς ναῦς ἐμπρήσειν, ἐκείνους δὲ ῥᾳδίως τὸ
στράτευμα προσβαλόντας τῷ σταυρώματι αἱρήσειν· εἶναι δὲ
ταῦτα τοὺς ξυνδράσοντας πολλοὺς Καταναίων καὶ ἡτοιμάσθαι 25
65 ἤδη, ἀφ᾽ ὧν αὐτὸς ἥκειν. οἱ δὲ στρατηγοὶ τῶν Συρακοσίων,
μετὰ τοῦ καὶ ἐς τὰ ἄλλα θαρσεῖν καὶ εἶναι ἐν διανοίᾳ καὶ
ἄνευ τούτων ἰέναι παρεσκευάσθαι ἐπὶ Κατάνην, ἐπίστευσάν
τε τῷ ἀνθρώπῳ πολλῷ ἀπερισκεπτότερον καὶ εὐθὺς ἡμέραν
ξυνθέμενοι ᾗ παρέσονται ἀπέστειλαν αὐτόν, καὶ αὐτοί (ἤδη 30
γὰρ καὶ τῶν ξυμμάχων Σελινούντιοι καὶ ἄλλοί τινὲς παρ-

1 αὐτοὶ Bekker : αὐτοῖς codd.   5 καταλαβεῖν A B E F M
suprascr. G   6 καὶ secl. Reiske, fort. non legit Schol.   22 τοὺς
C : αὐτοὺς cett.   24 σταυρώματι] στρατεύματι C G

ἦσαν) προεῖπον πανδημεὶ πᾶσιν ἐξιέναι Συρακοσίοις. ἐπεὶ δὲ
ἑτοῖμα αὐτοῖς καὶ τὰ τῆς παρασκευῆς ἦν καὶ αἱ ἡμέραι ἐν
αἷς ξυνέθεντο ἥξειν ἐγγὺς ἦσαν, πορευόμενοι ἐπὶ Κατάνης
ηὐλίσαντο ἐπὶ τῷ Συμαίθῳ ποταμῷ ἐν τῇ Λεοντίνῃ. οἱ 2
5 δ᾽ Ἀθηναῖοι ὡς ᾔσθοντο αὐτοὺς προσιόντας, ἀναλαβόντες
τό τε στράτευμα ἅπαν τὸ ἑαυτῶν καὶ ὅσοι Σικελῶν αὐτοῖς
ἢ ἄλλος τις προσεληλύθει καὶ ἐπιβιβάσαντες ἐπὶ τὰς ναῦς
καὶ τὰ πλοῖα, ὑπὸ νύκτα ἔπλεον ἐπὶ τὰς Συρακούσας.
καὶ οἵ τε Ἀθηναῖοι ἅμα ἕῳ ἐξέβαινον ἐς τὸ κατὰ τὸ Ὀλυμ- 3
10 πιεῖον ὡς τὸ στρατόπεδον καταληψόμενοι, καὶ οἱ ἱππῆς οἱ
Συρακοσίων πρῶτοι προσελάσαντες ἐς τὴν Κατάνην καὶ
αἰσθόμενοι ὅτι τὸ στράτευμα ἅπαν ἀνῆκται, ἀποστρέψαντες
ἀγγέλλουσι τοῖς πεζοῖς, καὶ ξύμπαντες ἤδη ἀποτρεπόμενοι
ἐβοήθουν ἐπὶ τὴν πόλιν. ἐν τούτῳ δ᾽ οἱ Ἀθηναῖοι, μακρᾶς 66
15 οὔσης τῆς ὁδοῦ αὐτοῖς, καθ᾽ ἡσυχίαν καθῖσαν τὸ στράτευμα
ἐς χωρίον ἐπιτήδειον, καὶ ἐν ᾧ μάχης τε ἄρξειν ἔμελλον
ὁπότε βούλοιντο καὶ οἱ ἱππῆς τῶν Συρακοσίων ἥκιστ᾽ ἂν
αὐτοὺς καὶ ἐν τῷ ἔργῳ καὶ πρὸ αὐτοῦ λυπήσειν· τῇ μὲν γὰρ
τειχία τε καὶ οἰκίαι εἶργον καὶ δένδρα καὶ λίμνη, παρὰ δὲ τὸ
20 κρημνοί. καὶ τὰ ἐγγὺς δένδρα κόψαντες καὶ κατενεγκόντες ἐπὶ 2
τὴν θάλασσαν παρά τε τὰς ναῦς σταύρωμα ἔπηξαν καὶ ἐπὶ τῷ
Δάσκωνι ἔρυμά τι, ᾗ εὐεφοδώτατον ἦν τοῖς πολεμίοις, λίθοις
λογάδην καὶ ξύλοις διὰ ταχέων ὤρθωσαν, καὶ τὴν τοῦ Ἀνάπου
γέφυραν ἔλυσαν. παρασκευαζομένων δὲ ἐκ μὲν τῆς πόλεως 3
25 οὐδεὶς ἐξιὼν ἐκώλυε, πρῶτοι δὲ οἱ ἱππῆς τῶν Συρακοσίων προσ-
εβοήθησαν, ἔπειτα δὲ ὕστερον καὶ τὸ πεζὸν ἅπαν ξυνελέγη.
καὶ προσῆλθον μὲν ἐγγὺς τοῦ στρατεύματος τῶν Ἀθηναίων τὸ
πρῶτον, ἔπειτα δὲ ὡς οὐκ ἀντιπροῆσαν αὐτοῖς, ἀναχωρήσαντες
καὶ διαβάντες τὴν Ἑλωρίνην ὁδὸν ηὐλίσαντο.
30   Τῇ δ᾽ ὑστεραίᾳ οἱ Ἀθηναῖοι καὶ οἱ ξύμμαχοι παρεσκευά- 67
ζοντο ὡς ἐς μάχην, καὶ ξυνετάξαντο ὧδε. δεξ ὸν μὲν κέρας

Ἀργεῖοι εἶχον καὶ Μαντινῆς, Ἀθηναῖοι δὲ τὸ μέσον, τὸ δὲ
ἄλλο οἱ ξύμμαχοι οἱ ἄλλοι. καὶ τὸ μὲν ἥμισυ αὐτοῖς τοῦ
στρατεύματος ἐν τῷ πρόσθεν ἦν τεταγμένον ἐπὶ ὀκτώ, τὸ δὲ
ἥμισυ ἐπὶ ταῖς εὐναῖς ἐν πλαισίῳ, ἐπὶ ὀκτὼ καὶ τοῦτο τετα-
γμένον· οἷς εἴρητο, ᾗ ἂν τοῦ στρατεύματός τι πονῇ μάλιστα, 5
ἐφορῶντας παραγίγνεσθαι. καὶ τοὺς σκευοφόρους ἐντὸς
2 τούτων τῶν ἐπιτάκτων ἐποιήσαντο. οἱ δὲ Συρακόσιοι ἔτα-
ξαν τοὺς μὲν ὁπλίτας πάντας ἐφ᾽ ἑκκαίδεκα, ὄντας πανδημεὶ
Συρακοσίους καὶ ὅσοι ξύμμαχοι παρῆσαν (ἐβοήθησαν δὲ αὐτοῖς Σελινούντιοι μὲν μάλιστα, ἔπειτα δὲ καὶ Γελῴων ἱππῆς, 10
τὸ ξύμπαν ἐς διακοσίους, καὶ Καμαριναίων ἱππῆς ὅσον εἴκοσι
καὶ τοξόται ὡς πεντήκοντα), τοὺς δὲ ἱππέας ἐπετάξαντο ἐπὶ
τῷ δεξιῷ, οὐκ ἔλασσον ὄντας ἢ διακοσίους καὶ χιλίους, παρὰ
3 δ᾽ αὐτοὺς καὶ τοὺς ἀκοντιστάς. μέλλουσι δὲ τοῖς Ἀθηναίοις
προτέροις ἐπιχειρήσειν ὁ Νικίας κατά τε ἔθνη ἐπιπαριὼν 15
ἕκαστα καὶ ξύμπασι τοιάδε παρεκελεύετο.

68 'Πολλῇ μὲν παραινέσει, ὦ ἄνδρες, τί δεῖ χρῆσθαι, οἳ
πάρεσμεν ἐπὶ τὸν αὐτὸν ἀγῶνα; αὐτὴ γὰρ ἡ παρασκευὴ
ἱκανωτέρα μοι δοκεῖ εἶναι θάρσος παρασχεῖν ἢ καλῶς λε-
2 χθέντες λόγοι μετὰ ἀσθενοῦς στρατοπέδου. ὅπου γὰρ Ἀργεῖοι 20
καὶ Μαντινῆς καὶ Ἀθηναῖοι καὶ νησιωτῶν οἱ πρῶτοί ἐσμεν,
πῶς οὐ χρὴ μετὰ τοιῶνδε καὶ τοσῶνδε ξυμμάχων πάντα τινὰ
μεγάλην τὴν ἐλπίδα τῆς νίκης ἔχειν, ἄλλως τε καὶ πρὸς
ἄνδρας πανδημεί τε ἀμυνομένους καὶ οὐκ ἀπολέκτους ὥσπερ
καὶ ἡμᾶς, καὶ προσέτι Σικελιώτας, οἳ ὑπερφρονοῦσι μὲν ἡμᾶς, 25
ὑπομενοῦσι δ᾽ οὔ, διὰ τὸ τὴν ἐπιστήμην τῆς τόλμης ἥσσω
3 ἔχειν. παραστήτω δέ τινι καὶ τόδε, πολύ τε ἀπὸ τῆς ἡμετέρας
αὐτῶν εἶναι καὶ πρὸς γῇ οὐδεμιᾷ φιλίᾳ, ἥντινα μὴ αὐτοὶ μαχόμενοι κτήσεσθε. καὶ τοὐναντίον ὑπομιμνῄσκω ὑμᾶς ἢ οἱ
πολέμιοι σφίσιν αὐτοῖς εὖ οἶδ᾽ ὅτι παρακελεύονται· οἱ μὲν γὰρ 30
ὅτι περὶ πατρίδος ἔσται ὁ ἀγών, ἐγὼ δὲ ὅτι οὐκ ἐν πατρίδι, ἐξ

ἧς κρατεῖν δεῖ ἢ μὴ ῥᾳδίως ἀποχωρεῖν· οἱ γὰρ ἱππῆς πολλοὶ
ἐπικείσονται. τῆς τε οὖν ὑμετέρας αὐτῶν ἀξίας μνησθέντες 4
ἐπέλθετε τοῖς ἐναντίοις προθύμως, καὶ τὴν παροῦσαν ἀνάγκην
καὶ ἀπορίαν φοβερωτέραν ἡγησάμενοι τῶν πολεμίων.'

5 Ὁ μὲν Νικίας τοιαῦτα παρακελευσάμενος ἐπῆγε τὸ 69
στρατόπεδον εὐθύς. οἱ δὲ Συρακόσιοι ἀπροσδόκητοι μὲν ἐν
τῷ καιρῷ τούτῳ ἦσαν ὡς ἤδη μαχούμενοι, καί τινες αὐτοῖς
ἐγγὺς τῆς πόλεως οὔσης καὶ ἀπεληλύθεσαν· οἱ δὲ καὶ διὰ
σπουδῆς προσβοηθοῦντες δρόμῳ ὑστέριζον μέν, ὡς δὲ ἕκαστός
10 πῃ τοῖς πλέοσι προσμείξειε καθίσταντο. οὐ γὰρ δὴ προθυμίᾳ ἐλλιπεῖς ἦσαν οὐδὲ τόλμῃ οὔτ' ἐν ταύτῃ τῇ μάχῃ οὔτ'
ἐν ταῖς ἄλλαις, ἀλλὰ τῇ μὲν ἀνδρείᾳ οὐχ ἥσσους ἐς ὅσον ἡ
ἐπιστήμη ἀντέχοι, τῷ δὲ ἐλλείποντι αὐτῆς καὶ τὴν βούλησιν
ἄκοντες προυδίδοσαν. ὅμως δὲ οὐκ ἂν οἰόμενοι σφίσι τοὺς
15 Ἀθηναίους προτέρους ἐπελθεῖν καὶ διὰ τάχους ἀναγκαζόμενοι
ἀμύνασθαι, ἀναλαβόντες τὰ ὅπλα εὐθὺς ἀντεπῇσαν. καὶ 2
πρῶτον μὲν αὐτῶν ἑκατέρων οἵ τε λιθοβόλοι καὶ σφενδονῆται
καὶ τοξόται προυμάχοντο καὶ τροπὰς οἵας εἰκὸς ψιλοὺς ἀλλήλων ἐποίουν· ἔπειτα δὲ μάντεις τε σφάγια προύφερον τὰ
20 νομιζόμενα καὶ σαλπιγκταὶ ξύνοδον ἐπώτρυνον τοῖς ὁπλίταις,
οἱ δ' ἐχώρουν, Συρακόσιοι μὲν περί τε πατρίδος μαχούμενοι 3
καὶ τῆς ἰδίας ἕκαστος τὸ μὲν αὐτίκα σωτηρίας, τὸ δὲ μέλλον
ἐλευθερίας, τῶν δ' ἐναντίων Ἀθηναῖοι μὲν περί τε τῆς ἀλλο-
τρίας οἰκείαν σχεῖν καὶ τὴν οἰκείαν μὴ βλάψαι ἡσσώμενοι,
25 Ἀργεῖοι δὲ καὶ τῶν ξυμμάχων οἱ αὐτόνομοι ξυγκτήσασθαί
τε ἐκείνοις ἐφ' ἃ ἦλθον καὶ τὴν ὑπάρχουσαν σφίσι πατρίδα
νικήσαντες πάλιν ἐπιδεῖν· τὸ δ' ὑπήκοον τῶν ξυμμάχων
μέγιστον μὲν περὶ τῆς αὐτίκα ἀνελπίστου σωτηρίας, ἢν μὴ
κρατῶσι, τὸ πρόθυμον εἶχον, ἔπειτα δὲ ἐν παρέργῳ καὶ εἴ τι
30 ἄλλο ξυγκαταστρεψαμένοις ῥᾷον αὐτοῖς ὑπακούσεται. γενο- 70

8 ἀπεληλύθεσαν recc.: ἐπεληλύθεσαν codd.   18 οἷα
ABEFM suprascr. G   23 δὲ ἀντίων ACEFM   30 συγκατα-
στρεψομένοις ABFM: συγκαταστρεφομένοι E: ξυγκαταστρεψάμενοι
F. Müller   ὑπακούσονται Schol.

μένης δ' ἐν χερσὶ τῆς μάχης ἐπὶ πολὺ ἀντεῖχον ἀλλήλοις,
καὶ ξυνέβη βροντάς τε ἅμα τινὰς γενέσθαι καὶ ἀστραπὰς
καὶ ὕδωρ πολύ, ὥστε τοῖς μὲν πρῶτον μαχομένοις καὶ ἐλάχιστα πολέμῳ ὡμιληκόσι καὶ τοῦτο ξυνεπιλαβέσθαι τοῦ
φόβου, τοῖς δ' ἐμπειροτέροις τὰ μὲν γιγνόμενα καὶ ὥρᾳ 5
ἔτους περαίνεσθαι δοκεῖν, τοὺς δὲ ἀνθεστῶτας πολὺ μείζω
2 ἔκπληξιν μὴ νικωμένους παρέχειν.   ὡσαμένων δὲ τῶν Ἀργείων πρῶτον τὸ εὐώνυμον κέρας τῶν Συρακοσίων καὶ μετ'
αὐτοὺς τῶν Ἀθηναίων τὸ κατὰ σφᾶς αὐτούς, παρερρήγνυτο
ἤδη καὶ τὸ ἄλλο στράτευμα τῶν Συρακοσίων καὶ ἐς φυγὴν 10
3 κατέστη.   καὶ ἐπὶ πολὺ μὲν οὐκ ἐδίωξαν οἱ Ἀθηναῖοι (οἱ
γὰρ ἱππῆς τῶν Συρακοσίων πολλοὶ ὄντες καὶ ἀήσσητοι εἶργον, καὶ ἐσβαλόντες ἐς τοὺς ὁπλίτας αὐτῶν, εἴ τινας προ-
διώκοντας ἴδοιεν, ἀνέστελλον), ἐπακολουθήσαντες δὲ ἁθρόοι
ὅσον ἀσφαλῶς εἶχε πάλιν ἐπανεχώρουν καὶ τροπαῖον ἵστα- 15
4 σαν.   οἱ δὲ Συρακόσιοι ἀθροισθέντες ἐς τὴν Ἑλωρίνην ὁδὸν
καὶ ὡς ἐκ τῶν παρόντων· ξυνταξάμενοι ἔς τε τὸ Ὀλυμπιεῖον
ὅμως σφῶν αὐτῶν παρέπεμψαν φυλακήν, δείσαντες μὴ οἱ
Ἀθηναῖοι τῶν χρημάτων ἃ ἦν αὐτόθι κινήσωσι, καὶ οἱ λοιποὶ
71 ἐπανεχώρησαν ἐς τὴν πόλιν.   οἱ δὲ Ἀθηναῖοι πρὸς μὲν τὸ 20
ἱερὸν οὐκ ἦλθον, ξυγκομίσαντες δὲ τοὺς ἑαυτῶν νεκροὺς καὶ
ἐπὶ πυρὰν ἐπιθέντες ηὐλίσαντο αὐτοῦ.   τῇ δ' ὑστεραίᾳ τοῖς
μὲν Συρακοσίοις ἀπέδοσαν ὑποσπόνδους τοὺς νεκρούς (ἀπέθανον δὲ αὐτῶν καὶ τῶν ξυμμάχων περὶ ἑξήκοντα καὶ διακοσίους), τῶν δὲ σφετέρων τὰ ὀστᾶ ξυνέλεξαν (ἀπέθανον δὲ 25
αὐτῶν καὶ τῶν ξυμμάχων ὡς πεντήκοντα), καὶ τὰ τῶν πολε-
2 μίων σκῦλα ἔχοντες ἀπέπλευσαν ἐς Κατάνην· χειμών τε
γὰρ ἦν, καὶ τὸν πόλεμον αὐτόθεν ποιεῖσθαι οὔπω ἐδόκει
δυνατὸν εἶναι, πρὶν ἂν ἱππέας τε μεταπέμψωσιν ἐκ τῶν
Ἀθηνῶν καὶ ἐκ τῶν αὐτόθεν ξυμμάχων ἀγείρωσιν, ὅπως μὴ 30
παντάπασιν ἱπποκρατῶνται, καὶ χρήματα δὲ ἅμα αὐτόθεν τε
ξυλλέξωνται καὶ παρ' Ἀθηναίων ἔλθῃ, τῶν τε πόλεών τινας

13 τινας E : τινες cett.   25 ἀνέλεξαν C

προσαγάγωνται, ἃς ἤλπιζον μετὰ τὴν μάχην μᾶλλον σφῶν
ὑπακούσεσθαι, τά τε ἄλλα καὶ σῖτον καὶ ὅσων δέοι παρα-
σκευάσωνται ὡς ἐς τὸ ἔαρ ἐπιχειρήσοντες ταῖς Συρακούσαις.

Καὶ οἱ μὲν ταύτῃ τῇ γνώμῃ ἀπέπλευσαν ἐς τὴν Νάξον 72
5 καὶ Κατάνην διαχειμάσοντες, Συρακόσιοι δὲ τοὺς σφετέρους
αὑτῶν νεκροὺς θάψαντες ἐκκλησίαν ἐποίουν. καὶ παρελθὼν 2
αὐτοῖς Ἑρμοκράτης ὁ Ἕρμωνος, ἀνὴρ καὶ ἐς τἆλλα ξύνεσιν
οὐδενὸς λειπόμενος καὶ κατὰ τὸν πόλεμον ἐμπειρίᾳ τε ἱκανὸς
γενόμενος καὶ ἀνδρείᾳ ἐπιφανής, ἐθάρσυνέ τε καὶ οὐκ εἴα
10 τῷ γεγενημένῳ ἐνδιδόναι· τὴν μὲν γὰρ γνώμην αὐτῶν οὐχ 3
ἡσσῆσθαι, τὴν δὲ ἀταξίαν βλάψαι. οὐ μέντοι τοσοῦτόν γε
λειφθῆναι ὅσον εἰκὸς εἶναι, ἄλλως τε καὶ τοῖς πρώτοις τῶν
Ἑλλήνων ἐμπειρίᾳ ἰδιώτας ὡς εἰπεῖν χειροτέχναις ἀνταγω-
νισαμένους. μέγα δὲ βλάψαι καὶ τὸ πλῆθος τῶν στρατηγῶν 4
15 καὶ τὴν πολυαρχίαν (ἦσαν γὰρ πέντε καὶ δέκα οἱ στρατηγοὶ
αὐτοῖς) τῶν τε πολλῶν τὴν ἀξύντακτον ἀναρχίαν. ἢν δὲ
ὀλίγοι τε στρατηγοὶ γένωνται ἔμπειροι καὶ ἐν τῷ χειμῶνι
τούτῳ παρασκευάσωσι τὸ ὁπλιτικόν, οἷς τε ὅπλα μὴ ἔστιν
ἐκπορίζοντες, ὅπως ὡς πλεῖστοι ἔσονται, καὶ τῇ ἄλλῃ μελέτῃ
20 προσαναγκάζοντες, ἔφη κατὰ τὸ εἰκὸς κρατήσειν σφᾶς τῶν
ἐναντίων, ἀνδρείας μὲν σφίσιν ὑπαρχούσης, εὐταξίας δ᾽ ἐς
τὰ ἔργα προσγενομένης· ἐπιδώσειν γὰρ ἀμφότερα αὐτά, τὴν
μὲν μετὰ κινδύνων μελετωμένην, τὴν δ᾽ εὐψυχίαν αὐτὴν ἑαυ-
τῆς μετὰ τοῦ πιστοῦ τῆς ἐπιστήμης θαρσαλεωτέραν ἔσεσθαι.
25 τούς τε στρατηγοὺς καὶ ὀλίγους καὶ αὐτοκράτορας χρῆναι 5
ἑλέσθαι καὶ ὀμόσαι αὐτοῖς τὸ ὅρκιον ἦ μὴν ἐάσειν ἄρχειν
ὅπῃ ἂν ἐπίστωνται· οὕτω γὰρ ἅ τε κρύπτεσθαι δεῖ μᾶλλον
ἂν στέγεσθαι καὶ τἆλλα κατὰ κόσμον καὶ ἀπροφασίστως
παρασκευασθῆναι. καὶ οἱ Συρακόσιοι αὐτοῦ ἀκούσαντες 73
30 ἐψηφίσαντό τε πάντα ὡς ἐκέλευε καὶ στρατηγὸν αὐτόν τε
εἵλοντο τὸν Ἑρμοκράτη καὶ Ἡρακλείδην τὸν Λυσιμάχου καὶ

2 παρασκευάσονται A E G M   3 ὡς ἐς recc.: ὥστε codd.   12 καὶ
recc.: om. codd.   13 χειροτέχναις F¹: χειροτέχνας cett.

2 Σικανὸν τὸν Ἐξηκέστου, τούτους τρεῖς, καὶ ἐς τὴν Κόρινθον
καὶ ἐς τὴν Λακεδαίμονα πρέσβεις ἀπέστειλαν, ὅπως ξυμμαχία τε αὐτοῖς παραγένηται καὶ τὸν πρὸς Ἀθηναίους
πόλεμον βεβαιότερον πείθωσι ποιεῖσθαι ἐκ τοῦ προφανοῦς
ὑπὲρ σφῶν τοὺς Λακεδαιμονίους, ἵνα ἢ ἀπὸ τῆς Σικελίας 5
ἀπαγάγωσιν αὐτοὺς ἢ πρὸς τὸ ἐν Σικελίᾳ στράτευμα ἧσσον
ὠφελίαν ἄλλην ἐπιπέμπωσιν.

74 Τὸ δ' ἐν τῇ Κατάνῃ στράτευμα τῶν Ἀθηναίων ἔπλευσεν
εὐθὺς ἐπὶ Μεσσήνην ὡς προδοθησομένην. καὶ ἃ μὲν ἐπράσ-
σετο οὐκ ἐγένετο· Ἀλκιβιάδης γὰρ ὅτ' ἀπῄει ἐκ τῆς ἀρχῆς 10
ἤδη μετάπεμπτος, ἐπιστάμενος ὅτι φεύξοιτο, μηνύει τοῖς τῶν
Συρακοσίων φίλοις τοῖς ἐν τῇ Μεσσήνῃ ξυνειδὼς τὸ μέλλον·
οἱ δὲ τούς τε ἄνδρας διέφθειραν πρότερον καὶ τότε στασιά-
ζοντες καὶ ἐν ὅπλοις ὄντες ἐπεκράτουν μὴ δέχεσθαι τοὺς
2 Ἀθηναίους οἱ ταῦτα βουλόμενοι. ἡμέρας δὲ μείναντες περὶ 15
τρεῖς καὶ δέκα οἱ Ἀθηναῖοι ὡς ἐχειμάζοντο καὶ τὰ ἐπιτήδεια
οὐκ εἶχον καὶ προυχώρει οὐδέν, ἀπελθόντες ἐς Νάξον καὶ
ὅρια καὶ σταυρώματα περὶ τὸ στρατόπεδον ποιησάμενοι αὐτοῦ διεχείμαζον· καὶ τριήρη ἀπέστειλαν ἐς τὰς Ἀθήνας ἐπί
τε χρήματα καὶ ἱππέας, ὅπως ἅμα τῷ ἦρι παραγένωνται. 20

75 Ἐτείχιζον δὲ καὶ οἱ Συρακόσιοι ἐν τῷ χειμῶνι πρός τε τῇ
πόλει, τὸν Τεμενίτην ἐντὸς ποιησάμενοι, τεῖχος παρὰ πᾶν
τὸ πρὸς τὰς Ἐπιπολὰς ὁρῶν, ὅπως μὴ δι' ἐλάσσονος εὐαποτεί-
χιστοι ὦσιν, ἢν ἄρα σφάλλωνται, καὶ τὰ Μέγαρα φρούριον,
καὶ ἐν τῷ Ὀλυμπιείῳ ἄλλο· καὶ τὴν θάλασσαν προυσταύ- 25
2 ρωσαν πανταχῇ ᾗ ἀποβάσεις ἦσαν. καὶ τοὺς Ἀθηναίους
εἰδότες ἐν τῇ Νάξῳ χειμάζοντας ἐστράτευσαν πανδημεὶ ἐπὶ
τὴν Κατάνην, καὶ τῆς τε γῆς αὐτῶν ἔτεμον καὶ τὰς τῶν
Ἀθηναίων σκηνὰς καὶ τὸ στρατόπεδον ἐμπρήσαντες ἀνεχώ-
3 ρησαν ἐπ' οἴκου. καὶ πυνθανόμενοι τοὺς Ἀθηναίους ἐς τὴν 30
Καμάριναν κατὰ τὴν ἐπὶ Λάχητος γενομένην ξυμμαχίαν
πρεσβεύεσθαι, εἴ πως προσαγάγοιντο αὐτούς, ἀντεπρε-

σβεύοντο καὶ αὐτοί· ἦσαν γὰρ ὕποπτοι αὐτοῖς οἱ Καμαριναῖοι
μὴ προθύμως σφίσι μήτ' ἐπὶ τὴν πρώτην μάχην πέμψαι ἃ
ἔπεμψαν, ἔς τε τὸ λοιπὸν μὴ οὐκέτι βούλωνται ἀμύνειν,
ὁρῶντες τοὺς Ἀθηναίους ἐν τῇ μάχῃ εὖ πράξαντας, προσ-
5 χωρῶσι δ' αὐτοῖς κατὰ τὴν προτέραν φιλίαν πεισθέντες.
ἀφικομένων οὖν ἐκ μὲν Συρακουσῶν Ἑρμοκράτους καὶ 4
ἄλλων ἐς τὴν Καμάριναν, ἀπὸ δὲ τῶν Ἀθηναίων Εὐφήμου μεθ' ἑτέρων, ὁ Ἑρμοκράτης ξυλλόγου γενομένου τῶν
Καμαριναίων βουλόμενος προδιαβάλλειν τοὺς Ἀθηναίους
10 ἔλεγε τοιάδε.

'Οὐ τὴν παροῦσαν δύναμιν τῶν Ἀθηναίων, ὦ Καμαρι- 76
ναῖοι, μὴ αὐτὴν καταπλαγῆτε δείσαντες ἐπρεσβευσάμεθα,
ἀλλὰ μᾶλλον τοὺς μέλλοντας ἀπ' αὐτῶν λόγους, πρίν τι καὶ
ἡμῶν ἀκοῦσαι, μὴ ὑμᾶς πείσωσιν. ἥκουσι γὰρ ἐς τὴν 2
15 Σικελίαν προφάσει μὲν ᾗ πυνθάνεσθε, διανοίᾳ δὲ ἣν πάντες
ὑπονοοῦμεν· καί μοι δοκοῦσιν οὐ Λεοντίνους βούλεσθαι
κατοικίσαι, ἀλλ' ἡμᾶς μᾶλλον ἐξοικίσαι. οὐ γὰρ δὴ εὔλογον
τὰς μὲν ἐκεῖ πόλεις ἀναστάτους ποιεῖν, τὰς δὲ ἐνθάδε κατοικίζειν, καὶ Λεοντίνων μὲν Χαλκιδέων ὄντων κατὰ τὸ ξυγγενὲς
20 κήδεσθαι, Χαλκιδέας δὲ τοὺς ἐν Εὐβοίᾳ, ὧν οἵδε ἄποικοί
εἰσι, δουλωσαμένους ἔχειν. τῇ δὲ αὐτῇ ἰδέᾳ ἐκεῖνά τε ἔσχον 3
καὶ τὰ ἐνθάδε νῦν πειρῶνται· ἡγεμόνες γὰρ γενόμενοι ἑκόντων τῶν τε Ἰώνων καὶ ὅσοι ἀπὸ σφῶν ἦσαν ξύμμαχοι ὡς
ἐπὶ τοῦ Μήδου τιμωρίᾳ, τοὺς μὲν λιποστρατίαν, τοὺς δὲ ἐπ'
25 ἀλλήλους στρατεύειν, τοῖς δ' ὡς ἑκάστοις τινὰ εἶχον αἰτίαν
εὐπρεπῆ ἐπενεγκόντες κατεστρέψαντο. καὶ οὐ περὶ τῆς 4
ἐλευθερίας ἄρα οὔτε οὗτοι τῶν Ἑλλήνων οὔθ' οἱ Ἕλληνες
τῆς ἑαυτῶν τῷ Μήδῳ ἀντέστησαν, περὶ δὲ οἱ μὲν σφίσιν
ἀλλὰ μὴ ἐκείνῳ καταδουλώσεως, οἱ δ' ἐπὶ δεσπότου μεταβολῇ
30 οὐκ ἀξυνετωτέρου, κακοξυνετωτέρου δέ.

''Ἀλλ' οὐ γὰρ δὴ τὴν τῶν Ἀθηναίων εὐκατηγόρητον οὖσαν 77
πόλιν νῦν ἥκομεν ἀποφανοῦντες ἐν εἰδόσιν ὅσα ἀδικεῖ, πολὺ
δὲ μᾶλλον ἡμᾶς αὐτοὺς αἰτιασόμενοι ὅτι ἔχοντες παραδεί-

γματα τῶν τ' ἐκεῖ Ἑλλήνων ὡς ἐδουλώθησαν οὐκ ἀμύνοντες
σφίσιν αὐτοῖς, καὶ νῦν ἐφ' ἡμᾶς ταὐτὰ παρόντα σοφίσματα,
Λεοντίνων τε ξυγγενῶν κατοικίσεις καὶ Ἐγεσταίων ξυμμάχων
ἐπικουρίας, οὐ ξυστραφέντες βουλόμεθα προθυμότερον δεῖξαι
αὐτοῖς ὅτι οὐκ Ἴωνες τάδε εἰσὶν οὐδ' Ἑλλησπόντιοι καὶ 5
νησιῶται, οἳ δεσπότην ἢ Μῆδον ἢ ἕνα γέ τινα αἰεὶ μετα-
βάλλοντες δουλοῦνται, ἀλλὰ Δωριῆς ἐλεύθεροι ἀπ' αὐτονόμου
2 τῆς Πελοποννήσου τὴν Σικελίαν οἰκοῦντες. ἢ μένομεν ἕως
ἂν ἕκαστοι κατὰ πόλεις ληφθῶμεν, εἰδότες ὅτι ταύτῃ μόνον
ἁλωτοί ἐσμεν καὶ ὁρῶντες αὐτοὺς ἐπὶ τοῦτο τὸ εἶδος τρεπο- 10
μένους ὥστε τοὺς μὲν λόγοις ἡμῶν διιστάναι, τοὺς δὲ ξυμμάχων ἐλπίδι ἐκπολεμοῦν πρὸς ἀλλήλους, τοῖς δὲ ὡς ἑκάστοις
τι προσηνὲς λέγοντες δύνανται κακουργεῖν; καὶ οἰόμεθα τοῦ
ἄπωθεν ξυνοίκου προαπολλυμένου οὐ καὶ ἐς αὐτόν τινα ἥξειν
τὸ δεινόν, πρὸ δὲ αὐτοῦ μᾶλλον τὸν πάσχοντα καθ' ἑαυτὸν 15
78 δυστυχεῖν; καὶ εἴ τῳ ἄρα παρέστηκε τὸν μὲν Συρακόσιον,
ἑαυτὸν δ' οὐ πολέμιον εἶναι τῷ Ἀθηναίῳ, καὶ δεινὸν ἡγεῖται
ὑπέρ γε τῆς ἐμῆς κινδυνεύειν, ἐνθυμηθήτω οὐ περὶ τῆς ἐμῆς
μᾶλλον, ἐν ἴσῳ δὲ καὶ τῆς ἑαυτοῦ ἅμα ἐν τῇ ἐμῇ μαχούμενος,
τοσούτῳ δὲ καὶ ἀσφαλέστερον ὅσῳ οὐ προδιεφθαρμένου ἐμοῦ, 20
ἔχων δὲ ξύμμαχον ἐμὲ καὶ οὐκ ἔρημος ἀγωνιεῖται· τόν τε
Ἀθηναῖον μὴ τὴν τοῦ Συρακοσίου ἔχθραν κολάσασθαι, τῇ δ'
ἐμῇ προφάσει τὴν ἐκείνου φιλίαν οὐχ ἧσσον βεβαιώσασθαι
2 βούλεσθαι. εἴ τέ τις φθονεῖ μὲν ἢ καὶ φοβεῖται (ἀμφότερα
γὰρ τάδε πάσχει τὰ μείζω), διὰ δὲ αὐτὰ τὰς Συρακούσας 25
κακωθῆναι μὲν ἵνα σωφρονισθῶμεν βούλεται, περιγενέσθαι
δὲ ἕνεκα τῆς αὑτοῦ ἀσφαλείας, οὐκ ἀνθρωπίνης δυνάμεως
βούλησιν ἐλπίζει· οὐ γὰρ οἷόν τε ἅμα τῆς τε ἐπιθυμίας καὶ
3 τῆς τύχης τὸν αὐτὸν ὁμοίως ταμίαν γενέσθαι. καὶ εἰ γνώμῃ
ἁμάρτοι, τοῖς αὑτοῦ κακοῖς ὀλοφυρθεὶς τάχ' ἂν ἴσως καὶ τοῖς 30
ἐμοῖς ἀγαθοῖς ποτε βουληθείη αὖθις φθονῆσαι. ἀδύνατον δὲ

1 ἐκεῖσε ABEFM   15 αὐτὸν ABEFM   19 μαχόμενος
ABEFM[G]   23. οὐχ f G (in rasura): οὓς cett.   27 αὐτοῦ
Stephanus: αὐτοῦ codd.   30 αὐτοῦ C: αὐτοῦ cett.

προεμένῳ καὶ μὴ τοὺς αὐτοὺς κινδύνους οὐ περὶ τῶν ὀνομάτων,
ἀλλὰ περὶ τῶν ἔργων, ἐθελήσαντι προσλαβεῖν· λόγῳ μὲν
γὰρ τὴν ἡμετέραν δύναμιν σῴζοι ἄν τις, ἔργῳ δὲ τὴν αὑτοῦ
σωτηρίαν.   καὶ μάλιστα εἰκὸς ἦν ὑμᾶς, ὦ Καμαριναῖοι, 4
5 ὁμόρους ὄντας καὶ τὰ δεύτερα κινδυνεύσοντας προορᾶσθαι
αὐτὰ καὶ μὴ μαλακῶς ὥσπερ νῦν ξυμμαχεῖν, αὐτοὺς δὲ πρὸς
ἡμᾶς μᾶλλον ἰόντας, ἅπερ ἂν εἰ ἐς τὴν Καμαριναίαν πρῶτον
ἀφίκοντο οἱ Ἀθηναῖοι δεόμενοι ἂν ἐπεκαλεῖσθε, ταῦτα ἐκ
τοῦ ὁμοίου καὶ νῦν παρακελευομένους ὅπως μηδὲν ἐνδώσομεν
10 φαίνεσθαι.   ἀλλ' οὔθ' ὑμεῖς νῦν γέ πω οὔθ' οἱ ἄλλοι ἐπὶ
ταῦτα ὥρμησθε.

' Δειλίᾳ δὲ ἴσως τὸ δίκαιον πρός τε ἡμᾶς καὶ πρὸς τοὺς 79
ἐπιόντας θεραπεύσετε, λέγοντες ξυμμαχίαν εἶναι ὑμῖν πρὸς
Ἀθηναίους· ἥν γε οὐκ ἐπὶ τοῖς φίλοις ἐποιήσασθε, τῶν δὲ
15 ἐχθρῶν ἥν τις ἐφ' ὑμᾶς ἴῃ, καὶ τοῖς γε Ἀθηναίοις βοηθεῖν, ὅταν
ὑπ' ἄλλων καὶ μὴ αὐτοὶ ὥσπερ νῦν τοὺς πέλας ἀδικῶσιν, ἐπεὶ 2
οὐδ' οἱ Ῥηγῖνοι ὄντες Χαλκιδῆς Χαλκιδέας ὄντας Λεοντίνους
ἐθέλουσι ξυγκατοικίζειν.   καὶ δεινὸν εἰ ἐκεῖνοι μὲν τὸ ἔργον
τοῦ καλοῦ δικαιώματος ὑποπτεύοντες ἀλόγως σωφρονοῦσιν,
20 ὑμεῖς δ' εὐλόγῳ προφάσει τοὺς μὲν φύσει πολεμίους βούλεσθε
ὠφελεῖν, τοὺς δὲ ἔτι μᾶλλον φύσει ξυγγενεῖς μετὰ τῶν
ἐχθίστων διαφθεῖραι.   ἀλλ' οὐ δίκαιον, ἀμύνειν δὲ καὶ μὴ 3
φοβεῖσθαι τὴν παρασκευὴν αὐτῶν· οὐ γὰρ ἦν ἡμεῖς ξυστῶμεν
πάντες δεινή ἐστιν, ἀλλ' ἤν, ὅπερ οὗτοι σπεύδουσι, τἀναντία
25 διαστῶμεν, ἐπεὶ οὐδὲ πρὸς ἡμᾶς μόνους ἐλθόντες καὶ μάχῃ
περιγενόμενοι ἔπραξαν ἃ ἐβούλοντο, ἀπῆλθον δὲ διὰ τάχους.
ὥστε οὐχ ἀθρόους γε ὄντας εἰκὸς ἀθυμεῖν, ἰέναι δὲ ἐς τὴν 80
ξυμμαχίαν προθυμότερον, ἄλλως τε καὶ ἀπὸ Πελοποννήσου
παρεσομένης ὠφελίας, οἳ τῶνδε κρείσσους εἰσὶ τὸ παράπαν
30 τὰ πολέμια· καὶ μὴ ἐκείνην τὴν προμηθίαν δοκεῖν τῳ ἡμῖν
μὲν ἴσην εἶναι, ὑμῖν δὲ ἀσφαλῆ, τὸ μηδετέροις δὴ ὡς καὶ

3 αὐτοῦ recc.: αὑτοῦ codd.   7 ἂν Μ : om. cett.   8 ἀφίκοντο
G : ἀφίκοιντο cett.   24 ὅπερ om. ABEFM   30 τῳ c : τῷ codd.

2 ἀμφοτέρων ὄντας ξυμμάχους βοηθεῖν. οὐ γὰρ ἔργῳ ἴσον
ὥσπερ τῷ δικαιώματί ἐστιν. εἰ γὰρ δι' ὑμᾶς μὴ ξυμμαχή-
σαντας ὅ τε παθὼν σφαλήσεται καὶ ὁ κρατῶν περιέσται, τί
ἄλλο ἢ τῇ αὐτῇ ἀπουσίᾳ τοῖς μὲν οὐκ ἠμύνατε σωθῆναι,
τοὺς δὲ οὐκ ἐκωλύσατε κακοὺς γενέσθαι; καίτοι κάλλιον 5
τοῖς ἀδικουμένοις καὶ ἅμα ξυγγενέσι προσθεμένους τήν τε
κοινὴν ὠφελίαν τῇ Σικελίᾳ φυλάξαι καὶ τοὺς Ἀθηναίους
φίλους δὴ ὄντας μὴ ἐᾶσαι ἁμαρτεῖν.

3 ' Ξυνελόντες τε λέγομεν οἱ Συρακόσιοι ἐκδιδάσκειν μὲν
οὐδὲν ἔργον εἶναι σαφῶς οὔτε ὑμᾶς οὔτε τοὺς ἄλλους περὶ ὧν 10
αὐτοὶ οὐδὲν χεῖρον γιγνώσκετε· δεόμεθα δὲ καὶ μαρτυρόμεθα
ἅμα, εἰ μὴ πείσομεν, ὅτι ἐπιβουλευόμεθα μὲν ὑπὸ Ἰώνων αἰεὶ
4 πολεμίων, προδιδόμεθα δὲ ὑπὸ ὑμῶν Δωριῆς Δωριῶν. καὶ
εἰ καταστρέψονται ἡμᾶς Ἀθηναῖοι, ταῖς μὲν ὑμετέραις
γνώμαις κρατήσουσι, τῷ δ' αὑτῶν ὀνόματι τιμηθήσονται, 15
καὶ τῆς νίκης οὐκ ἄλλον τινὰ ἆθλον ἢ τὸν τὴν νίκην παρα-
σχόντα λήψονται· καὶ εἰ αὖ ἡμεῖς περιεσόμεθα, τῆς αἰτίας
5 τῶν κινδύνων οἱ αὐτοὶ τὴν τιμωρίαν ὑφέξετε. σκοπεῖτε οὖν καὶ
αἱρεῖσθε ἤδη ἢ τὴν αὐτίκα ἀκινδύνως δουλείαν ἢ κἂν περιγενόμενοι μεθ' ἡμῶν τούσδε τε μὴ αἰσχρῶς δεσπότας λαβεῖν καὶ 20
τὴν πρὸς ἡμᾶς ἔχθραν μὴ ἂν βραχεῖαν γενομένην διαφυγεῖν.'

81 Τοιαῦτα μὲν ὁ Ἑρμοκράτης εἶπεν, ὁ δ' Εὔφημος ὁ τῶν
Ἀθηναίων πρεσβευτὴς μετ' αὐτὸν τοιάδε.

82 ''Ἀφικόμεθα μὲν ἐπὶ τῆς πρότερον οὔσης ξυμμαχίας
ἀνανεώσει, τοῦ δὲ Συρακοσίου καθαψαμένου ἀνάγκη καὶ 25
2 περὶ τῆς ἀρχῆς εἰπεῖν ὡς εἰκότως ἔχομεν. τὸ μὲν οὖν
μέγιστον μαρτύριον αὐτὸς εἶπεν, ὅτι οἱ Ἴωνες αἰεί ποτε
πολέμιοι τοῖς Δωριεῦσιν εἰσίν. ἔχει δὲ καὶ οὕτως· ἡμεῖς
γὰρ Ἴωνες ὄντες Πελοποννησίοις Δωριεῦσι καὶ πλέοσιν
οὖσι καὶ παροικοῦσιν ἐσκεψάμεθα ὅτῳ τρόπῳ ἥκιστα αὐτῶν 30
3 ὑπακουσόμεθα, καὶ μετὰ τὰ Μηδικὰ ναῦς κτησάμενοι τῆς
μὲν Λακεδαιμονίων ἀρχῆς καὶ ἡγεμονίας ἀπηλλάγημεν,

15 αὐτῶν C : αὑτῶν cett.

οὐδὲν προσῆκον μᾶλλόν τι ἐκείνους ἡμῖν ἢ καὶ ἡμᾶς ἐκείνοις
ἐπιτάσσειν, πλὴν καθ' ὅσον ἐν τῷ παρόντι μεῖζον ἴσχυον,
αὐτοὶ δὲ τῶν ὑπὸ βασιλεῖ πρότερον ὄντων ἡγεμόνες καταστάντες οἰκοῦμεν, νομίσαντες ἥκιστ' ἂν ὑπὸ Πελοποννησίοις
5 οὕτως εἶναι, δύναμιν ἔχοντες ᾗ ἀμυνούμεθα, καὶ ἐς τὸ ἀκριβὲς
εἰπεῖν οὐδὲ ἀδίκως καταστρεψάμενοι τούς τε Ἴωνας καὶ
νησιώτας, οὓς ξυγγενεῖς φασιν ὄντας ἡμᾶς Συρακόσιοι
δεδουλῶσθαι. ἦλθον γὰρ ἐπὶ τὴν μητρόπολιν ἐφ' ἡμᾶς μετὰ 4
τοῦ Μήδου καὶ οὐκ ἐτόλμησαν ἀποστάντες τὰ οἰκεῖα φθεῖραι,
10 ὥσπερ ἡμεῖς ἐκλιπόντες τὴν πόλιν, δουλείαν δὲ αὐτοί τε
ἐβούλοντο καὶ ἡμῖν τὸ αὐτὸ ἐπενεγκεῖν. ἀνθ' ὧν ἄξιοί τε 83
ὄντες ἅμα ἄρχομεν, ὅτι τε ναυτικὸν πλεῖστόν τε καὶ προθυμίαν ἀπροφάσιστον παρεσχόμεθα ἐς τοὺς Ἕλληνας, καὶ
διότι καὶ τῷ Μήδῳ ἑτοίμως τοῦτο δρῶντες οὗτοι ἡμᾶς
15 ἔβλαπτον, ἅμα δὲ τῆς πρὸς Πελοποννησίους ἰσχύος ὀρε-
γόμενοι. καὶ οὐ καλλιεπούμεθα ὡς ἢ τὸν βάρβαρον μόνοι 2
καθελόντες εἰκότως ἄρχομεν ἢ ἐπ' ἐλευθερίᾳ τῇ τῶνδε μᾶλλον
ἢ τῶν ξυμπάντων τε καὶ τῇ ἡμετέρᾳ αὐτῶν κινδυνεύσαντες.
πᾶσι δὲ ἀνεπίφθονον τὴν προσήκουσαν σωτηρίαν ἐκπορίζε-
20 σθαι. καὶ νῦν τῆς ἡμετέρας ἀσφαλείας ἕνεκα καὶ ἐνθάδε
παρόντες ὁρῶμεν καὶ ὑμῖν ταὐτὰ ξυμφέροντα. ἀποφαίνομεν 3
δὲ ἐξ ὧν οἵδε τε διαβάλλουσι καὶ ὑμεῖς μάλιστα ἐπὶ τὸ
φοβερώτερον ὑπονοεῖτε, εἰδότες τοὺς περιδεῶς ὑποπτεύοντάς
τι λόγου μὲν ἡδονῇ τὸ παραυτίκα τερπομένους, τῇ δ'
25 ἐγχειρήσει ὕστερον τὰ ξυμφέροντα πράσσοντας. τήν τε 4
γὰρ ἐκεῖ ἀρχὴν εἰρήκαμεν διὰ δέος ἔχειν καὶ τὰ ἐνθάδε διὰ
τὸ αὐτὸ ἥκειν μετὰ τῶν φίλων ἀσφαλῶς καταστησόμενοι,
καὶ οὐ δουλωσόμενοι, μὴ παθεῖν δὲ μᾶλλον τοῦτο κωλύσοντες.

'Υπολάβῃ δὲ μηδεὶς ὡς οὐδὲν προσῆκον ὑμῶν κηδόμεθα, 84
30 γνοὺς ὅτι σῳζομένων ὑμῶν καὶ διὰ τὸ μὴ ἀσθενεῖς ὑμᾶς
ὄντας ἀντέχειν Συρακοσίοις ἧσσον ἂν τούτων πεμψάντων

5 ἀμυνούμεθα recc. : ἀμυνόμεθα codd. (G)   ἐς] ὡς Krüger   16 οὐ
καλλιεπούμεθα recc.: οὐκ ἄλλο (ἄλλω F) ἐπόμεθα (vel ἐπ.) codd.
21 ταντὰ (sic) E : ταῦτα cett.

2 τινὰ δύναμιν Πελοποννησίοις ἡμεῖς βλαπτοίμεθα. καὶ ἐν
τούτῳ προσήκετε ἤδη ἡμῖν τὰ μέγιστα. διόπερ καὶ τοὺς
Λεοντίνους εὔλογον κατοικίζειν μὴ ὑπηκόους ὥσπερ τοὺς ξυγγενεῖς αὐτῶν τοὺς ἐν Εὐβοίᾳ, ἀλλ᾽ ὡς δυνατωτάτους, ἵνα ἐκ
τῆς σφετέρας ὅμοροι ὄντες τοῖσδε ὑπὲρ ἡμῶν λυπηροὶ ὦσιν. 5
3 τὰ μὲν γὰρ ἐκεῖ καὶ αὐτοὶ ἀρκοῦμεν πρὸς τοὺς πολεμίους,
καὶ ὁ Χαλκιδεύς, ὃν ἀλόγως ἡμᾶς φησὶ δουλωσαμένους τοὺς
ἐνθάδε ἐλευθεροῦν, ξύμφορος ἡμῖν ἀπαράσκευος ὢν καὶ
χρήματα μόνον φέρων, τὰ δὲ ἐνθάδε καὶ Λεοντῖνοι καὶ οἱ
85 ἄλλοι φίλοι ὅτι μάλιστα αὐτονομούμενοι. ἀνδρὶ δὲ τυράννῳ 10
ἢ πόλει ἀρχὴν ἐχούσῃ οὐδὲν ἄλογον ὅτι ξυμφέρον οὐδ᾽ οἰκεῖον
ὅτι μὴ πιστόν· πρὸς ἕκαστα δὲ δεῖ ἢ ἐχθρὸν ἢ φίλον μετὰ
καιροῦ γίγνεσθαι. καὶ ἡμᾶς τοῦτο ὠφελεῖ ἐνθάδε, οὐκ ἢν
τοὺς φίλους κακώσωμεν, ἀλλ᾽ ἢν οἱ ἐχθροὶ διὰ τὴν τῶν
2 φίλων ῥώμην ἀδύνατοι ὦσιν. ἀπιστεῖν δὲ οὐ χρή· καὶ γὰρ 15
τοὺς ἐκεῖ ξυμμάχους ὡς ἕκαστοι χρήσιμοι ἐξηγούμεθα, Χίους
μὲν καὶ Μηθυμναίους νεῶν παροκωχῇ αὐτονόμους, τοὺς δὲ
πολλοὺς χρημάτων βιαιότερον φορᾷ, ἄλλους δὲ καὶ πάνυ
ἐλευθέρως ξυμμαχοῦντας, καίπερ νησιώτας ὄντας καὶ εὐλή-
πτους, διότι ἐν χωρίοις ἐπικαίροις εἰσὶ περὶ τὴν Πελοπόννησον. 20
3 ὥστε καὶ τἀνθάδε εἰκὸς πρὸς τὸ λυσιτελοῦν, καὶ ὃ λέγομεν,
ἐς Συρακοσίους δέος καθίστασθαι. ἀρχῆς γὰρ ἐφίενται ὑμῶν
καὶ βούλονται ἐπὶ τῷ ἡμετέρῳ ξυστήσαντες ὑμᾶς ὑπόπτῳ,
βίᾳ ἢ καὶ κατ᾽ ἐρημίαν, ἀπράκτων ἡμῶν ἀπελθόντων, αὐτοὶ
ἄρξαι τῆς Σικελίας. ἀνάγκη δέ, ἢν ξυστῆτε πρὸς αὐτούς· 25
οὔτε γὰρ ἡμῖν ἔτι ἔσται ἰσχὺς τοσαύτη ἐς ἓν ξυστᾶσα
εὐμεταχείριστος, οὔθ᾽ οἶδ᾽ ἀσθενεῖς ἂν ἡμῶν μὴ παρόντων
86 πρὸς ὑμᾶς εἶεν. καὶ ὅτῳ ταῦτα μὴ δοκεῖ, αὐτὸ τὸ ἔργον
ἐλέγχει. τὸ γὰρ πρότερον ἡμᾶς ἐπηγάγεσθε οὐκ ἄλλον τινὰ
προσείοντες φόβον ἤ, εἰ περιοψόμεθα ὑμᾶς ὑπὸ Συρακοσίοις 30

16 τοῖς ... ξυμμάχοις Α Β Ε F ⟨G⟩ Μ   17 παροκωχῆ Stahl : παροχῇ
codd.   21 ἐνθάδε Α Β Ε F   22 καθίστασθαι Ε : καθίστανται F :
καθίσταται cett.   30 προσείοντες G M : προσιόντας C : προσιόντες
cett.

γενέσθαι, ὅτι καὶ αὐτοὶ κινδυνεύσομεν. καὶ νῦν οὐ δίκαιον, 2
ᾧπερ καὶ ἡμᾶς ἠξιοῦτε λόγῳ πείθειν, τῷ αὐτῷ ἀπιστεῖν, οὐδ᾽
ὅτι δυνάμει μείζονι πρὸς τὴν τῶνδε ἰσχὺν πάρεσμεν ὑποπτεύεσθαι, πολὺ δὲ μᾶλλον τοῖσδε ἀπιστεῖν. ἡμεῖς μέν γε οὔτε 3
5 ἐμμεῖναι δυνατοὶ μὴ μεθ᾽ ὑμῶν, εἴ τε καὶ γενόμενοι κακοὶ
κατεργασαίμεθα, ἀδύνατοι κατασχεῖν διὰ μῆκός τε πλοῦ καὶ
ἀπορίᾳ φυλακῆς πόλεων μεγάλων καὶ τῇ παρασκευῇ ἠπειρω-
τίδων· οἵδε δὲ οὐ στρατοπέδῳ, πόλει δὲ μείζονι τῆς ἡμετέρας
παρουσίας ἐποικοῦντες ὑμῖν αἰεί τε ἐπιβουλεύουσι καὶ ὅταν
10 καιρὸν λάβωσιν ἑκάστου, οὐκ ἀνιᾶσιν (ἔδειξαν δὲ καὶ ἄλλα 4
ἤδη καὶ τὰ ἐς Λεοντίνους), καὶ νῦν τολμῶσιν ἐπὶ τοὺς ταῦτα
κωλύοντας καὶ ἀνέχοντας τὴν Σικελίαν μέχρι τοῦδε μὴ
ὑπ᾽ αὐτοὺς εἶναι παρακαλεῖν ὑμᾶς ὡς ἀναισθήτους. πολὺ 5
δὲ ἐπὶ ἀληθεστέραν γε σωτηρίαν ἡμεῖς ἀντιπαρακαλοῦμεν,
15 δεόμενοι τὴν ὑπάρχουσαν ἀπ᾽ ἀλλήλων ἀμφοτέροις μὴ προ-
διδόναι, νομίσαι δὲ τοῖσδε μὲν καὶ ἄνευ ξυμμάχων αἰεὶ ἐφ᾽
ὑμᾶς ἑτοίμην διὰ τὸ πλῆθος εἶναι ὁδόν, ὑμῖν δ᾽ οὐ πολλάκις
παρασχήσειν μετὰ τοσῆσδε ἐπικουρίας ἀμύνασθαι· ἣν εἰ τῷ
ὑπόπτῳ ἢ ἄπρακτον ἐάσετε ἀπελθεῖν ἢ καὶ σφαλεῖσαν, ἔτι
20 βουλήσεσθε καὶ πολλοστὸν μόριον αὐτῆς ἰδεῖν, ὅτε οὐδὲν
ἔτι περανεῖ παραγενόμενον ὑμῖν.

    ''Ἀλλὰ μήτε ὑμεῖς, ὦ Καμαριναῖοι, ταῖς τῶνδε διαβολαῖς 87
ἀναπείθεσθε μήτε οἱ ἄλλοι· εἰρήκαμεν δ᾽ ὑμῖν πᾶσαν τὴν
ἀλήθειαν περὶ ὧν ὑποπτευόμεθα, καὶ ἔτι ἐν κεφαλαίοις
25 ὑπομνήσαντες ἀξιώσομεν πείθειν. φαμὲν γὰρ ἄρχειν μὲν 2
τῶν ἐκεῖ, ἵνα μὴ ὑπακούωμεν ἄλλου, ἐλευθεροῦν δὲ τὰ ἐνθάδε,
ὅπως μὴ ὑπ᾽ αὐτῶν βλαπτώμεθα, πολλὰ δ᾽ ἀναγκάζεσθαι
πράσσειν, διότι καὶ πολλὰ φυλασσόμεθα, ξύμμαχοι δὲ καὶ
νῦν καὶ πρότερον τοῖς ἐνθάδε ὑμῶν ἀδικουμένοις οὐκ ἄκλητοι,
30 παρακληθέντες δὲ ἥκειν. καὶ ὑμεῖς μήθ᾽ ὡς δικασταὶ γενό- 3
μενοι τῶν ἡμῖν ποιουμένων μήθ᾽ ὡς σωφρονισταί, ὃ χαλεπὸν

ἤδη, ἀποτρέπειν πειρᾶσθε, καθ᾽ ὅσον δέ τι ὑμῖν τῆς ἡμετέρας
πολυπραγμοσύνης καὶ τρόπου τὸ αὐτὸ ξυμφέρει, τούτῳ ἀπολαβόντες χρήσασθε, καὶ νομίσατε μὴ πάντας ἐν ἴσῳ βλάπτειν
4 αὐτά, πολὺ δὲ πλείους τῶν Ἑλλήνων καὶ ὠφελεῖν· ἐν παντὶ
γὰρ πᾶς χωρίῳ, καὶ ᾧ μὴ ὑπάρχομεν, ὅ τε οἰόμενος ἀδι- 5
κήσεσθαι καὶ ὁ ἐπιβουλεύων διὰ τὸ ἑτοίμην ὑπεῖναι ἐλπίδα
τῷ μὲν ἀντιτυχεῖν ἐπικουρίας ἀφ᾽ ἡμῶν, τῷ δὲ εἰ ἥξομεν,
μὴ ἀδεεῖ εἶναι κινδυνεύειν, ἀμφότεροι ἀναγκάζονται ὁ μὲν
5 ἄκων σωφρονεῖν, ὁ δ᾽ ἀπραγμόνως σῴζεσθαι. ταύτην οὖν
τὴν κοινὴν τῷ τε δεομένῳ καὶ ὑμῖν νῦν παροῦσαν ἀσφάλειαν 10
μὴ ἀπώσησθε, ἀλλ᾽ ἐξισώσαντες τοῖς ἄλλοις μεθ᾽ ἡμῶν τοῖς
Συρακοσίοις, ἀντὶ τοῦ αἰεὶ φυλάσσεσθαι αὐτούς, καὶ ἀντεπι-
βουλεῦσαί ποτε ἐκ τοῦ ὁμοίου μεταλάβετε.᾽
88   Τοιαῦτα δὲ ὁ Εὔφημος εἶπεν. οἱ δὲ Καμαριναῖοι ἐπε-
πόνθεσαν τοιόνδε. τοῖς μὲν Ἀθηναίοις εὖνοι ἦσαν, πλὴν
καθ᾽ ὅσον [εἰ] τὴν Σικελίαν ᾤοντο αὐτοὺς δουλώσεσθαι, τοῖς
δὲ Συρακοσίοις αἰεὶ κατὰ τὸ ὅμορον διάφοροι· δεδιότες δ᾽
οὐχ ἧσσον τοὺς Συρακοσίους ἐγγὺς ὄντας μὴ καὶ ἄνευ σφῶν
περιγένωνται, τό τε πρῶτον αὐτοῖς τοὺς ὀλίγους ἱππέας
ἔπεμψαν καὶ τὸ λοιπὸν ἐδόκει αὐτοῖς ὑπουργεῖν μὲν τοῖς 20
Συρακοσίοις μᾶλλον ἔργῳ, ὡς ἂν δύνωνται μετριώτατα, ἐν
δὲ τῷ παρόντι, ἵνα μηδὲ τοῖς Ἀθηναίοις ἔλασσον δοκῶσι
νεῖμαι, ἐπειδὴ καὶ ἐπικρατέστεροι τῇ μάχῃ ἐγένοντο, λόγῳ
2 ἀποκρίνασθαι ἴσα ἀμφοτέροις. καὶ οὕτω βουλευσάμενοι
ἀπεκρίναντο, ἐπειδὴ τυγχάνει ἀμφοτέροις οὖσι ξυμμάχοις 25
σφῶν πρὸς ἀλλήλους πόλεμος ὤν, εὔορκον δοκεῖν εἶναι
σφίσιν ἐν τῷ παρόντι μηδετέροις ἀμύνειν. καὶ οἱ πρέσβεις
ἑκατέρων ἀπῆλθον.
3   Καὶ οἱ μὲν Συρακόσιοι τὰ καθ᾽ ἑαυτοὺς ἐξηρτύοντο ἐς
τὸν πόλεμον, οἱ δ᾽ Ἀθηναῖοι ἐν τῇ Νάξῳ ἐστρατοπεδευμένοι 30

7 ἄν [τι] τυχεῖν Herwerden   8 ἀδεεῖ Krüger : ἀδεεῖς codd.
16 εἰ secl. Reiske   22 δοκῶσι νεῖμαι Valckenaer (ne minoris
facere viderentur Athenienses Valla : δοκῶσιν εἶναι codd.   29 τὰ]
τὸ G M

τὰ πρὸς τοὺς Σικελοὺς ἔπρασσον ὅπως αὐτοῖς ὡς πλεῖστοι
προσχωρήσονται. καὶ οἱ μὲν πρὸς τὰ πεδία μᾶλλον τῶν 4
Σικελῶν ὑπήκοοι ὄντες τῶν Συρακοσίων οἱ πολλοὶ ἀφειστή-
κεσαν· τῶν δὲ τὴν μεσόγειαν ἐχόντων αὐτόνομοι οὖσαι καὶ
5 πρότερον αἰεὶ ⟨αἱ⟩ οἰκήσεις εὐθὺς πλὴν ὀλίγοι μετὰ τῶν
Ἀθηναίων ἦσαν, καὶ σῖτόν τε κατεκόμιζον τῷ στρατεύματι
καὶ εἰσὶν οἳ καὶ χρήματα. ἐπὶ δὲ τοὺς μὴ προσχωροῦντας 5
οἱ Ἀθηναῖοι στρατεύοντες τοὺς μὲν προσηνάγκαζον, τοὺς δὲ
καὶ ὑπὸ τῶν Συρακοσίων φρουρούς τε πεμπόντων καὶ βοη-
10 θούντων ἀπεκωλύοντο. τόν τε χειμῶνα μεθορμισάμενοι ἐκ
τῆς Νάξου ἐς τὴν Κατάνην καὶ τὸ στρατόπεδ.ν ὃ κατεκαύθη
ὑπὸ τῶν Συρακοσίων αὖθις ἀνορθώσαντες διεχείμαζον. καὶ 6
ἔπεμψαν μὲν ἐς Καρχηδόνα τριήρη περὶ φιλίας, εἰ δύναιντό
τι ὠφελεῖσθαι, ἔπεμψαν δὲ καὶ ἐς Τυρσηνίαν, ἔστιν ὧν
15 πόλεων ἐπαγγελλομένων καὶ αὐτῶν ξυμπολεμεῖν. περιήγ-
γελλον δὲ καὶ τοῖς Σικελοῖς καὶ ἐς τὴν Ἔγεσταν πέμψαντες
ἐκέλευον ἵππους σφίσιν ὡς πλείστους πέμπειν, καὶ τἆλλα
ἐς τὸν περιτειχισμόν, πλινθία καὶ σίδηρον, ἡτοίμαζον, καὶ
ὅσα ἔδει, ὡς ἅμα τῷ ἦρι ἐξόμενοι τοῦ πολέμου.

20 Οἱ δ' ἐς τὴν Κόρινθον καὶ Λακεδαίμονα τῶν Συρακοσίων 7
ἀποσταλέντες πρέσβεις τούς τε Ἰταλιώτας ἅμα παραπλέοντες
ἐπειρῶντο πείθειν μὴ περιορᾶν τὰ γιγνόμενα ὑπὸ τῶν Ἀθηναίων, ὡς καὶ ἐκείνοις ὁμοίως ἐπιβουλευόμενα, καὶ ἐπειδὴ
ἐν τῇ Κορίνθῳ ἐγένοντο, λόγους ἐποιοῦντο ἀξιοῦντες σφίσι
25 κατὰ τὸ ξυγγενὲς βοηθεῖν. καὶ οἱ Κορίνθιοι εὐθὺς ψηφι- 8
σάμενοι αὐτοὶ πρῶτοι ὥστε πάσῃ προθυμίᾳ ἀμύνειν, καὶ ἐς
τὴν Λακεδαίμονα ξυναπέστελλον αὐτοῖς πρέσβεις, ὅπως καὶ
ἐκείνους ξυναναπείθοιεν τόν τε αὐτοῦ πόλεμον σαφέστερον
ποιεῖσθαι πρὸς τοὺς Ἀθηναίους καὶ ἐς τὴν Σικελίαν ὠφελίαν
30 τινὰ πέμπειν. καὶ οἵ τε ἐκ τῆς Κορίνθου πρέσβεις παρῆσαν 9
ἐς τὴν Λακεδαίμονα καὶ Ἀλκιβιάδης μετὰ τῶν ξυμφυγάδων

3 οἷ] οὐ Canter   5 αἱ add. Bekker   8 στρατεύσαντες C
9 τε πεμπόντων] ἐσπεμπόντων C   10 ἀπεκωλύοντο Döderlein : ἀπε-
κώλυον codd.

περαιωθεὶς τότ' εὐθὺς ἐπὶ πλοίου φορτηγικοῦ ἐκ τῆς Θουρίας
ἐς Κυλλήνην τῆς Ἠλείας πρῶτον, ἔπειτα ὕστερον ἐς τὴν
Λακεδαίμονα αὐτῶν τῶν Λακεδαιμονίων μεταπεμψάντων
ὑπόσπονδος ἐλθών· ἐφοβεῖτο γὰρ αὐτοὺς διὰ τὴν περὶ τῶν
10 Μαντινικῶν πρᾶξιν. καὶ ξυνέβη ἐν τῇ ἐκκλησίᾳ τῶν 5
Λακεδαιμονίων τούς τε Κορινθίους καὶ τοὺς Συρακοσίους
τὰ αὐτὰ καὶ τὸν Ἀλκιβιάδην δεομένους πείθειν τοὺς Λακεδαιμονίους. καὶ διανοουμένων τῶν τε ἐφόρων καὶ τῶν ἐν
τέλει ὄντων πρέσβεις πέμπειν ἐς Συρακούσας κωλύοντας μὴ
ξυμβαίνειν Ἀθηναίοις, βοηθεῖν δὲ οὐ προθύμων ὄντων, 10
παρελθὼν ὁ Ἀλκιβιάδης παρώξυνέ τε τοὺς Λακεδαιμονίους
καὶ ἐξώρμησε λέγων τοιάδε.

89   ''Ἀναγκαῖον περὶ τῆς ἐμῆς διαβολῆς πρῶτον ἐς ὑμᾶς
εἰπεῖν, ἵνα μὴ χεῖρον τὰ κοινὰ τῷ ὑπόπτῳ μου ἀκροάσησθε.
2 τῶν δ' ἐμῶν προγόνων τὴν προξενίαν ὑμῶν κατά τι ἔγκλημα 15
ἀπειπόντων αὐτὸς ἐγὼ πάλιν ἀναλαμβάνων ἐθεράπευον ὑμᾶς
ἄλλα τε καὶ περὶ τὴν ἐκ Πύλου ξυμφοράν. καὶ διατελοῦντός
μου προθύμου ὑμεῖς πρὸς Ἀθηναίους καταλλασσόμενοι τοῖς
μὲν ἐμοῖς ἐχθροῖς δύναμιν δι' ἐκείνων πράξαντες, ἐμοὶ δὲ
3 ἀτιμίαν περιέθετε. καὶ διὰ ταῦτα δικαίως ὑπ' ἐμοῦ πρός 20
τε τὰ Μαντινέων καὶ Ἀργείων τραπομένου καὶ ὅσα ἄλλα
ἐνηντιούμην ὑμῖν ἐβλάπτεσθε· καὶ νῦν, εἴ τις καὶ τότε ἐν
τῷ πάσχειν οὐκ εἰκότως ὠργίζετό μοι, μετὰ τοῦ ἀληθοῦς
σκοπῶν ἀναπειθέσθω. ἢ εἴ τις, διότι καὶ τῷ δήμῳ προσ-
εκείμην μᾶλλον, χείρω με ἐνόμιζε, μηδ' οὕτως ἡγήσηται 25
4 ὀρθῶς ἄχθεσθαι. τοῖς γὰρ τυράννοις αἰεί ποτε διάφοροί
ἐσμεν (πᾶν δὲ τὸ ἐναντιούμενον τῷ δυναστεύοντι δῆμος ὠνόμασται), καὶ ἀπ' ἐκείνου ξυμπαρέμεινεν ἡ προστασία ἡμῖν
τοῦ πλήθους. ἅμα δὲ καὶ τῆς πόλεως δημοκρατουμένης τὰ
5 πολλὰ ἀνάγκη ἦν τοῖς παροῦσιν ἕπεσθαι. τῆς δὲ ὑπαρχούσης 30
ἀκολασίας ἐπειρώμεθα μετριώτεροι ἐς τὰ πολιτικὰ εἶναι.

1 φορτηγικοῦ f: φορτικοῦ C E Pollux: φορτηκοῦ M: φορτητικοῦ cett.
15 ἐμῶν Haacke: ἡμῶν codd.   29 καὶ om. A B E F M

ἄλλοι δ' ἦσαν καὶ ἐπὶ τῶν πάλαι καὶ νῦν οἱ ἐπὶ τὰ πονηρό
τερα ἐξῆγον τὸν ὄχλον· οἵπερ καὶ ἐμὲ ἐξήλασαν. ἡμεῖς 6
δὲ τοῦ ξύμπαντος προέστημεν, δικαιοῦντες ἐν ᾧ σχήματι
μεγίστη ἡ πόλις ἐτύγχανε καὶ ἐλευθερωτάτη οὖσα καὶ ὅπερ
5 ἐδέξατό τις, τοῦτο ξυνδιασῴζειν, ἐπεὶ δημοκρατίαν γε καὶ
ἐγιγνώσκομεν οἱ φρονοῦντές τι, καὶ αὐτὸς οὐδενὸς ἂν χεῖρον,
ὅσῳ καὶ λοιδορήσαιμι. ἀλλὰ περὶ ὁμολογουμένης ἀνοίας
οὐδὲν ἂν καινὸν λέγοιτο· καὶ τὸ μεθιστάναι αὐτὴν οὐκ ἐδόκει
ἡμῖν ἀσφαλὲς εἶναι ὑμῶν πολεμίων προσκαθημένων.
10 ‘Καὶ τὰ μὲν ἐς τὰς ἐμὰς διαβολὰς τοιαῦτα ξυνέβη· περὶ 90
δὲ ὧν ὑμῖν τε βουλευτέον καὶ ἐμοί, εἴ τι πλέον οἶδα, ἐσηγη-
τέον, μάθετε ἤδη. ἐπλεύσαμεν ἐς Σικελίαν πρῶτον μέν, εἰ 2
δυναίμεθα, Σικελιώτας καταστρεψόμενοι, μετὰ δ' ἐκείνους
αὖθις καὶ Ἰταλιώτας, ἔπειτα καὶ τῆς Καρχηδονίων ἀρχῆς καὶ
15 αὐτῶν ἀποπειράσοντες. εἰ δὲ προχωρήσειε ταῦτα ἢ πάντα 3
ἢ καὶ τὰ πλείω, ἤδη τῇ Πελοποννήσῳ ἐμέλλομεν ἐπιχειρήσειν,
κομίσαντες ξύμπασαν μὲν τὴν ἐκεῖθεν προσγενομένην δύναμιν
τῶν Ἑλλήνων, πολλοὺς δὲ βαρβάρους μισθωσάμενοι καὶ
Ἴβηρας καὶ ἄλλους τῶν ἐκεῖ ὁμολογουμένως νῦν βαρβάρων
20 μαχιμωτάτους, τριήρεις τε πρὸς ταῖς ἡμετέραις πολλὰς
ναυπηγησάμενοι, ἐχούσης τῆς Ἰταλίας ξύλα ἄφθονα, αἷς
τὴν Πελοπόννησον πέριξ πολιορκοῦντες καὶ τῷ πεζῷ ἅμα
ἐκ γῆς ἐφορμαῖς τῶν πόλεων τὰς μὲν βίᾳ λαβόντες, τὰς δ'
ἐντειχισάμενοι, ῥᾳδίως ἠλπίζομεν καταπολεμήσειν καὶ μετὰ
25 ταῦτα καὶ τοῦ ξύμπαντος Ἑλληνικοῦ ἄρξειν. χρήματα δὲ 4
καὶ σῖτον, ὥστε εὐπορώτερον γίγνεσθαί τι αὐτῶν, αὐτὰ τὰ
προσγενόμενα ἐκεῖθεν χωρία ἔμελλε διαρκῆ ἄνευ τῆς ἐνθένδε
προσόδου παρέξειν. τοιαῦτα μὲν περὶ τοῦ νῦν οἰχομένου 91
στόλου παρὰ τοῦ τὰ ἀκριβέστατα εἰδότος ὡς διενοήθημεν
30 ἀκηκόατε· καὶ ὅσοι ὑπόλοιποι στρατηγοί, ἢν δύνωνται, ὁμοίως
αὐτὰ πράξουσιν. ὡς δέ, εἰ μὴ βοηθήσετε οὐ περιέσται τἀκεῖ,
μάθετε ἤδη. Σικελιῶται γὰρ ἀπειρότεροι μέν εἰσιν, ὅμως δ' 2

ἂν ξυστραφέντες ἀθρόοι καὶ νῦν ἔτι περιγένοιντο· Συρακόσιοι δὲ μόνοι μάχῃ τε ἤδη πανδημεὶ ἡσσημένοι καὶ ναυσὶν
ἅμα κατειργόμενοι ἀδύνατοι ἔσονται τῇ νῦν Ἀθηναίων ἐκεῖ
3 παρασκευῇ ἀντισχεῖν. καὶ εἰ αὕτη ἡ πόλις ληφθήσεται,
ἔχεται καὶ ἡ πᾶσα Σικελία, καὶ εὐθὺς καὶ Ἰταλία· καὶ ὃν ;
ἄρτι κίνδυνον ἐκεῖθεν προεῖπον, οὐκ ἂν διὰ μακροῦ ὑμῖν
4 ἐπιπέσοι. ὥστε μὴ περὶ τῆς Σικελίας τις οἰέσθω μόνον
βουλεύειν, ἀλλὰ καὶ περὶ τῆς Πελοποννήσου, εἰ μὴ ποιήσετε
τάδε ἐν τάχει, στρατιάν τε ἐπὶ νεῶν πέμψετε τοιαύτην ἐκεῖσε
οἵτινες αὐτερέται κομισθέντες καὶ ὁπλιτεύσουσιν εὐθύς, καὶ 10
ὃ τῆς στρατιᾶς ἔτι χρησιμώτερον εἶναι νομίζω, ἄνδρα Σπαρτιάτην ἄρχοντα, ὡς ἂν τούς τε παρόντας ξυντάξῃ καὶ τοὺς
μὴ ᾽θέλοντας προσαναγκάσῃ· οὕτω γὰρ οἵ τε ὑπάρχοντες ὑμῖν
φίλοι θαρσήσουσι μᾶλλον καὶ οἱ ἐνδοιάζοντες ἀδεέστερον
5 προσίασιν. καὶ τὰ ἐνθάδε χρὴ ἅμα φανερώτερον ἐκπολεμεῖν, 15
ἵνα Συρακόσιοί τε νομίζοντες ὑμᾶς ἐπιμέλεσθαι μᾶλλον
ἀντέχωσι καὶ Ἀθηναῖοι τοῖς ἑαυτῶν ἧσσον ἄλλην ἐπικουρίαν
6 πέμπωσιν. τειχίζειν τε χρὴ Δεκέλειαν τῆς Ἀττικῆς, ὅπερ
Ἀθηναῖοι μάλιστα αἰεὶ φοβοῦνται, καὶ μόνου αὐτοῦ νομίζουσι
τῶν ἐν τῷ πολέμῳ οὐ διαπεπειρᾶσθαι. βεβαιότατα δ᾽ ἄν 20
τις οὕτω τοὺς πολεμίους βλάπτοι, εἰ ἃ μάλιστα δεδιότας
αὐτοὺς αἰσθάνοιτο, ταῦτα σαφῶς πυνθανόμενος ἐπιφέροι·
εἰκὸς γὰρ αὐτοὺς ἀκριβέστατα ἑκάστους τὰ σφέτερα αὐτῶν
7 δεινὰ ἐπισταμένους φοβεῖσθαι. ἃ δ᾽ ἐν τῇ ἐπιτειχίσει αὐτοὶ
ὠφελούμενοι τοὺς ἐναντίους κωλύσετε, πολλὰ παρεὶς τὰ 25
μέγιστα κεφαλαιώσω. οἷς τε γὰρ ἡ χώρα κατεσκεύασται,
τὰ πολλὰ πρὸς ὑμᾶς τὰ μὲν ληφθέντα, τὰ δ᾽ αὐτόματα ἥξει·
καὶ τὰς τοῦ Λαυρείου τῶν ἀργυρείων μετάλλων προσόδους
καὶ ὅσα ἀπὸ γῆς καὶ δικαστηρίων νῦν ὠφελοῦνται εὐθὺς
ἀποστερήσονται, μάλιστα δὲ τῆς ἀπὸ τῶν ξυμμάχων προσόδου 30
ἧσσον διαφορουμένης, οἳ τὰ παρ᾽ ὑμῶν νομίσαντες ἤδη κατὰ

κράτος πολεμεῖσθαι ὀλιγωρήσουσιν. γίγνεσθαι δέ τι αὐτῶν 92
καὶ ἐν τάχει καὶ προθυμότερον ἐν ὑμῖν ἐστίν, ὦ Λακεδαιμόνιοι, ἐπεὶ ὥς γε δυνατά (καὶ οὐχ ἁμαρτήσεσθαι οἶμαι
γνώμης) πάνυ θαρσῶ.

5 ' Καὶ χείρων οὐδενὶ ἀξιῶ δοκεῖν ὑμῶν εἶναι, εἰ τῇ ἐμαυτοῦ 2
μετὰ τῶν πολεμιωτάτων φιλόπολίς ποτε δοκῶν εἶναι νῦν
ἐγκρατῶς ἐπέρχομαι, οὐδὲ ὑποπτεύεσθαί μου ἐς τὴν φυγαδικὴν
προθυμίαν τὸν λόγον. φυγάς τε γάρ εἰμι τῆς τῶν ἐξε- 3
λασάντων πονηρίας, καὶ οὐ τῆς ὑμετέρας, ἢν πείθησθέ μοι,
10 ὠφελίας· καὶ πολεμιώτεροι οὐχ οἱ τοὺς πολεμίους που βλά-
ψαντες ὑμεῖς ἢ οἱ τοὺς φίλους ἀναγκάσαντες πολεμίους
γενέσθαι. τό τε φιλόπολι οὐκ ἐν ᾧ ἀδικοῦμαι ἔχω, ἀλλ' 4
ἐν ᾧ ἀσφαλῶς ἐπολιτεύθην. οὐδ' ἐπὶ πατρίδα οὖσαν ἔτι
ἡγοῦμαι νῦν ἰέναι, πολὺ δὲ μᾶλλον τὴν οὐκ οὖσαν ἀνακτᾶσθαι.
15 καὶ φιλόπολις οὗτος ὀρθῶς, οὐχ ὃς ἂν τὴν ἑαυτοῦ ἀδίκως
ἀπολέσας μὴ ἐπίῃ, ἀλλ' ὃς ἂν ἐκ παντὸς τρόπου διὰ τὸ
ἐπιθυμεῖν πειραθῇ αὐτὴν ἀναλαβεῖν. οὕτως ἐμοί τε ἀξιῶ 5
ὑμᾶς καὶ ἐς κίνδυνον καὶ ἐς ταλαιπωρίαν πᾶσαν ἀδεῶς
χρῆσθαι, ὦ Λακεδαιμόνιοι, γνόντας τοῦτον δὴ τὸν ὑφ'
20 ἁπάντων προβαλλόμενον λόγον, ὡς εἰ πολέμιός γε ὢν
σφόδρα ἔβλαπτον, κἂν φίλος ὢν ἱκανῶς ὠφελοίην, ὅσῳ τὰ
μὲν Ἀθηναίων οἶδα, τὰ δ' ὑμέτερα ἤκαζον· καὶ αὐτοὺς νῦν
νομίσαντας περὶ μεγίστων δὴ τῶν διαφερόντων βουλεύεσθαι
μὴ ἀποκνεῖν τὴν ἐς τὴν Σικελίαν τε καὶ ἐς τὴν Ἀττικὴν
25 στρατείαν, ἵνα τά τε ἐκεῖ βραχεῖ μορίῳ ξυμπαραγενόμενοι
μεγάλα σώσητε καὶ Ἀθηναίων τήν τε οὖσαν καὶ τὴν μέλ-
λουσαν δύναμιν καθέλητε, καὶ μετὰ ταῦτα αὐτοί τε ἀσφαλῶς
οἰκῆτε καὶ τῆς ἁπάσης Ἑλλάδος ἑκούσης καὶ οὐ βίᾳ, κατ'
εὔνοιαν δὲ ἡγῆσθε.'

30 Ὁ μὲν Ἀλκιβιάδης τοσαῦτα εἶπεν, οἱ δὲ Λακεδαιμόνιοι 93
διανοούμενοι μὲν καὶ αὐτοὶ πρότερον στρατεύειν ἐπὶ τὰς

12 φιλόπολιν E F G M : φιλόπονον A B   21 κἂν B : καὶ ἂν cett.
28 πάσης B   29 ἡγῆσθε B : ἱ-γήσησθε C G : ἡγήσεσθε A E F M
30 τοιαῦτα B

Ἀθήνας, μέλλοντες δ' ἔτι καὶ περιορώμενοι, πολλῷ μᾶλλον
ἐπερρώσθησαν διδάξαντος ταῦτα ἕκαστα αὐτοῦ καὶ νομί-
2 σαντες παρὰ τοῦ σαφέστατα εἰδότος ἀκηκοέναι· ὥστε τῇ
ἐπιτειχίσει τῆς Δεκελείας προσεῖχον ἤδη τὸν νοῦν καὶ τὸ
παραυτίκα καὶ τοῖς ἐν τῇ Σικελίᾳ πέμπειν τινὰ τιμωρίαν. 5
καὶ Γύλιππον τὸν Κλεανδρίδου προστάξαντες ἄρχοντα τοῖς
Συρακοσίοις ἐκέλευον μετ' ἐκείνων καὶ τῶν Κορινθίων βου-
λευόμενον ποιεῖν ὅπη ἐκ τῶν παρόντων μάλιστα καὶ τάχιστά
3 τις ὠφελία ἥξει τοῖς ἐκεῖ. ὁ δὲ δύο μὲν ναῦς τοὺς Κορινθίους ἤδη ἐκέλευέν οἱ πέμπειν ἐς Ἀσίνην, τὰς δὲ λοιπὰς 10
παρασκευάζεσθαι ὅσας διανοοῦνται πέμπειν καί, ὅταν καιρὸς
ᾖ, ἑτοίμας εἶναι πλεῖν. ταῦτα δὲ ξυνθέμενοι ἀνεχώρουν ἐκ
τῆς Λακεδαίμονος.
4 Ἀφίκετο δὲ καὶ ἡ ἐκ τῆς Σικελίας τριήρης τῶν Ἀθηναίων,
ἣν ἀπέστειλαν οἱ στρατηγοὶ ἐπί τε χρήματα καὶ ἱππέας. καὶ 15
οἱ Ἀθηναῖοι ἀκούσαντες ἐψηφίσαντο τήν τε τροφὴν πέμπειν
τῇ στρατιᾷ καὶ τοὺς ἱππέας. καὶ ὁ χειμὼν ἐτελεύτα, καὶ
ἕβδομον καὶ δέκατον ἔτος τῷ πολέμῳ ἐτελεύτα τῷδε ὃν
Θουκυδίδης ξυνέγραψεν.
94 Ἅμα δὲ τῷ ἦρι εὐθὺς ἀρχομένῳ τοῦ ἐπιγιγνομένου θέρους 20
οἱ ἐν τῇ Σικελίᾳ Ἀθηναῖοι ἄραντες ἐκ τῆς Κατάνης παρέπλευσαν ἐπὶ Μεγάρων τῶν ἐν τῇ Σικελίᾳ, οὓς ἐπὶ Γέλωνος
τοῦ τυράννου, ὥσπερ καὶ πρότερόν μοι εἴρηται, ἀναστήσαντες
2 Συρακόσιοι αὐτοὶ ἔχουσι τὴν γῆν. ἀποβάντες δὲ ἐδῄωσαν
τούς [τε] ἀγροὺς καὶ ἐλθόντες ἐπὶ ἔρυμά τι τῶν Συρακοσίων 25
καὶ οὐχ ἑλόντες αὖθις καὶ πεζῇ καὶ ναυσὶ παρακομισθέντες
ἐπὶ τὸν Τηρίαν ποταμὸν τό τε πεδίον ἀναβάντες ἐδῄουν καὶ
τὸν σῖτον ἐνεπίμπρασαν, καὶ τῶν Συρακοσίων περιτυχόντες
τισὶν οὐ πολλοῖς καὶ ἀποκτείναντές τέ τινας καὶ τροπαῖον
3 στήσαντες ἀνεχώρησαν ἐπὶ τὰς ναῦς. καὶ ἀποπλεύσαντες 30
ἐς Κατάνην, ἐκεῖθεν δὲ ἐπισιτισάμενοι, πάσῃ τῇ στρατιᾷ

18 ἐτελεύτα τῷ πολέμῳ B   25 τε om. B   28 τισὶ περιτυχόντες B
29 τέ om. C G

ἐχώρουν ἐπὶ Κεντόριπα, Σικελῶν πόλισμα, καὶ προσαγαγό-
μενοι ὁμολογίᾳ ἀπῇσαν, πιμπράντες ἅμα τὸν σῖτον τῶν τε
Ἰνησσαίων καὶ τῶν Ὑβλαίων. καὶ ἀφικόμενοι ἐς Κατάνην 4
καταλαμβάνουσι τούς τε ἱππέας ἥκοντας ἐκ τῶν Ἀθηνῶν
5 πεντήκοντα καὶ διακοσίους ἄνευ τῶν ἵππων μετὰ σκευῆς, ὡς
αὐτόθεν ἵππων πορισθησομένων, καὶ ἱπποτοξότας τριάκοντα
καὶ τάλαντα ἀργυρίου τριακόσια.

Τοῦ δ᾽ αὐτοῦ ἦρος καὶ ἐπ᾽ Ἄργος στρατεύσαντες Λακε- 95
δαιμόνιοι μέχρι μὲν Κλεωνῶν ἦλθον, σεισμοῦ δὲ γενομένου
10 ἀπεχώρησαν. καὶ Ἀργεῖοι μετὰ ταῦτα ἐσβαλόντες ἐς τὴν
Θυρεᾶτιν ὅμορον οὖσαν λείαν τῶν Λακεδαιμονίων πολλὴν
ἔλαβον, ἣ ἐπράθη ταλάντων οὐκ ἔλασσον πέντε καὶ εἴκοσι.
καὶ ὁ Θεσπιῶν δῆμος ἐν τῷ αὐτῷ θέρει οὐ πολὺ ὕστερον 2
ἐπιθέμενος τοῖς τὰς ἀρχὰς ἔχουσιν οὐ κατέσχεν, ἀλλὰ
15 βοηθησάντων Θηβαίων οἱ μὲν ξυνελήφθησαν, οἱ δ᾽ ἐξέπεσον
Ἀθήναζε.

Καὶ οἱ Συρακόσιοι τοῦ αὐτοῦ θέρους, ὡς ἐπύθοντο τούς 96
[τε] ἱππέας ἥκοντας τοῖς Ἀθηναίοις καὶ μέλλοντας ἤδη ἐπὶ
σφᾶς ἰέναι, νομίσαντες, ἐὰν μὴ τῶν Ἐπιπολῶν κρατήσωσιν
20 οἱ Ἀθηναῖοι, χωρίου ἀποκρήμνου τε καὶ ὑπὲρ τῆς πόλεως
εὐθὺς κειμένου, οὐκ ἂν ῥᾳδίως σφᾶς, οὐδ᾽ εἰ κρατοῖντο
μάχῃ, ἀποτειχισθῆναι, διενοοῦντο τὰς προσβάσεις αὐτῶν
φυλάσσειν, ὅπως μὴ κατὰ ταύτας λάθωσι σφᾶς ἀναβάντες
οἱ πολέμιοι· οὐ γὰρ ἂν ἄλλῃ γε αὐτοὺς δυνηθῆναι. ἐξήρτηται 2
25 γὰρ τὸ ἄλλο χωρίον, καὶ μέχρι τῆς πόλεως ἐπικλινές τ᾽ ἐστὶ
καὶ ἐπιφανὲς πᾶν ἔσω· καὶ ὠνόμασται ὑπὸ τῶν Συρακοσίων
διὰ τὸ ἐπιπολῆς τοῦ ἄλλου εἶναι Ἐπιπολαί. καὶ οἱ μὲν 3
ἐξελθόντες πανδημεὶ ἐς τὸν λειμῶνα παρὰ τὸν Ἄναπον
ποταμὸν ἅμα τῇ ἡμέρᾳ (ἐτύγχανον γὰρ αὐτοῖς καὶ οἱ περὶ
30 τὸν Ἑρμοκράτη στρατηγοὶ ἄρτι παρειληφότες τὴν ἀρχήν)

1 Σικελῶν G : Σικελικὸν B : Σικελὸν cett.   2 ἐμπιπρῶντες
(sic) B   7 τριακόσια ἀργυρίου B   15 Θηβαίων B : Ἀθηναίων
cett.   ἐξέφυγον B   18 τε om. B E   23 ταῦτα A C E F M
28 λειμῶνα] λιμένα B M   post λειμῶνα add. τὸν Krüger

ἐξέτασίν τε ὅπλων ἐποιοῦντο καὶ ἑξακοσίους λογάδας τῶν
ὁπλιτῶν ἐξέκριναν πρότερον, ὧν ἦρχε Διόμιλος φυγὰς ἐξ
Ἄνδρου, ὅπως τῶν τε Ἐπιπολῶν εἶεν φύλακες, καὶ ἦν ἐς
97 ἄλλο τι δέῃ, ταχὺ ξυνεστῶτες παραγίγνωνται. οἱ δὲ Ἀθηναῖοι ταύτης τῆς νυκτὸς τῇ ἐπιγιγνομένῃ ἡμέρᾳ ἐξητάζοντο 5
καὶ ἔλαθον αὐτοὺς παντὶ ἤδη τῷ στρατεύματι ἐκ τῆς Κατάνης
σχόντες κατὰ τὸν Λέοντα καλούμενον, ὃς ἀπέχει τῶν Ἐπιπολῶν ἐξ ἢ ἑπτὰ σταδίους, καὶ τοὺς πεζοὺς ἀποβιβάσαντες,
ταῖς τε ναυσὶν ἐς τὴν Θάψον καθορμισάμενοι· ἔστι δὲ
χερσόνησος μὲν ἐν στενῷ ἰσθμῷ προύχουσα ἐς τὸ πέλαγος, 10
τῆς δὲ Συρακοσίων πόλεως οὔτε πλοῦν οὔτε ὁδὸν πολλὴν
2 ἀπέχει. καὶ ὁ μὲν ναυτικὸς στρατὸς τῶν Ἀθηναίων ἐν τῇ
Θάψῳ διασταυρωσάμενος τὸν ἰσθμὸν ἡσύχαζεν· ὁ δὲ πεζὸς
ἐχώρει εὐθὺς δρόμῳ πρὸς τὰς Ἐπιπολὰς καὶ φθάνει ἀναβὰς
κατὰ τὸν Εὐρύηλον πρὶν τοὺς Συρακοσίους αἰσθομένους ἐκ 15
3 τοῦ λειμῶνος καὶ τῆς ἐξετάσεως παραγενέσθαι. ἐβοήθουν
δὲ οἵ τε ἄλλοι, ὡς ἕκαστος τάχους εἶχε, καὶ οἱ περὶ τὸν
Διόμιλον ἑξακόσιοι· στάδιοι δὲ πρὶν προσμεῖξαι ἐκ τοῦ
λειμῶνος ἐγίγνοντο αὐτοῖς οὐκ ἔλασσον ἢ πέντε καὶ εἴκοσι.
4 προσπεσόντες οὖν αὐτοῖς τοιούτῳ τρόπῳ ἀτακτότερον καὶ 20
μάχῃ νικηθέντες οἱ Συρακόσιοι ἐπὶ ταῖς Ἐπιπολαῖς ἀνεχώρησαν ἐς τὴν πόλιν· καὶ ὅ τε Διόμιλος ἀποθνῄσκει καὶ τῶν
5 ἄλλων ὡς τριακόσιοι. καὶ μετὰ τοῦτο οἱ Ἀθηναῖοι τροπαῖόν
τε στήσαντες καὶ τοὺς νεκροὺς ὑποσπόνδους ἀποδόντες τοῖς
Συρακοσίοις, πρὸς τὴν πόλιν αὐτὴν τῇ ὑστεραίᾳ ἐπικατα- 25
βάντες, ὡς οὐκ ἐπεξῆσαν αὐτοῖς, ἐπαναχωρήσαντες φρούριον
ἐπὶ τῷ Λαβδάλῳ ᾠκοδόμησαν, ἐπ᾽ ἄκροις τοῖς κρημνοῖς τῶν
Ἐπιπολῶν, ὁρῶν πρὸς τὰ Μέγαρα, ὅπως εἴη αὐτοῖς, ὁπότε
προΐοιεν ἢ μαχούμενοι ἢ τειχιοῦντες, τοῖς τε σκεύεσι καὶ
98 τοῖς χρήμασιν ἀποθήκη. καὶ οὐ πολλῷ ὕστερον αὐτοῖς 30
ἦλθον ἔκ τε Ἐγέστης ἱππῆς τριακόσιοι καὶ Σικελῶν καὶ

---

1 ἑξακοσίους Aem. Portus (*sexcenti* Valla): ἑπτακοσίους codd.
20 ἀτακτότεροι B   24 τε om. B   29 προΐοιεν] *prodirent* Valla:
προσίοιεν codd.   31 ἱππῆς B: om. cett.

Ναξίων καὶ ἄλλων τινῶν ὡς ἑκατόν· καὶ Ἀθηναίων ὑπῆρχον
πεντήκοντα καὶ διακόσιοι, οἷς ἵππους τοὺς μὲν παρ' Ἐγεσταίων καὶ Καταναίων ἔλαβον, τοὺς δ' ἐπρίαντο, καὶ
ξύμπαντες πεντήκοντα καὶ ἑξακόσιοι ἱππῆς ξυνελέγησαν.
5 καὶ καταστήσαντες ἐν τῷ Λαβδάλῳ φυλακὴν ἐχώρουν πρὸς 2
τὴν Συκῆν οἱ Ἀθηναῖοι, ἵναπερ καθεζόμενοι ἐτείχισαν τὸν
κύκλον διὰ τάχους. καὶ ἔκπληξιν τοῖς Συρακοσίοις παρέσχον
τῷ τάχει τῆς οἰκοδομίας· καὶ ἐπεξελθόντες μάχην διενοοῦντο
ποιεῖσθαι καὶ μὴ περιορᾶν. καὶ ἤδη ἀντιπαρατασσομένων 3
10 ἀλλήλοις οἱ τῶν Συρακοσίων στρατηγοὶ ὡς ἑώρων σφίσι τὸ
στράτευμα διεσπασμένον τε καὶ οὐ ῥᾳδίως ξυντασσόμενον,
ἀνήγαγον πάλιν ἐς τὴν πόλιν πλὴν μέρους τινὸς τῶν ἱππέων·
οὗτοι δὲ ὑπομένοντες ἐκώλυον τοὺς Ἀθηναίους λιθοφορεῖν τε
καὶ ἀποσκίδνασθαι μακροτέραν. καὶ τῶν Ἀθηναίων φυλὴ 4
15 μία τῶν ὁπλιτῶν καὶ οἱ ἱππῆς μετ' αὐτῶν πάντες ἐτρέψαντο
τοὺς τῶν Συρακοσίων ἱππέας προσβαλόντες, καὶ ἀπέκτεινάν
τέ τινας καὶ τροπαῖον τῆς ἱππομαχίας ἔστησαν.

Καὶ τῇ ὑστεραίᾳ οἱ μὲν ἐτείχιζον τῶν Ἀθηναίων τὸ πρὸς 99
βορέαν τοῦ κύκλου τεῖχος, οἱ δὲ λίθους καὶ ξύλα ξυμφοροῦντες
20 παρέβαλλον ἐπὶ τὸν Τρωγίλον καλούμενον αἰεί, ᾗπερ βραχύτατον ἐγίγνετο αὐτοῖς ἐκ τοῦ μεγάλου λιμένος ἐπὶ τὴν
ἑτέραν θάλασσαν τὸ ἀποτείχισμα. οἱ δὲ Συρακόσιοι οὐχ 2
ἥκιστα Ἑρμοκράτους τῶν στρατηγῶν ἐσηγησαμένου μάχαις
μὲν πανδημεὶ πρὸς Ἀθηναίους οὐκέτι ἐβούλοντο διακιν-
25 δυνεύειν, ὑποτειχίζειν δὲ ἄμεινον ἐδόκει εἶναι, ᾗ ἐκεῖνοι
ἔμελλον ἄξειν τὸ τεῖχος καί, εἰ φθάσειαν, ἀποκλήσεις
γίγνεσθαι, καὶ ἅμα καὶ ἐν τούτῳ εἰ ἐπιβοηθοῖεν, μέρος
ἀντιπέμπειν αὐτοῖς τῆς στρατιᾶς καὶ φθάνειν αὐτοὶ προκαταλαμβάνοντες τοῖς σταυροῖς τὰς ἐφόδους, ἐκείνους δὲ ἂν
30 παυομένους τοῦ ἔργου πάντας ἂν πρὸς σφᾶς τρέπεσθαι.

5 ἐν] ἐπὶ B   8 ἐξελθόντες B   20 παρέβαλλον B : παρέβαλον
cett.   24 post πρὸς add. τοὺς B   28 αὐτοῖς Bekker : αὐτοὺς codd.
αὐτοὶ B : ἂν cett   29 τοῖς σταυροῖς προκαταλαμβάνοντες A C E F G M
ἀναπαυομένους B   30 ἂν om. B

3 ἐτείχιζον οὖν ἐξελθόντες ἀπὸ τῆς σφετέρας πύλεως ἀρξάμενοι, κάτωθεν τοῦ κύκλου τῶν Ἀθηναίων ἐγκάρσιον τεῖχος
ἄγοντες, τάς τε ἐλάας ἐκκόπτοντες τοῦ τεμένους καὶ πύργους
4 ξυλίνους καθιστάντες. αἱ δὲ νῆες τῶν Ἀθηναίων οὔπω ἐκ
τῆς Θάψου περιεπεπλεύκεσαν ἐς τὸν μέγαν λιμένα, ἀλλ᾿ ἔτι 5
οἱ Συρακόσιοι ἐκράτουν τῶν περὶ τὴν θάλασσαν, κατὰ γῆν
100 δ᾿ ἐκ τῆς Θάψου οἱ Ἀθηναῖοι τὰ ἐπιτήδεια ἐπήγοντο. ἐπειδὴ
δὲ τοῖς Συρακοσίοις ἀρκούντως ἐδόκει ἔχειν ὅσα τε ἐσταυρώθη
καὶ ᾠκοδομήθη τοῦ ὑποτειχίσματος, καὶ οἱ Ἀθηναῖοι αὐτοὺς
οὐκ ἦλθον κωλύσοντες, φοβούμενοι μὴ σφίσι δίχα γιγνομέ- 10
νοις ῥᾷον μάχωνται, καὶ ἅμα τὴν καθ᾿ αὑτοὺς περιτείχισιν
ἐπειγόμενοι, οἱ μὲν Συρακόσιοι φυλὴν μίαν καταλιπόντες
φύλακα τοῦ οἰκοδομήματος ἀνεχώρησαν ἐς τὴν πόλιν, οἱ δὲ
Ἀθηναῖοι τούς τε ὀχετοὺς αὐτῶν, οἳ ἐς τὴν πόλιν ὑπονομηδὸν
ποτοῦ ὕδατος ἠγμένοι ἦσαν, διέφθειραν, καὶ τηρήσαντες τούς 15
τε ἄλλους Συρακοσίους κατὰ σκηνὰς ὄντας ἐν μεσημβρίᾳ
καί τινας καὶ ἐς τὴν πόλιν ἀποκεχωρηκότας καὶ τοὺς ἐν τῷ
σταυρώματι ἀμελῶς φυλάσσοντας, τριακοσίους μὲν σφῶν
αὐτῶν λογάδας καὶ τῶν ψιλῶν τινὰς ἐκλεκτοὺς ὡπλισμένους
προὔταξαν θεῖν δρόμῳ ἐξαπιναίως πρὸς τὸ ὑποτείχισμα, ἡ 20
δ᾿ ἄλλη στρατιὰ δίχα, ἡ μὲν μετὰ τοῦ ἑτέρου στρατηγοῦ πρὸς
τὴν πόλιν, εἰ ἐπιβοηθοῖεν, ἐχώρουν, ἡ δὲ μετὰ τοῦ ἑτέρου
2 πρὸς τὸ σταύρωμα τὸ παρὰ τὴν πυλίδα. καὶ προσβαλόντες
οἱ τριακόσιοι αἱροῦσι τὸ σταύρωμα· καὶ οἱ φύλακες αὐτὸ
ἐκλιπόντες κατέφυγον ἐς τὸ προτείχισμα τὸ περὶ τὸν Τεμε- 25
νίτην. καὶ αὐτοῖς ξυνεσέπεσον οἱ διώκοντες, καὶ ἐντὸς
γενόμενοι βίᾳ ἐξεκρούσθησαν πάλιν ὑπὸ τῶν Συρακοσίων,
καὶ τῶν Ἀργείων τινὲς αὐτόθι καὶ τῶν Ἀθηναίων οὐ πολλοὶ
3 διεφθάρησαν. καὶ ἐπαναχωρήσασα ἡ πᾶσα στρατιὰ τήν τε
ὑποτείχισιν καθεῖλον καὶ τὸ σταύρωμα ἀνέσπασαν καὶ διε- 30
φόρησαν τοὺς σταυροὺς παρ᾿ ἑαυτοὺς καὶ τροπαῖον ἔστησαν.

---

7 post ἐπιτήδεια add. σιτία Β   9 αὐτοὺς om. Β   10 post
φοβούμενοι add. οἱ Ἀθηναῖοι Β   11 ἑαυτοὺς Β   19 ἐπιλέκτους Β
23 alterum τὸ om. Β   26 ξυνεσέπεσον Β Ε : ξυνέπεσον cett.

Τῇ δ' ὑστεραίᾳ ἀπὸ τοῦ κύκλου ἐτείχιζον οἱ Ἀθηναῖοι 101
τὸν κρημνὸν τὸν ὑπὲρ τοῦ ἕλους, ὃς τῶν Ἐπιπολῶν ταύτῃ
πρὸς τὸν μέγαν λιμένα ὁρᾷ, καὶ ᾗπερ αὐτοῖς βραχύτατον
ἐγίγνετο καταβᾶσι διὰ τοῦ ὁμαλοῦ καὶ τοῦ ἕλους ἐς τὸν
5 λιμένα τὸ περιτείχισμα. καὶ οἱ Συρακόσιοι ἐν τούτῳ ἐξελ- 2
θόντες καὶ αὐτοὶ ἀπεσταύρουν αὖθις ἀρξάμενοι ἀπὸ τῆς
πόλεως διὰ μέσου τοῦ ἕλους, καὶ τάφρον ἅμα παρώρυσσον,
ὅπως μὴ οἷόν τε ᾖ τοῖς Ἀθηναίοις μέχρι τῆς θαλάσσης
ἀποτειχίσαι. οἱ δ', ἐπειδὴ τὸ πρὸς τὸν κρημνὸν αὐτοῖς 3
10 ἐξείργαστο, ἐπιχειροῦσιν αὖθις τῷ τῶν Συρακοσίων σταυρώματι καὶ τάφρῳ, τὰς μὲν ναῦς κελεύσαντες περιπλεῦσαι
ἐκ τῆς Θάψου ἐς τὸν μέγαν λιμένα τὸν τῶν Συρακοσίων,
αὐτοὶ δὲ περὶ ὄρθρον καταβάντες ἀπὸ τῶν Ἐπιπολῶν ἐς τὸ
ὁμαλὸν καὶ διὰ τοῦ ἕλους, ᾗ πηλῶδες ἦν καὶ στεριφώτατον,
15 θύρας καὶ ξύλα πλατέα ἐπιθέντες καὶ ἐπ' αὐτῶν διαβαδί-
σαντες, αἱροῦσιν ἅμα ἕῳ τό τε σταύρωμα πλὴν ὀλίγου καὶ
τὴν τάφρον, καὶ ὕστερον καὶ τὸ ὑπολειφθὲν εἷλον. καὶ μάχη 4
ἐγένετο, καὶ ἐν αὐτῇ ἐνίκων οἱ Ἀθηναῖοι. καὶ τῶν Συρακοσίων οἱ μὲν τὸ δεξιὸν κέρας ἔχοντες πρὸς τὴν πόλιν
20 ἔφευγον, οἱ δ' ἐπὶ τῷ εὐωνύμῳ παρὰ τὸν ποταμόν. καὶ
αὐτοὺς βουλόμενοι ἀποκλῆσασθαι τῆς διαβάσεως οἱ τῶν
Ἀθηναίων τριακόσιοι λογάδες δρόμῳ ἠπείγοντο πρὸς τὴν
γέφυραν. δείσαντες δὲ οἱ Συρακόσιοι (ἦσαν γὰρ καὶ τῶν 5
ἱππέων αὐτοῖς οἱ πολλοὶ ἐνταῦθα) ὁμόσε χωροῦσι τοῖς τρια-
25 κοσίοις τούτοις, καὶ τρέπουσί τε αὐτοὺς καὶ ἐσβάλλουσιν ἐς
τὸ δεξιὸν κέρας τῶν Ἀθηναίων· καὶ προσπεσόντων αὐτῶν
ξυνεφοβήθη καὶ ἡ πρώτη φυλὴ τοῦ κέρως. ἰδὼν δὲ ὁ 6
Λάμαχος παρεβοήθει ἀπὸ τοῦ εὐωνύμου τοῦ ἑαυτῶν μετὰ
τοξοτῶν τε οὐ πολλῶν καὶ τοὺς Ἀργείους παραλαβών, καὶ
30 ἐπιδιαβὰς τάφρον τινὰ καὶ μονωθεὶς μετ' ὀλίγων τῶν ξυν-
διαβάντων ἀποθνήσκει αὐτός τε καὶ πέντε ἢ ἓξ τῶν μετ'

17 καὶ ὕστερον Β: om. cett.   18 ἐν αὐτῇ om. E, post ἐγένετο
habet Β   20 ἔφευγον Β: ἔφυγον cett.   27 φυλὴ Duker
(cohors Valla): φυλακὴ codd.

αὐτοῦ. καὶ τούτους μὲν οἱ Συρακόσιοι εὐθὺς κατὰ τάχος
φθάνουσιν ἁρπάσαντες πέραν τοῦ ποταμοῦ ἐς τὸ ἀσφαλές,
αὐτοὶ δὲ ἐπιόντος ἤδη καὶ τοῦ ἄλλου στρατεύματος τῶν Ἀθη-
102 ναίων ἀπεχώρουν. ἐν τούτῳ δὲ οἱ πρὸς τὴν πόλιν αὐτῶν
τὸ πρῶτον καταφυγόντες ὡς ἑώρων ταῦτα γιγνόμενα, αὐτοί 5
τε πάλιν ἀπὸ τῆς πόλεως ἀναθαρσήσαντες ἀντετάξαντο πρὸς
τοὺς κατὰ σφᾶς Ἀθηναίους, καὶ μέρος τι αὐτῶν πέμπουσιν
ἐπὶ τὸν κύκλον τὸν ἐπὶ ταῖς Ἐπιπολαῖς, ἡγούμενοι ἐρῆμον
2 αἱρήσειν. καὶ τὸ μὲν δεκάπλεθρον προτείχισμα αὐτῶν
αἱροῦσι καὶ διεπόρθησαν, αὐτὸν δὲ τὸν κύκλον Νικίας διε- 10
κώλυσεν· ἔτυχε γὰρ ἐν αὐτῷ δι᾽ ἀσθένειαν ὑπολελειμμένος.
τὰς γὰρ μηχανὰς καὶ ξύλα ὅσα πρὸ τοῦ τείχους ἦν κατα-
βεβλημένα, ἐμπρῆσαι τοὺς ὑπηρέτας ἐκέλευσεν, ὡς ἔγνω
ἀδυνάτους ἐσομένους ἐρημίᾳ ἀνδρῶν ἄλλῳ τρόπῳ περιγενέ-
3 σθαι. καὶ ξυνέβη οὕτως· οὐ γὰρ ἔτι προσῆλθον οἱ Συρακό- 15
σιοι διὰ τὸ πῦρ, ἀλλὰ ἀπεχώρουν πάλιν. καὶ γὰρ πρός τε
τὸν κύκλον βοήθεια ἤδη κάτωθεν τῶν Ἀθηναίων ἀποδιωξάντων τοὺς ἐκεῖ ἐπανῄει, καὶ αἱ νῆες ἅμα αὐτῶν ἐκ τῆς
4 Θάψου, ὥσπερ εἴρητο, κατέπλεον ἐς τὸν μέγαν λιμένα. ἃ
ὁρῶντες οἱ ἄνωθεν κατὰ τάχος ἀπῇσαν καὶ ἡ ξύμπασα 20
στρατιὰ τῶν Συρακοσίων ἐς τὴν πόλιν, νομίσαντες μὴ ἂν
ἔτι ἀπὸ τῆς παρούσης σφίσι δυνάμεως ἱκανοὶ γενέσθαι
κωλῦσαι τὸν ἐπὶ τὴν θάλασσαν τειχισμόν.

103 Μετὰ δὲ τοῦτο οἱ Ἀθηναῖοι τροπαῖον ἔστησαν καὶ τοὺς
νεκροὺς ὑποσπόνδους ἀπέδοσαν τοῖς Συρακοσίοις καὶ τοὺς 25
μετὰ Λαμάχου καὶ αὐτὸν ἐκομίσαντο· καὶ παρόντος ἤδη
σφίσι παντὸς τοῦ στρατεύματος καὶ τοῦ ναυτικοῦ καὶ τοῦ
πεζοῦ, ἀπὸ τῶν Ἐπιπολῶν καὶ τοῦ κρημνώδους ἀρξάμενοι
ἀπετείχιζον μέχρι τῆς θαλάσσης τείχει διπλῷ τοὺς Συρα-
2 κοσίους. τὰ δ᾽ ἐπιτήδεια τῇ στρατιᾷ ἐσήγετο ἐκ τῆς Ἰταλίας 30

---

2 post ἁρπάσαντες add καὶ διαβιβάσαντες B   6 ἀπὸ τῆς πόλεως
om. C   7 αὐτῶν Bekker: αὐτῶν codd.   14 post ἀδυνάτους
add. αὐτοὺς M   17 ἀποδιωξάντων B : ἀποδιωξόντων cett.   20 ἀπῄ-
εσαν (sic) κατὰ τάχος B   ἐπῄεσαν (sic) A E F M suprascr. G

πανταχόθεν. ἦλθον δὲ καὶ τῶν Σικελῶν πολλοὶ ξύμμαχοι
τοῖς Ἀθηναίοις, οἳ πρότερον περιεωρῶντο, καὶ ἐκ τῆς Τυρσηνίας νῆες πεντηκόντοροι τρεῖς. καὶ τἆλλα προυχώρει
αὐτοῖς ἐς ἐλπίδας. καὶ γὰρ οἱ Συρακόσιοι πολέμῳ μὲν οὐκέτι 3
5 ἐνόμιζον ἂν περιγενέσθαι, ὡς αὐτοῖς οὐδὲ ἀπὸ τῆς Πελοποννήσου ὠφελία οὐδεμία ἧκε, τοὺς δὲ λόγους ἔν τε σφίσιν
αὐτοῖς ἐποιοῦντο ξυμβατικοὺς καὶ πρὸς τὸν Νικίαν· οὗτος
γὰρ δὴ μόνος εἶχε Λαμάχου τεθνεῶτος τὴν ἀρχήν. καὶ 4
κύρωσις μὲν οὐδεμία ἐγίγνετο, οἷα δὲ εἰκὸς ἀνθρώπων ἀπο-
10 ρούντων καὶ μᾶλλον ἢ πρὶν πολιορκουμένων, πολλὰ ἐλέγετο
πρός τε ἐκεῖνον καὶ πλείω ἔτι κατὰ τὴν πόλιν. καὶ γάρ
τινα καὶ ὑποψίαν ὑπὸ τῶν παρόντων κακῶν ἐς ἀλλήλους
εἶχον, καὶ τοὺς στρατηγούς τε ἐφ' ὧν αὐτοῖς ταῦτα ξυνέβη
ἔπαυσαν, ὡς ἢ δυστυχίᾳ ἢ προδοσίᾳ τῇ ἐκείνων βλαπτόμενοι,
15 καὶ ἄλλους ἀνθείλοντο, Ἡρακλείδην καὶ Εὐκλέα καὶ Τελλίαν.

Ἐν δὲ τούτῳ Γύλιππος ὁ Λακεδαιμόνιος καὶ αἱ ἀπὸ τῆς 104
Κορίνθου νῆες περὶ Λευκάδα ἤδη ἦσαν, βουλόμενοι ἐς τὴν
Σικελίαν διὰ τάχους βοηθῆσαι. καὶ ὡς αὐτοῖς αἱ ἀγγελίαι
ἐφοίτων δειναὶ καὶ πᾶσαι ἐπὶ τὸ αὐτὸ ἐψευσμέναι ὡς ἤδη
20 παντελῶς ἀποτετειχισμέναι αἱ Συράκουσαί εἰσι, τῆς μὲν
Σικελίας οὐκέτι ἐλπίδα οὐδεμίαν εἶχεν ὁ Γύλιππος, τὴν δὲ
Ἰταλίαν βουλόμενος περιποιῆσαι αὐτὸς μὲν καὶ Πυθὴν ὁ
Κορίνθιος ναυσὶ δυοῖν μὲν Λακωνικαῖν, δυοῖν δὲ Κορινθίαιν
ὅτι τάχιστα ἐπεραιώθησαν τὸν Ἰόνιον ἐς Τάραντα, οἱ δὲ
25 Κορίνθιοι πρὸς ταῖς σφετέραις δέκα Λευκαδίας δύο καὶ Ἀμπρακιώτιδας τρεῖς προσπληρώσαντες ὕστερον ἔμελλον πλεύ-
σεσθαι. καὶ ὁ μὲν Γύλιππος ἐκ τοῦ Τάραντος ἐς τὴν Θουρίαν 2
πρῶτον πρεσβευσάμενος καὶ τὴν τοῦ πατρὸς ἀνανεωσάμενος
πολιτείαν καὶ οὐ δυνάμενος αὐτοὺς προσαγαγέσθαι, ἄρας
30 παρέπλει τὴν Ἰταλίαν, καὶ ἁρπασθεὶς ὑπ' ἀνέμου κατὰ τὸν

1 Σικελιωτῶν B   3 τἆλλα] πάντα B   4 ἐλπίδα B M   8 δὴ]
ἤδη B   10 πρὶν om. C   15 Εὐρυκλέα B   28 καὶ B: κατὰ
cett.   ἀνανεωσάμενος B: ποτε cett.   30 παρέπλευσε B
ἀνάρπασθείς (sic) M

Τεριναῖον κόλπον, ὃς ἐκπνεῖ ταύτῃ μέγας κατὰ βορέαν ἑστη-
κώς, ἀποφέρεται ἐς τὸ πέλαγος, καὶ πάλιν χειμασθεὶς ἐς τὰ
μάλιστα τῷ Τάραντι προσμίσγει· καὶ τὰς ναῦς, ὅσαι μάλιστα
3 ἐπόνησαν ὑπὸ τοῦ χειμῶνος, ἀνελκύσας ἐπεσκεύαζεν. ὁ δὲ
Νικίας πυθόμενος αὐτὸν προσπλέοντα ὑπερεῖδε τὸ πλῆθος τῶν 5
νεῶν, ὅπερ καὶ οἱ Θούριοι ἔπαθον, καὶ λῃστικώτερον ἔδοξε
παρεσκευασμένους πλεῖν, καὶ οὐδεμίαν φυλακήν πω ἐποιεῖτο.

105 Κατὰ δὲ τοὺς αὐτοὺς χρόνους τούτου τοῦ θέρους καὶ Λακεδαιμόνιοι ἐς τὸ Ἄργος ἐσέβαλον αὐτοί τε καὶ οἱ ξύμμαχοι
καὶ τῆς γῆς τὴν πολλὴν ἐδῄωσαν, καὶ Ἀθηναῖοι Ἀργείοις 10
τριάκοντα ναυσὶν ἐβοήθησαν· αἵπερ τὰς σπονδὰς φανερώ-
2 τατα τὰς πρὸς τοὺς Λακεδαιμονίους αὐτοῖς ἔλυσαν. πρότερον μὲν γὰρ λῃστείαις ἐκ Πύλου καὶ περὶ τὴν ἄλλην
Πελοπόννησον μᾶλλον ἢ ἐς τὴν Λακωνικὴν ἀποβαίνοντες
μετά τε Ἀργείων καὶ Μαντινέων ξυνεπολέμουν, καὶ πολλάκις 15
Ἀργείων κελευόντων ὅσον σχόντας μόνον ξὺν ὅπλοις ἐς τὴν
Λακωνικὴν καὶ τὸ ἐλάχιστον μετὰ σφῶν δῃώσαντας ἀπελθεῖν οὐκ ἤθελον· τότε δὲ Πυθοδώρου καὶ Λαισποδίου καὶ
Δημαράτου ἀρχόντων ἀποβάντες ἐς Ἐπίδαυρον τὴν Λιμηρὰν
καὶ Πρασιὰς καὶ ὅσα ἄλλα ἐδῄωσαν τῆς γῆς, καὶ· τοῖς 20
Λακεδαιμονίοις ἤδη εὐπροφάσιστον μᾶλλον τὴν αἰτίαν ἐς
3 τοὺς Ἀθηναίους τοῦ ἀμύνεσθαι ἐποίησαν. ἀναχωρησάντων
δὲ τῶν Ἀθηναίων ἐκ τοῦ Ἄργους ταῖς ναυσὶ καὶ τῶν Λακεδαιμονίων οἱ Ἀργεῖοι ἐσβαλόντες ἐς τὴν Φλειασίαν τῆς τε
γῆς αὐτῶν ἔτεμον καὶ ἀπέκτεινάν τινας, καὶ ἀπῆλθον ἐπ᾽ 25
οἴκου.

---

3 alt. μάλιστα Β : om. cett.   5 προσπλέοντα Β : πλέοντα cett.
7 παρασκευασαμένους ΑΕΦΜ   φυλακήν πω ἐποιεῖτο] πως φυλακὴν
ἐποιοῦντο Β   12 τὰς Β : om. cett.   τοὺς Β : om. cett.   15 ξυνεπολέμουν Β : ἐπολέμουν cett.   16 ἔχοντας Β   19 Λιμηρὰν Β :
Λιμέραν cett.   20 Πρασιὰς Β : Πρασίαν (-σσ- F) cett.   ὅσα ἄλλα]
ἄλλα ἄττα Β   23 ἐξ Ἄργους Β   25 post ἀπέκτεινάν add. τε Β

COMMENTARY

COMMENTARY

COMMENTARY

DECEMBER 416–FEBRUARY 415

1. Athenian Designs on Sicily

1. 1. τοῦ δ' αὐτοῦ χειμῶνος: i.e. the winter of 416/5. Thucydides divides each year of the war into two parts, θέρος and χειμών; normally he regards θέρος, the larger of the two parts, as running from the middle of March to the end of October, and he sometimes further specifies its beginning and end as ἔαρ and φθινόπωρον.

παρασκευῇ: Here, as often in Thucydides, 'force'; sometimes 'fleet' or 'army' is an appropriate translation, while elsewhere it means 'equipment and support' (e.g. 31. 3) or 'preparation' (e.g. 26. 2).

τῆς μετὰ Λάχητος κτλ.: Laches was one of the two generals sent to Sicily with twenty ships to help Leontinoi in 427 (iii. 86. 1); he was relieved in the winter of 426/5 by Pythodoros (iii. 115. 2 ff.); and in the spring of 425 Eurymedon and Sophokles were sent out with forty ships (iv. 2. 2).

καταστρέψασθαι: To *subjugate* Sicily, not simply to create a favourable political situation. Thucydides represents the Athenians as entertaining this ambition in 427–424 (iii. 86. 4, iv. 65. 3).

ἄπειροι . . . τοῦ μεγέθους . . . καὶ ὅτι κτλ.: 'Ignorant of the size of the island . . . and of the fact that . . .' (cf. Intr. I. 3. 17). Thucydides' words suggest that he thought the subjugation of Sicily an impossibly large and difficult undertaking; but he expresses the opposite view in ii. 65. 11, and his narrative shows how very close to success the Athenians came.

2. **οὐ πολλῷ τινι ἔλασσον κτλ.**: lit. 'for a sailing-round of Sicily is, for a merchant ship, of days not by any large amount less than eight'. In numerical expressions of this type ἔλασσον is not declined; cf. 67. 2. The distance is *c.* 500 nautical miles; since ancient data as a whole suggest that a merchant ship could maintain a speed of 4-4·5 knots under reasonable conditions of wind and weather, the estimate 'not much less than eight days' is very high. Probably Thucydides is thinking in terms of sailing by day only; Ephoros' estimate (fr. 135) for the circumnavigation of Sicily in a merchant ship is five days and nights.

ἐν εἰκοσισταδίῳ . . . μέτρῳ: The strait at its narrowest measures

2,800 m., and in this context Thucydides must be referring to the narrowest part. His datum therefore implies that 1 stade = 140 m. Unfortunately, other data in his work imply other values for the stade, ranging from 130 m. to 175 m. or more, and we must suppose either that the majority of his data are wrong or that 'stade' (like 'block' in America) was a rather subjective term.

τὸ μὴ ἤπειρος εἶναι: τὸ μή c. inf. is an occasional alternative to μή c. inf. after verbs meaning 'prevent' and with other types of consecutive infinitive.

2–5. The Colonization of Sicily

We might have expected Thucydides to give us an account of the population and resources of Sicily as they were in 415. Instead, he tells us about the origin of each element in its population. These chapters therefore constitute a digression, of a kind which Thucydides sometimes inserts in order to correct current inaccuracies or to give us interesting and out-of-the-way information which he thinks we are unlikely to obtain elsewhere.

He distinguishes three categories of incomers: 2. 1, mythical; 2. 2–2. 6, non-Greek; and 3–5, Greek. The dates which he gives are all in terms of intervals, and are incomplete; no intervals of time are given for the foundations of Zankle and Himera, and some others are vague (3. 3–4. 1: 'after Leontinoi . . . about the same time . . . and later . . . for a short time . . .'). He anchors his figures to later times at one point only, by saying (4. 2) that Megara had existed for 245 years when it was destroyed by Gelon, the tyrant of Syracuse. Since Gelon died in 478/7, after ruling Syracuse for seven years, and had already destroyed Megara when envoys from Greece approached him for help against the Persians in 481 (Hdt. vii. 156. 2–157. 1), he must have destroyed Megara in 483 ($\pm$ 1). Thus we can present Thucydides' chronology of the Sicilian colonies as follows, calling the interval between Leontinoi and Megara x and the interval between Leontinoi and Katane y: ('$c.$' represents Thucydides' ἐγγύς or ἐγγύτατα):

Sikel migration from Italy	$c.$ $1033+x$
Naxos	$733+x$
Syracuse	$732+x$
Leontinoi	$728+x$
Katane	$728+x-y$
Megara	728
Gela	$688+x$
Akrai	$662+x$
Kasmenai	$c.$ $642+x$

Selinus	628
Kamarina	c. 597+x
Akragas	c. 580+x

These figures, with x treated as one year and y as negligible, recur in later writers (who are not 'confirming' Thucydides, but simply repeating him) and have been accepted as valid by many modern scholars. Where did Thucydides get them?

It is certain that he is following in this digression a written source. The terms which he uses here for 'approximately', ἐγγύς and ἐγγύτατα, occur nowhere else in his work in that sense, for which he uses as a rule μάλιστα and sometimes ὡς, ὅσον, περί, or ἐς. Presumably, therefore, he found the figures which he here qualifies by ἐγγύς or ἐγγύτατα so qualified in his source, and used the exact words because he could not know how far they meant what he himself would have meant by μάλιστα. τοῦ ἐχομένου ἔτους in 3. 2 and ὅστις in 3. 1 may also indicate the influence of an alien style.

Three authors have a prima-facie claim to be considered as sources for these chapters:

(i) Hellanikos of Lesbos, whose chronological work *Priestesses of Hera at Argos*—we know that it included references to the founding of colonies in Sicily—appeared some time during the last quarter of the fifth century. But we know Hellanikos' views on some of the matters mentioned in these chapters of Thucydides (e.g. the origin of the name 'Italy'), and they are invariably different from Thucydides'. Moreover, Thucydides criticized Hellanikos' *Attic Chronicle* as inadequate and chronologically inaccurate (i. 97. 2). It is therefore unlikely that he would value Hellanikos' *Priestesses* as an authority on the colonization of Sicily; and even if he did, it was too well-known a work to justify reproduction in a digression.

(ii) Hippys of Rhegion, a shadowy figure of uncertain date. Even if he was earlier than Thucydides, he is not likely as a source for this digression; for the dates which Thucydides does not give, the foundation-dates of Zankle and Himera, are precisely those in which we would expect a man of Rhegion to be interested.

(iii) Antiochos of Syracuse, described by Dionysios of Halikarnassos as πάνυ ἀρχαῖος, wrote a history of Sicily from the earliest times down to 424, and a similar work on Italy. Where we have any information on his opinions, they coincide with Thucydides'; we would expect him, as a Syracusan, to be well informed on the foundation-dates of such unimportant places as the Syracusan colonies Akrai and Kasmenai, but less interested in Zankle and Himera; also, if his work was little known in Greece and the Aegean, it is understandable that Thucydides should summarize part of it in a digression.

Our question then becomes: where did Antiochos himself get these foundation-dates?

(i) 'Official records' is an exceedingly unlikely answer. Such evidence as we have indicates that even bare lists of eponymous magistrates or priests were not kept by Greek states until the sixth century B.C.; the Olympic victor-list compiled and put into circulation by Hippias of Elis at the end of the fifth century began with the first Olympiad, i.e. 776 B.C., but it is noteworthy that Plutarch questioned the authenticity of its early portion. There is no good evidence that official 'chronicles' were kept by any Greek states at any time in the archaic and classical periods. A more positive argument against the use of official records by Antiochos is that the Antiochos–Thucydides chronology of the Sicilian colonies is only one of a set of alternative chronologies. For example, Ephoros adopted a tradition which made Megara earlier than Syracuse, Timaios dated Selinus to 651, and variant foundation-dates for some of the other colonies are to be found in Hellenistic and Roman chronographers. If official records existed and were drawn upon by Antiochos, how was disagreement possible?

(ii) Calculation certainly played a part, and probably the chief part. The Greeks of the fifth century commonly expressed intervals of time in terms of generations, and 'm generations' could be converted into 'n years' by assigning a constant value to the unit 'generation'. Thus Herodotos (ii. 142. 2) tells us that he himself reckons 3 generations = 100 years. Now, it is noticeable that two of Thucydides' intervals of time in this digression, 245 years (4. 2) and 70 years (5. 2), are multiples of 35. If we suppose that Antiochos, like later writers, treated the interval between Leontinoi and Megara as one year and the interval between Leontinoi and Katane as negligible, other multiples of 35 become conspicuous in the table of dates given above. The foundation of Selinus is 3×35 years after Syracuse; that of Kamarina, 3×35 years earlier than its refoundation by Hippokrates in 493/2; and that of Akragas is 3×35 years earlier than the event which, as it were, put Akragas on the map of the Greek world as a whole, the Olympic victory won by Theron, the tyrant of Akragas, in 476/5. Since different historians in the ancient world used at least three different generation-values—35, 33⅓, and 30 years—it is understandable that they should offer us different dates for the Sicilian colonies; the dates offered for the foundations of Rome and Carthage can be shown to differ for precisely this reason.

(iii) Oral tradition. The interval of one year between Naxos and Syracuse cannot easily be explained as the product of calculation by generations; the priority of Naxos was presumably a widespread tradition which Antiochos could not reject. The priority of Megara, on the other hand, he did reject, but Ephoros did not; which of the two was right, we do not know. Nor do we know the nature and content of other traditions which may have played a part, side by side with calculation, in building up the Antiochos–Thucydides chronology.

The Greek colonies in the central Mediterranean have been extensively excavated and have yielded large quantities of Corinthian pottery. It is possible to construct a chronological sequence of styles in this fabric, and to relate it to similarly constructed sequences in other fabrics with which it is associated in some Aegean sites. Until quite recently it was generally accepted that the 'internal' chronology of Corinthian pottery was fully consistent with the sequence of foundations as given by Thucydides and consistent on the whole with the intervals of time which he gives and with the absolute chronology which emerges from these intervals. At present, however, fresh finds suggest that Thucydides' date for Selinus (628) might be too low and Timaios' date (651) nearer the mark, and even that the priority of Megara over Syracuse must be seriously considered. Archaeological evidence accumulates year by year, and no one can predict now what we shall be saying about the Antiochos–Thucydides chronology in ten years' time.

Note. In the following notes on chapters 2–5 no comment is made on:

(1) Thucydides' dates: these are discussed above.

(2) The location of places; these may be found in an atlas.

(3) Founders of colonies, Sikel kings, &c.

(i) 2. 1. *Introduction; Mythical Inhabitants*

2. 1. ᾠκίσθη δὲ ὧδε τὸ ἀρχαῖον: 'I will now describe its original settlement.'

ἔσχε: ἔθνη is the subject, and 'Sicily' is understood as the object; cf. i. 12.3 Δωριῆς Πελοπόννησον ἔσχον, 'the Dorians occupied the Peloponnese'.

Κύκλωπες κτλ.: As early as the Hesiodic poems we find indications that the peoples and places of *Od.* ix–x were regarded as having existed in the central and western Mediterranean, and this was taken for granted by Thucydides' time.

ποιηταῖς: Thucydides refrains from speculation on mythical creatures, but this does not mean that he dismisses the whole of Homer as fiction; in i. 10 he treats the *Iliad* as an historical source.

(ii) 2. 2–2. 6. *Settlement before the Greeks*

2. ὡς μὲν αὐτοί φασι: These words qualify καὶ πρότεροι κτλ., 'even earlier ⟨than the Laistrygones, &c.⟩ . . .'.

Ἴβηρες . . . ἀναστάντες: Later writers differed on the identification of the river Sikanos, while agreeing that it was on the east coast of Spain. Ligurians are nowhere else mentioned as living in Spain, except in the extreme north-eastern corner.

Σικανία: In *Od*. xxiv. 307 Σικανίη is mentioned without further explanation; Hdt. vii. 170. 1 accepts it as the name of Sicily in the time of 'Minos'.

Τρινακρία: Θρινακίη νῆσος is where Odysseus' men ate the cattle of the Sun (*Od*. xi. 107). Thucydides is our first evidence for the form Τρινακρία; it would seem that when Θρινακίη had been identified with Sicily and the general shape of Sicily (with its 'three capes') had become known, Θρινακίη was believed to be a corruption or modification of *Τρινακρία, and the allegedly 'correct' name prevailed.

τὰ πρὸς ἑσπέραν: lit. 'they inhabit Sicily its western parts', i.e. '. . . the western parts of Sicily'; the emphasized part and the un-emphasized whole stand in apposition to each other. On the Sikan expulsion from the eastern parts cf. § 5 *infra*.

3. Ἰλίου δέ . . . Σικελίαν: The story that Aineias and other Trojans escaped from the fall of Troy and sailed to Italy and Sicily was accepted by Hellanikos (frr. 31 and 84), and there is reason to think that it was told also by the early lyric poet Stesichoros. The nature of the story suggests that Ἰλίου ἁλισκομένου should be translated '*during* the capture of Troy', although grammatically '*when* Troy was captured' is possible; cf. νικᾶν = 'be the winner', 'have won'. πλοίοις belongs with ἀφικνοῦνται; the sea-voyage of the Trojans is contrasted with the land-lubberly procedure of the Sikels described in § 4.

Ἔλυμοι . . . καὶ Ἔγεστα: Hellanikos (fr. 31) spoke of Trojan heroes 'Elymos' and 'Egestos'.

Φωκέων τινές: All our other evidence for stories attributing the foundation of western colonies to the Phokians of the heroic age is later than Thucydides. Possibly the Phokians figured in an epic poem about the wanderings of the Greeks in their attempts to get home from Troy.

4. Σικελοὶ δ' . . . Ὀπικούς: The theory that the Sikels migrated from Italy under pressure from the Oscans (Ὀπικοί) was universally accepted in antiquity. Archaeological evidence confirms that there was a great disturbance in eastern Sicily, involving the obliteration of some earlier sites, in the thirteenth century B.C. (not in the eleventh, which is the date Thucydides offers), but it was not accompanied by the extension to Sicily of any specifically Italic cultural features.

ὡς μὲν εἰκός: 'As one would expect' of a people which was not sea-faring.

κατιόντος τοῦ ἀνέμου: We say 'the wind rises'; the Greeks said 'the wind comes down'. South, south-east, and east winds, needed for a crossing from the toe of Italy to Sicily on rafts, are rare in the Straits of Messina.

ἐν τῇ Ἰταλίᾳ: Where, is not known.

5. πρὸς τὰ μεσημβρινά . . . αὐτῆς: The boundary between the western (Sikan) and eastern (Sikel) cultures seems to have lain well within the eastern half of the island at the end of the eighth century, and to have retreated westwards during the seventh. Therefore, unless the material remains are misleading as an indication of political and linguistic divisions, the Sikan withdrawal before Sikel pressure was later and slower than Thucydides suggests.

6. ἄκρας τε . . . νησίδια: If this is true, it is surprising that no trace of Phoenician occupation has been revealed by the excavation of Ortygia (cf. 3. 2 n.) and Thapsos, for no sites would have suited the Phoenicians better. Thucydides has probably inferred from the situation as he knew it that Phoenician settlement of the same type as Motya must have existed throughout Sicily before the arrival of the Greeks. Possible Phoenician etymologies have been sought for place-names all over Sicily, but must be treated cautiously; many of these names may have much simpler etymologies in the Sikan and Sikel languages, about which we know almost nothing.

(iii) 3–5. Greek Colonies

3. 1. Χαλκιδῆς . . . ᾤκισαν: The island of Naxos in the Aegean also had a share in this venture, according to Hellanikos (fr. 82).

Ἀρχηγέτου: Apollo was given this title in so far as he enjoined or sanctioned colonizing enterprises through his oracle; hence it often figures in his cult in colonies.

ὅστις νῦν . . . ἐστιν: We might have expected ὅσπερ, 'the self-same one which . . .'. Possibly Thucydides meant 'and there is one there now', but he probably adopted ὅστις direct from Antiochos; cf. Antiochos fr. 2 τὴν γῆν ταύτην, ἥτις νῦν Ἰταλία καλεῖται . . . εἶχον Οἴνωτροι.

Naxos was obliterated by Dionysios in 403/2, but it does not follow that Thucydides must have written these words before then; he is concerned only with the location of the altar, and in such a context ἔξω τῆς πόλεως can just as well mean 'outside where the city was until lately' as 'outside where the city is now'.

θεωροί: Delegates to international festivals, e.g. the Olympic Games.

2. τοῦ ἐχομένου ἔτους: An abnormal expression for 'in the following year', possibly adopted from Antiochos.

τῶν Ἡρακλειδῶν: The aristocracy of Corinth, like other Dorian aristocracies, regarded itself as directly descended from Herakles.

ἐκ τῆς νήσου: i.e. Ortygia. It is clear from the archaeological evidence that settlement on the mainland (ἡ ἔξω πόλις) was very early, and the connecting mole existed by the last part of the sixth century, as the lyric poet Ibykos refers to it (fr. 21).

3. **μετὰ Συρακούσας οἰκισθείσας**: The so-called 'ab urbe condita' construction is abnormal in Greek and confined to expressions of time.

4. 1. **ἐς Λεοντίνους ... ξυμπολιτεύσας**: When movement in space or time is implied, ἐς or ἐκ is commonly used instead of ἐν; so here Lamis and his Megarians went *to* Leontinoi in order to become part of it. See further 7. 2 n.

ὑπὸ αὐτῶν ἐκπεσών: This outbreak of hostility between Megarians and Leontinians may reflect the relations between their mother-cities in Greece; there is evidence to suggest that at the end of the eighth century Corinth, Chalkis, and Samos co-operated against Megara, Eretria, and Miletos.

αὐτὸς μὲν ἀποθνῄσκει: The one very early Greek grave found on Thapsos could conceivably be that of Lamis himself.

προδόντος: This seems to need fuller explanation; Classen conjectured παραδόντος, but possibly Thucydides forgot that the details of a story familiar to him from Antiochos would not be known to his readers.

2. **ὑπὸ Γέλωνος ... ἀνέστησαν**: Gelon, who succeeded Hippokrates as tyrant of Gela in 491/0, became tyrant of Syracuse in 485/4; two years later he captured and destroyed Megara, making its upper class citizens of Syracuse and selling its common people into slavery (Hdt. vii. 156. 2).

ὕστερον ... ἢ αὐτοὺς οἰκίσαι: 'After founding (sc. Hyblaean) Megara itself' (cf. Μεγαρέας ᾤκισαν in § 1), not 'after they themselves had founded (sc. Megara)', which would require αὐτοί.

καὶ ἐκ Μεγάρων ... ξυγκατῴκισεν: lit. 'and coming from Megara (sc. in Greece), their mother-city, he helped them to found it'. But something is wrong here: (i) the connexion—καί rather than ὅς—is odd, and (ii) if Pammilos (that, not 'Pamillos', is the correct form of the name) was the founder of Selinus, and was sent by the Megarians to found it, he would not be said to 'help the Megarians to found it'. Plainly a proper name has fallen out: 'Sending out Pammilos, they founded Selinus, and ... coming from Megara, their mother-city, was co-founder ⟨with Pammilos⟩.'

3. **ἐποίκους**: ἄποικοι and ἔποικοι are somewhat like the English 'emigrants' and 'immigrants'; the same people can be called either, according to the end from which their movement is viewed.

ἀπὸ τοῦ Γέλα ποταμοῦ: γέλας (cf. the Latin *gelu*) was the native word for 'ice'.

Λίνδιοι: The name attests the Rhodian element in Gela, for Lindos was one of the three cities of Rhodes.

νόμιμα: 'Institutions', not simply 'customs'.

5. Ζάγκλη . . . ῳκίσθη: λῃσταί are not necessarily 'pirates', i.e. state-less outlaws, but 'raiders'. Thucydides must mean that a force which came out from Kyme to raid Sicily settled on the site of Zankle, intermarried with the natives, and made itself an independent state.

ζάγκλον: Zankle calls itself δανκλε on its coins; ζ and δ must be two different Greek approximations to the initial consonant of the Sikel word.

ὑπὸ Σαμίων . . . Σικελίᾳ: According to Hdt. vi. 22–24 Zankle had issued an invitation to the Ionians, during the Ionian revolt against Persian rule, to take part in the foundation of a new colony at Kale Akte. After the fall of Miletos in 494 and the collapse of the revolt the Samians responded to this invitation. When the Samian contingent arrived in the west it was persuaded by Anaxilas, the tyrant of Rhegion, to seize Zankle itself.

6. Ἀναξίλας . . . ἀντωνόμασεν: Hdt. says nothing of the expulsion of the Samians, but mentions the change of name in another connexion (vii. 164. 1). At the time of the Spartan conquest of Messenia in the late eighth century some Messenians left their homeland and joined with the Chalkidians in the foundation of Rhegion. Some of the leading families of Rhegion were proud of their Messenian descent and sentimentally attached to the name of Messene; understandably, since their original home, reduced to servitude by the Spartans, no longer bore it. ξυμμείκτων ἀνθρώπων is treated syntactically exactly as if it were a predicative adjective: lit., 'having ⟨re-⟩founded the city him-self ⟨as a city⟩ of mixed population', just as one might say τὴν πόλιν μεγάλην οἰκίσας.

5. 1. Ἱμέρα: Diod. xiii. 62. 4 dates the foundation of Himera 649; he will have taken this date from Timaios, who may have taken it from Philistos.

Μυλητίδαι: We do not know whether these were a family group (cf. Πεισιστρατίδαι &c.) or a class; they should not be confused (as they are by Strabo) with the inhabitants of Mylai, another colony of Zankle.

καὶ φωνὴ μέν . . . ἐκράθη: There are very few extant inscriptions of Himera, but so far as they go they show the Doric ā.

3. ἀναστάτων δέ . . . δι' ἀπόστασιν: No other Greek historian refers to this, but the Scholiast on Pi. O. 5 dates it—we do not know his source—to 552–549.

δι' ἀπόστασιν does not necessarily imply that Kamarina had had 'colonial' status under Syracuse—not a common phenomenon in the Greek world—ever since its foundation; it may have been reduced to

tributary status by Syracuse only a short time before its 'revolt'.
Thucydides' words (cf. τὴν γῆν *infra*) suggest that Kamarina was
wholly destroyed and depopulated on this occasion, but excavation of
the site has shown that this was not so; and cf. the next note.

Ἱπποκράτης . . . Καμάριναν: Hippokrates was tyrant of Gela (498–
491) before Gelon. According to Hdt. vii. 154 Kamarina (Hdt. does
not say 'the *site* of Kamarina') was awarded to him by Corinthian and
Kerkyrean arbitrators in settlement of his war against Syracuse.

καὶ αὖθις . . . ὑπὸ Γελῴων: Gelon, as tyrant of Syracuse, destroyed
the citadel of Kamarina and enrolled all the inhabitants of the city as
citizens of Syracuse (Hdt. vii. 156. 2). Diod. x. 76. 5 dates the third
founding of Kamarina to 461, long after Gelon's death, and ascribes it
to Γελῷοι.

6. The Segestan Embassy at Athens

6. 1. τῇ ἀληθεστάτῃ προφάσει: πρόφασις is not necessarily 'pretext' or
'excuse', i.e. a false reason given to conceal the true one, but simply
'reason', 'motive', or 'cause'. Thucydides means that anyone who gave
'desire to become rulers of the whole of Sicily' as the Athenians' reason
for embarking on the Sicilian expedition would be telling the truth.
Cf. i. 23. 6, where he says that the 'real cause' (τὴν ἀληθεστάτην πρόφασιν)
of the Peloponnesian War was that the growth of the power of Athens
alarmed the Spartans and forced them to fight.

εὐπρεπῶς: cf. 8. 2 n.

τοῖς ἑαυτῶν . . . ξυμμάχοις: It is clear from the instructions given to
the generals (8. 2, q.v.) that the 'kinsmen' are Leontinoi (the Chalkidians, who founded Leontinoi [3. 3], were Ionian, and Athens regarded herself as the mother-city of the Ionians) and the 'allies'
Segesta. Thucydides assumes our knowledge of what he has said in
Book V (4. 2 ff.) about the depopulation of Leontinoi by Syracuse in
423/2. Racial affinities and antipathies were fully exploited in the
language of diplomacy, as we shall see later in this book, and there is
no doubt that on occasion they affected policy and political views.

προσ- and προ- are constantly confused in MSS., and EM are probably
right here in having προ-, 'those who were already their allies'; this
gives much more point to εὐπρεπῶς than προσ-, 'those who had adhered
to them as allies'.

2. περί τε γαμικῶν τινῶν: The right to choose a wife from another
state without thereby depriving one's children of citizen rights was
a subject of inter-state agreement and therefore, on occasion, of inter-
state disputes.

τὴν γενομένην . . . ξυμμαχίαν: Λεοντίνων goes with ξυμμαχίαν, 'alliance with Leontinoi' (cf. 2. 6), not with πολέμου, which would mean

'war against Leontinoi' or 'war conducted by Leontinoi', not 'war *over* Leontinoi'. The reason for the abnormal word-order is that whereas we should have expected Segesta to remind the Athenians of their alliance with herself she in fact reminded them of their alliance with Leontinoi; the juxtaposition of Λεοντίνων and οἱ Ἐγεσταῖοι brings this out. In his description of the fighting in Sicily in 427–425 Thucydides says nothing about the making of an alliance with Leontinoi; it had been made long before that, and had been renewed, as we know from an inscription (*GHI* 57), in 433/2. But since (i) Greek alliances tended to be of short duration and were frequently renewed, (ii) the inscription recording the renewal in 433/2 says τὴν ξυμμαχίαν ἐποιήσαντο (not ἀνενεώσαντο), and (iii) γενέσθαι serves regularly as the passive of ποιήσασθαι, there is no difficulty in 'the alliance which was made' (= 'renewed') 'with Leontinoi in the time of Laches and the previous war'.

τοὺς λοιποὺς . . . αὐτῶν: It looks at first as if αὐτῶν referred to Leontinoi; but αὐτ- takes its reference from the sense of the context, and αὐτῶν here must mean Athens, for the envoys are speaking of the eventual danger to Athens and recommending action by Athens. In the next part of the sentence 'the allies still remaining' can only mean allies of *Athens*. The fact that the Athenians are ἐκείνων in τὴν ἐκείνων δύναμιν is no obstacle to their being αὐτῶν in τούς . . . αὐτῶν; cf. Pl. *Euthyphr.* 14 D αἰτεῖν . . . αὐτοὺς καὶ διδόναι ἐκείνοις, 'to make requests of them and give to them'.

Δωριῆς τε . . . βοηθήσαντες: 'Coming to assist the Peloponnesians ⟨as⟩ Dorians to Dorians, in accordance with ⟨the claims of⟩ kinship, and also ⟨as⟩ colonists to those who had sent them forth.'

σφῶν: i.e. Segesta; cf. Intr. I. 3. 13.

3. τῶν ξυναγορευόντων αὐτοῖς: Athenians who spoke in favour of Segesta.

εἰ ὑπάρχει: 'To see whether it was there'. An ancient state commonly borrowed from its temple treasures, with the intention of repaying the loan with interest; hence the amount of money 'in the temples' at Segesta was relevant.

καὶ τὰ τοῦ πολέμου . . . εἰσομένους: 'And to discover', lit., 'the things of the war . . . in what they were', i.e. 'what stage the progress of the war . . . had reached'.

7. Operations in Greece and Macedonia

(i) **7.** 1–2. *The Argolid*

7. 1. Λακεδαιμόνιοι δέ . . . ἐς τὴν Ἀργείαν: After the battle of Mantinea in 418 Sparta established a friendly oligarchy in Argos, but this lasted only a few months, and hostilities broke out again in the winter of 417/6. Then, as here, the Corinthians took no part in the Spartan invasion of the Argolid (v. 83. 1); we do not know why, but relations between Sparta and Corinth had been cool ever since the Peace of Nikias, to which Corinth had objected.

καὶ σῖτον . . . κομίσαντες: The word-order and the absence of a neuter plural τινα elsewhere in Thucydides show that the meaning is: 'they brought in wagons and brought home some grain'. For the repetition of the verb-stem cf. Pl. *Prt.* 328 E ὃ . . . ῥᾳδίως ἐπεκδιδάξει, ἐπειδὴ καὶ τὰ πολλὰ ταῦτα ἐξεδίδαξε. As it is winter, the Peloponnesians are carrying off stored grain, and their 'ravaging of the land' is destruction of buildings, vineyards, and trees.

καὶ ἐς Ὀρνεάς . . . ὀλίγους: Orneai, 20 km. north-west of Argos, had been an ally of Argos in 418 (v. 67. 2); Sparta must have gained control of it after the battle of Mantinea and kept it even after she lost control of Argos. The 'Argive exiles' are pro-Spartan Argives thrown out when the Argive democracy took power in 417.

καὶ σπεισάμενοι . . . τὴν ἀλλήλων: That is to say, the Spartans, on behalf of Orneai, negotiated through a herald with Argos itself (Ἀργείους, without the definite article, is the state of Argos, not the Argive exiles) and persuaded Argos to make a truce with Orneai.

2. ἐλθόντων δὲ Ἀθηναίων: The Argive democracy in 417 had renewed the alliance with Athens.

ἐπολιόρκουν: Whether or not this was a violation of the truce depends on whether the 'certain time' for which the truce was made had expired.

οἱ ἐκ τῶν Ὀρνεῶν: We should say 'the men *in* Orneai escaped', but cf. 4. 1 n. and (e.g.) ἔμαθον ἐκ νέου = 'I learnt it when I was young', ἥξω εἰς τὸ ἔαρ = 'I'll come in the spring'.

(ii) 7. 3–4 *Macedonia*

3. καὶ ἐς Μεθώνην . . . Μακεδονίᾳ: Methone, which lay just north of Pynda and about 10 km. from the mouth of the Haliakmon—there was another Methone in Lakonia—had become a tributary ally of Athens before 432/1. It was treated indulgently and protected against the tentative aggressions of Perdikkas, the king of Macedon. At the time of the Peace of Nikias Perdikkas had been in alliance with Athens (v. 6. 2), but in 417 he was persuaded by Sparta to abandon this alliance (v. 80. 2), and in the winter of 417/6 an Athenian fleet blockaded the Macedonian coast (v. 83. 4).

ἱππέας . . . φυγάδας: 'Cavalry of their own and the Macedonian exiles who were at Athens': cf. Intr. I. 3. 15(a).

4. παρὰ Χαλκιδέας . . . σπονδάς: The people of Chalkidike—Olynthos was their city—had been seduced from allegiance to Athens by

Perdikkas before the Peloponnesian War began, and heartened by Brasidas in 424–423. The Peace of Nikias provided that they should resume the payment of tribute to Athens, but they did not do so. A 'ten-day truce' was a truce which could be denounced at ten days' notice.

SEVENTEENTH YEAR OF THE WAR, 415/4
MARCH–APRIL 415

8. 1–2. Decision on the Expedition

8. 1. ἑξήκοντα τάλαντα . . . μισθόν: The crew of a trireme numbered about 200 (Hdt. vii. 184. 1, viii. 17); hence the rate of pay envisaged (ὡς) was 1 drachma per sailor per day, which in the late fifth century was a reasonable wage for a skilled man.

2. καὶ οὐκ ἀληθῆ: cf. 46 on the manner in which the Athenian envoys were deceived.

στρατηγοὺς αὐτοκράτορας: αὐτοκράτωρ means 'empowered to act without reference to the appointing body'. Usually (e.g. 26. 1) the particular respect in which an official or body is given such powers is specified. The context here indicates that the generals were empowered to decide, without referring back to Athens, when the objects detailed in βοηθοὺς κτλ. had been attained, or when they had become impossible to attain. Being empowered to act αὐτοκράτωρ in no way saved a general from the wrath of the assembly if it was thought that his judgement had been at fault or his energy and loyalty deficient.

Ἀλκιβιάδην . . . Νικίαν . . . Λάμαχον: Nikias and Lamachos had both held generalships during the Archidamian War; Nikias was a man of great wealth, and Lamachos is caricatured in Aristophanes' *Acharnians* (at the beginning of 425) as opposed to any talk of peace with Sparta. Alkibiades was a younger man, probably not yet forty; he had held his first generalship in 419, but, quite apart from his own talents, he had one advantage which Nikias and Lamachos lacked: distinguished forebears and connexions. He was descended on both sides from families which had (according to tradition) opposed and eventually expelled the Peisistratid tyranny in the sixth century; and Perikles had become his guardian when his father was killed.

In accordance with Athenian practice, the three generals appointed were of equal authority; no one of them could give orders to the other two, and nothing could be done until at least two of them agreed. Later writers naturally found this practice hard to understand (as we do, too), and Plutarch, at the cost of serious inconsistency, imports an 'order of seniority' into some passages of his *Nicias*.

The fragmentary inscription (*GHI* 77A) relating to the appointment of the generals shows that the Athenians had contemplated the possibility of appointing only one general, but decided against this. The one in mind was no doubt Alkibiades, the chief proponent of the expedition; had he by himself held so large a command so far from home for so long, it would have been a striking departure from normal Athenian practice, at least in the fifth century.

ξυγκατοικίσαι δὲ καὶ Λεοντίνους: 'To co-operate ⟨with the survivors of Leontinoi⟩ in ⟨re-⟩establishing ⟨the city of⟩ Leontinoi.'

ἤν τι περιγίγνηται αὐτοῖς τοῦ πολέμου: Possibly (*a*) 'if anything of the state of Leontinoi survived the war ⟨between Syracuse and the survivors⟩', but this is not easy (we would expect ἤν τινες αὐτῶν . . . περιγίγνωνται), and since Athens hoped (cf. 50. 4) to seduce those former citizens of Leontinoi who were now part of Syracuse they can hardly have envisaged the possibility that there would be no one at all to re-establish at Leontinoi (and cf. on ξυγκατοικίσαι above). Hence (*b*), lit., 'if anything were on the right side of the war for them' (= the generals), i.e. 'if the development of operations were favourable'; cf. περιγίγνεσθαι = 'be victorious', 'be a credit surplus'.

καὶ τἆλλα . . . Ἀθηναίοις: The phraseology is characteristic of documentary inscriptions, but here it is of exceptional weight, since it covers what everyone at Athens knew to be the real purpose of the expedition, the conquest of Syracuse. The Athenians preserved appearances (cf. εὐπρεπῶς, 6. 1) by telling the generals to help their ally Segesta, re-establish Leontinoi ('if the situation permits'), 'and to execute the other measures required in Sicily in whatever manner they judge to be in the best interests of Athens'. This εὐπρέπεια was important diplomatically, as the goodwill of other states in Italy and Sicily would have to be won (cf. 48).

8. 3–26. Debate at Athens

8. 3–8. 4. *Introduction*

8. 3. ἡμέρᾳ πέμπτῃ: With ordinal numerals the count is inclusive; we would say '*four* days later'.

καθ' ὅτι χρή . . . ἐς τὸν ἔκπλουν: lit., 'according to what it is right . . .', i.e. 'to decide what provision should be made . . .'. γίγνεσθαι, as usual, serves as the passive of the middle ποιεῖσθαι.

ψηφισθῆναι: 'In order that . . . should be voted', or 'for voting . . .'; the infinitive is similarly used in 30. 2.

4. ἀκούσιος μὲν ᾑρημένος ἄρχειν: He was not necessarily unwilling

to be one of the ten generals for the year 415/4, but unwilling to be appointed to the command of the Sicilian expedition.

βραχείᾳ: 'Inadequate'; βραχύς covers our 'short', but is a word of much wider application.

9–14. *First Speech of Nikias*

9. 1. **καθ' ὅτι χρὴ κτλ.**: cf. 8. 3 n.

εἰ ἄμεινόν ἐστιν . . . ἄρασθαι: ἄμεινον = 'advisable', as often in the language of oracular responses. **καὶ μή . . . ἄρασθαι** is co-ordinated with σκέψασθαι and dependent on χρῆναι: '. . . that we ought to consider again this very question, whether . . . and ⟨ought⟩ not to take upon ourselves a war . . .'

ἀλλοφύλοις: This is a hit at non-Greek Segesta (cf. 2. 3); here Nikias ignores Leontinoi, but later (12. 1) he ignores Segesta in order to sneer at Leontinoi.

2. **τιμῶμαι ἐκ τοῦ τοιούτου**: He means that he owes to war his own rise to prominence; cf. τιμᾶσθαι ἐκ τοῦ πολεμεῖν (referring to Brasidas) in v. 16. 1.

νομίζων . . . προνοῆται: νομίζων, ἐπιστάμενος, ἐλπίσας, &c., are so often used by Thucydides in a causal sense, explaining someone's motives, that we would naturally expect here: '*because* I believe that a man who takes some thought both for his personal safety and for his property is just as good a citizen', but (i) this provokes the question 'just as good as who?', and (ii) it deprives the following sentence, 'for such a man is more likely than anyone to want his country's enterprises to succeed, for his own sake', of any point. νομίζων must therefore be concessive: '*although* I believe that a man who takes some thought . . . is just as good a citizen (sc. as I, who am reckless of my own safety)'. Stobaios' quotation of this passage has προῆται, 'sacrifices', which does not help at all, for it gives no reference for ὁμοίως and no logical sequence with μάλιστα γὰρ ἂν κτλ.

οὔτε νῦν . . . ἐρῶ: Apparently 'nor ⟨will I⟩ now, but, as I judge best, ⟨so⟩ will I speak'. But Thucydides may have intended ἄλλα ἢ ἄν, 'nor now will I say anything other than what I judge best'; Valla, whose translation is *ita nunc quae optima esse sentio dicam*, must have had ἄλλα ἢ ἄν in his Greek text, and the reading ἀλλα ἦι αν in a newly discovered fragmentary MS. of the tenth century reveals a copyist with some grounds for uncertainty about the accents and breathings.

10. 1. **καὶ ἑτέρους . . . ἐπαγαγέσθαι**: καί is adverbial, and πλεύσαντας refers to ὑμᾶς.

2. **τάς . . . σπονδάς**: The Peace of Nikias (421).

ὀνόματι: The parenthesis ('for that is the consequence . . .') shows that Nikias means not '*so long as* you are inactive it will be a peace *at* *any rate* in name', but '*even if* you are inactive, it will be a peace *only* in name'.

οὕτω γάρ . . . καὶ ἐκ τῶν ἐναντίων: The active opponents of a lasting peace had been Alkibiades at Athens (v. 43. 2 f.) and Kleobulos and Xenares at Sparta (v. 36. 1). αὐτά refers not to the peace treaty itself but to the whole train of events of which the treaty was a part; cf. αὐτά in § 5 = 'the considerations I have mentioned' or 'the situation I have described', and Intr. I. 3. 12.

τὴν ἐπιχείρησιν: The article implies that an attack is ultimately inevitable; only its timing and nature are open to discussion.

διὰ ξυμφορῶν . . . ἐγένετο: The notable ξυμφοραί for Sparta were the capture of the Spartiates at Sphakteria (cf. v. 15. 1 f.) and the death of Brasidas (cf. v. 13, 16. 1). Lit., 'from the more disgraceful than for us' = 'in a situation less creditable than ours'; cf. iii. 37. 4, ἀμαθέστεροι τῶν νόμων = 'less wise than the law', And. ii. 1 ἐμοῦ κακίων = 'not as good a man as I'.

τὰ ἀμφισβητούμενα: The continued refusal of Chalkidike to accept Athenian rule, and the Athenian retention of Pylos (v. 56. 2 f., cf. 115. 2), were contrary to the provisions of the peace treaty.

3. εἰσὶ δ' οἳ . . . ἐδέξαντο: Within the Peloponnesian League, Corinth and Megara had resisted the Spartan proposals for a peace treaty and were not parties to it (v. 17. 2); Sparta's ally Thebes also refused it.

οἱ μὲν ἄντικρυς πολεμοῦσιν: For some years after the treaty relations between Athens and Corinth were 'a suspension of hostilities, without a truce' (v. 32. 5 ff.), but in the summer of 416 there was outright fighting between them (v. 115. 3).

οἱ δέ . . . κατέχονται: Thebes made a 'ten-day truce' (cf. 7. 4 n.) with Athens shortly after the peace treaty (v. 26. 2).

4. οὓς πρὸ πολλῶν . . . χρόνῳ: cf. Intr. II. 1.

5. αὐτά: cf. § 2 n.

μὴ μετεώρῳ τε . . . κινδυνεύειν: μετέωρος is literally 'up in the air', 'off the ground', and among its many metaphorical meanings are 'out on the open sea', 'in suspense', 'unsettled', and (as here) 'insecure'. κινδυνεύειν c. dat. = 'run a risk *with*', i.e. 'endanger'.

πρίν . . . βεβαιωσώμεθα: In fifth-century prose, as in poetry, πρίν or πρότερον . . . ἤ with the subjunctive is not uncommon; in fourth-century prose πρὶν ἄν with the subjunctive prevails completely.

εἰ Χαλκιδῆς γε: 'When . . .' or 'considering that . . .'; on Chalkidike cf. 7. 4 n.

κατὰ τὰς ἠπείρους: So far as the Athenian Empire is concerned, the two ἤπειροι are (i) Thrace and Macedonia, and (ii) Asia Minor. Independent evidence for 'hesitant obedience' among Athenian subject-allies in 415 is lacking; Nikias' rhetorical statement is of a type which cannot be effectively challenged.

'Εγεσταίοις δὴ οὖσι ξυμμάχοις: δή obviously has its sceptical sense here; we might expect its force to extend to ξυμμάχοις (implying 'they are hardly real allies') or to ἀδικουμένοις (implying 'they are not really the innocent victims of aggression'), but there are no other passages in which δή precedes the words which it colours, unless it is itself preceded by ἵνα, ὅτι, ὡς, etc., or by a word meaning 'say' or 'think'. It is therefore likely that δή here colours the whole clause, including 'Εγεσταίοις; Nikias implies, rightly, that the desire to help Segesta is only a pretext.

ἔτι μέλλομεν ἀμύνεσθαι: 'We still delay measures against . . .'; ἀμύνεσθαι, which can mean 'requite', 'take revenge on', 'punish', does not imply waiting to be attacked.

11. 1. τοὺς μέν . . . τῶν δ': τοὺς μέν refers to the rebellious allies, τῶν δ' to Sicily.

διὰ πολλοῦ γε . . . δυναίμεθα: The difficulty of *maintaining* dominion over Sicily was, of course, by far the strongest argument against the Sicilian expedition, and it is surprising that it is not developed in more detail in this speech.

ἀνόητον δ' . . . ἔσται: 'It is foolish to attack an enemy of such a kind that if you overcome him you will not hold him down and if you fail you will not be in the same position as before making the attempt' (i.e. you will be in a much *weaker* position, in consequence of your failure, than you were before making the attempt).

2. Σικελιῶται δ' ἄν μοι . . . Συρακόσιοι: 'It seems to me that the Greeks of Sicily, to judge from their present condition, would be still (καὶ ἔτι) less formidable (sc. than they are now) if they were ruled by Syracuse.' The sentence has a partial resemblance to the first sentence of § 3: 'For as it is now, they might come . . . but ἐκείνως (i.e. if they were ruled by Syracuse), it is not likely . . .' Some editors have therefore suspected that a group of words is missing here, and that Thucydides wrote: 'It seems to me that the Greeks of Sicily, in their present condition, *are no danger to us*, and (καί) that they would be still less formidable, &c.' The first ἄν, however, showing that the opinion delivered is *wholly* about a hypothetical situation, tells against this conjecture; so does γε, which deprives 'as they are now' of the character of an antithesis to 'if they were ruled by Syracuse'; and for the adverbial καί with ἔτι cf. καὶ πάνυ in 10. 4. (The belief that Valla's Greek MS. had the words which are alleged to have fallen out is unfounded; it rests on Stephanus' drastic revision of Valla's translation of this sentence.)

3. **οὐκ εἰκός . . . στρατεῦσαι:** A remarkable piece of nonsense, which would not have seemed to the Athenians consonant either with their own proverbial beliefs about κόρος and ὕβρις or with their own elementary knowledge of history.

διὰ τοῦ αὐτοῦ: = τῷ αὐτῷ τρόπῳ; cf. Intr. I. 3. 17.

4. **δι' ὀλίγου:** 'After a short time' (cf. v. 14. 1); the phrase can mean 'for a short time' (e.g. i. 77. 6) or 'at close quarters' (e.g. ii. 89. 9). 'For a short time' would be possible here (taken with δείξαντες), but 'at close quarters' would not, for Nikias goes on to say that what is διὰ πλείστου ('farthest away') is most respected.

τὰ γὰρ διὰ πλείστου . . . δόντα: In the manuscripts these words come after ἐπιθοῖντο, and should have been allowed to stay there. The three possibilities envisaged by Nikias are (i) not to go at all, (ii) to go briefly and safely, and (iii) the danger of defeat; and his view of the consequences of defeat in the particular case of the proposed expedition is supported by his generalization about the contrary situation, in which θαυμαζόμενα is contrasted with ὑπεριδόντες and πεῖραν picks up σφαλείημεν. The next statement, ὅπερ . . . ἐφίεσθε, is related to the generalization just as in 33. 6 ὅπερ . . . ηὐξήθησαν is related to the preceding generalization (33. 5) 'few overseas expeditions succeed, and when they fail they bring great renown to their adversaries', a generalization which itself follows from the particularization (33. 4) 'if we defeat Athens, we shall win great renown'. The transposition, which has been followed by all recent editors, has a further disadvantage: it brings into close proximity (linking them by γάρ) δι' ὀλίγου and διὰ πλείστου, which at first glance appear to be opposites but in fact are not, and this creates ambiguity.

5. **διὰ τὸ παρὰ γνώμην αὐτῶν . . . περιγεγενῆσθαι:** 'Because you have got the better of them contrary to (sc. your) expectation, considering your original fears.' On αὐτῶν cf. Intr. I. 3. 11.

6. **τὰς διανοίας . . . θαρσεῖν:** Elsewhere in Thucydides κρατεῖν has an accusative object only when it means 'defeat in battle' and is accompanied by μάχῃ or μαχόμενοι; hence 'get the better of them in planning', for which the nearest parallel is D. xxi. 18 κρατούσῃ τὸν ἀγῶνα.

δόξαν ἀρετῆς μελετῶσιν: ἀρετή here is primarily the selfless courage and endurance which bring victory, the qualities of the ἀνὴρ ἀγαθός in the usual Greek sense of the term.

7. **δι' ὀλιγαρχίας ἐπιβουλεύουσαν:** The city referred to is Sparta, but the precise meaning of διά here is uncertain; does Nikias mean 'plotting against us by means of oligarchy', i.e. trying to foment oligarchic

conspiracy in Athens, or 'plotting against us under oligarchic rule', implying that the Spartans are bound to have hostile designs on Athens because they are oligarchic and that their hostility is particularly dangerous for that same reason? Probably the latter, because the former would seem to need somewhat more explicit development; and cf. D. xv. 19 εἰ δι' ὀλιγαρχίας ἅπαντα συστήσεται, 'if everything alike is going to be united under oligarchic rule'.

12. 1. νεωστί ... ηὐξῆσθαι: It was now fifteen years since the major attack of the plague, and six years since the peace treaty. When Thucydides himself comments on the extent of Athens' recovery (26. 2) he omits any such qualification as βραχύ τι. In so doing he possibly underestimates the effects of the plague, for nothing could or did replace the thousands of citizens who died in it (cf. iii. 87), and his Nikias perhaps underestimates Athens' financial strength. We do not know how large a reserve of money had been accumulated by 415, for the statement of And. iii. 8, 'because of the Peace of Nikias we put 7,000 talents on to the Akropolis' represents as an achievement what was in fact a programme only partly fulfilled; but they had, after all, a big enough reserve to sustain the Sicilian expedition and its reinforcements.

καὶ ταῦτα ... ἀναλοῦν: C omits εἶναι, giving excellent sense: 'and this (sc. it is) right to spend here on us.' With εἶναι there must be a variation of construction : 'we must remember that (ὅτι) we have recovered ... and that' (infinitive construction) 'it is right ...'; but we would expect καὶ ταῦτα to introduce a reflection upon what has just been stated (cf. 17. 1, 23. 3, &c.), not part of what 'we must remember'. ἐνθάδε εἶναι = ἐνθάδε would be inappropriate, since εἶναι with νῦν, ἐνθάδε, &c., has the limiting sense 'at any rate'.

φυγάδων: This refers to Leontinoi; so does 'themselves providing only talk' in the next part of the sentence, for Segesta at least had offered some cash.

οἷς ... χρήσιμον ... ξυναπολέσαι: The point is : it suits them to persuade someone else to run risks on their behalf; if, then, the outcome is favourable, they show no gratitude to those who helped them, and, if it is unfavourable, they drag down their helpers with them. The skeleton of the sentence is : χρήσιμον (sc. ἐστι) ψεύσασθαι ... καὶ ... ἢ ... μὴ ... εἰδέναι ἢ ... ξυναπολέσαι. For τοῦ πέλας cf. archaic 'my neighbour', modern 'the next man', = 'someone else'.

2. εἰ τέ τις ... παραινεῖ: Nikias does not name Alkibiades, but immediately makes his reference clear by closer specification of Alkibiades' characteristics.

νεώτερος ὢν ἔτι: Items of information on Alkibiades in Plato make it clear that he was born not later than 452; he was therefore at least 36 now. We do not know whether a minimum age for generals was laid down at Athens, as it was for (e.g.) jurymen and members of the Council; but it is always rhetorically possible to suggest that a man younger than oneself is too young, and Greek sentiment was amenable to warnings against 'youthful folly'.

ὅπως θαυμασθῇ μέν . . . ἐκ τῆς ἀρχῆς: The μέν-clause is subordinate in sense, for admiration of Alkibiades as the owner of a racing stable would not itself be a consequence of his commanding an expedition to Sicily; hence: 'so that, while being admired for the horses he keeps, he may διὰ πολυτέλειαν derive some benefit from his command.' διὰ πολυτέλειαν may mean either (i) 'as his (sc. previous) expenditure (sc. on horses) necessitates', the 'benefit' to be gained from command being financial, or (ii) 'by means of expenditure (sc. in command)', the 'benefit' being political. The latter interpretation is by no means far-fetched—in Lys. xix. 56 f. it is taken for granted that lavish expenditure while in office is designed to secure popularity and political advancement—but in this context it is likely that Nikias is making the more damaging accusation that Alkibiades hopes to recoup his finances by abuse of high office. Cf. 15. 2, where Th. seems to accept the accusation as just.

τὰ μέν . . . ἀναλοῦν: ἀδικεῖν suggests—as βλάπτειν, for example, would not—deliberate damage, in this case embezzlement to make up for private extravagance; hence the relationship between μέν and δέ has a strong causal flavour.

οἷον νεωτέρῳ . . . μεταχειρίσαι: νεωτέρου, νεωτέρων, νεώτερον, νεωτέρους, would all be possible, but νεωτέρῳ has a parallel in A. Th. 731 f. χθόνα ναίειν . . . ὁπόσαν καὶ φθιμένοισιν κατέχειν.

13. 1. οὕς: i.e. young men.

παρακελευστούς: 'Supporters', lit. 'called upon'.

εἴ τῳ τις παρακάθηται τῶνδε: 'Any older man (τῳ) who has one of the young men (τις . . . τῶνδε) sitting next to him.' This clause functions as the subject of καταισχυνθῆναι; Nikias' 'counter-exhortation' to the older men is (i) that an older man who has a young man sitting next to him should 'not be shamed into making sure that he is not thought—through voting against war—cowardly', and (ii) that the older men as a whole (here we return to the plural) should not be δυσέρωτας τῶν ἀπόντων.

ὅπερ ἂν αὐτοὶ πάθοιεν: As ἄν shows, these words are a warning, not an imprecation: 'and not to conceive an ill-starred (δυσ-) desire—as it may prove to be for the young men themselves—for distant gains.'

τῶν ἀπόντων: This word has much more emotional associations for the Greeks than for us; cf. Pi. P. 3. 19 ff. ἤρατο τῶν ἀπεόντων and Pindar's reflections thereon.

κατορθοῦνται: Thucydides predicates the intransitive active κατορ-θοῦν of persons, the passive of enterprises. Hence ἐλάχιστα and πλεῖστα are the only possible subjects of κατορθοῦνται, and the plural verb is questionable. There are, however, many exceptions to the general rule that a neuter plural subject takes a singular verb; some of them are classifiable and explicable, but there remain passages in which no special reason for abnormality can be discerned. Some, no doubt, are corrupt; but which?

ὅροις: Nikias clearly envisages possible boundaries other than those existing, and is thus not merely reminding us that Sicily is separated from Greece by natural barriers. Nor, on the other hand, need he be referring to any explicit provision, e.g. in the treaty of Gela. His point is that warships and troops from Sicily have not in fact intervened in Greece.

τῷ τε Ἰονίῳ κόλπῳ: Hdt. vi. 127. 2 so names the sea off Epidamnos; from there to Brindisi is the only stretch of open sea which is unavoidable in travelling between Greece and Italy or Sicily.

τῷ Σικελικῷ: sc. κόλπῳ, which is freely applied to expanses of water wide enough to be called also πόντος or πέλαγος; cf. 62. 2 Τυρσηνικὸς κόλπος ∼ vii. 58. 2 Τυρσηνικὸς πόντος.

2. ἰδίᾳ: 'In particular', as distinct from the view which they are to take of the Sicilian states as a whole.

μετὰ σφῶν αὐτῶν: Not normal Greek for 'by themselves', but prompted by the antitheses 'without'/'with' and 'Athens'/'themselves'.

14. ὦ πρύτανι: Nikias is addressing the chairman (ἐπιστάτης) of the body of fifty (πρυτάνεις) which presided over the Council and the Assembly; it is the chairman's job to put an issue to the vote (ἐπι-ψηφίζειν) and to invite the Assembly (γνώμας προτιθέναι) to give its opinions on a proposal.

ἀναψηφίσαι: A procedural term, 'to put to the vote for a second time a proposal on which a decision has already been taken'.

τὸ μὲν λύειν . . . σχεῖν: 'In the realization that with so many witnesses you cannot be charged with (or blamed for) λύειν τοὺς νόμους.' αἰτίαν σχεῖν, as normally, has a personal subject and a dependent infinitive. The interpretation of λύειν τοὺς νόμους is difficult:

(i) 'Rescinding an enactment.' This is a possible meaning in so far as (a) a distinction between νόμος, 'law', and ψήφισμα, 'decree', is not always observed, (b) whoever proposes the rescinding of an enactment or takes any steps which imply or lead to its rescinding can be said to λύειν that enactment, (c) even if only one enactment is involved, it can be referred to as οἱ νόμοι, just as 'the law' in English can have a collective or an individual sense. But since Nikias is asking the chairman to put the issue of the expedition to the vote again, and hopes that the earlier decision will be rescinded (cf. 15. 1 τὰ ἐψηφισμένα . . . μὴ λύειν), he cannot mean 'with so many witnesses you will not be accused of rescinding an enactment', for the more witnesses there are, the more clearly will the chairman be seen to do what Nikias wants him to do.

(ii) 'Breaking the law.' Is it possible that the action for which Nikias asks could in some circumstances be illegal, but is not (or is not so regarded by Nikias) in the existing circumstances? In point of fact, it was *not* illegal to put an issue to the vote for a second time; the decision to massacre the Mytileneans was so put, and annulled, and in Thucydides' account of the debate on that occasion Kleon, although he fiercely attacks the reopening of the issue as foolish, does not raise any issue of legality. Moreover, λύειν νόμον (or νόμους) is not used in Classical Greek of an individual's contravention of the law of his state.

(iii) 'Abolishing' (sc. by setting a precedent) 'our established procedure.' It was *unusual* to have a second vote on a decision, and νόμος in Greek covers 'custom' and 'traditional practice' as well as 'law'. The chairman might well be afraid, for an Athenian citizen could be tried (and executed) for acting against the interests of the state, whether or not he had contravened any explicit law. Nikias' reference to the number of witnesses implies 'all these witnesses will testify that the Assembly is genuinely divided, and you will not be accused of acting frivolously or maliciously'.

ἄρξαι: Not 'rule', but 'hold office'; all officials and magistrates, however brief and limited their power, are said to ἀρχὰς ἄρχειν.

15. *Introduction to Alkibiades*

15. 1. τῶν δὲ Ἀθηναίων . . . ἀντέλεγον: lit., 'of the Athenians, coming forward, the majority urged . . . while others, a certain number, spoke *against* that', i.e. 'The majority of those members of the Assembly who came forward urged . . . while there were some others who did speak against that.'

2. βουλόμενος κτλ.: lit., 'wishing to oppose Nikias . . . and, more than anything, desiring to serve as general . . .'; on the position of the first τε cf. I. 3. 15 (a).

ὧν . . . ἐμνήσθη: The causal participle ὥν (= 'since he was . . .') and the causal clause ὅτι κτλ. (= 'because . . .') are co-ordinated by καί, and the clause is foreshadowed by the adverbial καί in καὶ ἐς τἄλλα. Nikias' attack (διαβόλως ἐμνήσθη) is a particular example of general political hostility.

It is noteworthy that Thucydides puts 'desire to oppose Nikias' first among Alkibiades' motives in making so strong a plea for the expedition. He often represents political issues in terms of personal rivalries (cf. especially 28. 2), and this is sometimes taken as an indication that he failed to see the 'real' causes of political decisions. It is, however, in fact a reminder that he knew more about the actual conditions of Greek political life than we do. During the first twenty years of the Peloponnesian War, although there were sharp divisions of opinion on strategic issues, there was no consistent 'party system' in Athenian politics; men who took part in public life accepted the radical democracy as it was, and contended with each other for high standing within it, while those who were not reconciled to democracy had no public life. The schematic reconstruction of fourth-century historians, in which Nikias becomes the leader and representative of the 'better' men, rests on Nikias' *strategic* conservatism, and is not warranted by any suggestion in Thucydides that Nikias was *constitutionally* conservative.

καὶ Καρχηδόνα: It is remarkable that Thucydides baldly states that Alkibiades entertained this ambition, when his Alkibiades says nothing about it in this debate, nor does Nikias attack it. We next encounter it in 90. 2, where the exiled Alkibiades is trying to frighten the Spartans by painting a picture of Athenian plans for the Western Mediterranean. In Ar. *Eq.* 1303 f. (produced in 424) Hyperbolos is credited with 'asking for 100 triremes εἰς Καρχηδόνα', but that is not unambiguous: to attack Carthage, or to go to Carthage and co-operate with Carthage against Syracuse?

3. **ὑπὸ τῶν ἀστῶν**: ὑπό is used as if ὢν ἐν ἀξιώματι were a passive participle, e.g. τιμώμενος.

μείζοσιν . . . οὐσίαν: lit., 'greater than in-accordance-with the already-existing estate', i.e. 'greater than his actual estate could support'.

ἱπποτροφίας: cf. 12. 2.

ὅπερ καὶ καθεῖλεν . . . οὐχ ἥκιστα: The interpretation of this and the following sentence is controversial, since there were two occasions on which Alkibiades fell out with his fellow citizens and was driven into exile. The first, shortly to be described in this book, was in 415. In 411 he was accepted by the Athenian fleet stationed at Samos, and after four years of energetic and successful action as one of its commanders he returned to Athens itself in 407 and was given over-riding powers. In the following winter, however, one of his subordinates suffered a defeat, feeling against Alkibiades ran high again, and he went into exile for the second and last time in 406, eighteen months before the final defeat of Athens at Aigospotamoi.

Since § 4 in many particulars would be an appropriate description of what happened in 415 (and has verbal resemblances to 28. 2), it is believed by some historians that §§ 3–4 refer solely to 415 and that Thucydides, in saying that the extravagance of Alkibiades 'contributed as much as anything to the overthrow of Athens', means by 'overthrow' the defeat of the Sicilian Expedition. There are, however, two strong objections to this interpretation:

(i) καθαιρεῖν is a very strong word, used elsewhere of final and decisive defeat (cf. especially v. 103. 1 κἂν βλάψῃ, οὐ καθεῖλεν). The defeat of the Sicilian Expedition did not καθαιρεῖν the Athenians; they recovered from it and fought on, with a fair prospect of success; it by no means rendered their final defeat inevitable. And it will not do to argue (as has been argued) that Thucydides wrote these words soon after 413 in the (mistaken) belief that the defeat in Sicily had rendered final defeat absolutely inescapable; for no historian has ever been so well aware as Thucydides of the role of the unexpected in war, or of the extent to which the Peloponnesians could lose an opportunity through delay. It is therefore certain that § 3 refers to the final defeat of Athens in 405, and it follows from this that § 4, the explanation (note γάρ) of § 3, refers to the *second* exile of Alkibiades.

(ii) In § 4 Thucydides says that the Athenians resented Alkibiades' behaviour 'although in the sphere of public life his conduct of strategy was superior to all'. This judgement is inexplicable if it refers to the period down to 415; Alkibiades' strategy in the Peloponnese (on which cf. 16. 6 n.) had ended in failure, and his plan for the conduct of the Sicilian Expedition (48) not only proved unsuccessful when applied but was pretty certainly not highly regarded by Thucydides, if we consider the approval which Thucydides gives in vii. 42. 3 to the principle of *speed* in attacking the main enemy. If, on the other hand, the judgement 'his conduct of strategy was superior to all' refers to the period 411–406, it is justified by the narrative of Book VIII of Thucydides and by Xenophon's *Hellenica*.

Thus ὕστερον refers to 407–405, οὐ διὰ μακροῦ (§ 4) to that interval of two years, and καθεῖλεν and ἔσφηλαν (§ 4) both to 405.

4. αὐτοῦ: cf. 11. 5 n.

παρανομίας: Just as νόμος covers 'custom' as well as 'law', so παρανομία is not always or necessarily 'illegality' but also unconventional behaviour or violation of accepted ideas of right and wrong.

καὶ τῆς διανοίας ... ἔπρασσεν: lit., 'and of the thinking of the things which he carried out along each one thing in whatever he was involved', i.e. 'the ambition (διάνοια denotes not an *attitude*, which would be denoted by φρονεῖν and its derivatives, but systematic thinking; cf. 11. 6) apparent in all his actions in everything with which he was concerned'.

ὡς τυραννίδος ἐπιθυμοῦντι: Although ninety-five years had passed since the expulsion of the last Athenian tyrant, allegation of tyrannical ambitions was still current coin in politics (cf. Ar. *V.* 488 ff.); it had a foundation in fact, as was shown by the establishment of the 'Four

Hundred' in 411 and, more dramatically, by the tyranny of Dionysios which in 406 brought to an end the sixty-year-old democracy of Syracuse.

διαθέντι τὰ τοῦ πολέμου: διαθέντι is the reading of H^c; the other MSS. have διαθέντα, which cannot be adopted unless we suppose that some such words as 'deprived him of his office' have fallen out. But διαθέντι is not free from difficulty either, as it gives a clumsy sentence: 'and although in the sphere of public life his conduct of strategy was superior to all, in the private sphere they, as individuals, resenting (sc. αὐτῷ = him) *because of* his behaviour . . .' It is preferable to adopt the conjecture διαθέντος, treat δημοσίᾳ . . . πολέμου as a genitive absolute clause, and then take τοῖς ἐπιτηδεύμασιν αὐτοῦ as the object of ἀχθεσθέντες (= 'resenting his behaviour').

καὶ ἄλλοις ἐπιτρέψαντες: It is not necessary to 'supply' τὴν πόλιν (or anything else) as the object of ἐπιτρέψαντες, which can be used absolutely in the sense 'hand over to', 'trust', or 'follow the lead of'. Thucydides does not have in mind the transfer of any specific powers; he means simply that in driving out Alkibiades in 406 Athens necessarily 'handed over' to others.

16–18. *Speech of Alkibiades*

16. 1. ἀνάγκη γάρ . . . ἄρξασθαι: Speakers in Thucydides commonly begin by defending themselves against actual or potential accusations; cf. 82. 1, 89. 1.

ἐπιβόητος: Picked up by ἐπιβοώμενος in § 6; unlike περιβόητος, which can denote the object of admiration, it implies notoriety and hostile criticism.

τοῖς μὲν προγόνοις . . . ταῦτα: He means either (i) that the credit for what he does belongs also to his ancestors, since they accumulated wealth and established a tradition, or (ii) that it brought renown to them and brings it still to him.

2. τῷ ἐμῷ διαπρεπεῖ . . . θεωρίας: cf. Intr. I. 3. 8 on this remarkable substantival complex: 'the splendour of my participation in the Olympic festival.'

καθῆκα: 'Entered', 'put into the race'.

οὐδείς πω ἰδιώτης: The implied contrast is not simply with the famous tyrants of an earlier age but also with states, which could enter chariots in the Olympic games (cf. v. 50. 4).

ἐνίκησα δέ . . . ἐγενόμην: In 420 the chariot race was won by Lichas (v. 50. 4), and since 'believing that Athens had been beaten down in war' can hardly refer to 424, even making allowances for rhetorical exaggeration, the occasion of Alkibiades' victory must have been 416.

A victory ode for this occasion, attributed to Euripides and quoted by Plutarch, spoke of Alkibiades' chariots as coming first, second, and *third*, and that is also the version given by Isokrates in a speech delivered eighteen years after the event (xvi. 34). Possibly the third place was disputed, Alkibiades thinking that a chariot of his 'really' came first, and the judges thinking otherwise (popular opinions on the award of bronze medals in the modern Olympic Games provide parallels enough). Alternatively, the poem attributed to Euripides may be wrongly attributed—Plutarch himself (*Dem.* 1. 1) casts doubt on its authenticity— and actually based on a distortion popularized by Isokrates.

νόμῳ μὲν γὰρ τιμὴ τὰ τοιαῦτα: lit., 'by custom such things are honour', i.e. 'it is the way of men to respect such achievements'.

3. **χορηγίαις**: χορηγία, the obligation to pay for a dramatic production or for the training and dressing of a non-dramatic chorus, was imposed on the rich, and its lavish discharge was commonly regarded as a means of winning the favour of the citizen body.

ἥδ' ἡ ἄνοια: Alkibiades is speaking sarcastically, as he does in 17. 1, ἡ . . . ἄνοια . . . δοκοῦσα εἶναι. Nikias, however, has not accused Alkibiades of 'folly', and used the word ἀνόητος only with a highly general reference to the extension of empire; no doubt there was at times a slight discrepancy between what Thucydides had actually written and what he thought he had written.

4. **οὐδέ γε ἄδικον κτλ.**: The sequence of thought in this rather sophistic argument is: 'there is no reason why a man who has reason to be proud of himself should behave towards others as an equal; an unfortunate man does not expect others to share his misfortune; the prosperous man is to the ordinary man as the ordinary man is to the unfortunate; just as the unfortunate is not treated as an equal by the ordinary, so the ordinary must tolerate not being treated as an equal by the prosperous; or, if he will not tolerate this, he must himself treat the unfortunate better.' Understand τινα as the subject of εἶναι, and in the last clause put the emphasis on the participial group: 'or let him treat (sc. his inferior) as an equal and only then demand like treatment (sc. from his superior).'

5. **τοὺς τοιούτους**: The proud and successful, those like Alkibiades himself.

ἔν τινος λαμπρότητι: lit., 'in brilliance of something', i.e. 'in any brilliant quality or achievement'.

λυπηρούς . . . ξυνόντας: 'Objectionable above all to their peers, and in the second place', lit., 'to the rest when they are with them', i.e. 'when they associate with others'.

προσποίησιν . . . καταλιπόντας: μὴ οὖσαν = 'which is no claim', i.e. 'untrue', 'unfounded'; cf. S. *El.* 584 σκῆψιν οὐκ οὖσαν = 'an untrue excuse'.

Alkibiades' generalization was borne out in later times by the historian Duris of Samos, who claimed to be a descendant of Alkibiades himself; Thucydides probably had in mind men who claimed descent from Odysseus (e.g. the orator Andokides), Ajax (e.g. his own family), or other figures of heroic times.

6. ὧν: 'Fame of this kind.'

Πελοποννήσου . . . ξυστήσας: Alkibiades could fairly claim to have been the architect of the Athenian alliance with Argos, Elis, and Mantinea; it was his persuasiveness, on an embassy to Argos in 418 (v. 61. 2 f.), which set in motion the campaign which was ended by the Spartan victory at Mantinea. The Argives, Eleans, and Mantineans would no doubt have been pleased to be described as 'the most powerful elements in the Peloponnese', but the description has little bearing on the realities of the time.

Λακεδαιμονίους . . . ἀγωνίσασθαι: The battle of Mantinea was in fact a decisive Spartan victory, in consequence of which Spartan prestige was enhanced, the Argive alliance fell to pieces, and Mantinea lost her hold on the minor communities of Arkadia. Alkibiades puts the best face he can on these disagreeable events; the one part of his claim which is justified is that the battle of Mantinea was fought 'without any considerable danger or expense to Athens'.

οὐδέπω . . . θαρσοῦσιν: It would be surprising if this was true to any significant extent; but Alkibiades could perhaps point to the fact that the pro-Spartan oligarchy established in Argos in the winter of 418/7 was thrown out within a few months, so that Argos again constituted a focus of opposition to Sparta in the Peloponnese.

17. 1. ταῦτα: Almost = 'thus'; ταῦτα . . . ὡμίλησε καί . . . ἔπεισεν is to be analysed as 'dealt these dealings and persuaded these persuadings'.

ἡ ἐμὴ νεότης . . . δοκοῦσα εἶναι: We say 'what is regarded as my youth . . .'; Greek says not τὸ ἐμὴ νεότης δοκοῦν εἶναι but, with assimilation of gender, ἡ ἐμὴ νεότης δοκοῦσα εἶναι.

παρὰ φύσιν: 'Contrary to the natural state', i.e. 'insane'; cf. 16. 3 n.

ἐς τὴν Πελοποννησίων δύναμιν: Since everywhere else in Thucydides Πελοποννήσιοι means not 'the inhabitants of the Peloponnese' but 'Sparta and her allies', Alkibiades represents himself as dealing with 'the area controlled by Sparta and her allies'; for this sense of δύναμις cf. ii. 7. 1 ἐκτὸς τῆς ἑαυτῶν δυνάμεως 'outside the areas which they themselves controlled'.

ὀργῇ πίστιν παρασχομένη: Probably 'offering, in its spirit, a guarantee'; cf. λόγους παρασχομένους in 12. 1 and προθυμίαν . . . παρεσχόμεθα in 83. 1. But 'inspiring confidence (sc. in them) by its spirit' is possible. The arguments (λόγοις) were what the occasion required (πρέπουσιν), but it was the sincerity underlying them (ὀργῇ) which achieved conviction. The variant reading παρασχομένῃ makes as good sense as the nominative.

εὐτυχής: Good luck was a proof of the gods' favour (highly desirable in a general). Nikias so far had not been associated with any setbacks; he was also outstandingly wealthy, and that also was proof of divine favour (cf. 103. 4 n.).

2. ὄχλοις τε γάρ . . . αἱ πόλεις: The Sicilian tyrants at the beginning of the fifth century carried out wholesale transplantations of population, and their settlements were upset, after they and their power had gone, by a fresh set of transplantations. Between then and 415 the only transplantation of which we know was the Syracusan incorporation of the upper class of Leontinoi, with the expulsion of its remaining population, in 423/2 (v. 4. 2 ff.). This recent case would naturally be uppermost in the minds of Alkibiades' audience; but the basis of his generalization is a conception of Sicilian affairs formed early in the fifth century and no doubt deeply rooted in Athens.

3. νομίμοις κατασκευαῖς: κατασκευαί, as often in Thucydides, means 'farms', the buildings and the fittings and accessories (e.g. wine-presses, sheep-pens, &c.) that go with them; and νόμιμος = 'of the usual kind', 'normal', 'regular'.

ὅτι δὲ ἕκαστος . . . ἑτοιμάζεται: Instead of spending his money on personal arms and the equipment of his farm, the Sicilian 'accumulates it in readiness'; the reference is to the behaviour of individuals, not to the policy of states. ὅτι is the object of λαβών, and ὅτι . . . οἴεται . . . λαβών . . . οἰκήσειν = ὅτι ἂν λάβῃ, οἰόμενος οἰκήσειν, 'what he has taken, in the belief that he will live . . .'. ἢ ἐκ τοῦ λέγων πείθειν . . . ἢ στασιάζων denote the means by which he 'gets money from public funds', and μὴ κατορθώσας (= 'if he fails', sc. in his political career) denotes the circumstances in which, he thinks, he will go and live somewhere else, for which he will naturally need the money which he has accumulated. Hence: 'What each individual has got from public funds, either by persuasive oratory or by faction, in the confidence that if his career is a failure he will go and live elsewhere—this he accumulates in readiness.' Alkibiades is casting a double slur on the Siceliots, affirming not only that they keep their money ready in the expectation of emigration, but that the money itself is acquired by dishonest means. It is taken for granted by the Greeks, as we see from the comedians' and orators' references to men whom they dislike, that a dishonest man makes money out of prominence in public life. 'Persuasive oratory or faction' is only a variant form of the very common antitheses 'words/deeds' and 'persuasion/force'.

This difficult sentence has often been misinterpreted by editors through failure to see that it is simply an explanation of καὶ οὐδείς ... κατασκευαῖς and not a fresh point about Siceliot finances.

4. **ὡς ἕκαστοι**: = ἕκαστοι; in view of what is said in § 2, the reference must be to groups or elements between which the boundaries are not those of state or party.

στασιάζουσιν: This normally refers to faction within a state; it is used of interstate warfare only when the speaker wishes to suggest that the states concerned are, or ought to be, members of a higher unity. Here any suggestion of the natural unity of Sicily would be contrary to the tenor of Alkibiades' argument.

5. **οὔτε οἱ ἄλλοι ... ἠρίθμουν**: Rhetorical statements of this kind are as much favoured by an ancient as by a modern speaker; they can be denied by his opponent, but they cannot be refuted except by laborious research, by which time it is too late to counteract their effect on the audience. The modern student of Thucydides (or of the orators) must constantly be on his guard against a natural tendency to treat such statements as if they were true; as a rule, we have no idea whether they are true or not.

ἡ Ἑλλάς: Personification of a geographical entity is not common; usually 'Greece' = οἱ Ἕλληνες, 'Sparta' = Λακεδαιμόνιοι, &c. Here variation after οἱ ἄλλοι Ἕλληνες is sought.

ἐν τῷδε τῷ πολέμῳ: In v. 26. 2 ff. Thucydides defends his own view that the Archidamian War, the period of the Peace of Nikias, the Sicilian Expedition, and the subsequent fighting all constituted a single war, and accordingly he describes each year in his narrative as 'the *n*th year of this war'. Thucydides' view was not held universally in the fourth century, as we see from the orators. Here, however, he represents Alkibiades, speaking in 415, not only as holding the view which he held himself but as taking it for granted in arguing before the Assembly. This may be an anachronism; but it may also be true that both Alkibiades and Nikias (cf. 10. 2 f.) in 415 regarded the 'peace' as unreal, and that Thucydides in writing v. 26. 2 ff. was arguing against a view which predominated *after* the end of the war.

6. **βαρβάρους [τε] γάρ ... αὐτοῖς**: τε is indefensible, as it does not co-ordinate βαρβάρους with anything else. The βάρβαροι whom Alkibiades especially has in mind are the Sikels, many of whom were subjects of Syracuse (cf. 88. 3 f.).

7. **οἱ γὰρ πατέρες ... ἐκτήσαντο**: Alkibiades is not arguing that because the Athenians in the past had survived desperate situations they should now deliberately create another one, but, as his continuation shows, that they had in the past taken calculated risks as the only way of acquiring their empire. In saying τὴν ἀρχὴν ἐκτήσαντο he ignores

the fact that the Delian League was created, on the initiative of the Ionian states, at a time when Athens and Sparta were still allies, and the essential steps towards the conversion of the League into an Empire were taken while the Spartan alliance was still in force; but his point is valid so far as the decade 460–450 is concerned.

8. ἀνέλπιστοι: An active sense here: 'without hope.'

ὑπόλοιπον γάρ . . . ναυτικόν: This is true, for Alkibiades in 415 could not reasonably have envisaged that it would be necessary, two years later, to send to Sicily a force almost as large as the original expedition; it was this reinforcement which denuded Athens of ships.

18. 1. ὥστε τί ἄν . . . μὴ βοηθοῖμεν;: If ἤ . . . ἤ belong logically where they are placed, the sense is: 'With what plausible argument could we ourselves shrink from the enterprise or, making it an excuse to our allies in Sicily, fail to help them?' But it is possible that the first ἤ is 'delayed' (cf. 7. 3 n.), in which case the sense is: 'With what plausible argument could we ourselves shrink . . . or with what excuse to our allies . . .?' The latter interpretation is supported by viii. 46. 1 μηδὲ βουληθῆναι ἢ ναῦς Φοινίσσας . . . ἢ Ἕλλησι πλέοσι μισθὸν πορίζοντα τοῖς αὑτοῖς . . . τὸ κράτος δοῦναι, 'not to be willing either by bringing in Phoenician ships . . . or by providing pay for an increased number of Greeks . . . to give superiority . . . to the same state'.

ἐκεῖνοι: sc. ἐπήμυνον.

ἀντιβοηθῶσι: Alkibiades is speaking of Athenian intentions, not of the formal terms of the Athenian alliances with Segesta and Leontinoi. We know of no Greek alliance in which A promises to help B but B does not promise to help A; since, however, neither party would be expected to help the other until called upon to do so, alliances which were formally reciprocal could be unilateral in practice.

δεῦρο . . . ἐπιέναι: Alkibiades, like Nikias (10. 1), but for different reasons, affects to believe that there was a significant likelihood of Sicilian help for the Peloponnesians.

2. παραγιγνόμενοι προθύμως: Readiness to help injured friends is a common theme in laudations of Athens; Alkibiades amplifies it here, as the occasion demands, by including βάρβαροι.

εἴ γε ἡσυχάζοιεν πάντες: After the preceding words, we would expect πάντες to mean 'all imperial powers', but it is clear from what follows that Alkibiades means 'all of us', i.e. all Athenians.

τὸν γὰρ προύχοντα . . . προκαταλαμβάνει: 'One does not simply repel the stronger when they attack; one catches them in time, to ensure that they do not attack.' To us, surveying Greek history as a whole, this generalization does not seem conspicuously true; but Perikles no doubt regarded his own policy towards the Peloponnesians in the 430's in this light, and Alkibiades will have been among those who shared his view.

3. καὶ οὐκ ἔστιν ἡμῖν . . . ἄρχοιμεν: The danger of inactivity on the part of an imperial city is a recurrent theme in the speeches of Thucydides' Perikles. ἄρχειν is used here straightforwardly, and without apology, of Athens' relation to her Empire.

4. τάδε . . . ἐκεῖνα: 'Our empire *here* . . . our enemies in *Sicily*.'

εἰ δόξομεν: '(sc. as we shall) if it is seen (sc. as it will be) that we . . .'

ἄρξομεν . . . κακώσομεν: Although these words are co-ordinated with the final clause ἵνα . . . στορέσωμεν, the mood (in both senses of the word) changes, the change being helped by εἰ δόξομεν; emendation to produce grammatical uniformity would spoil the rhetorical effect.

5. τὸ δὲ ἀσφαλὲς κτλ.: lit., 'safety, both for staying . . . and for departing'. The infinitives simply amplify τὸ ἀσφαλές, and ἀσφαλές should not be regarded as an attributive adjective qualifying a substantival infinitive τὸ μένειν. Cf. X. *An.* i. 3. 13 ἀπορία . . . καὶ μένειν καὶ ἀπιέναι.

6. τοῖς νέοις: Used instead of the expected objective genitive, for variation after Νικίου τῶν λόγων.

ἐς τάδε κτλ.: The sentiment is that of Thucydides' Perikles, i. 144. 4 οἱ γοῦν πατέρες ἡμῶν . . . ἐς τάδε προήγαγον αὐτά, and immediately below we find another 'Periklean' phrase, ὥσπερ καὶ ἄλλο τι; cf. i. 142. 9 τέχνης ἐστί, ὥσπερ καὶ ἄλλο τι.

τό τε φαῦλον κτλ.: The idea that health in the body depends on the right 'mixture' (κρᾶσις) of unlike elements in its constitution is a commonplace in the earlier Greek medical works; and the ethical doctrine that right action is a mean between extremes is related to this.

ἐγγηράσεσθαι: 'The skill of all' is the subject, the point of ἐγ- being 'in the city', but with ἀγωνιζομένην we return to 'the city' as subject; for the succession of subjects A–B–A cf. 86. 2 n.

7. γιγνώσκω . . . δοκεῖν: There is no tautology here; Alkibiades is delivering his γνώμη, i.e. his opinion on the matter under debate, and γιγνώσκω formally indicates that.

ἀπραγμοσύνης μεταβολῇ: 'By a change *to* inactivity'. The 'philosophy' of πολυπραγμοσύνη, advocated in § 3 on the grounds that any alternative is dangerous for a city that rules an empire, is defended also in 87. 2 (v. n.) and by Perikles in ii. 63. 2 f.

οἳ ἂν . . . πολιτεύωσιν: Appeal to traditional practice and character was always rhetorically cogent; Kleon is represented as exploiting it in the debate on Mytilene, iii. 37. 3 f.

19. *Nikias' Change of Tactics*

19. 2. τάχ' ἂν μεταστήσειεν αὐτούς: This was a miscalculation, from some points of view; if a smaller force had been sent, it might not have secured in the first year success enough to justify prolonging its efforts, and the whole adventure might have ended more in accordance with Nikias' wishes.

20. *Second Speech of Nikias*

20. 1. ξυνενέγκοι μὲν ταῦτα κτλ.: A rhetorical equivalent of the expression τύχῃ ἀγαθῇ with which a decree recorded in an inscription sometimes opens.

2. ὡς ἐγὼ ἀκοῇ αἰσθάνομαι: Nikias is explicitly denying the argument expounded by Alkibiades in 17. 2 ff., and his words, though in writing identical with Alkibiades' (17. 6), must be spoken in different tones.

ἐς ῥᾴω μετάστασιν: As a democracy, Athens could sometimes exploit political discontent among her adversaries; but since Syracuse was herself a democracy, Athens could not pose as the champion of the Syracusan *demos* against the governing class.

3. ἐπὶ ἃς μᾶλλον πλέομεν: μᾶλλον, with the opening words of § 2, shows that Nikias recognizes that the essential Athenian objective is the subjugation of Sicily.

4. χρήματά τ' . . . Σελινουντίοις: Although χρήματα and τὰ μέν are objects of ἔχουσι, with τὰ δέ we pass into a fresh finite clause, of which τὰ δέ is the subject.

ἱεροῖς: The archaic and classical temples of Selinus constituted as splendid a group as could be found anywhere in the Greek world; no doubt they contained many rich dedications, but we do not know whether they enjoyed any exceptional revenue such as would justify Nikias' statement.

ἀπὸ βαρβάρων τινῶν ἀπαρχὴ ἐσφέρεται: ἀπαρχὴ φέρεται is the text required, 'a tithe is paid as tribute'; φέρειν, φόρος, and φορά are used of payment of tribute by subject to ruler, εἰσφέρειν and εἰσφορά of payment by individuals into public funds or by members of an association into a common treasury.

σίτῳ: The contrast with Athens, which imported a large part of the grain which she consumed, is pointed. A country which grew its own was naturally less vulnerable to naval interference with its trade-routes.

21. 1. οὐ ναυτικῆς . . . ξυμπλεῖν: δεῖ is constructed both with a genitive and with an infinitive : 'there is a need not simply of a naval and ⟨otherwise⟩ inadequate force but that a lot of infantry should sail with it.'

εἰ ξυστῶσιν: The grammar is eccentric—there is no certain example of εἰ with the subjunctive in Attic prose—and εἰ should be emended to ἤν.

μὴ ἀντιπαράσχωσιν . . . ἱππικόν: 'Furnish us with cavalry for our protection to match (ἀντι-) ⟨the Syracusan cavalry⟩.' It is noteworthy that Nikias does not think in terms of transporting cavalry from Athens; cf. 22, 'archers and slingers, so that we may hold our own against the enemy cavalry'. Presumably it was not practicable to transport enough cavalry with their horses to make much difference; cf. 94. 4.

ἐπιέναι: sc. δεῖ.

πολύ τε . . . ἐπί τινα: 'far (πολύ) . . . and not to conduct a campaign in the same conditions as ⟨καί⟩ when . . .' The MSS. have καὶ οὐκ ἐν, which makes no sense ; καὶ οὗ ἐν is an alternative emendation to καὶ ὅτε ἐν, but καὶ ὅτε is perhaps the best, since 'to help (ξύμμαχοι) our subjects in the Aegean' is better sense than 'as allies (sc. of somebody) in our empire in the Aegean'.

ὅθεν . . . ὧν προσέδει: '*Where* the supply . . .'; 'static' words meaning 'in', 'at', 'where', 'here', &c., constantly become 'to', 'from', 'whither', 'whence', &c., when direction of movement is indicated (as here) in the rest of the clause.

ἀλλ' . . . ἀπαρτήσοντες: ἀλλ' is in antithesis to οὐκ in καὶ οὐκ ἐν τῷ ὁμοίῳ κτλ. The intransitive ἀπαρτᾶν does not occur elsewhere in extant Attic literature ; but its meaning, 'be separate', 'be detached', is clear enough from the context and from the usage of the passive and the transitive active.

μηνῶν οὐδὲ τεσσάρων: Adverbial οὐδέ cannot be detached in sense from the word which follows it ; 'from which it is not easy for a messenger to return *even* within four months, during the winter.' Nikias exaggerates (cf., inter alia, 74. 2 and 88. 7, where journeys by sea from Sicily to Greece in winter are accomplished satisfactorily) but he is true to Greek sentiment ; cf. And. i. 137, 'what greater peril is there than to sail the sea in winter ?'

22. ἢ πεῖσαι ἢ μισθῷ προσαγαγέσθαι: 'Persuasion' would be applied to allies, notably Argos, 'inducement by pay' to Arcadian mercenaries.

τὸν δὲ καὶ αὐτόθεν σῖτον: lit., 'and the other ⟨necessary⟩ thing actually from *here*, ⟨namely⟩ grain'; in the pronoun τόν the gender of σῖτον is anticipated.

πρὸς μέρος ἠναγκασμένους: 'Fairly' (or 'proportionately') 'conscripted'; but it is not clear whether this implies 'assigned proportionately to the various units of the force' or 'conscripted in such a way

that the burden is equally spread over the mills here'. The word
σιτοποιοί commonly denotes female slaves, but here, plainly, 'master-
bakers' who were free men and would each be accompanied by his
own slaves.

λόγῳ: Nikias was right; cf. 46.

23. 1. ἦν γὰρ αὐτοί . . . μόλις οὕτως κτλ.: 'For if we go *ourselves*, from
Athens' (this is in keeping with the emphasis in 21. 2–22 on the danger of
depending on others) 'not simply with forces which are a *match* for
them—though not, of course, for their *fighting* element, their hoplites—
but superior in all arms, even so we shall only just be able . . .' The
parenthesis is enigmatic; but since Nikias' whole argument up to this
point has been 'we must take *enough hoplites*' he clearly cannot be
taking it for granted that whatever happens the Athenians will be
a match for the Sicilian hoplites. Nor can he be suggesting that whatever they did they could *not* be a match, for he envisages circumstances
in which they might be superior in *everything*. It is therefore probable
that he is contrasting the kind of force which has so far been assumed—
a force of sixty ships (8. 2), which he has in mind when he speaks (21. 1)
of ναυτικῆς καὶ φαύλου στρατιᾶς—with the desirable force which would
be superior in hoplites and other arms as well as in ships. The Athenians
have thought of the proposed force as a 'match' for the enemy; Nikias
reminds them that it is not a match in the arm that will be needed for
the decisive fighting.

A variant in H has πλεῖν for πλήν: '—for going by sea, remember, to
meet their fighting force, their hoplites—.' This would be a reminder of
the difficulty attendant on *any* force, whether a 'match' or superior; to
that extent it makes sense; but linguistically ἀντίπαλον . . . παρασκευασάμενοι πλεῖν has no true parallel, and stylistically the opposition of ideas
between 'sail' and 'fighting' is too heavily veiled.

τῶν μέν . . . διασῶσαι: The point is: 'conquer what (or whom) we
want to conquer and also save what we want to save', i.e. 'conquer our
enemies and also bring our own forces safely home'. Nikias is hinting
that a safe return cannot be taken for granted.

2. ᾗ ἂν κατάσχωσιν: ᾗ agrees with ἡμέρᾳ, since '*where*ver they land'
would require οἷ.

ᾗ εἰδέναι: ('They must . . .) *or* know . . .' = 'for if they do not—
and this they must recognize . . .'.

3. ἐκπλεῖν . . . ἐκπλεῦσαι: The semantics of verbal aspect in Greek
prose literature have not yet been investigated with sufficient care to
provide an objective explanation of the change of aspect here.

παρασκευῇ δὲ κτλ.: lit., 'by equipment from what is likely', i.e.

'by provision' (of troops of all arms, &c.) 'on a scale dictated by rational planning'.

παρίημι αὐτῷ τὴν ἀρχήν: 'I *offer* to resign . . .'; neither an Athenian nor a modern general can divest himself of office merely by his own declaration. On another famous occasion, when Kleon was appointed to clear up the situation on Sphakteria (iv. 28. 3), Nikias' bluff was called.

24-26. *Outcome of the Debate*

24. 1. ⟨ἄν⟩: The addition of ἄν is not necessary, since, although νομίζων ἐκπλεῦσαι in isolation would naturally be taken to mean 'thinking that he had sailed out', the aorist or imperfective infinitive may have a potential sense when the context makes this quite clear; cf. its use with ἐλπίζειν and εἰκός.

ἀσφάλεια . . . ἔσεσθαι: sc. ἔδοξε.

2. τὸ μὲν ἐπιθυμοῦν τοῦ πλοῦ: This unusual form of expression occurs with reference to other emotions: i. 36. 1 τὸ δεδιὸς αὐτοῦ . . . τὸ θαρσοῦν, 'his fear . . . his confidence', vii. 68. 1 and Antiphon ii. γ. 3 τῆς γνώμης τὸ θυμούμενον.

3. τοῖς μὲν γὰρ πρεσβυτέροις κτλ.: Thucydides divides 'everyone alike' into (*a*) 'the older men', (*b*) 'the men of military age', and (*c*) ὁ πολὺς ὅμιλος καὶ στρατιώτης; this, of course, involves cross-division, since anyone in (*c*) must be in either (*a*) or (*b*) also. γάρ introduces the amplification of 'everyone alike'. ὡς = 'in the belief that . . .'. In καὶ εὐέλπιδες κτλ. the construction changes from the dative to the nominative, as in ii. 53. 4 νόμος οὐδεὶς ἀπεῖργε (sc. αὐτούς), τὸ μὲν κρίνοντες κτλ. (= '. . . for they thought . . .').

ὁ δὲ . . . στρατιώτης: 'The mass of the people, including the members of the expedition.' στρατιώτης is a member of a στρατιά, and may be a sailor, not always a soldier. With the words which follow understand 'thought'.

ἀίδιον μισθοφοράν: The greater the imperial revenue (of which tribute was the main item) and the wider the responsibilities of empire, the more would be spent on administration (especially the empanelling of juries) and on the maintenance of fleets at sea. This passage, like Ar. *V*. 684 f., shows that imperial revenue was available for general purposes of state and was not all set aside as a war fund.

Thucydides appears to adopt here the common view of Athenian conservatives that the poor welcome war and (by implication) the rich fear it. This was sometimes true, but not always; τιμή, the enhancement of one's standing in society, was more easily pursued in war than in peace.

4. **κακόνους . . . τῇ πόλει:** 'Unpatriotic', with the overtone 'un-democratic'.

25. 1. **παρελθών τις:** A certain Demostratos, according to Plu. *Nic.* 12. 6; but that may be only an inference from a passage of Aristophanes (*Lys.* 387 ff.) which mentions Demostratos as speaking at some stage in the debates on the expedition.

2. **ὁ δὲ ἄκων μὲν εἶπεν:** δέ refers back, contrasting Nikias with τις, and μέν refers forward, contrasting him with οἱ Ἀθηναῖοι (26. 1); the meaning is something which cannot be said in Greek, *ὁ δὲ μέν.

αὐτῶν δ' Ἀθηναίων . . . εἶναι: This text is plainly unsatisfactory, since it is the Athenian proportion of the whole fleet which matters, not their proportion of the troop-transports. The right reading is provided by Hᶜ (and had already been conjectured by Krüger): αὐτῶν Ἀθηναίων, ὧν ἔσεσθαι κτλ., which requires us to move the position of the brackets: '. . . from Athens itself—of which as many as they thought necessary would be troop-transports—and they must send for others . . .'; a double parenthesis, since ὁπλίταις resumes the construction of τριήρεσι. We see from 31. 3 and 43 that the expedition did in fact comprise one hundred Athenian triremes, of which forty were troop-transports, and thirty-six allied ships. On the nature of 'troop-transports' cf. 31. 3 n.

πεντακισχιλίων: The total in fact was 5,100 (43).

ἐκ Κρήτης: Except for a small-scale Athenian intervention in 429 (ii. 85. 5 f.), the Peloponnesian War did not involve Crete; the Cretans who served in the Athenian expedition were mercenaries (vii. 57. 9).

26. 1. **αὐτοκράτορας:** cf. 8. 2 n.
Ἀθηναίοις: Thucydides is reproducing the formula actually used in the decree, and Ἀθηναίοις should not be deleted.

2. **καταλόγους:** The expressions ἐκ καταλόγου (e.g. vii. 16. 1) and ὑπὲρ τὸν κατάλογον (D. xiii. 4), and the antithesis in 43 between hoplites ἐκ καταλόγου and hoplites who were θῆτες (see ad loc.), show that there was a single list (κατάλογος), at the disposal of the board of generals, containing the names of all those who were fit, by virtue of their age and property rating, for service as hoplites. The lists compiled for the purposes of any particular expedition represented a selection from *the* list.

ἀνειλήφει . . . ἑαυτήν: cf. 12. 1 n.
ξυνεχοῦς πολέμου: i.e. the Archidamian War.

MAY–JUNE 415

27–29. Mutilation of the Herms and Profanation of the Mysteries

27. 1. ἐν δὲ τούτῳ: There is no justification, either in Thucydides or in Andokides i (*De Mysteriis*), for the common modern belief that the herms were mutilated *immediately* before the sailing of the expedition.

ἡ τετράγωνος ἐργασία: The characteristic Athenian herm was a small pillar, square in section, topped by a bearded head and adorned on the front with an erect phallos.

τὰ πρόσωπα: The obvious way to mutilate a herm is to knock off the phallos, and Ar. *Lys.* 1094, where some men who enter *membro erecto* are warned ' Mind the Hermokopidai don't see you like that!', shows that this in fact was done. But πρόσωπον means 'face', and although it occasionally, in poetry, has the sense 'façade', Thucydides can hardly have used the ordinary word for 'face' of a part of a statue other than the statue's face. It is not credible that Thucydides is falsifying the facts in order to avoid an indecent word, especially as he was under no obligation to specify in what respect the herms were damaged. Possible explanations are: (i) The mutilators damaged both the face and the phallos, where there was a phallos to damage; but wear and tear is likely to have deprived most herms of their phalloi very early in their lives. (ii) By the end of the fifth century herms without erect phalloi were coming into fashion—there are some archaeological grounds for thinking that this was the case—and the mutilation of the face was felt to be a much more serious sacrilege.

2. ἀδεῶς: = 'with ἄδεια', a guarantee of immunity from prosecution.

3. οἰωνός: An omen, as a rule, either symbolizes a future event or gives an indication (recognized sometimes by everybody, at other times only by a professional seer) of the wishes and mood of the gods. The mutilation of herms was not an omen in either of these senses, but it was an event regarded as affecting the success of the expedition. If the gods were offended by the action of some members of the community, they might punish the whole community, especially if the real offenders were not found and punished by the community itself; this was especially important on the eve of a naval expedition, for the belief that it was dangerous to sail in the same ship as a man guilty of impiety was one of the strongest of Greek superstitions.

ἐπὶ ξυνωμοσίᾳ . . . γεγενῆσθαι: Why an oligarchic conspiracy should advertise itself by mutilating statues is not immediately clear to us, especially since (28. 1) statues *could* be mutilated 'by young men in

drunken sport', in those days as now; and according to Plu. *Alc.* 18. 8
(source unknown) some people regarded even the wholesale mutilation
of the herms as mere drunken vandalism. But Andokides, who was
deeply implicated in the mutilation, throws a little light on it by saying
(i. 67) that it was suggested as a πίστις in the club of well-to-do young
men to which he belonged, i.e. as a concerted crime which would bind
together the members of the club by putting them all in each other's
power. Clubs of this kind were not necessarily 'political', in the sense
of seriously contemplating revolution; the members of a club did, however, support one another in political life. In so far as νόμος, to the
ordinary fifth-century Athenian, embraced not only the code of laws
and the inherited constitution (democracy) but also social custom and
traditional religious observances (cf. 15. 4 n.), a man guilty of παρανομία
in any of these spheres was automatically suspected in the others also.

28. 1. ἀπὸ μετοίκων τέ τινων κτλ.: According to And. i. 11 f., 15, 34 f.,
embodying documents of unquestionable authenticity, the most important of the informers, the metic Teukros, did name certain men as
guilty of mutilating the herms, as well as others who had profaned the
mysteries (v. infra), although the slave who first gave information
about the mysteries gave none about the herms. Thucydides is therefore misleading in saying 'information from certain metics and slaves—
nothing about the herms . . .'; the rhetorical point underlying what he
says becomes apparent in 53. 2, where he emphasizes that many good
men were arrested on evidence from unworthy sources.

καὶ τὰ μυστήρια . . . ἐφ' ὕβρει: At an assembly held when the expedition was almost ready to sail (And. i. 11 f.) Alkibiades and others
were dramatically denounced for parodying mysteries in private
houses; the immediate source of information was a slave. Subsequently
further information was given by the metic Teukros, by a woman, and
by another slave.

2. ἐμποδὼν ὄντι σφίσι . . . προεστάναι: Thucydides often represents
Athenian political life as a competition for προστασία; this is especially
prominent in his survey (ii. 65. 11) of Athenian politics after the death
of Perikles, and in his remarks (viii. 89. 3) on the weakness of oligarchies.
Here there is an interesting difference in that he treats Alkibiades'
enemies as a group temporarily suspending their mutual rivalries in
order to combine against Alkibiades. Only two of these men are
identifiable: Androkles, a member of the Council and 'as responsible as
anyone for driving Alkibiades into exile' (viii. 65. 2, cf. And. i. 27), and—
a strange ally for a demagogue, but an indication that opposition to
Alkibiades came from more than one quarter—Thessalos, son of Kimon
(Plu. *Alc.* 19. 3, 22. 4). Peisandros, almost certainly the opportunist who

engineered the oligarchic revolution of 411, raised to 10,000 drachmai the reward offered for information on the profanation of the mysteries (And. i. 27), but we know nothing of his previous relations with Alkibiades.

μετ' ἐκείνου: As is clear both from Thucydides and from the narrative and the documents of And. i, Alkibiades was not accused of mutilating herms; the idea that he was grew up during the fourth century, by a natural enough process. The allegation to which Thucydides refers was simply that he was 'behind' the mutilations, in the sense that they were a manifestation of the same movement as the profanation of the mysteries.

ἐπιλέγοντες . . . παρανομίαν: The fact that Alkibiades flouted convention was treated as evidence that he also despised the democratic constitution; cf. 27. 3 n. δημοτικός describes not only a man's loyalty to the democratic constitution but also his treatment of his fellow citizens as equals; so X. *Mem.* i. 2. 60 describes Sokrates as δημοτικὸς καὶ φιλάνθρωπος.

29. 1. **κρίνεσθαι, εἴ τι . . . ἦν**: 'To be tried, to establish whether he had committed any of these acts.'

καὶ εἰ μέν . . . ἄρχειν: 'And (he was ready), if he had committed any of these acts, to be punished, or, if he were acquitted, to hold his command.' The latter part of the sentence represents the *oratio recta*: ἑτοῖμός εἰμι, ἐὰν ἀπολυθῶ, ἄρχειν while the former represents: ἑτοῖμός εἰμι, εἴ τι τούτων εἴργασμαι, δίκην δοῦναι.

2. **καὶ ὅτι κτλ.**: sc. 'he said'.

3. **δεδιότες . . . ἔχῃ**: 'Fearing that he might have the expeditionary force well disposed (sc. to him).' This reading is recorded as a variant by Σᴹ, whose paraphrase points to something rather different: . . . μὴ εὔνουν οὐκ ᾖ, '. . . that the expeditionary force might not be well disposed (sc. to them)'; but in the context we would more naturally expect 'well disposed' to mean 'well disposed *to the accused*'.

The nature of the Greek state normally precluded a difference of allegiance between 'civilians' and 'the army'; but in the present case, if the soldiers and sailors who were going on the expedition had been listed at an early stage of the preparations, there had been time for them to acquire a unity of spirit and interest.

θεραπεύων ὅτι κτλ.: 'Protecting his interests, because . . .'

δι' ἐκεῖνον: Because of his personal influence at Argos and with friends of Argos, dating from his efforts to create an anti-Spartan alliance in the Peloponnese after the Peace of Nikias.

καὶ τῶν Μαντινέων τινές: Mantinea, when we last heard of her (v. 81. 1), had unwillingly come to terms with Sparta. The Mantineans who went to Sicily with the Athenians are classified as mercenaries in 43 and vii. 57. 9, but no doubt there were also some (τινες here) who came as volunteers with the connivance of their city.

πλεῖν . . . μὴ κατασχεῖν . . . κρίνεσθαι: The infinitive after a verb meaning 'say' may represent the imperative of direct speech.

ἐν ἡμέραις ῥηταῖς: '*Within* a prescribed period', sc. from receipt of the summons.

μετάπεμπτον κομισθέντα: Neither word is superfluous, since κομισθῆναι can be used of voluntary action or as a true passive; hence 'returning under summons'.

JUNE 415

30–32. 2. Departure of the Expedition

30. 1. θέρους μεσοῦντος ἤδη: i.e. after the middle period of the summer had begun. Cf. 1. 1 n.

ἐς Κέρκυραν: The natural place to assemble, since (i) Kerkyra was an ally, (ii) from Kerkyra to Iapygia was the only stage of the journey which would be out of sight of land, and (iii) this stage was the natural boundary between the Aegean world and the Western Greeks; cf. 13. 1.

ἐπὶ ἄκραν 'Ιαπυγίαν: The tip of the 'heel' of Italy.

τὸν 'Ιόνιον: sc. κόλπον; cf. 13. 1 n.

2. οἱ μὲν ἐπιχώριοι: μέν looks forward to οἱ δὲ ξένοι in 31. 1.

τὰ μὲν . . . ὄψοιντο: ⟨In the expectation⟩ that they would conquer Sicily'—this explains ἐλπίδος—'but ⟨wondering⟩ whether they would see their men ⟨again⟩'—this explains ὀλοφυρμῶν. 'See' in Greek often implies 'see *again*', just as 'come' often implies 'come *back*'.

31. 1. τῇ παρούσῃ ῥώμῃ . . . ἀνεθάρσουν: lit., 'with the present strength, because of the quantity of each category which they saw, at the sight they took heart'. ῥώμη cannot here mean 'confidence' or 'energy' (as it does, e.g., in vii. 18. 2), for Thucydides is not speaking of a handful of doubters but of the spectators as a whole, and he has just described them as apprehensive; and if he meant the confidence of the soldiers and sailors who were leaving, διὰ τὸ πλῆθος κτλ. would be a *different* reason for the spectators' taking heart and would thus have to be co-ordinated with ῥώμη by a conjunction. On the other hand, if he means by ῥώμη 'material strength', διὰ τὸ πλῆθος κτλ. seems tautologous; and in either case the attachment of two different 'causal' datives to 'they took heart', ῥώμη and ὄψει, is stylistically objectionable. This last objection would be easily removed by punctuating after ὄψει, not after ἑώρων: '. . . which they saw with sight' = 'which they saw with their own eyes'; cf. iii. 112. 4 οὐ καθορωμένους τῇ ὄψει, [Lys.] vi. 51 εἶπε τῇ φωνῇ = 'spoke out loud'. The other difficulties remain, and the least unsatisfactory solution is to accept διὰ τὸ πλῆθος . . . τῇ ὄψει as Thucydides' own amplification of the otherwise ambiguous expression τῇ παρούσῃ ῥώμῃ : 'through the *strength* around them — ⟨I mean⟩, because of the *quantity* . . .'

παρασκευὴ γάρ . . . ἐγένετο: lit., 'for this (force), (as) a force having sailed out of one city with Greek strength, (was the) first (which) was more expensive and splendid than any of those up to that time'. The point is clear enough : no previous force sailing from a single Greek city had been as splendid as this (presumably the mid-century armadas, e.g. the 200 ships sent to Cyprus in 460/459 [i. 104. 2], assembled in the theatre of war and did not 'sail from one city', unless perhaps Thucydides is misleading us in his love of exaggeration). But Thucydides appears to have run together two alternative ways of saying that : 'this was more splendid . . .' and 'this was the first to be so splendid . . .'. Sense is restored by Dobree's addition of ἡ before πρώτη : 'this first force (as a force), having sailed . . . was more . . .'; cf. 44. 1, where the force is referred to as ἡ πρώτη παρασκευή, to distinguish it from the reinforcement, on a comparable scale, which was sent in 413.

2. ἡ ἐς Ἐπίδαυρον: Perikles took this force out in the summer of 430 (ii. 56), ravaging places in the north-east Peloponnese ; Hagnon and Kleopompos relieved him and took it to Poteidaia later in the summer (ii. 58).

ξυνέπλευσαν: This does duty both for the 'sailed' required with τετράκις γάρ . . . πεντήκοντα and for the 'sailed with them' required with 'and many allies besides'.

3. παρασκευῇ φαύλῃ: Whereas παρασκευή in § 1 meant 'force' (cf. 1. 1), here it must mean 'equipment', covering both supplies and supporting arms.

κατ' ἀμφότερα: Specified by καὶ ναυσὶ καὶ πεζῷ.

τὸ μὲν ναυτικὸν κτλ.: τὸ μὲν ναυτικόν . . . ἐκπονηθέν and τὸ δὲ πεζόν . . . ἁμιλληθέν are in apposition to ὁ στόλος (sc. ὡρμήθη) . . . ἐξαρτυθείς, and represent an exhaustive division of ὁ στόλος. τοῦ μὲν δημοσίου . . . καὶ τῷ ταχυναυτεῖν is an amplification of μεγάλαις . . . ἐκπονηθέν, τοῦ μὲν δημοσίου picking up τῆς πόλεως and τῶν ⟨δὲ⟩ τριηράρχων picking up τῶν τριηράρχων.

τῶν τε τριηράρχων: A trierarch was a rich man to whom a trireme had been allotted for (i) maintenance and equipment, (ii) enrolment of the crew, and (iii) command at sea ; he was not responsible for building the trireme or for replacing it when it was lost or for paying the crew.

δράχμην: This was a higher rate of pay than was customary later, when Athens was compelled to economize, but not higher than during the previous twenty years; cf. 8. 1 n.

κενάς: Elsewhere in Thucydides νῆες κεναί are ships without men; the point here is that the trierarchs were responsible for engaging the crews.

ὁπλιταγωγούς: Thucydides never tells us how many men a troop-transport (ὁπλιταγωγός or στρατιῶτις) carried or how it differed from a fighting trireme. In 43, where he catalogues the forces sent to Sicily, he does not say how many of the 36 ships provided by the allies were troop-transports. If all of them were, so that 4,400 hoplites (I exclude the epibatai, who are part of the normal complement of a fighting ship) and 1,300 light-armed troops were carried in 40 Athenian and 36 allied transports, each transport carried about 75 soldiers. Plainly a transport cannot have been a normal trireme with a large number of soldiers crammed on board; for if there had been room for the soldiers at all, it would mean that the trireme normally was bigger, heavier, and therefore slower, than it need have been for ordinary fighting. There remain three possibilities:

(i) It could not be used as a fighting trireme at all. In that case, it is strange that on several occasions (e.g. viii. 30. 2, 62. 2), Thucydides mentions that troop-transports were included in a fleet but does not trouble to say how many, and particularly strange that he says nothing at all about troop-transports in describing the reinforcements brought by Demosthenes and Eurymedon in 413 (vii. 42. 1). Of the 110 ships which the Athenians manned for the final battle in the harbour (vii. 60. 4), which represented the total available to them at that time, including those in poor condition (vii. 60. 2), a proportion must have come to Sicily as troop-transports.

(ii) It was a normal trireme with a skeleton crew of sailors and a full complement of soldiers, who manned the oars, as soldiers on occasion could. This does not account for the use of the terms ὁπλιταγωγός and στρατιῶτις; one would expect, e.g., 'the troops themselves rowed 40 of the ships', using the word αὐτερέται, rather than '40 of the ships were ὁπλιταγωγοί'. Nor does it explain the transfer of the *entire* crew of the *Paralos* to a στρατιῶτις in 411 (viii. 74. 2~86. 9) in order to render them less dangerous.

(iii) It differed structurally from the normal trireme, having an upper deck for the accommodation of soldiers, but was (given time) reconvertible into a fighting ship. This hypothesis accounts for all the passages in which the term is used, as well as those in which we are surprised to find that it is not.

ὑπηρεσίας: The ὑπηρεσία of a trireme was its complement of 'petty officers' and 'tradesmen'; in D. l. 25 al. (misinterpreted by LSJ) a distinction between ὑπηρεσία and ναῦται is consistently made.

θρανίταις: The θρανῖται sat outside the ζύγιοι and, by virtue of the θρᾶνοι after which they were named, slightly above them, while the θαλαμιοί sat with their heads on the level of the seats of the ζύγιοι. The superior status and (on this occasion) extra pay of the θρανῖται were based upon an estimation of their work as harder and more skilled and by their greater exposure to injury in fighting. In Ar. *Ach.* 162 ὁ θρανίτης λεὼς ὁ σωσίπολις are the sailors *par excellence*.

σημείοις: σημεῖα were used in an elementary signalling system— 'raising the σημεῖον' is the signal to attack in i. 49. 1—but the word is also used (e.g. Ar. *Ra.* 933) of devices painted on ships purely for show.

προθυμηθέντος . . . προέξει: lit., 'each one man having been zealous how for a man (τινι) himself (αὐτῷ) the ship shall be superior', i.e. 'and each individual trierarch took pains to ensure that his own ship should be superior'.

καταλόγοις τε χρηστοῖς: cf. 26. 2 n. A 'good' list is a list which includes all the men who were fit for hoplite service, and them alone; a bad list would include men who were poor, disabled, exiled, dead, or fictitious, and exclude men who were fit and available.

4. **ἔριν:** 'Rivalry', the beneficial one of Hesiod's two ἔριδες.

ἐπίδειξιν . . . εἰκασθῆναι: 'It was *as if* a display . . . *were being made* . . .'; here, as commonly in other authors, εἰκάζειν = 'represent' or 'portray', and not, as usually in Thucydides, 'infer' or 'conjecture'. No one would have been so silly as to 'conjecture' that the expedition was only a display and did not mean business.

5. **δημοσίαν:** The word-order is highly suspect, and δημοσίαν should be deleted as a gloss on τῆς πόλεως; cf. viii. 23. 5, where B has τὸν ἑαυτοῦ στρατὸν πεζὸν ἀναλαβών and the other MSS., together with a papyrus, omit πεζόν.

καὶ τριήραρχος ἐς τὴν ναῦν . . . καὶ κτλ.: 'Both, if he was a trierarch, on his ship, and . . .'

ἐπὶ μεταβολῇ: lit., 'with a view to exchange', i.e. 'for trade'.

πολλὰ ἂν τάλαντα: This seems to us as striking anticlimax, but πολλὰ τάλαντα suggests to a Greek 'a vast sum of money'; cf. Ar. *Nu.* 1065 f. 'Hyperbolos has gained πλεῖν ἢ τάλαντα πολλά', i.e. '. . . a whole fortune'.

6. **στρατιᾶς . . . ὑπερβολῇ:** lit., 'by excess of forces in relation to ⟨those against⟩ whom they were proceeding'. It was evidently Alkibiades' view of the Siceliots which prevailed at this moment, not Nikias'; cf. Athenian hopes of 'subjugating Sicily' (iv. 65. 3) with a far less imposing force ten years earlier, and the assumptions which Nikias attacks in 20–25.

πρὸς τὰ ὑπάρχοντα: 'In relation to their existing possessions'; the point is that no state had ever before aimed at acquiring *so great an increase on* what it had already.

32. 1. ὑπὸ κήρυκος: i.e. one herald spoke for them all.

οἵ τε ἐπιβάται: 'The soldiers on board'; the term is used of whatever categories of troops on board a ship are spoken of in the context, and not always of the particular category mentioned in 43 (q.v.).

2. εἴ τις ἄλλος 'And all others who . . .'; unlike 'if', εἰ is not always sceptical.

ἤδη: 'Then' or 'thereafter', contrasted with τὸ πρῶτον.

32. 3–41. Debate at Syracuse

32. 3. *The News Comes to Syracuse*

32. 3. ἐλέχθησαν τοιοίδε λόγοι ἀπό τε ἄλλων . . . καὶ Ἑρμοκράτης . . . ἔλεγε . . . τοιάδε: lit., 'speeches were made by others . . . and Hermokrates . . . spoke . . . to the following effect', i.e. 'speeches were made, and in particular Hermokrates . . . spoke . . .' The meaning of τοιοίδε is obscure. When τοιόσδε refers forwards, it immediately, or almost immediately, precedes the subject of reference (cf. τοιάδε at the end of the sentence); it is therefore unlikely that Thucydides means 'speeches of the kinds which I will illustrate', referring to the whole content of 33–41. The alternative explanation is that τοιοίδε refers back, 'to that effect', i.e. 'speeches of the kind we should expect, given that the news was brought but for a long time was not believed'. Cf. A. *Ch.* 480 κἀγώ . . . τοιάδε, lit. 'and I am such', i.e. 'I make the same prayer', and Pi. *P.* 4. 156 ἔσομαι τοῖος, lit. 'I will be such', i.e. 'I will do as you ask'.

Ἑρμοκράτης ὁ Ἕρμωνος: This man was the moving spirit of the conference at Gela in 424, when the Siceliot states made peace among themselves and left the Athenian force then in Sicily no pretext for further intervention (iv. 58 ff.). We know nothing of his career before that time. His enemy Athenagoras (36 ff.) treats him as an oligarchic conspirator, but we are under no obligation to believe Athenagoras. In 412 Hermokrates came to the Aegean as one of the commanders of a Syracusan contingent helping the Peloponnesians; sentence of exile fell on him when the Syracusan democracy came under the control of the democratic extremists, but Xenophon represents him (*HG* i. 1. 28) as ostentatiously correct in accepting this sentence.

33–34. *Speech of Hermokrates*

33. 1. ἄπιστα μέν: μέν may look forward to εἰ δέ τῳ καὶ πιστά in § 4; but in the opening words of a speech μέν is not always answered by a subsequent δέ.

2. ξυμμαχίᾳ . . . κατοικίσει . . . ἐπιθυμίᾳ: '. . . because of their alliance with Segesta, and in order to re-establish Leontinoi, but in fact because they desire Sicily.' The dative κατοικίσει is a little strained—ἐπί . . . κατοικίσει would be normal—for the sake of conformity with the other two datives, which have a familiar sense.

3. τοῦ ξύμπαντος: If they despise the Athenians, they will take inadequate precautions; if they disbelieve the news, they will take none; hence τοῦ ξύμπαντος = 'everything' (cf. τοῦ παντός in 40. 1).

4. εἰ δέ τῳ καὶ πιστά: 'If anyone does believe the news'; cf. § 1 n.

οὔθ' . . . ἀνωφελεῖς: lit., 'nor ⟨are they⟩ to our disadvantage'; we would say 'nor is it to our disadvantage'. Cf. 84. 3, where 'the Chalkidian is to our advantage being unarmed'='it is to our advantage that the Chalkidians are unarmed'.

μᾶλλον γάρ . . . ξυμμαχεῖν: cf. § 5, πάντα γὰρ . . . ξυνίσταται. Both Hermokrates and Athenagoras (37. 2) take it for granted that the Siceliots will unite if Syracuse is threatened by Athens. In this they were too optimistic, just as the Athenians were too optimistic about their own chances of uniting Sicily against Syracuse. What is surprising is that no reference is made to the events of 424, which might have provided Syracuse with reasonable grounds for optimism in 415 (contrast Nikias' foreboding in 21. 1). Thucydides almost certainly wrote his account of the conference at Gela after the Sicilian expedition of 415 had taken place, for otherwise his Hermokrates' reference (iv. 60. 1) to the Athenian fleet present in Sicily in 424 as 'a few ships' is inexplicable; sixty is not 'a few' except by contrast with a quite extraordinary expedition. The silence of the Syracusan speakers on the events of 424 in the present debate may justify us in going a stage farther: Thucydides turned his attention to the conference at Gela, and wrote iv. 58–65, *after* he wrote vi. 32. 3–41.

6. ὅπερ . . . ηὐξήθησαν: lit., 'and this increase they were increased', i.e. 'and this was their glory'.

τοῦ Μήδου . . . σφαλέντος: The disastrous expedition of Xerxes illustrates the generalization of § 5; cf. i. 69. 5 (Corinthian speaker at Sparta): 'most of the barbarian's setbacks were of his own making.'

34. 1. ἐς τοὺς Σικελούς: Many Sikel tribes were in fact subject to Syracuse; they are the βαρβάρων τινῶν of 20. 4.

πέμπωμεν πρέσβεις: These embassies, and those advocated later by the general (41. 4), were not undertaken until the end of the campaigning season (73. 2, 75. 3), when Athenian superiority in the field had been demonstrated. There was much latent hostility to Syracuse in Sicily, and the Syracusans may have decided that to ask for help too soon might only hearten their enemies.

ξυμμαχίαν ποιώμεθα ἡμῖν: We cannot import an alien idiom from modern European languages and translate 'make . . . for ourselves'; ἡμῖν must therefore go with ξυμμαχίαν, the sense being ἵνα ξυμμάχους ἡμῖν ποιῶμεν αὐτούς. Cf. E. El. 1229 φονέας ἔτικτες ἀρά σοι, and 57. 2 infr. τῶν ξυνωμοτῶν σφίσι.

2. ἐς Καρχηδόνα: There is no evidence that Syracuse made any approach to Carthage; the Athenians did.

ἄμεινον: cf. 9. 1 n.

οὐ γὰρ ἀνέλπιστον αὐτοῖς: sc. a threat from Athens. We do not know whether Hermokrates' statement about Carthaginian fears is true.

τάδε: 'Sicily.'

ἢ ἐξ ἑνός γέ του τρόπου: 'Secretly' and 'openly' are exhaustive alternatives, as ΣM observes; but bad logic may be good rhetoric. Cf. E. IT 895 ff. 'what god or mortal or what unexpected thing . . .?'

δυνατοὶ δέ εἰσι: sc. ἀμῦναι ἡμῖν.

4. ὅμως: i.e. in spite of the unlikelihood that you will do it.

οὐ περὶ τῆς Σικελίας . . . τὸν Ἰόνιον: lit., 'that the contest will not be about Sicily before ⟨it is about⟩ their crossing of the Ionian sea'. The MSS. have περὶ τῇ Σικελίᾳ, which is appropriate with ἀγών, cf. Pl. Prt. 313 E μὴ περὶ τοῖς φιλτάτοις . . . κινδυνεύῃς. As for the genitive, ἀγών . . . τοῦ περαιωθῆναι, cf. S. Aj. 1239 f. τῶν Ἀχιλλείων ὅπλων ἀγῶνας, 'contests for the arms of Achilles'.

Τάρας: Hermokrates' confidence in the sympathy of Taras seems to have been justified; cf. 44. 2.

εἴη: sc. ἡ παρασκευή.

5. εἰ δ' αὖ . . . προσβάλοιεν: 'If, on the other hand, they disembarrassed themselves (sc. of merchant ships and transports) and attacked with their fast warships concentrated.' κουφίζειν is intransitive here, as (in different senses) in poetry and Ionic prose.

εἰ δὲ μὴ δοκοίη: The logic of antithesis suggests at first sight that this refers to an Athenian decision: 'if they decided not ⟨to use oars⟩', i.e. to sail across. But it is possible for μὲν / δέ to contrast not the two protases but the two complexes, and the point of the argument is much stronger if εἰ δὲ μὴ δοκοίη refers to a Siceliot decision: 'if we decided not', i.e. not to attack them. The unemphatic position of ἡμῖν in the next clause is also in favour of this interpretation; not 'we, for our part, can retire into Taras', but 'it is open to us . . .'.

τὰ τῶν πόλεων . . . εἰ ὑποδέξοιντο: 'Not being assured of the attitude of the cities (sc. along the coast), not knowing whether they would receive them.'

6. **τούτῳ τῷ λογισμῷ**: With ἀποκληρομένους; cf. ἐς λογισμὸν καταστήσαιμεν in § 4. Hermokrates is sanguine. At this time no Siceliot state had a fleet comparable with the Athenian in experience and efficiency, and even if there had been time (as there was not) to put Hermokrates' plan into effect its probable outcome would have been the destruction of the Siceliot fleets and the rapid subjugation of South Italy and Sicily by Athens. The sheer impracticability of the plan has an important bearing on the question of the essential authenticity of the Thucydidean speeches; if Thucydides made them all up, why did he attribute this plan to the man who was later the driving force behind the Syracusan victory?

ὡς ἐγὼ ἀκούω: The volume of maritime traffic throughout the eastern Mediterranean must have ensured that the gossip of every port was soon known in every other.

7. **ἀγγελλοίμεθα δ' ἄν . . . ἐπὶ τὸ πλέον**: lit., 'we would be reported . . . on to the more', i.e. 'our strength would be exaggerated in the reports'.

καὶ τοὺς προεπιχειροῦντας . . . πεφόβηνται: ἤ = 'or', and with μᾶλλον understand ἤ τοὺς μὴ τοῦτο ποιοῦντας.

ἰσοκινδύνους: lit., 'having equal danger', i.e. 'running no *greater* a risk' (sc. than themselves). ('Equal to the danger' would be an Anglicism quite out of keeping with the ἰσο- compounds in general.)

8. **τῇ ἀπὸ τοῦ ἀληθοῦς δυνάμει**: lit., 'the power based on the truth', i.e. 'our true power'.

9. **καὶ παραστῆναι κτλ.**: πείθεσθε . . . παραστῆναι παντί, 'be so persuaded that everyone realizes . . .' is impossible Greek when thus isolated, but is facilitated here by the intervening ἑτοιμάζειν: 'Do as I suggest, preferably . . . or, failing that, ⟨let me persuade you⟩ to prepare . . . and ⟨let⟩ everyone realize . . .' Then: 'that contempt for the aggressor' (the accusative after καταφρονεῖν is abnormal but not unparalleled) 'is shown . . . but to act now (τὸ δ' ἤδη . . . πράσσειν) . . .'

οἱ δὲ ἄνδρες: 'They', i.e. 'the enemy' or 'our men', according to context, in the language of the battlefield.

35. *Reactions to Hermokrates' Speech*

35. 1. **ὁ δῆμος**: This debate is taking place in the Assembly of the whole Syracusan people, not in any kind of Council.

οἱ μέν: sc. 'saying'.

τοῖς δέ: If this is right, Thucydides' reasons for writing it, rather than οἱ δέ ('and others ⟨asked⟩'), are obscure; the problem is not unlike those of 76. 3 and 77. 2, but harder. Conceivably we are to understand ἔρις ἦν; cf. ii. 54. 3, ἐγένετο . . . ἔρις τοῖς ἀνθρώποις μὴ λοιμὸν ὠνομάσθαι . . . ἀλλὰ λιμόν, 'people contended that the word was not "plague" but "famine" '.

2. Ἀθηναγόρας: We know nothing else about this man. As 'champion of the people', i.e. spokesman of the Left in the Assembly, he makes much of his own role as watchdog and protector of the people against its internal enemies.

36–40. *Speech of Athenagoras*

36. 1. οὐκ εὔνους: Cf. 24. 4 n.

2. τὸν σφέτερον: The MSS. have τό, not τόν, and this may mean (i) 'their own *fear*', understanding δέος from δεδιότες, despite the intervening masculine φόβῳ and the antithesis between κοινῷ and σφέτερον, or (ii) 'their own *purpose*', which is improbable, since τὰ σφέτερα would be normal and here specially desirable to minimize ambiguity. As Σ^M in his paraphrase, Valla in his translation, and the late historian Dexippos in his imitation all adopted (i), they possibly had τόν in their texts. Athenagoras' point is that Hermokrates and his friends are afraid that their anti-democratic plots are about to be 'unmasked' and accordingly try to divert public attention by false reports of an impending Athenian attack.

τοῦτο δύνανται: 'This is the *significance* of these reports'; cf. 40. 2 τοὺς λόγους . . . ὡς ἔργα δυναμένους κρινεῖ. τοῦτο thus refers back to the previous sentence, not forward to the next, which makes a statement about the *origin* of the reports. It is therefore necessary to insert a connective with οὐκ, and Classen's ⟨αἱ⟩ οὐκ is the easiest answer: 'and they . . .'

3. ὥσπερ . . . ἀξιῶ: 'For that is how I rate the Athenians', i.e. as intelligent and experienced people. Cf. E. *El.* 70 ἰατρὸν εὑρεῖν, ὡς ἐγώ σε λαμβάνω.

4. μήπω βεβαίως καταλελυμένους: Athenagoras adopts the same mistrustful view of the peace treaty of 421 as Nikias (10. 2 ff.) and Alkibiades (17. 5).

37. 1. οἷς γ᾽ ἐπίσταμαι κτλ.: 'Since I understand that no horses will be coming with them . . .' For the purposes of this argument Athenagoras treats the report as true.

ἐπὶ νεῶν γε ἐλθόντας: 'Considering that they will have come by sea.'

τήν τε ἄλλην . . . οὖσαν: τε co-ordinates this generalization with the particular statement οὔθ᾽ ἵππους κτλ. The punctuation of the Oxford

Text is defective; either there should be no comma after πορισθῆναι or another comma after παρασκευήν.

2. **παρὰ τοσοῦτον**: 'By so large a margin' or 'by so small a margin', according to context; here almost 'I will go so far as to say'.

μόλις ἄν μοι δοκοῦσιν . . . διαφθαρῆναι: 'I think it would be hard for them to escape total destruction.'

πόλιν . . . οἰκίσαντες: cf. Nikias' words in 23. 2: 'you must think of us as going to found a city in an alien land.'

σκηνιδίων: The diminutive is contemptuous.

38. 2. **αὐτούς . . . ἄρχειν**: The procedure which Athenagoras has in mind here and in 40. 2 is (i) establishing a reputation for sagacity and patriotism by giving timely warning of an impending danger, (ii) being elected to office with special powers to deal with the danger, (iii) using such office to establish one's own rule. The circumstances in which Dionysios, not long afterwards, obtained tyrannical power had something in common with this process.

μήποτε: = μή ποτε, and better printed as two words. In later Greek μήποτε = 'perhaps'.

κακοί . . . προφυλάξασθαι: 'Bad at taking precautions', as in S. *OT* 545 μανθάνειν . . . κακός.

3. **τυραννίδας δὲ ἔστιν ὅτε**: Since the Deinomenid tyranny at Syracuse ended over fifty years before, Athenagoras is abusing history rather as Alkibiades did in saying of the Siceliots (17. 2) 'their cities are full of a medley of peoples'. Conceivably Thucydides composed this speech after Dionysios had established himself as tyrant in 406, and did not reflect that 'sometimes tyrannies' would be a strange thing for a Syracusan speaker to say in 415. More probably, however, he classifies as 'tyrannies' the troubles caused by a certain Tyndaridas in 454 (Diod. xi. 86 f.).

δυναστείας: The exercise of unconstitutional power by a group.

4. **μὴ μόνον . . . προπείσεται**: These words constitute a parenthesis, within which there are two minor parentheses.

εἴπερ καὶ μὴ κτλ.: 'Since (εἴπερ) if a man takes no precautions in time he will be worsted before he can take any.'

τοὺς δ' αὖ ὀλίγους: As the text stands, there are three separate categories : (*a*) 'you, the people', (*b*) 'those who design plots like these', and (*c*) 'the few'. But (*b*) are part of (*c*); and δ' αὖ in Thucydides is used with the second of two alternatives, not with the third of three. There is therefore much to be said for Weil's emendation : delete δέ in line 5, change κολάζων to κολάζειν, and do not punctuate after πείθων.

Then: 'persuading you, the people, to punish those who contrive . . . and accusing, watching, or admonishing the upper class.'

5. τί καὶ βούλεσθε: 'What do you *want*?', with a rhetorical affectation of impatient bewilderment.

ὦ νεώτεροι: Hermokrates himself cannot have been young at this time, for he had been chosen as an envoy to the conference at Gela nine years earlier, and the Greeks tended always to choose older men for such an office; but Athenagoras finds it politically advantageous to treat Hermokrates as the leader of a group of ambitious and irresponsible young men.

ἀλλ' οὐκ ἔννομον: It was normal in Greek states to lay down minimum ages for various offices.

μᾶλλον ἤ: = 'and not', as often in Thucydides.

ἰσονομεῖσθαι: ἰσονομία, the situation in which all have the same rights under the law, is one face of democracy; δημοκρατία, 'power in the hands of the people', is another.

τοὺς αὐτούς: cf. Hdt. iii. 142. 3, where Maiandrios defends ἰσονομίη and attacks tyranny on the grounds that a tyrant is 'master of men who are like himself'.

39. 1. φύλακας μέν . . . τοὺς πλουσίους: Athenagoras is thinking not of the competence of the rich to look after their own property, but of their part in the administration of the state. We may compare the Athenian practice of restricting offices such as that of the Treasurers of Athena to the highest property class.

βουλεῦσαι δ' ἄν . . . τοὺς ξυνετούς: This implies appointment to the Council by election, not by lot; but possibly Athenagoras would not have accepted this implication.

κρῖναι δ' ἄν . . . τοὺς πολλούς: The theory that the mass of the people was best *fitted* to decide issues was traditionally defended on the grounds that the larger the sovereign body, the more completely sectional and private interests would cancel each other out and the more the deficiencies of some individuals would be offset by the capacities of others. The argument that, whether fitted or not, the mass of the people *ought* to decide issues rests partly on the observation that decisions taken on their behalf by a governing class tend to be in the interest of that class (cf. § 2 infra), and partly on the faith that a habit of decision makes a better man than a habit of ignorant obedience (cf. the remarks attributed to Perikles in the Funeral Speech, ii. 40. 2). It may also be argued that poor men, who stand to lose everything (cf. ii. 65. 2), have a right to decide whether or not they shall risk losing it.

καὶ ταῦτα . . . ἰσομοιρεῖν: Whether ταῦτα means 'these three classes' or 'these three capacities' (viz. administration, deliberation, and decision), it is hard to attach any meaning to the distinction between κατὰ μέρη, 'taken separately', and ξύμπαντα, 'all together', and it is possible that Thucydides, whose political sympathies did not lie with people like Athenagoras, is deliberately introducing an element of woolly rhetoric.

2. ἀλλ' ἔτι καὶ νῦν ... τολμᾶτε: lit., 'yet even now, most stupid of all men, if you do not realize that your aims are wrong, you are either the most unintelligent of all Greeks known to me, or the most immoral, if your attempts are made with understanding'. The sequence 'if A, either P, or Q, if B' is un-English but has an affinity with 18. 1 (v. n.). The real difficulty lies in the logical sequence 'Most stupid men, you are either stupid or immoral'; but this difficulty is removed by inserting (as Gomme suggested) γάρ after the first εἰ: 'Most stupid of all men— for if ... you are ... unintelligent, or ... immoral, if ...' Then ἀλλά before ἤτοι resumes the ἀλλά with which the sentence begins, and ἀλλ' ἔτι καὶ νῦν belongs in sense with the imperative αὔξετε. For the repetition of ἀλλά cf. Herodas 1. 20 f. ἀλλ'—οὐ τοῦτο μή σε θερμήνῃ— ἀλλ' ὦ τέκνον κτλ.

40. 1. τοῦτο μὲν ἄν ... στερηθῆναι: Given the antithesis between τοῦτο μέν and εἰ δ' ἄλλα βουλήσεσθε, τοῦτο must mean 'in this way', 'if you do this'; cf. 33. 6 ὅπερ ... ηὐξήθησαν and Pl. *Smp.* 204 A αὐτὸ τοῦτο (= 'in precisely this respect') χαλεπὸν ἀμαθία. οἱ ἀγαθοὶ ὑμῶν is not an afterthought, but is to be taken closely with πλέον, the point being 'those of you who play the game will get a fair share, and those who play it well will get an extra share'. ἤπερ is unique in Attic prose, and it seems likely that Σᴹ, to judge from his paraphrase, had ὧνπερ, not ἤπερ, in his text; this makes excellent sense: 'In the realization that in this way you can have a fair share, and, the good among you, a greater share, *in what* the people of the city ⟨shares⟩.'

2. αὐτά: 'The matter'; cf. 10. 2 al.
ὥσπερ οὐκ οἴομαι: '—and I think it is not—.'
ἐπιτρέπειν: 'Let you do what you like', 'yield to you'. Cf. 15. 4 n.

41. *Speech of the General*

41. 1. ἄλλον μέν ... παρελθεῖν: 'He would not let anyone else come forward' does not necessarily mean that the generals presided over the Assembly and had a constitutional right to close a debate; οὐκ ἐᾶν often means 'urge ... not to ...', 'say that ... ought not to ...', just as κελεύειν often means 'urge', even 'entreat', without any implication of superior authority.

2. πρὸς δέ ... ὁρᾶν: sc. σῶφρόν ἐστι.

3. **οἷς ὁ πόλεμος ἀγάλλεται:** A highly poetic expression, prompted by κοσμηθῆναι ('adorned', 'bedecked'); the credit for it may belong to the general himself and not to Thucydides, for memorable metaphors (such as Perikles' 'the spring is taken out of the year') were remembered and transmitted.

4. **τῶν . . . διαπομπῶν:** The definite article looks back to 34. 1.

τὰ δὲ καὶ ἐπιμεμελήμεθα ἤδη: 'And there are other matters which . . .'; cf. τὰ δέ = 'and apart from that' in iii. 11. 7. The wrong translation 'the latter' (referring to the embassies) has led critics into much needless difficulty here.

JUNE–JULY 415

42–46. The Athenians Sail from Kerkyra to Rhegion

42. 1. **ἐν ἑκάστῳ ἐκλήρωσαν:** For the use of the lot in dividing a command between colleagues of equal authority, cf. 62. 1.

ἅμα πλέοντες: The point of dividing the fleet into smaller units was that the crew of a trireme could not sleep or cook on board, and were thus compelled to land every night. This limitation did not apply to merchant ships.

2. **προαπαντᾶν:** Not before the fleet left Kerkyra, but before it reached the toe of Italy; cf. 44. 4 n.

43. στρατιώτιδες: Thucydides does not tell us how many of the *allied* ships were troop-transports.

πεντηκοντόροιν: The pentekonter (-ερος is the correct spelling) was obsolescent after the invention of the trireme.

Χίων καὶ τῶν ἄλλων ξυμμάχων: After the suppression of the revolt of Mytilene in 427 the only two states in the Athenian Empire left with fleets of their own were Chios and Methymna; cf. 85. 2. 'The other allies' here probably includes ships from Kerkyra and Kephallenia.

θῆτες: The lowest property rating, comprising all those whose capital was too low to enable them to arm themselves as hoplites; they could, however, be armed at the public expense. There were normally ten men equipped as soldiers allocated to each trireme on active service.

Μαντινέων καὶ μισθοφόρων: In vii. 57. 9, where Thucydides catalogues the forces present at the last battle at Syracuse, he makes it clear that the Mantineans were mercenaries, despite their political friendship with Athens; hence here 'Mantineans and other mercenaries'.

Κρῆτες: cf. 25. 2 n.

Ῥοδίων: Rhodes was a subject-ally of Athens. The Rhodians had a great reputation as slingers; cf. X. *An*. iii. 3. 16.

Μεγαρεῦσι ψιλοῖς φυγάσιν: The pro-Athenians in Megara had taken refuge at Athens in 424. 'Exiles' explains 'bare' (i.e. 'without hoplite arms'); exile impoverished them.

ἱππέας: We hear no more of these; in 64. 1 the Athenians have no cavalry.

44. 1. **ἡ πρώτη παρασκευή:** 'First' to distinguish it from the reinforcements of 413.

διέπλει: This should be followed by a comma, not a full stop; understand διέπλεον with τούτοις δὲ κτλ.

τὰ ἐπιτήδεια ἄγουσαι: Contrasted with πρὸς τὸν πόλεμον, which = lit., 'to deal with the fighting', i.e. 'as a fighting force'.

ὁλκάδες μέν ... πλοῖα δέ: Thucydides commonly distinguishes between ὁλκάς and πλοῖον, but the grounds of the distinction are never clear; probably πλοῖον is the less specific word and ὁλκάς is a ship of more than a certain size. Neither word means 'barge' or 'lighter'.

2. **Τάραντος δέ ... οὐδὲ τούτοις:** Taras was consistently hostile (cf. 34. 4); Lokroi had been strongly hostile during the Athenian intervention in the west in 427–424 (v. 5. 2 f.).

3. **Χαλκιδέας ὄντας:** cf. 4. 6 f. on the origins of Rhegion.

ὅτι ἄν ... ξυνδοκῇ: There is no explicit indication that representatives of the Italiot cities met, either regularly or in an emergency, to discuss matters of common interest.

4. **τὰς προπλους ναῦς:** Three in number (46. 1). In 42. 2 we were told that three ships were sent ahead from Kerkyra 'to Italy and Sicily'. Presumably these ships went as far as Rhegion, came back to the fleet as it was sailing along the Italian coast, and were sent off again to Segesta.

45. **ἀπὸ τῶν κατασκόπων:** cf. 41. 4.

ἔνθα μέν ... πρέσβεις: 'To some places ... and to others (sc. of the Sikel tribes) envoys.' Some tribes were under Syracusan control, but many were independent; cf. 88. 4. For demonstrative ὁ governed by a preposition cf. 66. 1 παρὰ δὲ τό.

ἐπὶ ταχεῖ πολέμῳ: 'For a war which would soon be upon them.'

46. 2. **καὶ σφίσιν αἰεὶ ἐπιτηδείους:** Thucydides nowhere mentions the fact that in 433/2 Athens renewed an alliance 'for all time' with Rhegion (*IG* i². 51, *GHI* 58). Presumably Rhegion's attitude of consistent friendliness seemed to Thucydides so much more important

than a formal alliance that he thought it unnecessary, in stating the
former, to mention the latter. Rhegion was obviously now waiting to
see how the situation would develop before she committed herself;
but we know that the Athenians extracted at least 50 talents from her
(*SEG* xvii. 7. 11 f.).

τοῖν δὲ ἑτέροιν καὶ ἀλογώτερα: The comparative is antithetical, of
the type found in (e.g.) **εὖ τε καὶ χεῖρον**: 'To Nikias . . . was expected,
but to the other two it was quite *inexplicable*.'

3. **οἱ πρῶτοι πρέσβεις**: cf. 6. 3, 8. 1.

ἀργυρᾶ: The point must be that the temple at Eryx received dedications from many places besides Segesta; hence the expensive dedications
did not reveal the comparative poverty of the state which controlled
the famous sanctuary. Emendation to **ἐπάργυρα** (Meineke), 'of silver
plate over base metal', or **ὑπάργυρα** (Naber), 'of gold plate over silver',
entails the unlikely hypothesis that the majority of dedications in the
sanctuary were of a peculiar kind.

ἐκπώματα: Gold and silver drinking-vessels were a standard manifestation of wealth in the Greek world.

καὶ Φοινικικῶν καὶ Ἑλληνίδων: The only Greek city 'near' was
Selinus, with which Segesta was at war; and the only Greek city on the
north coast was Himera (62. 2), which was unfriendly to Athens and
unlikely to co-operate in a scheme designed to stimulate Athenian
interest in Sicily. It seems that the story exaggerated 'from everywhere they could' into 'from all the neighbouring cities, Greek and
Phoenician alike', and Thucydides accepted the story in that form. In
extenuation we must remember that an ancient historian, unlike
a modern historian, did not form a mental picture of a map whenever
he heard a place-name.

αἰτησάμενοι: 'Borrowing'; this common usage is not recognized by
LSJ.

4. **παρεῖχε**: The understood subject is the *fact* that they passed round
the goblets; cf. **ἐφαίνετο** in 60. 2.

46. 5–50. 1. Conference of the Athenian Generals

(i) *Sources of Information*. Lamachos was killed in 414, Nikias in 413.
If, therefore, no one but the three generals took part in this conference,
and if Thucydides is not deliberately writing plausible fiction, he had
two possible sources of information: (a) Alkibiades, and (b) anyone to
whom any of the generals may have talked, complacently or com-
plainingly, at the time. Certainly if Thucydides had had the opportunity to learn anything from Alkibiades he would not have let it slip,
but that is not to say that he had such an opportunity before he wrote
this narrative.

(ii) *The Collegiate Principle.* Since there were three generals of equal status, no decision could be taken until at least two of them agreed. Therefore, when each had put forward a different plan, one of them had to withdraw his own plan and support one of the other two. It was in fact Lamachos who withdrew and supported Alkibiades; we do not know whether he was persuaded that Alkibiades was right or simply decided to end the deadlock. He was of lower political standing than either Alkibiades or Nikias, and he may have realized that if his own plan were adopted and failed his career would be at an end.

(iii) *The Three Plans.* Nikias and Alkibiades both put forward plans consistent with their arguments before the Assembly; Nikias aims at a limited objective, avoiding direct conflict with Syracuse unless a favourable opportunity to help Leontinoi presents itself, and not 'wasting' Athenian money (cf. 10. 5, 12. 1, 22 f.), while Alkibiades is confident that other states can be persuaded to join them (cf. 17. 4). Lamachos strikes a note which we have not heard before; to him the problem is one of military tactics, not of finance or diplomacy or even of strategy.

(iv) *Thucydides' Opinion.* Most readers of Thucydides feel that Lamachos is right. Nikias is simply dishonest in pretending that Selinus is the main objective; he could fall back on the actual words of the Athenian decision (8. 2), but Thucydides represents him as recognizing, in the letter which he wrote to the Assembly at the end of 414, that Syracuse was the objective (vii. 11. 2). Alkibiades' plan, when tried, proved unsuccessful. But Lamachos' prediction that Syracusan morale would rise if the Athenian attack on the city were delayed was apparently fulfilled (63. 2). There is some reason to think that Thucydides may have sympathized with Lamachos; for in vii. 42. 3, in describing the situation as it was when Demosthenes and Eurymedon arrived with reinforcements in 413, he expresses in parenthesis his own view that speed was all-important and that Nikias (he should have said, Nikias and Lamachos) ought to have pressed at once the advantage gained by their victory in the autumn of 415. It is not, however, an absolutely certain inference from this that Thucydides believed that the Athenians should have landed at Syracuse in force—as Lamachos wanted them to—*before* the autumn of 415 or that Alkibiades was mistaken in attaching importance to the winning of allies in the West.

47. *Nikias' Opinion*

48. *Alkibiades' Opinion*

48. ἦν μὴ κτλ.: Strictly speaking Alkibiades is making the attack on Selinus and Syracuse conditional on their refusal to fulfil certain

demands. These demands, however, are not trivial, and their accep-
tance would be an acknowledgement of defeat; cf. Perikles' insistence
that the Athenians could not afford to avert the Peloponnesian War by
yielding to Sparta's demand for the rescinding of the Megarian Decree
(i. 140. 4–141. 1).

ἐν πόρῳ γάρ ... τῆς Σικελίας: 'Where ships cross and land in
Sicily.'

49. Lamachos' Opinion

49. 1. ἄντικρυς: With πλεῖν, 'straight', not with ἔφη, 'outright'.

2. πείσονται: sc. οἱ Συρακόσιοι.

4. ἐφορμηθέντας: Neither the aorist passive of ἐφορμᾶν ('having been
impelled') nor that of ἐφορμεῖν ('having been blockaded') makes sense;
the simplest emendation is ἐφορμισθέντας (Schaefer), 'having anchored
off it'. The text of H at this point is not legible, but it does not seem
to have had ἐφορμηθέντας.

JULY 415

50. 1–53. The Athenians at Katane; the Recall of Alkibiades

50. 1–51. Messene, Naxos, Katane

50. 1. τῇ αὐτοῦ νηί: Literally his own (cf. 61. 6). His great-grandfather
Kleinias similarly owned the ship in which he fought at Artemision.

2. ἐκ πασῶν: i.e. without regard for the three divisions in which the
fleet had sailed.

ἕνα σφῶν αὐτῶν: It is curious that Thucydides does not say which
one; it was not Alkibiades, as we see from 51. 1. Cf. the similar—and
equally inexplicable—reticence in 100. 1.

3. δεξαμένων τῇ πόλει: Money was raised from Naxos, as we know
from *SEG* xvii. 7. 1 f.

τὰ Συρακοσίων βουλόμενοι: 'Partisans of Syracuse.'

4. Τηρίαν: Now Fiume di San Leonardo.

τὰς ἄλλας: The original sixty minus the ten mentioned in the next
clause.

τοὺς οὖν ὄντας ... ἀπιέναι: This accusative and infinitive represents
what would have been either accusative and infinitive or nominative
and imperative in the proclamation.

51. 1. κακῶς: With ἐνῳκοδομημένην.

2. **ξυμμαχίαν**: Katane also contributed something over 30 talents (*SEG* xvii. 7. 7 f.).

52. *Kamarina*

52. 1. τὰ ὅρκια . . . μεταπέμπωσιν: The reference is to the treaty which Laches made with Kamarina in 427–425 (first mentioned in 75. 3 infra); Kamarina must have sworn on that occasion that she would always receive a single Athenian ship, while the Athenians for their part swore that they would not attempt to bring in more than one except at Kamarina's own request. The reference cannot possibly be either to the undertaking which Sparta in 431 requested from her friends in the West (ii. 7. 2) or to the treaty of Gela, for a declaration by Kamarina 'I will not receive more than one Athenian ship unless I have asked for more' would have been no use to anyone.

53. *Recall of Alkibiades*

53. 1. Σαλαμινίαν: The *Salaminia* and *Paralos* were based at Peiraieus and were used for purposes of state.

ὡς κελεύσοντας: The ship is not unnaturally treated as masculine plural.

ἐπ' ἄλλους τινάς . . . περὶ τῶν Ἑρμῶν: 'Some other members of the expedition who were among those who had been informed against as committing impieties, some of them with Alkibiades in connexion with the mysteries and others in connexion with the herms.' It would have been clearer, but clumsier, if Thucydides had written . . . στρατιωτῶν, τοὺς μὲν τῶν μετ' αὐτοῦ περὶ τῶν μυστηρίων ὡς ἀσεβούντων μεμηνυμένων γενομένους, τοὺς δὲ τῶν καὶ περὶ τῶν Ἑρμῶν μεμηνυμένων.

2. **πάντα ὑπόπτως ἀποδεχόμενοι**: Not 'receiving everything suspiciously', i.e. being reluctant to accept anything, but 'in their readiness to suspect ⟨the men accused⟩ accepting every accusation'.

πονηρῶν ἀνθρώπων: Cf. 28, 1 n.

τινά: This is the subject of διαφυγεῖν and does not agree with πονηρίαν.

54–59. The End of the Tyranny at Athens

Family Tree of the Peisistratidai according to Thucydides

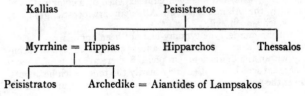

Kallias   Peisistratos

Myrrhine = Hippias   Hipparchos   Thessalos

Peisistratos   Archedike = Aiantides of Lampsakos

Chronology of the Life of Hippias

528/7 (?)	Death of Peisistratos. Hippias inherits his power as tyrant.
526/5	Hippias holds eponymous archonship.
522/1	Hippias' son Peisistratos holds eponymous archonship.
514, late summer	Hipparchos murdered by Harmodios and Aristogeiton.
513 or 512	Hippias' daughter Archedike marries Aiantides of Lampsakos.
511/10	Hippias and his children expelled from Athens; they go to Persia.
490	Hippias accompanies Persian expedition against Athens; Persians defeated at Marathon.
Soon after 490	Hippias dies.

Thucydides' Contentions. In i. 20. 1 f., speaking of the unreliability of tradition, Thucydides says: 'Most people at Athens think that Hipparchos was tyrant when he was killed by Harmodios and Aristogeiton, and they do not know that Hippias, as the eldest of the sons of Peisistratos, was reigning, while Hipparchos and Thessalos were his brothers, and that Harmodios and Aristogeiton, suspecting that their plot' (sc. to kill Hippias) '. . . had been given away, killed Hipparchos when they came upon him . . . marshalling the Panathenaic procession.' Now Thucydides devotes six chapters to expounding in detail his version of the famous story of the tyrannicides and the end of the tyranny at Athens. This long digression has only a marginal relevance to the main narrative of Book VI, and it is marked by a strongly polemical tone. Its four chief contentions are:

A. When Hipparchos was killed not he, but Hippias, was the reigning tyrant.

B. The murder did not originate in any determination on the part of the Athenians to rid themselves of tyranny, but was the accidental product of an emotional relationship between Hipparchos, Harmodios, and Aristogeiton.

C. The murder did not end the tyranny, for Hippias reigned for a further three years, and was eventually expelled by a combination of Sparta with the Alkmeonidai, an Athenian aristocratic group of families which was in exile.

D. Until the murder, the tyranny had not been oppressive.

Internal Consistency. On points C and D there is no sign of inconsistency within the digression. On point B there are parts of Thucydides' account which do not entirely justify the tone which he adopts. Whatever the reason for Aristogeiton's emotion, he and Harmodios did after all plan *the overthrow of the tyranny*, not mere personal revenge on Hipparchos; and it was presumably in the overthrow that their fellow conspirators were interested. Thucydides is so anxious to ensure that we understand the seed from which the conspiracy grew that he does nothing to make us understand the fact that it did grow. On point A, there is one sentence (54. 5 οὐδὲ γάρ . . . κατεστήσατο) which, as it stands, creates an inconsistency so serious as to be incredible, and emendation is inescapable (v. n. ad loc.).

Relation to Other Accounts. Of extant writers before Thucydides, only Herodotos (v. 55 f., 62 ff.) gives us an account of the end of the tyranny; of later writers, the fullest is Aristotle, Ἀθ. π. 17 ff. Aristotle draws on both Thucydides and Herodotos; he includes some matter which is drawn from neither and is probably to be attributed, as matter in other parts of Ἀθ. π. certainly is, to the (now lost) *Atthis* of the fourth-century Athenian historian Androtion. The other relevant evidence is:

(i) Some Attic skolia (i.e. drinking-songs), which are known to us in their full form only from later writers but certainly go back to the fifth century B.C., since they are referred to and partially quoted by Aristophanes.

(ii) The dialogue *Hipparchos*, which, although probably not written by Plato himself, cannot be dated much later than Plato's time.

(iii) The 'Parian Marble', a summary of dates and events erected on the island of Paros in the third century B.C.

In essentials there is agreement between Thucydides and Herodotos and, needless to say, between them and Aristotle. Herodotos expresses no opinion on how the conspiracy of Harmodios and Aristogeiton began, and it is unlikely—in view of his general attitude to tyrants— that he would ever have shared Thucydides' evident partiality for the Peisistratidai. One of the skolia, however, says that Harmodios and Aristogeiton 'slew the tyrant (τὸν τύραννον) and made Athens free (ἰσονόμους)'. Similarly, in the *Hipparchos* and in the Parian Marble we find Hipparchos treated as the eldest son and successor of Peisistratos, and the Parian Marble even represents the murder of Hipparchos as the end of the tyranny, dating the event 511/10 and omitting all mention of the three further years of Hippias' reign. The view that Hipparchos was the reigning tyrant is precisely the view which Thucydides attributes to 'most people at Athens' in his own day. Since it is unlikely that the person who compiled the Parian Marble would have chosen a version of events known to him only through its explicit rejection by Thucydides and implicit rejection by Herodotos and Aristotle, there must have been an historian who agreed with 'most people' against Herodotos and Thucydides; and Hellanikos, whose history of Athens is criticized by Thucydides for chronological inaccuracy in i. 97. 2, is the likeliest candidate. It should be noted that the wide sense of τύραννος which we find, for example, in the epigram quoted in 59. 3 will naturally have helped to generate alternative traditions.

Thucydides' Sources. Herodotos and Hellanikos were available to Thucydides, but he did more than follow the former and reject the latter. He speaks of himself (55. 1) as having access to accurate tradition—that is to say, to a source of tradition which he regarded, for reasons unknown to us, as reliable—but he mentions this only in connexion with the seniority of Hippias, leaving us to guess at the extent to which he is drawing upon it in connexion with other points. He quotes or mentions inscriptions: (i) To show that Peisistratos, son of Hippias, held the archonship, and thus to support his contention that the tyrants 'always took care that one of themselves should hold office'. (ii) To prove that Archedike was a daughter of Hippias and wife of Aiantides, and that Hippias sought alliances with friends of Persia. (iii) To prove that Hippias was the eldest son of Peisistratos. In connexion with the date of composition of Book VI it is important to remember that Thucydides was in exile from 424 to 404 and could not personally have inspected (i) or (iii) during that period; (ii) was at Lampsakos.

Political Relevance. The issue between Herodotos and Thucydides on one side and the beliefs which Thucydides rejects on the other was not just an academic difference of opinion. If the popular version was right, all the credit for ending the tyranny belonged to Harmodios and Aristogeiton. If Herodotos and Thucydides were right, no credit belonged to the tyrannicides, but great credit to the Alkmeonidai. Now, Perikles belonged to this family through his mother's side, and so did Alkibiades. In the fifth century the relations between a man's ancestors and the Peisistratid tyranny were politically important; therefore it was not possible to express an opinion about the manner in which the tyranny was overthrown without either augmenting or diminishing the political standing of the living representatives of the Alkmeonidai. Thucydides' digression was in fact, whatever his own intention, a contribution to the political controversy of his own time. (See further the note on 54. 6.)

Relation of the Digression to its Context. In 53. 3 Thucydides tells us that the Athenian people's fear of tyranny in 415 was accentuated by the belief, derived from tradition, that the tyranny of the Peisistratidai had in its last stages been oppressive (sc. however mild it might have been before) and that it had not been ended by the murder of Hipparchos or by any effort of their own but by Sparta in co-operation with the Alkmeonidai. The digression, which is introduced in 54. 1 by γάρ, gives in detail the vindication of this belief, and the main narrative is resumed in 60. 1 with the words 'Reflecting on these events, and recalling all that they knew about them by tradition, the Athenian people . . .'.

And yet in the very first sentence of the digression Thucydides appears to say that the Athenians did *not* know precisely what he has just told us they *did* know: 'In describing these circumstances in some detail I shall show that even the Athenians themselves, not to mention others, give a thoroughly inexact account of the tyrants, their own tyrants, and of what actually happened.' This apparent contradiction has given rise to the hypothesis that 53 and 60 were written at a time when Thucydides believed that the Athenians knew the truth about the end of the tyranny, and 54–59, together with the Introduction of which i. 20 is a part, at a later date, when he discovered that they did not know the truth. This hypothesis (which has been propounded in several forms) founders on 60. 1, which both recapitulates 53. 3 and presupposes the intervention of a digression. If there is really a contradiction between 53. 3 and 54–59, then neither Thucydides nor a posthumous 'editor' can have written 60. 1 after inserting 54–59. We therefore have to consider the possibility that the contradiction is illusory; and if we find that it is, no grounds remain for supposing that 54–59 were composed at a different time from 53 and 60.

When Thucydides speaks of the Athenians (54. 1) as ἀκριβὲς οὐδὲν λέγοντας about the end of the tyranny, he does not mean 'everything that the Athenians say about the end of the tyranny is untrue'. Indeed, as he has just told us that in one important matter they were right, he cannot have imagined that any reader would take him to mean 'everything they say is untrue'. Moreover, as he knows what he is going to say in this digression—and we do not, until we have read it— it does not occur to him that any reader would perceive any contradiction between 53. 3 and 54. 1. He means 'the Athenians give an account which is not at all exact'; cf. the common expression οὐδὲν ὑγιές, e.g. in Ar. *Ach.* 956 οἴσεις οὐδὲν ὑγιές, which means not 'everything which you will be taking is worthless' but 'you will be taking something which is thoroughly worthless'. Popular tradition in all ages easily digests inconsistencies and contradictions which are intolerable to an historian; tradition notoriously lacks ἀκρίβεια. The fact is, then, that Athenian tradition asserted:

both (*a*) Hipparchos was the reigning tyrant when he was killed in 514, and the credit for overthrowing the tyranny belonged essentially to Harmodios and Aristogeiton,

and (*b*) Hippias reigned after the death of Hipparchos, and was expelled by the Spartans and the Alkmeonidai.

Thucydides' argument is that this tradition *does not make historical sense* and that the evidence justifies rejection of (*a*); when (*a*) is rejected, (*b*) does make sense.

Motive for the Digression. Why did Thucydides *want* to correct tradition about the end of the tyranny? Not simply to make people think kindly of the ancestors of Pericles and Alkibiades, for his references to the role of the Alkmeonidai are entirely subservient to his essentially destructive purpose. Nor again to suggest similarities between the situations of 514 and 415; to discover such similarities we have to adopt a standpoint far removed from that of a candid reader. The most plausible explanation is that he succumbed to the temptation before which all historians and commentators are by their very nature weak, the temptation to correct historical error wherever they find it, regardless of its relevance to their immediate purpose. The seed from which the digression grew may have been the use, by opponents of Alkibiades in 415, of the argument: 'Beware, men of Athens, of the would-be tyrant; for nothing is easier than to give yourselves into the hands of a tyrant, but nothing harder to escape from him again. Why, not even the Peisistratidai fled at once when Harmodios and Aristogeiton slew the tyrant Hipparchos . . .'

54. 1. **ἐπὶ πλέον διηγησάμενος:** The comparative in the sense 'more than you might have expected' is common enough, and it is not necessary to understand here 'in more detail than in i. 20. 2'.

2. **ἐραστὴς ὢν εἶχεν αὐτόν:** Greek society in general, at least from the sixth century onwards, was bisexual; a man's sexual appetite could be aroused both by women and by younger men or boys, and the deep and powerful emotions which we regard as proper to love between men and women seem to have been more often experienced by the Greeks in relations between men and youths. Except for the isolated case of Sappho, we are not well informed on bisexuality in women and girls.

3. **ἐρωτικῶς περιαλγήσας:** Aristogeiton is tormented by a lover's violent jealousy of a rival; cf. 57. 3.

ὡς ἀπὸ τῆς ὑπαρχούσης ἀξιώσεως: 'So far as his status ("rank", "standing") permitted'; it would have been easier for the head of an aristocratic family, or a man of great wealth, than for a μέσος πολίτης.

4. **ἀφανεῖ:** i.e. in such a manner that the reason for the insult would not be apparent to people in general.

παρεσκευάζετο προπηλακιῶν αὐτόν: παρασκευάζεσθαι is commonly followed by ὡς with the future participle, but Thucydides sometimes omits the ὡς (e.g. vii. 17. 3).

5. **οὐδὲ γὰρ τὴν ἄλλην ἀρχήν . . . κατεστήσατο:** Since Hipparchos was the subject of the previous sentence, we naturally assume that he is the subject of this sentence too; but κατεστήσατο is appropriate only to

the *ruling tyrant*, as is clear from 55. 3, 'if . . . he himself (sc. Hippias) had tried to establish himself in power (καθίστατο) on the same day'. But the whole point of this digression is that Hipparchos was *not* the ruling tyrant. Therefore, either we must understand Hippias as the subject of ἦν and κατεστήσατο, or the sentence is corrupt. Reference to Hippias, without naming him, in this context would be impossibly obscure, and Hude removed the difficulty by a neat emendation: ἐπαχθεῖς ἦσαν . . . κατεστήσαντο, referring to Peisistratos and his sons as a whole, as the following words do unambiguously. -εῖς and -ής were pronounced alike from late antiquity onwards, and once ἐπαχθεῖς had become corrupted to ἐπαχθής it would not be long before the verbs were corrected to conform.

ἐπὶ πλεῖστον δὴ τύραννοι οὗτοι: If Thucydides had meant 'these tyrants', he would have used the definite article before τύραννοι. The analysis is: 'these, to the greatest extent (sc. of all), (as) tyrants', i.e. 'these men, to a greater extent than any other tyrants'.

ἀρετὴν καὶ ξύνεσιν: Thucydides is sparing of encomia, and calls few men 'good'. What he means by 'goodness' is apparent from v. 105. 4, where it is contrasted with 'regarding what is pleasant as honourable and what is advantageous as just'. A 'good' man, therefore, is a man who sacrifices his own pleasure and advantage; and the Peisistratid tyrants were 'good' in so far as they exercised power without forcing the will of others blatantly or recklessly.

εἰκοστήν: A 5 per cent. tax on the year's produce; 10 per cent. (δεκάτη), according to Ἀθ. π. 16. 4, but δεκάτη, like the English 'tithe', can be used generically and the specific εἰκοστή subsumed under it.

τοὺς πολέμους διέφερον: 'Carried their wars through to a conclusion'; cf. viii. 75. 2, 'they bound all the soldiers by an oath that they would wholeheartedly διοίσειν the war against the Peloponnesians'.

6. αὐτή: This is part of the predicate, not of the subject; 'the city observed *without interference* the laws previously in force'; elsewhere αὐτός is found in the senses 'by oneself', 'of one's own accord', and 'on one's own initiative'. Here the existence of the concept αὐτόνομος helps to explain αὐτή.

αἰεί τινα . . . εἶναι: If σφῶν αὐτῶν is taken literally, it means the Peisistratid family itself, and no doubt it was always possible for a member of a family to hold one or other of the principal offices of that period: the eponymous archonship, the office of polemarch, and that of the archon basileus. Thucydides may, however, mean σφῶν αὐτῶν to include political associates.

A fragment of an archon-list erected in the last quarter of the fifth century (*SEG* x. 352) gives us the names of Hippias, Kleisthenes, Miltiades, Kalliades, and .....]stratos in successive years. Miltiades, as we know from other evidence, was eponymous archon in 524/3; it follows that Hippias himself held the archonship in 526/5, and the mutilated name for 522/1 is probably that of his son Peisistratos. The archonship of Kleisthenes is of peculiar interest, since it disproves Herodotos' claim (i. 64. 3, vi. 123. 1) that the Alkmeonidai, of whom Kleisthenes was the leading representative, were in exile continuously, and implacably opposed to the tyrants, from before the death of Peisistratos to the expulsion of Hippias. (Cf. 59. 4 n.)

The mechanism by which the Peisistratidai ensured that 'one of themselves should always be in office' is not known; πλὴν καθ' ὅσον κτλ. suggests that it was not simply a matter of influence over a loyal electorate but a breach of the existing constitution, probably the substitution of nomination for election.

ἦρξαν . . . ἀρχήν: i.e. 'held the annual eponymous archonship'; ἦρξεν Ἀθηναίοις is the technical term for 'held the eponymous archonship at Athens'.

Πεισίστρατος . . . υἱός: Probably in 522/1 (cf. n. supra). The aorist τοῦ τυραννεύσαντος does not imply that Hippias had already finished being tyrant at the time of his son's archonship, but only that the tyranny lies in the past from the reader's standpoint; hence 'Hippias, the tyrant'.

τῶν δώδεκα θεῶν βωμόν: This altar and its sanctuary are now excavated; the original altar is archaeologically reconcilable with the date 522/1 for Peisistratos' archonship, and its enlargement (cf. § 7) is datable to 430–420.

καὶ τὸν τοῦ Ἀπόλλωνος ἐν Πυθίου: 'And the (sc. altar) of Apollo in (sc. the sanctuary) of (Apollo) Pythios.' This sanctuary lay in the south-east part of the city.

7. ἀμυδροῖς γράμμασι: Part of this inscription survives, and its letters do not seem 'faint' to us, as Greek inscriptions go; but no doubt they seemed faint to Thucydides by contrast with the great number of much more recent inscriptions, and possibly they had originally been painted in red but had lost most of their paint. The script is identical with that on a dedication by Hipparchos at a sanctuary in Boeotia, but otherwise ahead of its time, resembling Attic decrees of the first quarter of the fifth century rather than dedications of the sixth.

55. 1. τῶν γνησίων ἀδελφῶν: By 'the legitimate brothers' Thucydides means 'the brothers who were the sons of Peisistratos by his Athenian wife'. He is guilty of anachronism, since it was not until the middle of the fifth century that the Athenians denied legitimacy to the children of an Athenian father and a non-Athenian mother.

ὡς ὅ τε βωμὸς σημαίνει: The altar by itself does not in the least tell us whether any of Hippias' brothers had sons, but only that Hippias had one.

περὶ τῆς τῶν τυράννων ἀδικίας: The archaic and classical periods yield no examples of narrative inscriptions. The stele to which Thucydides refers must have recorded a decision to outlaw in perpetuity the surviving Peisistratidai and their issue, and anyone who might be discovered to be a descendant of any member of the family. A reason for this decision was perhaps given in general form, e.g. 'These men inflicted great wrongs upon the Athenian people'. The stele may have been of bronze, as other stelai on the Akropolis outlawing traitors and their issue are known to have been.

Θεσσαλοῦ μὲν οὐδ' Ἱππάρχου: Obviously Thessalos and Hipparchos were, in Thucydides' view, the two other 'legitimate' sons; and the distinction which he makes implies that 'illegitimate' sons were also named on the stele. Herodotos says nothing of Thessalos, but mentions (v. 94. 1) a certain Hegesistratos, a son of Peisistratos by his Argive wife. Aristotle (Ἀθ. π. 17. 4) adds Iophon, another son of the Argive wife. He also describes 'Thessalos' as an extra name of Hegesistratos; we do not know the origin or grounds of that view.

Μυρρίνης . . . θυγατρός: Nothing is known of this Kallias. According to the early-fourth-century Athenian historian Kleidemos (fr. 15), Hippias married the daughter of one Charmos after the return of Peisistratos from his first exile, and this datum accords with the existence of a Hipparchos son of Charmos in the early years of the fifth century. Textual corruption, Χάρμου > Καλλίου, has been suspected in Thucydides; but it is also possible that the daughter of Charmos died childless soon after her marriage to Hippias, so that the daughter of Kallias would be his second wife.

2. ἀπεοικότως: Attic writers (including Thucydides himself elsewhere) say ἀπεικός and ἀπεικότως; ἀπεοικ- is Hellenistic.

3. εἰ Ἵππαρχος μέν . . . καθίστατο: 'If Hipparchos had been killed and Hippias himself had been establishing himself', i.e. 'had tried to establish himself'. The imperfect indicative is used in stating hypotheses about the past whenever the meaning requires it, whether or not the resulting conditional sentence conforms to one of the types recognized in grammars.

διὰ τό . . . ἀκριβές: cf. Intr. I. 3. 7–8.

τοὺς ἐπικούρους: The bodyguard of mercenaries on whom the Peisistratidai, like other tyrants, relied.

ἐν ᾧ κτλ.: 'At a time when he had not been continuously familiar . . .' (sc. as he would not have been, if he had been a younger brother).

56. 1. κόρην . . . κανοῦν οἴσουσαν: It was normal for girls to serve as

κανηφόροι in religious processions, carrying offerings of food in baskets on their heads.

ἐπαγγείλαντες . . . ἀπήλασαν λέγοντες: Here Thucydides seems to speak of Hippias and Hipparchos as acting in concert; but naturally he could not know precisely who organized the procession in question.

διὰ τὸ μὴ ἀξίαν εἶναι: The κανηφόροι were supposed to be daughters of citizens of good standing; thus the rejection of the girl necessarily touched her brother's status. Harmodios, who was perhaps not wholly displeased that his good looks had caught the eye of Hipparchos, was ready to avenge an insult to his family by murder.

2. Παναθήναια τὰ μεγάλα: The Panathenaia were celebrated annually on 28 Hekatombaion; from 566/5 onwards the celebration was on a bigger scale ('the great Panathenaia') in every fourth year.

ἐν ὅπλοις: cf. 58. 2 n.

καὶ ἔδει . . . ἐκείνους: 'And the plan was (ἔδει) that they themselves (αὐτούς) should strike the first blow (ἄρξαι), and that the men in the procession (ἐκείνους) should then come to their help in dealing with the bodyguard'; 'the inevitable (τά) dealing . . .' is an internal accusative with ξυνεπαμύνειν.

57. 1. ἔξω . . . καλουμένῳ: The Kerameikos, in the north-west of the city, was divided in half by the city wall, as the location of its extant boundary-stones shows; for the present expression cf. Pl. *Prm.* 127 B 'outside the wall, in the Kerameikos'.

2. τῶν ξυνωμοτῶν σφίσι: = τῶν ξυνομωμοκότων σφίσι.

3. προτιμωρήσασθαι: i.e. before they could be arrested.

παρὰ τὸ Λεωκόρειον καλούμενον: Literary references suggest that the Leokoreion was in the western part of the Agora, but it has not been found. The name of the sanctuary reflects a myth of familiar type: the daughters of the Attic hero Leos were sacrificed with their father's consent when an oracle made their sacrifice a condition of the city's preservation.

ἔτυπτον . . . αὐτόν: The narrative present is especially frequent with words denoting violence and death (cf. vii. 30. 2), which need not be 'sudden' or 'unexpected'. The imperfect ἔτυπτον may be explicable as denoting repeated action: 'they rained blows on him'.

4. καὶ ὁ μέν . . . ὁ Ἀριστογείτων: 'And one of them . . . Aristogeiton.'

οὐ ῥᾳδίως διετέθη: Aristotle (Ἀθ. π. 18. 4 ff.) relates how Aristogeiton was long tortured until he was able to provoke Hippias, by insults, into killing him and ending his suffering.

58. I. τοὺς πομπέας τοὺς ὁπλίτας: 'The members of the procession who were fully armed'; ὁπλίτας is treated here as if it were a participle or adjective.

ἀδήλως . . . πρὸς τὴν ξυμφοράν: lit., 'having feigned with his sight unclearly with reference to the disaster', i.e. 'composing his appearance so as not to betray what had befallen him'.

ἐκέλευσεν αὐτούς . . . ἀπελθεῖν κτλ.: A similar anecdote was told of Peisistratos.

2. μετὰ γὰρ ἀσπίδος . . . ποιεῖν: An ἐγχειρίδιον (short stabbing sword) was a normal part of a hoplite's equipment for battle. Thucydides' point is that the hoplites in the Panathenaic procession carried *only* shield and spear, so that possession of any other weapon was suspicious. Aristotle (*Ἀθ. π.* 18. 4) denies what Thucydides says here, and asserts that procession with arms was an innovation of the democracy. The available evidence does not enable us to decide who is right, but it is easy to see why the issue was important to Athenian historians. If the men in the procession carried no arms, their failure to sweep away the tyranny is excusable; if they did carry arms, they must have been loyal to the tyranny through several Great Panathenaia and stupid enough to be disarmed by a trick.

59. 2. εἰ ποθεν . . . ὑπάρχουσάν οἱ: lit., 'to see if he could see from some source some safety being available to him if a revolution occurred', i.e. 'to see if he could discover anywhere a safe refuge for himself in the event of a revolution'.

3. Ἱππόκλου γοῦν . . . τυράννου: Hippoklos of Lampsakos was one of the Greek tyrants of the Asiatic coast who enjoyed Persian support, and he may have been a Persian imposition from the first. He accompanied Dareios on the expedition across the Danube, and was among those who opposed Miltiades' proposal to destroy the Danube bridge and allow Dareios' army to perish (Hdt. iv. 138. 1).

Ἀθηναῖος ὢν Λαμψακηνῷ: The point of the rhetorical juxtaposition (cf. 6. 2 n.) is that there had previously been enmity between Lampsakos and the Peisistratidai (Hdt. vi. 37 ff.).

ἐπίγραμμα ἔχον τόδε: Aristotle (*Rhet.* 1367ᵇ19) attributes this epigram to Simonides, and he might—by chance—be right. Sepulchral epigrams of the sixth and early fifth centuries do not include any reference to their composers, and Simonides, as the most famous epigrammatist of that period, came to be credited with far more than he actually composed.

4. ἐν τῷ τετάρτῳ: 511/10.

Ἀλκμεωνιδῶν τῶν φευγόντων: Not 'those of the Alkmeonidai who were in exile', but 'among the exiles, the Alkmeonidai'. Cf. Hdt. v. 62. 2 and Ἀθ. π. 19. 3, where the Alkmeonidai appear only as the most active and prominent among the exiles. For the detailed story of the respective parts played by the Alkmeonidai and Sparta, cf. Hdt. v. 55 f., 62 ff. As the Alkmeonidai had not been continuously in exile (supra, 54. 6 n.) since the time of Peisistratos, it is probable that they went into exile after the murder of Hipparchos, when 'the tyranny became harsher and Hippias . . . killed many citizens' (§ 2 supra).

ἔς τε Σίγειον: Sigeion, in the Troad, had been won by Athens from Mytilene after a lengthy war (cf. Hdt. v. 94f.); the chronology of this war is full of difficulties, but at least it is not disputed that Sigeion was controlled by Athens at the time of which Thucydides is speaking.

ὕστερον ἔτει εἰκοστῷ: Marathon was fought in 490, in the twenty-second year (by inclusive reckoning) after the expulsion of Hippias; cf. i. 18. 2, where Thucydides dates Xerxes' expedition against Greece 'in the tenth year' after Marathon. Either Thucydides is using round numbers, or he means by ὕστερον 'after his arrival at the court of Dareios'; the latter, however, is highly improbable, since (a) Thucydides is unlikely to have had any information on how long Hippias spent at Sigeion, and (b) coming after 'overthrown in the fourth year', 'in the twentieth year' naturally implies 'after his overthrow'.

60–61. Flight of Alkibiades

60. 1. **τότε:** In English historical narrative we tend to say 'now'; Greek does not use νῦν in this way.

ἐπὶ ξυνωμοσίᾳ κτλ.: cf. 27. 3 n.

2. **ἐφαίνετο:** sc. 'the process'.

εἷς τῶν δεδεμένων: Andokides. According to his own story, as told sixteen years later when he was charged with an offence to which his alleged impieties in 415 were relevant, he had promised his friends that he would join them in mutilating the herms, but was prevented from doing so by an accident (And. i. 61 ff.).

ὑπὸ τῶν ξυνδεσμωτῶν τινος: Andokides' cousin Charmides (And. i. 48 ff.).

τὸ δὲ σαφές . . . εἰπεῖν: According to Andokides, there were three occasions on which information was laid about the mutilation: (i) By the metic Teukros. Eighteen men were named by him, some of whom escaped execution by flight. Andokides, so far from challenging Teukros' information, implies that it was true (52, 59). (ii) By a certain Diokleides, who stated that some three hundred men were involved, and actually named forty-two, including Andokides and many of his relations. Diokleides later confessed that his information had been false, and he was accordingly executed (65). (iii) Andokides himself, who claims that he named only four men not already named by Teukros, and these four all saved themselves by flight. Although Andokides claims that his information was accepted as true at the time and was regarded as clearing up the case of the mutilation once for all—and Thucydides bears this out—Thucydides' own informants evidently did not regard it in this light; we do not know why.

3. εἰ μὴ καὶ δέδρακεν: '⟨Even⟩ if he had not *done* it.'
ἄδειαν ποιησάμενον: 'Having obtained immunity'; cf. ἀδεῶς in 27. 2.

4. καὶ δεινὸν ποιούμενοι πρότερον: This imperfective participle must be translated as a past participle in English: 'and having previously thought it intolerable that . . .'
ἐπανεῖπον ἀργύριον τῷ ἀποκτείναντι: 'Proclaimed a monetary reward to anyone who should kill them.'

61. 1. ὧν ἐπαίτιος ἦν: Alkibiades had been denounced by a slave and by a woman for complicity in the profanation of the mysteries. Neither Thucydides nor Andokides claims that he was innocent, and there is no reason why we should think him so. Alkibiades and his friends were not remarkable for simple piety, and their parodies of the mysteries must have been extremely funny.
μετὰ τοῦ αὐτοῦ λόγου κτλ.: 'With the same idea (*or* design), that is, the conspiracy against the democracy.'

2. καὶ στρατιὰ Λακεδαιμονίων: And. i. 45 has a slightly different version; after Diokleides had laid information and wholesale arrests were being made, 'the Boeotians learnt what was going on and were out in force on our borders'. We do not know what this activity on the part of the Spartans and Boeotians was all about.
ἐν Θησείῳ τῷ ἐν πόλει: The Theseion (which was not the temple commonly given that name in modern times) lay south-east of the Agora; ἐν πόλει here = 'in the city', not, as commonly, 'on the Akropolis', and the point of the specification is that there were four sanctuaries of Theseus in Attica, including at least one at Peiraieus.

3. καὶ τοὺς ὁμήρους τῶν Ἀργείων: In the summer of 416 the Argive democrats, having successfully revolted against the oligarchy imposed by Sparta, handed over to Alkibiades three hundred of their opponents as hostages, and these were put on Aegean islands under Athenian control (v. 84. 1).

5. θεραπεύοντες . . . παραμεῖναι: θεραπεύοντες agrees with the logical subject of εἴρητο, the Athenians. τε is deferred, as in 7. 3 (q.v.). Lit., 'taking care not to cause a disturbance in relation to those in Sicily,

soldiers of their own and of the enemy', i.e. 'for they were anxious not to cause any disturbance which would have an effect on their own men in Sicily or on the enemy', disheartening the former and encouraging the latter.

δι' ἐκείνου: cf. 29. 3.

7. ἐρήμῃ δίκῃ: A man could be condemned if, after due notice, he failed to appear to answer the charge against him.

AUGUST–OCTOBER 415

62. Operations in Northern and Eastern Sicily

Although Alkibiades has now gone, Nikias and Lamachos continue to carry out his plan, upon which they agreed at Rhegion: 'communicate with all the Greek cities except Selinus and Syracuse . . . win over the Sikels . . . *and then* attack Selinus and Syracuse.' They therefore make overtures to Himera, the only Greek city on the north coast, oblige their ally Segesta by destroying her Sikan enemy Hykkara, 'show the flag' to the Sikels, and attack Hybla Geleatis, probably to oblige their Sikel friends.

62. 1. ἐπὶ Σελινοῦντος καὶ Ἐγέστης: They did not in fact go as far as Selinus, and only Nikias went as far as Segesta; the words therefore simply describe the *direction* in which they went, naming the remoter place first.

2. ἥπερ μόνη κτλ.: Himera was totally destroyed by the Carthaginians in 409. Thucydides' statement, repeated in different words, but still in the present tense, in vii. 58. 2, would therefore seem to have been written before 409; since it is a statement about the *race* of the Himeraeans, and not about the *location* of Himera, it differs from some other passages which have been thought to afford evidence for date of composition. However, a community calling itself Ἱμεραῖοι existed in the same area after the destruction of the city, and Thucydides may have thought of this community and the city as a continuous entity.

3. Ὕκκαρα: The modern Carini, 24 km. west of Palermo.

τὰ ἀνδράποδα ἄγουσαι: The importance of getting the enslaved Hykkarans back to the east coast in marketable condition, and therefore in the troop-transports, was the chief reason for taking the troops back overland.

4. τάλαντα τριάκοντα: All that Segesta could contribute; cf. 46. 1.

παρῆν ἐς τὸ στράτευμα: 'Rejoined the force.'

4. ἀπέδοσαν: This must mean 'sold', although 'sell' is normally ἀποδίδοσθαι, not ἀποδιδόναι; the active, however, means 'sell' in E. *Cy.* 239.

ἐγένοντο: cf. 13. 1 n.

5. καὶ ἐς τοὺς τῶν Σικελῶν ξυμμάχους περιέπλευσαν: 'They sailed round to the allies of the Sikels' makes little sense, for who could 'the allies of the Sikels' be? τῶν Σικελῶν must be partitive, 'their allies among the Sikels', and Thucydides perhaps wrote it before ἐς or after ξυμμάχους. περιέπεμψαν (H⁸) also gives much better sense than περιέπλευσαν, since the Sikels were an inland people. The jingle περιέπεμψαν . . . πέμπειν is unobjectionable; cf. 88. 6.

5. ἐπὶ Ὕβλαν τὴν Γελεᾶτιν: Probably Paterno, some 14 km. west-north-west of Catania.

OCTOBER 415

63–71. Athenian Landing and Victory at Syracuse

63–65. 1. *The Athenian Plan*

63. 2. **οἷον δὴ ὄχλος φιλεῖ ποιεῖν:** A characteristic comment of Thucydides on the behaviour of men in the mass.

3. ἄλλα τε καὶ εἰ ξυνοικήσοντες κτλ.: 'And, in particular, ⟨asked them⟩ whether they (= the Athenians) had come to live with them (= the Syracusans) themselves (= the Athenians) on alien soil rather than to establish the people of Leontinoi on their (= Leontinoi) own soil.'

64. 1. **ὅτι πλεῖστον:** 'As *far* as possible.'

οὐκ ἂν ὁμοίως . . . καὶ εἰ κτλ.: lit., '. . . that they would not be able in the same way as if . . .', i.e. '. . . that ⟨in this way⟩ they would be able ⟨to do so⟩ *better* than ⟨they would⟩ if . . .'. Cf. 34. 7, where ἰσοκινδύνους = 'running no *greater* risk'. Both Σᴹ in his paraphrase and Valla in his translation ignore καί and therefore interpret οὐχ ὁμοίως as 'not so well'; but it does not follow that there was no καί in their texts.

τοὺς γὰρ ἂν ψιλοὺς τοὺς σφῶν: The position of ἄν between article and noun is most exceptional in Attic, though there are parallels from other dialects. τοὺς σφῶν is also odd Greek—just as τοὺς ἡμῶν would be—and it is possible that the second τούς should be deleted.

τῶν Συρακοσίων: With τοὺς ἱππέας, subject of βλάπτειν; καὶ τὸν ὄχλον refers to the Athenian unarmed men.

σφίσι δ': The connective is justified by the clausular status of πολλοὺς ὄντας: '—which were numerous, while they themselves had no
cavalry—.'

οὕτω δέ: i.e. if they carried out the plan indicated in the first part of
the sentence.

τοιόνδε τι οὖν: Unlike English 'therefore', οὖν is not commonly used
with a main clause which follows a subordinate or participial clause,
but in the present case the participial clause is exceptionally long and
complex. The same phenomenon occurs in vii. 42. 3.

2. ἔφη: sc. to the Syracusan generals, who are the subject of the
following relative clause.

ὑπολοίπους ὄντας: In 51. 2 we were told that the pro-Syracusans in
Katane departed when the Athenians came in.

3. αὐτοὶ μέν: The pro-Syracusans in Katane.

65. 1. καὶ εἶναι . . . παρεσκευάσθαι: lit., 'and being in planning', and
then either (a) 'even without these things to be prepared to go against
Katane' or (b) 'and being prepared ⟨even⟩ without these things to go
against Katane'. (a), involving 'being in planning to be prepared . . .',
is strikingly verbose, and (b) condemns itself by requiring us first to
translate as 'and' a word which can mean 'even' and then to *understand*
'even'. παρεσκευάσθαι is probably an interpolated gloss on εἶναι ἐν
διανοίᾳ, though not a very accurate one, since they were not yet 'prepared'. For εἶναι ἐν διανοίᾳ = 'be in process of planning' cf. ἐν ἐλπίσιν
εἶναι = 'be hopeful' in vii. 25. 9 and ἐν φόβῳ γενέσθαι = 'fear' in Pl. *R.*
578 E. Hence: '. . . and the fact that even without this news they were
thinking of moving against Katane.'

πολλῷ ἀπερισκεπτότερον: sc. 'than one might expect' or 'than they
ought to have done'; cf. 54. 1.

ἤδη γάρ . . . παρῆσαν: This explains why they were able to go out
πανδημεί; the protection of the city would be left to their allies.

65. 1–67. *The Athenian Landing*

65. 1. καὶ αἱ ἡμέραι . . . ἐγγὺς ἦσαν: 'The *days* were at hand', since
they could not arrive at Katane on the same day as they left Syracuse.
ἐγγύς sometimes denotes closer contact than the English 'near'; when
the poet Tyrtaios exhorts the Spartan soldier to fight ἐγγὺς ἰών, he
means 'hand to hand', 'at close quarters'.

Συμαίθῳ: The modern Giarretta.

2. προσεληλύθει: προσεληλύθεσαν would have been more logical, the
subject being 'as many of the Sikels or anyone else', but the number of
the words nearest the verb prevails. Cf. vii. 44. 1.

καὶ τὰ πλοῖα: ὁλκάδες, distinguished from πλοῖα hitherto, must here
be subsumed.

3. ἐς τὸ κατὰ τὸ 'Ολυμπιεῖον: The original text was probably ἐς τὸν
μέγαν λιμένα κατὰ τὸ 'Ολυμπιεῖον; this is indicated by Valla, by H (with
some disturbance of the word-order), and by the fact that ABCFM
have τόν, not τό.

The Olympieion, i.e. the sanctuary of Zeus Olympios, lay on high
ground south of the Anapos, 1·3 km. inland from the (modern) coast-
line in the very centre of the Great Harbour; the two surviving columns
catch the eye at once as one enters the Harbour by sea or looks westwards from the old city. The sanctuary was not isolated, but was part
of an inhabited locality; cf. 70. 4, 75. 1, and vii. 4. 7.

66. 1. μακρᾶς οὔσης τῆς ὁδοῦ αὐτοῖς: αὐτοῖς refers to the Syracusans,
and the clause explains why the Athenians were able to establish themselves καθ' ἡσυχίαν.

ἥκιστ' ἄν ... λυπήσειν: Unanimous manuscript testimony for ἄν
with the future in Attic Greek is very rare; Thucydides probably
wrote λυπῆσαι.

τῇ μὲν γάρ ... κρημνοί: 'For one way walls and houses and trees
and standing water kept off ⟨enemy cavalry⟩, and along the other side
precipitous ground.' These conditions are satisfied by a position facing
west or north-west, with the high ground (on which the Olympieion
stands) on the left and Lysimeleia (the λίμνη) *and also the river Anapos*
on the right. But if this is the position which Thucydides means, we
are entitled to ask (a) Why does he omit to mention the major protection afforded by the river and specify only less important features?
(b) Why does the river play no part whatsoever in his account of the
battle, impeding the movements of neither side, especially since the
Athenians 'destroyed the bridge over the Anapos' (§ 2)? We may
readily believe (we may, indeed, conclude that we *must* believe) that
he had no accurate mental picture of the scene, but it is another
matter to say that such data as he does give are false, and these data
are reconcilable with the following hypothesis. The Athenians landed
on *both* sides of the river-mouth; thus the whole force, as it landed, had
precipitous ground on its left, and a substantial part of the force had
on its right the river and, beyond that, standing water. The bridge
destroyed was just below the Olympieion, well upstream; but either
there was another bridge, nearer the mouth, which the Athenians did
not destroy, or they built some bridges themselves. When drawn up for
battle the force was north of the river, facing north, with the standing
water on its right and its own bridge behind it.

2. **σταύρωμα ἔπηξαν**: On shore, to facilitate re-embarkation, under the protection of a small defensive force, if they were defeated.

καὶ ἐπὶ τῷ Δάσκωνι: Daskon is a bay (κόλπος) in Diod. xiii. 13. 3; it is probably to be identified with the beach in the south-western portion of the Great Harbour and the fertile land lying behind that beach. This was an obvious place for a protective stockade, since between the higher ground inland and the shore there is a gap, a gentle slope (editors' maps are wrong in marking continuous precipitous ground) through which enemy cavalry could easily attack.

ἔρυμά τι: The MSS. have ἔρυμά τε, which makes quite a difference to the sense: 'they planted a stockade along by the ships and in the region of Daskon, and erected ... a strongpoint where it was easiest for the enemy to attack.' τι gives the sense '. . . by the ships; and upon Daskon, where it was easiest for the enemy to attack, they erected a strongpoint . . .'. But this emendation is unnecessary, and even misleading; the place where the Athenians thought 'it was easiest for the enemy to attack' may well have been at the *northern* end of their beachhead.

καὶ τὴν τοῦ Ἀνάπου γέφυραν ἔλυσαν: cf. on § 1 supra.

3. **τὴν Ἑλωρινὴν ὁδόν**: This road ran west and then south-west from Syracuse and eventually, after crossing the river, south towards Heloron, which lay on the coast 27 km. south of Syracuse. We do not know where it crossed the river (but cf. § 1 n. supra); the modern road does so close to the mouth. By 'crossing the road to Heloron' the Syracusans were moving north-westwards, far enough off to threaten the Athenians' left flank if the latter moved north-eastwards towards the city, but not so far off as to allow the Athenians to establish themselves in strength between them and their city.

67. *Preparations for Battle*

67. 1. **τὸ μὲν ἥμισυ**: *c.* 2,550 men (cf. 43).

ἐπὶ ὀκτώ: The same depth as at the battle of Delion (iv. 94. 1); the weight behind the attack was important in hoplite tactics.

ἐν πλαισίῳ: This formation, a hollow rectangle, could be used either stationary or on the move; in the latter case it had a 'mouth' and a 'tail', which suggests resemblance to a snake rather than to a square. In the present instance approximation to a square is probable, to create the maximum space in the centre for the carriers and baggage; calculation from the data given here and in 43 suggests that the space in the centre would have been rather less than 5,000 square metres and perhaps not much more than 3,000.

2. **τὸ ξύμπαν ἐς διακοσίους**: If this means the Selinuntines and Geloans together, we are not told whether the Selinuntines were

infantry or cavalry; if it means the Geloan cavalry only, we may presume that the Selinuntines were infantry but we are given no indication of their numbers. As it would be contrary to Thucydides' general practice to reckon cavalry and infantry together, it should be presumed that although he knew that the Selinuntines contributed the largest number of troops he did not know how many, and contented himself with μάλιστα. It should be observed also that 200 is the total of the Geloan cavalry in 413 (vii. 33. 1).

68. *Speech of Nikias*

Thucydides here combines in a single speech the various exhortations which he believes Nikias to have uttered (67. 3) 'nation by nation, as he passed by them separately, and to all of them together'.

68. 1. ὦ ἄνδρες . . . ἀγῶνα: 'You who are here, as we all are, to fight the same battle!' Cf. iii. 30. 1 Ἀλκίδα . . . καὶ ὅσοι πάρεσμεν κτλ. Nikias was aware of the very mixed composition of his force, as his speech in vii. 63 shows, and he therefore chooses a form of address which emphasizes their unity.

2. **Ἀργεῖοι καὶ Μαντινῆς:** It is sound tactics to pay the compliment of first mention to the allies who were present of their own free will.
νησιωτῶν: Since the Aegean islands were the nearest and most familiar part of the Athenian Empire to the Athenians themselves and the states of mainland Greece, and since they included some particularly large and important states—e.g. Chios, Lesbos, and Samos— there was a tendency to speak of the Empire loosely as 'the islands' and of the subject peoples as 'the islanders'.
διὰ τό . . . ἔχειν: On the inferiority of the Syracusans' ἐπιστήμη to their τόλμα cf. 69. 1, 72. 2.

3. **πρὸς γῇ . . . κτήσεσθε:** 'Not on the shores of any friendly land which you will acquire without fighting ⟨for it⟩ yourselves.'
οἱ πολέμιοι σφίσιν αὐτοῖς . . . παρακελεύονται: Either 'the enemy . . . are exhorting one another', or, more probably, 'the enemy commanders . . . are exhorting their own men'.
οἱ μὲν γάρ . . . ἐγὼ δέ: sc. παρακελεύονται . . . ὑπομιμνήσκω.
οὐκ ἐν πατρίδι . . . ἀποχωρεῖν: lit., 'not in ⟨your⟩ native land, from which it is necessary to be victorious or not easily to retreat', i.e. 'in a land which is not your own, a land which you must conquer, for otherwise ⟨you can⟩ not easily retreat from it'. 23. 2 is similar but much less elliptical.

4. **καὶ τὴν παροῦσαν ἀνάγκην κτλ.:** It is remarkable, though perhaps

characteristic of Thucydides' Nikias, that at this first encounter with
an anxious and unpractised enemy he should talk as if the Athenians
had their backs to the wall; there is no suggestion that the Athenians
are superior in spirit. Contrast Phormion at Naupaktos in ii. 89.

69–71. *The Battle*

69. 1. ἀπροσδόκητοι: Usually 'unexpected', but here 'not expecting'.

οἱ δέ: 'But they', i.e. the men who had gone off to the city.

οὐχ ἥσσους: sc. *ἦσαν*; then with *τῷ δὲ κτλ.* we pass into a fresh finite
clause.

αὐτῆς: This refers to *ἐπιστήμη*.

2. λιθοβόλοι: These threw their stones by hand, as is clear from Pl.
Lg. 834 A *λίθῳ ἐκ χειρός τε καὶ σφενδόναις ἁμιλλωμένων.*

μάντεις τε κτλ.: These were a normal feature of all battles. Thucydides is 'setting the stage' with an abundance of detail for this first encounter between Athenians and Syracusans.

3. καὶ τῆς ἰδίας κτλ.: 'And each individual for his own preservation
at this moment and his own freedom in future.'

οἱ αὐτόνομοι: The distinction between *αὐτόνομοι* and *ὑπήκοοι* among
the Athenian allies is essentially between (*a*) true allies, who paid no
tribute but stood in the relationship to Athens which was normally
denoted by *ξυμμαχία*, and (*b*) subjects, who paid tribute, and, though
as a rule formally called *ξύμμαχοι*, could also be called *ὧν Ἀθηναῖοι
ἄρχουσιν.*

περὶ τῆς αὐτίκα . . . κρατῶσι: 'For their own immediate preservation, for which they could have no hope if they did not win.'

καὶ εἴ τι ἄλλο . . . ὑπακούσεται: Hᶜ has the right text, with the
nominative *ξυγκαταστρεψάμενοι* and the plural *ὑπακούσονται*: lit., 'if
having joined in subduing something else they will be subject to them
more easily', i.e. 'in the hope that if they helped Athens to make
a further conquest they would find Athenian rule less oppressive'.
Σᴹ also seems to have had that text. The singular *ὑπακούσεται*,
strangely accepted as an impersonal passive by LSJ, makes no sense.

70. 1. ὕδωρ: sc. *ἐξ οὐρανοῦ*, i.e. 'rain', as commonly in Thucydides.

ξυνεπιλαβέσθαι τοῦ φόβου: The inexperienced men plainly took the
storm to be a sign of divine displeasure. Cf. vii. 79. 3, where Thucydides
comments that the rain was to be expected at the season in question.

2. ἐς φυγὴν κατέστη: Once a hoplite phalanx was broken, it could
not easily re-form more quickly than the victorious unbroken phalanx

could follow it up; for that reason the τροπή of a Greek battle tends to be more dramatic and decisive than the turning-point of a modern battle.

4. ὡς ἐκ τῶν παρόντων: 'As best they could in their present situation.' But this was not bad; they were, after all, on the Heloron road, and not beyond it, as they were before the battle began (66. 3), and the Athenians were not able to prevent their dispatch of a garrison to the Olympieion.

71. 1. πρὸς μὲν τὸ ἱερὸν οὐκ ἦλθον: Seizure of the treasure of the sanctuary would have been a sacrilege, before which the Athenians would at least have hesitated.

τὰ ὀστᾶ ξυνέλεξαν: These charred bones would be sent back to Athens for public interment in the Kerameikos.

2. ὅπως μὴ παντάπασιν ἱπποκρατῶνται: The achievement of the Syracusan cavalry in preventing the Athenians from following up their victory was one of the decisive factors in the whole campaign. The Athenians had brought with them plenty of archers and slingers, whose function it was (22) to prevent this fatal domination of the battlefield by enemy cavalry. Thucydides makes no comment here on their failure to do so, or on the wisdom of the generals' decision to put off to the spring further operations against Syracuse; yet in vii. 42. 3 he reveals his opinion that this decision was wrong.

OCTOBER–NOVEMBER 415

72–73. Reorganization at Syracuse

72. 2. ἀνὴρ κτλ.: It seems a little surprising that Hermokrates should be 'introduced' to us when we have already seen him in action (32–34); but whereas in English 'a man who was . . .' would be most appropriate when a character is mentioned for the first time, this is not necessarily true of ἀνήρ . . ., which merely distinguishes a general statement about a man's quality and characteristics from statements about individual actions of his.

κατὰ τὸν πόλεμον: Since ὁ πόλεμος very commonly means 'war' in the abstract, evidence of Hermokrates' martial qualities may have been of much longer standing than the battle just described.

3. τὴν μὲν γὰρ γνώμην αὐτῶν κτλ.: From here to the end of the chapter summarizes Hermokrates' advice, with a reminder (ἔφη) in line 20 that this is the case.

ἰδιώτας ὡς εἰπεῖν χειροτέχναις: '—laymen, as it were, against crafts-men—.' Cf. Pl. *Sph.* 221 c, where ἰδιώτης is contrasted with 'a man who possesses some τέχνη'.

4. καὶ τὸ πλῆθος . . . καὶ τὴν πολυαρχίαν: 'Multiplication of authority' is a result of the 'number'; the parenthesis ἦσαν γὰρ κτλ. simply comments on the number, the multiplication of authority needing no separate comment.

οἷς τε ὅπλα μὴ ἔστιν ἐκπορίζοντες: If this was done on a substantial scale it would have given Syracuse a very large hoplite force; but Thucydides never gives us any indication of the size of the Syracusan land forces.

καὶ τῇ ἄλλῃ μελέτῃ προσαναγκάζοντες: 'And compelling them to train too.'

ἀμφότερα αὐτά: Courage and discipline; then we revert to the femi-nine gender, τὴν μέν referring to εὐταξία and εὐψυχία being synonymous with ἀνδρεία.

5. καὶ ὀλίγους καὶ αὐτοκράτορας: 'Few' is a cure for πολυαρχία, and 'with power to act at their own discretion'—the power being reinforced by an oath of the Assembly—is a cure for the 'disorderly indiscipline' of the ranks.

73. 1. ἐψηφίσαντό τε κτλ.: Evidently Athenagoras was no longer in-fluential; it must have been amusing to watch his face as he swore an oath which gave such wide powers to Hermokrates.

2. ἀπαγάγωσιν . . . ἐπιπέμπωσιν: The subject of the former verb is Sparta, and of the latter, Athens.

74. Athenian Attempt on Messene

74. 1. οἱ δέ . . . βουλόμενοι: 'They' (the friends of Syracuse) 'had al-ready' (before the arrival of the Athenians just mentioned) 'killed the conspirators'; then lit., 'and then, forming a faction and being in arms, prevailed not to receive the Athenians those who wished this', i.e. 'and now those who were opposed to receiving the Athenians, organizing themselves as an armed faction, prevailed on the city not to receive them'. Cf. v. 46. 4: 'the Spartans told the Boeotians that they would not give up the alliance; it was the party of Xenares the ephor whose view that this should be done prevailed' (ἐπικρατούντων . . . ταῦτα γίγνεσθαι, where ταῦτα refers to 'saying that they would not give up the alliance').

2. ὅρια: Normally 'boundary-markers', but the word must have some technical military sense here.

NOVEMBER 415–FEBRUARY 414

75. 1–2. Activity at Syracuse

75. 1. **τὸν Τεμενίτην**: Recent excavations have revealed an archaic sanctuary immediately adjoining the Theatre on the west, and there is no reasonable doubt that this is the sanctuary of Apollo Temenites. Cic. *Verr.* iv. 119 mentions the theatre and Apollo Temenites as both belonging to what in his day was called 'Neapolis'.

παρὰ πᾶν τὸ πρὸς τὰς Ἐπιπολὰς ὁρῶν: 'Epipolai' is briefly described in 96. 2, and it seems from that description to have been the plateau above the city. It would therefore appear at first sight that the Syracusans built a wall from the coast at a point north of the city, westwards and south-westwards to include Temenites, and then south and south-east to the Harbour. But this hypothesis is open to serious objections: it is impossible to reconcile with Thucydides' description (vii. 5 f.) of the building of the Third Counterwall and the fighting connected with that, and it would not have served particularly well the purpose 'that Syracuse might not be walled off easily at close quarters'. This purpose would best have been served by building a wall *northwards* from the region of Temenites to reach the sea near Santa Panagia; and if this is what the Syracusans actually did, the narrative of vii. 5 f. becomes fully intelligible. It follows that (a) 'all the part which looks towards Epipolai' includes the (mainly uninhabited) eastern end of the pleateau itself, (b) when in 96. 2 Thucydides describes Epipolai as 'all visible inside' he means that the centre and west of the plateau were visible from what was by then (summer 414) 'inside', and (c) when he says in vii. 4. 1 that the Third Counterwall began 'from the city' he includes in 'the city' the eastern end of the plateau.

καὶ τὰ Μέγαρα φρούριον: sc. *ἐτείχιζον*; 'and ⟨they fortified⟩ Megara ⟨as⟩ a garrison-post'. Megara was an uninhabited site (49. 4).

καὶ ἐν τῷ Ὀλυμπιείῳ: cf. 65. 3 n.

2. **σκηνάς**: Obviously not 'tents', which the Athenians would have taken with them, but wooden structures which it was not worth while to dismantle and erect elsewhere.

75. 3–88. 2. The Envoys at Kamarina

75. 3–4. *Introduction*

75. 3. **ἐπὶ Λάχητος**: Thucydides did not mention this alliance in his account of Laches' operations in Sicily; on its content, cf. 52. 1.

ἦσαν γὰρ ὕποπτοι . . . ἀμύνειν: lit., 'were suspected . . . not to have sent enthusiastically . . . and lest they might not in the future . . .'

4. **Εὐφήμου**: Nothing else is known of him.

καὶ ἄλλων . . . μεθ' ἑτέρων: There is no distinction of meaning here, but only stylistic variation.

76-80. Speech of Hermokrates

76. 1. **δείσαντες**: With ἐπρεσβευσάμεθα, not with καταπλαγῆτε.

2. **κατοικίσαι . . . ἐξοικίσαι**: Assonances of this kind may possibly have characterized the oratory of Hermokrates—cf. οὐκ ἀξυνετωτέρου, κακοξυνετωτέρου δέ in § 4 and εὐπρεπῶς ἄδικοι ἐλθόντες εὐλόγως ἄπρακτοι ἀπίασιν in iv. 61. 7—but they were certainly a conspicuous feature of Gorgias' style and are therefore liable to occur in any speech of the late fifth and early fourth centuries.

εὔλογον: The antithesis εὔλογος / ἄλογος recurs in 79. 2 and is picked up by Euphemos in 84. 2–85. 1. εὔλογον is almost 'consistent' here; it is used of that which can be plausibly explained and defended by rational argument.

ἀναστάτους: The reference is to those cities which Athens punished by expelling (and in some cases killing or enslaving) the whole population, e.g. Hestiaia (i. 114. 3), Poteidaia (ii. 70. 3), and Skione (v. 32. 1), all of them allies who had revolted, and Melos (v. 115. 4), for us the most notorious case because of the attention which Thucydides gives it.

οἵδε: Leontinoi.

3. **καὶ τὰ ἐνθάδε νῦν πειρῶνται**: Probably sc. ἔχειν; or, less effectively, 'they are making the attempts which they are now making here'.

ἑκόντων . . . τιμωρίᾳ: In 478 the states of the Aegean islands and coasts newly liberated from Persian rule invited Athens to become the head of an alliance of which the original purpose was to carry on a war of reprisals against Persia in Asia Minor (i. 95. 1, 96. 1); it was this alliance which Athens transformed into an empire.

καὶ ὅσοι ἀπὸ σφῶν ἦσαν ξύμμαχοι: 'Those allies who were of Athenian origin.' Thucydides accepted the general view that all the Ionians of the Aegean had originally come from Attica, so that unless ὅσοι κτλ. is completely tautologous it must refer to colonies in the ordinary sense, e.g. Lemnos and Imbros. By no means all the states which came under Athenian ἡγεμονία in 478 were of Ionic or Attic descent—Lesbos, for example, was Aeolic, and Rhodes was Doric—but to take account of that would have weakened the point which Hermo krates is making and part (77. 1) of his later argument.

τοὺς μέν . . . κατεστρέψαντο: lit., '⟨they subjected⟩ some ⟨having brought against them an accusation of⟩ failure to provide troops, ⟨they subjected⟩ others ⟨having brought against them an accusation of⟩ attacking one another, and against others, according as they had some plausible accusation ⟨to bring⟩ against them separately, having brought ⟨it⟩, they subjected ⟨them⟩'. λιποστρατία, the failure to take part in expeditions organized and led by Athens, was a cause of trouble from an early date (cf. i. 99); the war between Samos and Miletos, which led to the revolt of Samos from Athens (i. 115. 2 ff.), is an example of ἐπ' ἀλλήλους στρατεύειν.

4. **περὶ δέ ... καταδουλώσεως**: 'But the Athenians to secure enslavement ⟨of the Greeks⟩ to themselves instead of to the Persian.'

77. 1. **ἡμᾶς αὐτούς**: Whereas the subject of ἥκομεν is 'we, the envoys from Syracuse', he means by 'ourselves' the Siceliots as a whole.

ἔχοντες ... Ἑλλήνων: The normal Greek for 'with the example of the Greeks before us' would be παράδειγμα ἔχοντες τοὺς Ἕλληνας. Translate, therefore: 'having examples furnished by the Greeks of the Aegean ...'

σφίσιν αὐτοῖς: The whole trend of the argument points to 'one another' rather than 'themselves'.

οὐκ Ἴωνες τάδε εἰσίν: 'It's not Ionians here.'

Δωριῆς: At Gela, ten years earlier, Hermokrates had decried racial divisions and stressed the unity of Sicily. Now, with Leontinoi obliterated and Naxos and Katane irretrievably committed to Athens, he exploits the racial pride of the Dorian states in the maintenance of freedom by valour.

ἐπὶ τοῦτο τὸ εἶδος ... κακουργεῖν: ὥστε controls the three infinitives διιστάναι, ἐκπολεμοῦν, and κακουργεῖν, not the indicative δύνανται; cf. viii. 56. 2 τρέπεται ἐπὶ τοιόνδε εἶδος ὥστε τὸν Τισσαφέρνην ... μὴ ξυμβῆναι. κακουργεῖν normally takes an accusative (in Pl. R. 416 A ἐπιχειρῆσαι τοῖς προβάτοις κακουργεῖν it is perhaps treated as epexegetic), so that the analysis of τοῖς δέ is obscure. 'And, saying something attractive to others, according as they are able ⟨to say it⟩ to them separately, damage ⟨them⟩' is contorted; possibly it is better to allow κακουργεῖν to govern τοῖς, 'and damage others, according as they are able ⟨to do so⟩ by saying something attractive to them separately', but the parallel of 76. 3 supports the former analysis. It is obvious that Thucydides does not like the monotony of the sequence τοὺς μέν / τοὺς δέ / τοὺς δέ; cf. 35. 1.

καὶ οἰόμεθα ... δυστυχεῖν: 'And do we believe, when a distant neighbour is being destroyed first, that this peril will not come to oneself (αὐτόν τινα), but that the man who is the victim before one (αὐτοῦ) is alone in his misfortune?'

78. 1. **ἑαυτὸν δ' οὔ**: The accent on οὐ in the O.C.T. is intended to clarify the grouping of the words: 'that the Syracusan, and not he himself, is an enemy of the Athenian.' The reflexive pronoun as subject of an

infinitive is not common, but cf. D. xxi. 74 ἐμαυτὸν μέν γε ... σωφρό-
νως ... οἶμαι βεβουλεῦσθαι.

οὐ περὶ τῆς ἐμῆς ... μαχούμενος: Although Hermokrates at Gela
urged that neutrality was only a postponement of disaster, he did not
there draw attention to any possible divergence of interest between
Syracuse and other Siceliot states, much less suggest that any state
would actually welcome the downfall of Syracuse. Now he has to
speak in plainer terms.

τὴν ἐκείνου φιλίαν ... βεβαιώσασθαι: φιλία is a diplomatic relationship, not an emotion; in a fifth-century inscription of Selinus φιλίας
γενομένας = 'when peace has been made'. Hermokrates' words are not,
therefore, sarcastic, but they have a sinister undertone; a state of whose
φιλία the Athenians 'make sure' loses its freedom of action.

2. ἀμφότερα γάρ ... τὰ μείζω: 'For greatness' (lit., 'the greater
things', including great nations, such as Syracuse) 'incurs both these'
(i.e. resentment and fear).

οὐ γὰρ οἷόν τε ... γενέσθαι: lit., 'for ⟨it is⟩ not possible that the
same man should be similarly dispenser at the same time of his desire
and of his fortune', i.e. 'for though a man may desire what he will, he
cannot also decide what fortune is to grant him'.

3. καὶ εἰ γνώμῃ ἁμάρτοι: i.e. if, having decided that it was best to let
Syracuse be defeated by Athens, he later realized that his decision had
been wrong.

ὀλοφυρθείς: 'Lamented' for the evil fate which he has suffered. There
is no adequate justification for LSJ's treatment of this participle as
active in sense.

ἀδύνατον δὲ προεμένῳ: lit., 'but ⟨it is⟩ impossible for ⟨him⟩ having
abandoned ⟨me⟩'.

οὐ περὶ τῶν ὀνομάτων: As the next sentence shows, the point is that
the issues at stake are not in reality what they might appear to be.

4. ὁμόρους ὄντας: Kamarina was originally a colony of Syracuse, but
Hermokrates makes no sentimental appeal on those grounds; wisely,
since the mother-city had in earlier times done her best to exterminate
the recalcitrant colony (5. 3).

ὅπως μηδὲν ἐνδώσομεν: This clause simply amplifies ταῦτα.

79. 1. δειλίᾳ: A harsh word, which it would be wrong to soften in
translation. Hermokrates hopes by this taunt to make a legalistic
standpoint uncomfortable for Kamarina.

τῶν δὲ ἐχθρῶν ... ἴῃ: 'But against the possibility that one of your
enemies might attack you.'

ὑπ' ἄλλων: sc. ἀδικῶνται.

2. **τὸ ἔργον τοῦ καλοῦ δικαιώματος**: 'The reality in the specious claim.'

ἀλόγως σωφρονοῦσιν: Rhegion 'holds back' (or 'refrains from aggression') ἀλόγως because she acts on suspicion and, as an ally of Athens summoned to help kinsmen, could not easily make a plausible case for abstention; Kamarina acts εὐλόγῳ προφάσει because she could make such a case for helping Athens.

τοὺς δὲ ἔτι μᾶλλον φύσει ξυγγενεῖς: lit., 'those who are even more by nature ⟨your⟩ kin', i.e. 'your kinsmen, whose natural claim is stronger', the implication being that whereas it may often be right to refrain from attacking one's 'natural enemies' (i.e. men of another racial division) it is never right to refuse the claim of kinsmen for help.

3. **πρὸς ἡμᾶς μόνους**: For rhetorical purposes the help already received from Selinus and elsewhere (65. 1, 67. 2) is ignored.

80. 1. ἰέναι ἐς τὴν ξυμμαχίαν: Not 'enter into the alliance' in the sense 'make a pact of alliance, as is being proposed' (its meaning v. 30. 5), for Kamarina is already an ally of Syracuse, but 'join the allied forces'; cf. ξυμμαχία = 'allied force' in 73. 2.

ἐκείνην τὴν προμηθίαν: Amplified by τὸ μηδετέροις δή . . . βοηθεῖν.
ἴσην: 'Fair', 'just'.

2. **εἰ γάρ . . . γενέσθαι**: lit., 'for if . . . the victim is going to be worsted and he who has the upper hand' (virtually, 'the aggressor') 'is going to come out on top, surely (τί ἄλλο ἤ) by the same absence you did not protect the former ⟨so as to⟩ be preserved and you did not prevent the latter from being bad', i.e. '. . . surely by your abstention you have both failed to protect the victim and ensure his preservation and failed to restrain the aggressor from crime'. The infinitive σωθῆναι stands in a looser syntactical relation to the rest of its clause than almost any other 'consecutive' or 'final' infinitive in Thucydides.

φίλους: sc. 'of yours'.

3. **οὐδὲν ἔργον εἶναι**: lit., 'that it is not at all a task to . . .', i.e. 'that there is no need to . . .'.

4. **οἱ αὐτοί**: 'You, again.'

5. **τὴν αὐτίκα ἀκινδύνως δουλείαν**: The abstract noun δουλεία is treated here as if it were an infinitive, and so is qualified by adverbs; cf. ξυμμαχίαν . . . ἡμῖν in 34. 1.

κἂν περιγενόμενοι . . . διαφυγεῖν: 'The chance of winning, with us, and so both avoiding the shame of servitude to Athens' (lit., 'not to take these shamefully ⟨as⟩ masters') 'and escaping the ⟨sc. otherwise necessarily following⟩ feud with us, which would not be short-lived.'

Notice that the first μή negatives αἰσχρῶς . . . λαβεῖν, whereas the second μή negatives only the adjective βραχεῖαν.

81. (*Formula of Transition*)

82–87. *Speech of Euphemos*

82. 2. μαρτύριον: He means: Hermokrates' view of the hereditary enmity between Ionians and Dorians is testimony in favour of us, the defendants, who are charged with ruling an empire.

ἔχει δὲ καὶ οὕτως: 'And that is indeed the case'; cf. E. *El.* 1102 f. 'it is your nature always to love your father; ἔστιν δὲ καὶ τόδ'· some are on the side of the male . . .'.

Ἴωνες ὄντες . . . ὑπακουσόμεθα: lit., 'for we, being Ionians for the Peloponnesians, who are Dorians and more numerous and live beside us, considered how we should least be subject to them'. This, however, is unsatisfactory; we cannot take Πελοποννησίοις to mean '*in the eyes of* the Peloponnesians', for there was no room for doubt as to whether or not the Athenians were Ionians. Herwerden's deletion of αὐτῶν is the simplest remedy, making Πελοποννησίοις the object of ὑπακουσόμεθα.

3. μετὰ τὰ Μηδικὰ ναῦς κτησάμενοι: Not 'having obtained a fleet after the Persian Wars', for the great expansion of the Athenian fleet came *before* the invasion of Xerxes, but 'after the Persian Wars, as we had obtained a fleet'.

ἀρχῆς: The Spartans would not have accepted this word as describing their relation to their allies in 478.

ἡγεμόνες καταστάντες οἰκοῦμεν: = ἡγεμὼν ἡ πόλις ἡμῶν καθέστηκε. Cf. ii. 37. 1, 'the name of our political structure is "democracy" διὰ τὸ ἐς πλέονας οἰκεῖν', i.e. 'because the city is in the hands of a majority'.

ἐς τὸ ἀκριβὲς εἰπεῖν: The implication is: the explanation already given suffices for practical purposes, but, for the benefit of those who bother about rights and wrongs . . .

4. ἐπὶ τὴν μητρόπολιν ἐφ' ἡμᾶς: lit., 'against their mother-city, against us', i.e. 'against us, their mother-city'.

ὥσπερ ἡμεῖς ἐκλιπόντες τὴν πόλιν: The fact that the Athenians had voluntarily sacrificed their city in 480 was (rightly) a focus of Athenian pride ever afterwards. Contemptuous animosity against the Ionians for their failure to make similar sacrifices and their consequent inclusion in Xerxes' forces must always have played a part in rhetorical justifications of the Athenian Empire.

δουλείαν δέ . . . ἐπενεγκεῖν: δουλείαν ἐβούλοντο is doubtful Attic usage, with no closer parallel than τὸ βουλόμενον τὴν πολιτείαν πλῆθος and οἱ δημοκρατίαν βουλόμενοι in Arist. *Pol.* 1309ᵇ17, 1310ᵃ21. It can, however, be defended: (i) Abstract nouns are sometimes treated syntactically as if they were infinitives, e.g. τὴν αὐτίκα ἀκινδύνως δουλείαν in 80. 5. (ii) The expression τὰ Συρακοσίων βουλόμενοι in 50. 3 is not so very far removed from the combination of βούλεσθαι with an abstract noun as object. (iii) δουλείαν here is one of two objects of ἐβούλοντο, the other being the infinitive ἐπενεγκεῖν. Hence: 'they willingly accepted servitude themselves and ⟨were willing⟩ to impose that same servitude upon us.' An alternative interpretation is: 'they were willing ⟨to bear⟩ servitude themselves . . .', understanding φέρειν in the first part of the sentence from ἐπενεγκεῖν in the second; cf. 79. 1, where ἀδικῶνται in the first part is understood from ἀδικῶσιν in the second.

83. 1. ἅμα: He offers two justifications of the empire: first, 'we deserve it, because . . . and because . . .', and secondly (ἅμα δέ) 'we aim . . .'.
τοῦτο δρῶντες: i.e. providing ships and enthusiasm.

2. μόνοι καθελόντες: While dismissing this and other boasts as mere καλλιεπεῖσθαι (cf. the Athenian rejection of ὀνόματα καλά in the Melian Dialogue, v. 89), Euphemos is careful to mention them.
πᾶσι δὲ ἀνεπίφθονον κτλ.: A similar sentiment occurs in the speech attributed to the Athenians at Sparta before the outbreak of the war (i. 72 ff.): πᾶσι δὲ ἀνεπίφθονον τὰ ξυμφέροντα τῶν μεγίστων πέρι κινδύνων εὖ τίθεσθαι (i. 75. 5), as part of the argument: 'we could not let our empire go, because that would strengthen Sparta, whom we naturally feared.'
λόγου μέν . . . τερπομένους: He means: those who are suspicious (as Kamarina is) accept, for the moment, arguments (such as those of Hermokrates) which accord with their suspicious mood; but on reflection, &c. The point is a little forced in order to draw the familiar rhetorical contrast between disagreeable truth and specious oratory which is at once acceptable to the audience.

4. ἥκειν: sc. φαμέν.
καὶ οὐ δουλωσόμενοι κτλ.: sc. ὑμᾶς.

84. 1. καὶ διὰ τὸ μὴ κτλ.: μή negatives only ἀσθενεῖς.
τούτων . . . Πελοποννησίοις: The idea that Syracuse might actively help the Peloponnesians was used by Nikias (10. 4, 11. 3, 13. 1) as a good reason for not provoking her. Alkibiades did not for a minute regard it as a serious possibility. Now Euphemos exploits it as a justification of Athenian intervention in Sicily.

2. μὴ ὑπηκόους . . . ἀλλ' ὡς δυνατωτάτους: '⟨To make them⟩ not our subjects but as powerful as possible.'
τοῖσδε: Syracuse.

3. καὶ Λεοντῖνοι κτλ.: sc. ξύμφοροί εἰσιν ἡμῖν.

85. 1. ἀνδρὶ δέ ... ἐχούσῃ: The comparison implicit here first occurs in a Periklean speech, ii. 63. 2 ὡς τυραννίδα γὰρ ἤδη ἔχετε αὐτήν (sc. τὴν ἀρχήν); Kleon converts the comparison into an equation, iii. 37. 2 τυραννίδα ἔχετε τὴν ἀρχήν.

τοῦτο: Amplified by οὐκ ἦν κτλ.

2. ἀπιστεῖν δὲ οὐ χρή: sc. ὑμᾶς ἡμῖν.

νεῶν παροκωχῇ αὐτονόμους: After the suppression of the revolt of Mytilene, Chios and Methymna were the only remaining states in the Athenian Empire which had their own fleets. This privileged status carried with it not only freedom from monetary tribute but some degree of immunity from Athenian legal and political control; what degree exactly, we do not know.

ἐλευθέρως ξυμμαχοῦντας: i.e. as 'allies' in the proper sense of the word; the primary reference is to Kephallenia and Zakynthos (cf. vii. 57. 7), and an Athenian speaker would also have Kerkyra in mind; Kerkyra, however, would not have liked to be called εὔληπτος.

3. ὥστε καὶ τἀνθάδε ... καθίστασθαι: lit., 'so that ⟨it is⟩ rational to establish also what is here with a view to what is profitable and ⟨with a view to⟩ that of which we speak, fear into Syracuse'. This last phrase is ambiguous: 'frightening Syracuse' or 'our fear of Syracuse'? The latter is, on the whole, suggested by the argument of the previous chapter, and is supported by 'you have the same lack of fear into your allies' = 'you are similarly unafraid of your allies' in iii. 37. 2, and 'the hopes of the Greeks into you' = 'the Greeks' hopes of you' in iii. 14. 1.

ξυστήσαντες ὑμᾶς: ὑμᾶς refers not simply to Kamarina, but to the Siceliot states other than Syracuse; and this reference is present, in greater or lesser degree, wherever the second person plural is used in this speech.

βίᾳ ἢ καὶ κατ' ἐρημίαν: With ἄρξαι: 'to become rulers of Sicily either by force' (i.e. by attacking and defeating the other Siceliot states) 'or through the lack of anyone to help you' (in which case the threat of force, without its application, will suffice); κατ' ἐρημίαν is then explained: 'when we have failed and gone away.'

86. 1. ἐπηγάγεσθε: Kamarina was among the allies of Leontinoi who asked Athens for help in 427.

2. ἀπιστεῖν ... ὑποπτεύεσθαι ... ἀπιστεῖν: The understood subject of ἀπιστεῖν in both cases is 'you'; the subject of ὑποπτεύεσθαι is either 'we' or 'the fact that ...' (ὅτι ... πάρεσμεν). ὑποπτεύεσθαι elsewhere in Th. is always passive (e.g. 87. 1, 92. 2), and nowhere middle in Attic. For the changes of subject in the sequence A–B–A cf. 18. 6.

δυνάμει ... ἰσχύν: Prima facie, 'with a force out of proportion to their strength' (cf. 31. 6). But the question : 'if your force is bigger than your war against Syracuse requires, for what purpose is it bigger?' would be awkward, for Euphemos would naturally want to stress Athenian conformity with *necessity*. Therefore: 'with a force larger ⟨than before⟩, as the enemy's strength requires.'

3. ἀδύνατοι κατασχεῖν: Euphemos uses Nikias' argument (11. 1) in order to achieve the purpose which Nikias believed to be impossible.

τῆς ἡμετέρας παρουσίας: 'Than our force which is here now.'

4. ἔδειξαν δέ . . . καὶ τὰ ἐς Λεοντίνους: Despite the plural verb, 'their treatment of Leontinoi, among other things' is probably to be regarded as the subject; cf. viii. 96. 5 ἔδειξαν δὲ οἱ Συρακόσιοι, 'and Syracuse was the proof of this'.

ἐπὶ τούς . . . εἶναι: i.e. the Athenians.

5. διὰ τὸ πλῆθος: 'Because of their ⟨greater⟩ numbers.'

87. 2. πολλὰ δ' . . . πράσσειν: cf. τῆς ἡμετέρας πολυπραγμοσύνης in § 3 and the famous reproach which the Theban herald addresses to Theseus in E. *Su.* 576 πράσσειν σὺ πόλλ' εἴωθας ἥ τε σὴ πόλις.

3. τῶν ἡμῖν ποιουμένων: The position of ἡμῖν shows that it is emphatic.

4. διὰ τὸ ἑτοίμην . . . κινδυνεύειν: lit., 'through the fact that the expectation is there at hand, for the former, to get compensating help from us, and for the latter, if we are going to come, to be not unafraid to take a risk'. The MSS. have ἀδεεῖς, which is grammatically impossible; the best emendation is not ἀδεεῖ (for to say that the potential aggressor *expects* that he will be afraid is a little odd), but Reiske's ἀδεές, giving the sense: 'the expectation . . . in the latter that, if we are going to come, making the venture' (sc. of attacking his victim) 'will not be without danger.' Cf. i. 36. 1: 'his confidence, if it is not backed by strength and his enemies are strong, will be ἀδεέστερον', i.e. 'will not frighten them'.

ἀναγκάζονται . . . σῴζεσθαι: The senses 'they are compelled' and 'it necessarily follows' are combined: 'the aggressor has to hold back, whether he likes it or not, and the victim is necessarily kept safe without any action on his part.'

5. ἀλλ' ἐξισώσαντες . . . μεταλάβετε: It is doubtful whether this can mean 'behaving like other states, with our help change your policy . . . to one of attacking Syracuse', since the only certain example of intransitive ἐξισοῦν is in v. 71. 3, where it appears to be a military technical term, meaning 'extend one's front (in conformity with the enemy)'. Such a technical term would be rhetorically effective here,

but it requires us to delete τοῖς ἄλλοις, giving: 'make your forces, with us, equal to Syracuse', understanding 'them' with ἀντεπιβουλεῦσαι. Another possibility (W. A. Camps) is to emend τοῖς Συρακοσίοις to τοὺς Συρακοσίους: 'by joining forces with us, make Syracuse equal to the other states', i.e. 'no longer superior'. Cf. Hdt. viii. 13 ὅκως ἂν ἐξισωθείη τῷ Ἑλληνικῷ τὸ Περσικὸν μηδὲ πολλῷ πλέον εἴη.

88. 1–2. *Outcome of the Debate*

88. 1. [εἰ]: εἰ is indefensible; καθάπερ εἰ and ὡς εἰ are semantically quite different.

τοὺς ὀλίγους: Those mentioned in 67. 2, cf. 75. 3.

88. 3–88. 6. Athenian Activities

88. 3. αὐτοῖς: Here = σφίσιν.

4. οἱ πολλοὶ ἀφεισττήκεσαν: Since ἀφειστήκεσαν must here mean 'had revolted from Syracuse' (cf. vii. 58. 3, where the Sikels who helped Syracuse are described as ὅσοι μὴ ἀφέστασαν πρὸς τοὺς Ἀθηναίους), and there is a contrast between the Sikels of the plains and those of the hills, the MSS.' text is untenable unless we understand (as we cannot) an emphatic 'already' in antithesis to the εὐθύς of the next clause. Canter's emendation of οἱ to οὐ is therefore necessary: 'the Sikels of the plains . . . had not revolted in great numbers, but the inland settlements . . . at once, with few exceptions, joined the Athenians.' Later in the summer (103. 2) 'many of the Sikel tribes' (sc. of the plains) 'who had previously stood by (περιεωρῶντο) came to join the Athenians'.

ὀλίγοι: This conforms in gender with the inhabitants of the οἰκήσεις; cf. 53. 1.

5. ἀπεκωλύοντο: sc. προσαναγκάζειν; cf. Intr. I. 3. 18.

τόν τε χειμῶνα . . . διεχείμαζον: lit., 'and ⟨as for⟩ the winter, having moved . . . and having re-erected . . . they began to pass ⟨the rest of⟩ the winter ⟨there⟩'; τὸν χειμῶνα is the 'internal' object of διεχείμαζον.

6. ἐς Καρχηδόνα: We do not know how this overture was received at Carthage.

καὶ ἐς Τυρσηνίαν: Hostility between Syracuse and the Etruscans went back at least to the 470's. In 413 Etruscan troops actually served in the Athenian force at Syracuse (vii. 53. 2, 57. 11).

πλινθία: 'Bricks' or 'small blocks', but the Patmos Scholiast read πλινθεῖα, 'wooden frames for the making of bricks' (on the spot, as by the Peloponnesians at Plataia, ii. 78. 1), and that makes very much better sense. The transport of a significant quantity of bricks or blocks from Katane to Syracuse would have been a tall order for the Athenians.

88. 7–93. Alkibiades at Sparta

88. 7–88. 8. *Arrival of Syracusan Envoys*

88. 7. οἱ δ' ἐς τὴν Κόρινθον . . . πρέσβεις: 73. 2.

κατὰ τὸ ξυγγενές: Since Syracuse was a Corinthian colony; cf. 3. 2.

88. 8. αὐτοὶ πρῶτοι: i.e. they took this decision before anyone else, and they took it on their own initiative.

αὐτοῦ: 'On the spot', i.e. 'in Greece'.

88. 9–88. 10. *Arrival of Alkibiades*

88. 9. τότ': 61. 6 f.

ἐπὶ πλοίου φορτηγικοῦ: This had the advantage that it could go directly across the open sea and therefore could not be pursued or intercepted by the *Salaminia*.

ἐς Κυλλήνην τῆς Ἠλείας: After the Peace of Nikias Elis had joined the anti-Spartan alliance of Argos and Mantinea. This alliance was broken up by the Spartan victory at Mantinea. We do not know precisely what the relations between Sparta and Elis were from that time to the outbreak of war between them in 402; but a Corinthian fleet on its way to help Syracuse anchored at Pheia in Elis in 413 (vii. 31. 1). If this means that Elis was under Spartan control, Alkibiades went straight to 'enemy territory', and not, as Isokrates alleged fifteen years later (xvi. 9), to Argos.

ἐφοβεῖτο γάρ: *γάρ* introduces the reason why he would not go unless *ὑπόσπονδος*.

διὰ τὴν περὶ τῶν Μαντινικῶν πρᾶξιν: cf. 16. 6.

10. **καὶ τῶν ἐν τέλει ὄντων:** The meaning of this expression in any given passage depends on the state concerned and on the level of authority required for the issue concerned; thus one could say '*οἱ ἐν τέλει* declared war on Athens' and '*οἱ ἐν τέλει* fined the butcher for giving short weight', and the phrase would not denote the same people in both cases. In the present passage we are not told (yet) of a decision to help Syracuse, but only of the consideration given to this, and *οἱ ἐν τέλει* here may be either a little more or a little less than the kings and the Council of Elders. In certain passages of Thucydides (e.g. iv. 88. 1) and Xenophon (e.g. *HG* iii. 2. 23) *τὰ τέλη τῶν Λακεδαιμονίων* means the whole Spartiate assembly.

89–92. *Speech of Alkibiades*

89. 1. περὶ τῆς ἐμῆς διαβολῆς: 'On the allegations made against me.'

2. **τὴν προξενίαν ὑμῶν:** It was his grandfather (v. 43. 2) who renounced the proxeny (i.e. the hereditary, but voluntary, task of entertaining,

helping, and representing Spartan visitors to Athens). The most likely
time for the renunciation is the late 460's, when the pro-Spartan sentiment championed by Kimon received its decisive setback.

καὶ περὶ τὴν ἐκ Πύλου ξυμφοράν: Alkibiades looked after the wel-
fare of the Spartiate prisoners taken at Sphakteria.

τοῖς μὲν ἐμοῖς ἐχθροῖς . . . περιέθετε: Nikias and Laches put the
Spartan proposals for peace to the Athenians in 422/1 (v. 43. 2). For the
highly personal conception of politics implied in 'my enemies'—a conception which recedes later in the chapter—cf. 15. 2.

3. δικαίως: The conception of retaliatory justice implied in this
argument is characteristically Greek.

οὐκ εἰκότως: '—as he ought not to have been—.'

καὶ τῷ δήμῳ . . . μᾶλλον: Alkibiades is contrasting himself not with
Nikias or others who sometimes advocated policies at variance with
the popular mood, but with other members of his class (we meet some
of them in the pages of Plato) who professed contempt for democracy
and sympathy with Sparta.

4. τοῖς γὰρ τυράννοις . . . διάφοροί ἐσμεν: Alkibiades' paternal and
maternal ancestors (the latter were the Alkmeonidai) took part in the
expulsion of Hippias (cf. 59. 4), but αἰεί ποτε is an exaggeration (cf.
54. 6 n.).

πᾶν δὲ τὸ ἐναντιούμενον . . . ὠνόμασται: This definition is the con-
verse of the prevailing Athenian assumption (cf. 60. 1) that oligarchy
and tyranny amounted to much the same thing. δυναστεύειν = 'exercise δυναστεία'; cf. 38. 3.

ἡ προστασία ἡμῖν τοῦ πλήθους: cf. 28. 2.

τὰ πολλά: With ἕπεσθαι; τῆς δὲ κτλ. states the exception.

5. ἀκολασίας: ἀκολασία, the opposite of σωφροσύνη, was a characteristic of democracy in the eyes of its critics; the use of the word
reflects the familiar resentment felt by the rich and powerful against
initiative on the part of the poor and weak.

καὶ ἐπὶ τῶν πάλαι: The chronological reference is vague; probably
the 460's are intended.

6. τοῦ ξύμπαντος προέστημεν: Most men in politics claim to represent
the true interests of the whole community. Cf. the modern usages
'non-political' (= 'excluding all political views but mine') and 'putting
party before country' (= 'opposing the policy of my party').

ἐν ᾧ σχήματι . . . ξυνδιασῴζειν: 'To help to preserve the form ⟨of
government⟩ under which our city was in fact most powerful and least
subject to others' (ἐλεύθερος, of a state, = 'not ruled by other states')
'and which was inherited.'

ἐπεὶ δημοκρατίαν γε . . . καὶ λοιδορήσαιμι: lit., 'since those of us
who had any sense knew democracy ⟨for what it was⟩, and I myself
would ⟨know it⟩ as well as anyone by the extent to which I abused it'.
But this does not make sense; Valla's translation, *tum vero ipse, quo
maiore iniuria affectus sum, eo magis vitupero*, and the paraphrase of
Σᴹ point to a text which had the words μέγιστα ἠδίκημαι between ὅσῳ
καί and λοιδορήσαιμι: 'and I myself could abuse it as much as anyone,
in so far as I have been wronged ⟨by it⟩ more than anyone.' Cf. i. 68. 2
προσήκει ἡμᾶς οὐχ ἥκιστα εἰπεῖν, ὅσῳ καὶ μέγιστα ἐγκλήματα ἔχομεν.

90. 1. εἴ τι πλέον οἶδα: 'Whatever confidential information I have';
cf. 91. 1.

2. ἔπειτα . . . ἀποπειράσοντες: cf. the ambition ascribed to Alkibiades in 15. 2.

3. καὶ Ἴβηρας: From the Καρχηδονίων ἀρχή in Spain.

ἐχούσης . . . ἄφθονα: This fact was familiar to the Spartans, who had
(vainly) requested their 'friends in the West' in 431 to make them
a great number of ships.

πέριξ πολιορκοῦντες: This is essentially a metaphor; the fleet corresponds to a circumvallation which seals off the enemy from supplies
and communications, whereas operations on land correspond to the
assaults on a besieged city.

τῶν πόλεων . . . ἐντειχισάμενοι: βίᾳ ('by assault') and ἐντειχισάμενοι
('by building forts in their territories') are alternative methods of
λαβεῖν.

4. ὥστε εὐπορώτερον γίγνεσθαί τι αὐτῶν: εὔπορος is commonly used
of that *for* which provision is easily made; γίγνεσθαι here serves, as
often, as the passive of ποιεῖν.

91. 1. καὶ ὅσοι ὑπόλοιποι στρατηγοί: Only two were in fact left in
Sicily; but Alkibiades may mean the whole college of ten, or he may
assume that others will be sent to Sicily.

3. ἔχεται . . . Σικελία: This at least is not an unreasonable exaggeration.

4. τάδε: Amplified by στρατιάν τε κτλ.

ἄνδρα Σπαρτιάτην ἄρχοντα: Spartan commanders of allied troops
were not all an unqualified success; but Brasidas had won great respect
in the north, and on Gylippos and his father cf. 104. 2 and vii. 5. 3.

6. Δεκέλειαν: 18 km. north of Athens, on the route to Oropos and
thereafter to the Euripos.

καὶ μόνου αὐτοῦ . . . οὐ διαπεπειρᾶσθαι: The possibility of establishing a fortified position in Attica was actually entertained by the
Spartans at the beginning of 421 (v. 17. 2).

εἰ ἃ μάλιστα . . . ἐπιφέροι: lit., 'if, what he realized that they feared
more than anything, this, being clearly informed ⟨about it⟩, he brought
to bear ⟨on them⟩'. But it is not clear what distinction between
'realizing' and 'obtaining information' is intended; the Spartans could
be said to 'realize' *or* 'obtain information' on the importance of Dekeleia
now, but we do not want both, and πυνθανόμενος may be an intrusive
gloss occasioned by a misunderstanding of σαφῶς, which with ἐπιφέροι
would mean 'outright' or 'without hesitation'; cf. τὸν . . . πόλεμον
σαφέστερον ποιεῖσθαι in 88. 8.

εἰκὸς γάρ . . . φοβεῖσθαι: 'For it is to be expected that each state
would itself know more accurately than anyone what its own peculiar
perils are, and fear them.'

7. οἷς τε γάρ . . . κατεσκεύασται: This includes all the tangible means
of human utilization of the land : farms, livestock, equipment, orchards,
slave workers, and mines. Cf. 17. 3.

αὐτόματα: This refers to the desertion of slaves.

τοῦ Λαυρείου: The mines of this region, the southern tip of Attica,
were a rich source of silver in the fifth century.

καὶ δικαστηρίων: Loss of revenue 'from the law courts' can only mean
that if a high proportion of the citizens are continuously under arms
(which did in fact happen [vii. 28. 2]) it is difficult to find juries for the
hearing of lawsuits; in consequence there is less paid jury-service
available to the ordinary citizen. Since this *saves* the state money,
Thucydides must be speaking throughout not simply of state revenue
but also of the citizens' sources of income as individuals; even the
tribute, mentioned at the end of the section, is regarded as affecting this
indirectly (cf. 24. 3). προσόδους is quite acceptable in this sense; cf. D.
xxvii. 18 al. The idea that jury pay was a significant part of the
Athenian national income was ludicrous, but highly acceptable to
a Spartan audience, which no doubt entertained as many misconcep-
tions about the Athenian economy as Americans and Russians do
about each other's economy. The hearing of private lawsuits was
suspended during the last years of the Peloponnesian War, as we learn
from Lys. xvii. 3; there were similar suspensions in the fourth century,
cf. D. xxxix. 17, xlv. 4. In this passage Thucydides is attributing to
a speaker a brief allusion which becomes fully intelligible to us only in
the light of our evidence for later events; if, however, private lawsuits
had been suspended during the earlier Peloponnesian invasions, the
allusion would not seem to him obscure.

92. 1. γίγνεσθαι δέ τι αὐτῶν: lit., 'that something of them (= the

building of the fort and the consequences which Alkibiades has pre-
dicted) should come about'. Cf. Intr. I. 3. 11.

ὥς γε δυνατά: 'That it *can* be done'; the understood subject of δυνατά
(sc. ἐστι) is just what αὐτῶν above refers to.

2. ἐς τὴν φυγαδικὴν προθυμίαν: 'The usual (τήν) zeal of exiles.'

4. τό τε φιλόπολι . . . ἐπολιτεύθην: The two relative clauses must be
treated as if they were nouns in the dative, or nouns governed by ἐς:
'I have a patriotic loyalty not to conditions in which I am wronged but
to those in which I exercised my rights as a citizen in security.' Alkibiades cannot mean 'I was once patriotic, but am so no longer', for he goes
on to define the true φιλόπολις in terms which are meant to apply to
himself.

5. τοῦτον δή . . . λόγον: At this point Alkibiades' attempt to dis-
sociate himself from the common run of exiles breaks down; but he is
possibly referring to an adage of wider application, cf. 'set a thief to
catch a thief'.

ἤκαζον: sc. 'only'.

93. *Consequences of Alkibiades' Speech*

93. 2. προσεῖχον ἤδη τὸν νοῦν: Yet a full year passed before they
carried it out. It has been suggested that Thucydides attributed to
Alkibiades' speech on arrival advice which he did not actually give until
much later; but the explanation which Thucydides offers (vii. 18. 2) of
Spartan delay, their anxiety to have a case which would afford the gods
no excuse to punish them for breaking a peace treaty, is adequate.

3. ἐς Ἀσίνην: This is probably the Asine which lies in the south-west
corner of the Messenian Gulf, not its namesake in the Lakonian Gulf.
ἀνεχώρουν: sc. the Syracusans and Corinthians.

4. ἢν ἀπέστειλαν: 74. 2.
τήν τε τροφήν: Money for the purchase of food, as commonly.

EIGHTEENTH YEAR OF THE WAR

MARCH–APRIL 414

94. Athenian Activities in Eastern Sicily

94. 1. ἐπὶ Μεγάρων: B has the ethnic Μεγαρέων, which is superficially
easier as the antecedent of οὕς. But since the site of Megara was uninhabited, 'sailed to Μεγαρῆς, whom the Syracusans expelled' is not

really easier than 'sailed to Megara, whom (= the population of which)
...' (cf. 88. 4 n.). Elsewhere Thucydides uses the place-name Μέγαρα
when referring to the site as it was in 415–413.
εἴρηται: 4. 2.

2. ἔρυμά τι: We were told in 75. 1 that the Syracusans made the site of
Megara a φρούριον. If the ἔρυμά τι and the φρούριον are the same, τι
betrays absent-mindedness in Thucydides; but perhaps a system of
ἐρύματα could be called φρούριον.
ἐπὶ τὸν Τηρίαν: cf. 50. 4.
καὶ τὸν σῖτον ἐνεπίμπρασαν: A Sicilian cornfield in March is more
combustible than its English counterpart at the same season.

3. ἐπὶ Κεντόριπα: The modern Centorbi, 40 km. north-west of Katane.
τῶν τε Ἰνησσαίων καὶ τῶν Ὑβλαίων: After the end of the Deinomenid tyranny the colonists whom Hieron had established at Katane
(which he had renamed Aitna) were expelled, and occupied Inessa,
which they called Aitna, Katane reverting to its original name.
Evidently by Thucydides' time the town had come into the possession
of Sikels who were under the control of Syracuse. On Hybla cf. 62. 5.

4. τούς τε ἱππέας ἥκοντας: cf. 93. 4.
καὶ τάλαντα ἀργυρίου τριακόσια: The record of this payment survives in the accounts of the Treasurers of Athena for 417/16–415/14, *IG*
i². 302 (*GHI* 75), 73 ff.: 'In the eighth prytany ... on the third day of
the prytany, to the hellenotamiai and their assessors, Aristokrates
Euonymeus and his colleagues, 300 talents; and these gave it to the
army [in Sicily].'

MARCH–APRIL 414

95. Fighting in Greece

95. 1. μέχρι μὲν Κλεωνῶν: Kleonai was an ally of Argos in 418, and presumably remained under Argive control after the democratic counter-
revolution in Argos. As it lay *c.* 23 km. north-north-east of Argos, and
yet the Spartan invasion was interrupted by the earthquake, the
Spartans must first have gone northwards through Arcadia to Phleius,
their ally, to join with troops from Phleius, and then begun their
operations with an attack on the territory of Kleonai, intending to work
southwards.
σεισμοῦ δὲ γενομένου: It was normal for a Spartan force to turn
back at this sign of divine displeasure.
ἐς τὴν Θυρεᾶτιν: This territory on the east coast of the Peloponnese
was in Spartan possession, but Argos never abandoned her claim to it.

2. **καὶ ὁ Θεσπιῶν δῆμος**: Thespiai, like Plataiai, tended to look towards Athens and away from the Boeotian confederation. Evidently there had been some doubt of its loyalty to Thebes during the Athenian invasion of Boeotia in 424, for in the following year Thebes compelled it to demolish its walls, 'accusing it of *ἀττικισμός*' (iv. 133. 1).

οὐ κατέσχεν: 'Did not achieve its purpose.'

ἐξέπεσον: Almost any compound of *πίπτειν* may serve as the passive of the corresponding compound of *βάλλειν*.

APRIL–JUNE 414

96–103. The Athenians Begin the Siege

96–98. *The Athenians Secure Control of the Plateau*

96. 1. **τοὺς [τε] ἱππέας**: τε (om. BE) is probably sound; the Syracusans learnt (a) that the Athenians had received cavalry, and (b) that ⟨the Athenians⟩ were going to attack Syracuse.

τῶν Ἐπιπολῶν: cf. 75. 1 n.

τὰς προσβάσεις αὐτῶν: The points at which it was easy for an army to ascend the plateau, notably Euryelos (97. 2 n.) and 'Scala Greca', where the modern road from Syracuse descends the northern edge and goes towards Megara.

2. **ἐξήρτηται**: lit., 'is hung', i.e. 'is steep'. There are few places where the edges of the plateau present any difficulty to a man picking his way up or down, but even fewer where a body of troops could move straight up in formation.

καὶ μέχρι τῆς πόλεως . . . ἔσω: The plateau 'slopes down towards the city', but the greater part of its surface is not visible from Ortygia or the older parts of the city; see 75. 1 n. for the interpretation of Thucydides' words here.

3. **ἄρτι παρειληφότες τὴν ἀρχήν**: They were elected at the beginning of the winter (73. 1), but probably at Syracuse (as at Athens) there was a considerable interval between election to military office and assumption of that office. This, then, will have been the generals' first review.

φυγὰς ἐξ Ἄνδρου: Andros was a subject-ally of Athens, and Diomilos had possibly incurred exile for anti-Athenian activities.

ὅπως . . . εἶεν . . . καί . . . παραγίγνωνται: There is no reason to suppose that the optative and subjunctive differ in 'vividness' or 'remoteness'; the same co-ordination of moods, but in reverse order, is to be found in vii. 17. 4.

97. 1. ταύτης τῆς νυκτός . . . ἔλαθον κτλ.: This is nonsense: 'the
Athenians, on the day which followed this night' (i.e. the night at
the end of which the Syracusans mustered at dawn) 'were mustered for
review and . . . landed unperceived by the Syracusans.' When the
Athenians, marching from a landing place some distance to the north,
appeared on the plateau, the Syracusan muster was still in progress
(§§ 2 f.); but they cannot have carried out a muster at Katane, em-
barked, sailed to Leon, disembarked, and marched on Epipolai, all
between the dawn and the end of the Syracusan muster, nor, if they
needed an ἐξέτασις at all, would they have put it off to this morning
when they were able to hold it the previous day. Nor, again, is the
sequence of tenses in ἐξητάζοντο καὶ ἔλαθον acceptable in the sense
'mustered their forces and then escaped notice . . .'. The simplest
solution is Krüger's: to delete τῇ ἐπιγιγνομένῃ ἡμέρᾳ ἐξητάζοντο as an
explanatory gloss on ταύτης, and to delete καί as syntactical padding
inserted after the gloss had been incorporated in the text. Hence:
'during this night the Athenians, unknown to the Syracusans, came
from Katane with their entire force and landed at Leon . . .', dis-
embarking at first light.

ἐξ ἢ ἑπτὰ σταδίους: Presumably in a straight line from the nearest
point of the edge of the plateau.

Θάψον: cf. 4. 1 n.

2. Εὐρύηλον: The fact that this was the place of ascent from the
north, but also, on a later occasion, from the south (vii. 43. 3), suffices
to show that it was the 'waist' of the plateau, just east of the modern
village of Belvedere.

5. Λαβδάλῳ: Nothing more is known of this locality than what
Thucydides tells us.

98. 1. ἔλαβον: 'Were given', not 'requisitioned'.

2. Συκῆν: The capital letter is not justified. συκῆ = 'figtree', and
a tree of exceptional size, shape, or antiquity may easily acquire the
status of a place in terms of which directions are given. Thucydides
writes here, as in 97. 5 (the definite article with 'Labdalon') and 100. 1
('the pyramid'), as if objects and places familiar to him from eye-
witness accounts of the fighting at Syracuse were equally familiar to
his readers. (There was a later tradition which confused 'the figtree'
with the area—the eastern part of the plateau—which in Hellenistic
times contained a sanctuary of Tyche, 'Fortune', and was named
Tyche after the sanctuary; hence in this passage f has Τυκήν, cf. Ἰτυκήν
in the MSS. of Diod. xi. 68. 1).

ἐτείχισαν τὸν κύκλον: For convenience we may call this structure 'the
Circle', but it was not necessarily circular; κύκλος is used of a perimeter

wall enclosing an area of any shape. The aorist ἐτείχισαν ('they *completed* the building of . . .', not 'they *began* to build . . .') and later references to the Circle (e.g. 101. 1) show that it cannot possibly mean 'the wall encircling Syracuse'; it was simply the main Athenian fortified position on the plateau. Thucydides writes '*the* Circle' as if his readers must know that a building of this kind played a prominent part in the story of the fighting at Syracuse.

4. **φυλή**: When the whole hoplite force of Athens was in the field it operated in ten tribal 'regiments', but we do not know how far this was true of small forces. The Athenian hoplites at Syracuse numbered 1,500 (excluding epibatai), and if they were drawn from all the tribes equally, 'one tribe of hoplites' was about 150 strong. The allied hoplites were drawn unequally from many states, and it appears from 67. 1 and 101. 6 that men of the same nationality were kept together, not distributed among the Athenian tribal contingents. Thucydides would probably use the term 'tribe of hoplites' to denote any contingent of about 150 hoplites which was composed of all the available members of either (a) one Athenian tribe, or (b) one tribe of any other nation which contributed several hundred hoplites, or (c) one smaller nation, or (d) a homogeneous group of very small nations.

99–100. *The Athenian Northern Wall and the First Syracusan Counterwall*

99. 1. **τὸ πρὸς βορέαν τοῦ κύκλου τεῖχος**: 'The wall northwards from the Circle'; cf. ii. 96. 4. οἰκοῦσι δ' οὗτοι πρὸς βορέαν τοῦ Σκόμβρου ὄρους, 'these people live to the north of Mt. Skombros'.

Τρώγιλον: A deep gully runs down to the sea at the cove of Santa Panagia; the west side of this gully is a naturally strong position, and an obvious course for the Athenian northward wall. Livy xxv. 23. 10 speaks of *portus Trogilorum*, which can only be Santa Panagia; Trogilos was therefore the cove or the gully. In strict mathematical terms, it does not offer exactly 'the shortest route to the sea', but any point in the region of Scala Greca or Santa Panagia satisfies that description by contrast with the coast further west.

2. **ἀποκλῄσεις . . . γίγνεσθαι**: The alternative interpretations are: (a) lit., 'and ⟨they decided⟩ that, to see if they could anticipate ⟨the Athenians⟩, debarments ⟨of the Athenians⟩ should be effected', referring to something which the Syracusans thought they should do themselves, and (b) 'and cuttings off ⟨of Syracuse⟩ ⟨were going⟩ to be effected, if they (the Athenians) were to anticipate ⟨the Syracusans⟩', making ἀποκλῄσεις a further subject of ἔμελλον and referring to the

Athenian threat. The plural ἀποκλῄσεις suits (a) better, implying 'wherever the Athenians try to build a siege-wall, we will build a counter-wall in the way of it'; it would be an odd way of expressing (b). The only prima-facie argument in favour of (b) is that in the following part of the sentence φθάνειν αὐτοὶ κτλ., 'and that they *themselves* should get in first by occupying . . .' refers to the Syracusans and that accordingly the subject of φθάσειαν ought, by contrast, to be the Athenians. This argument, however, can be met by associating the emphatic αὐτοί with προκαταλαμβάνοντες rather than with φθάνειν.

εἰ ἐπιβοηθοεῖν: 'In case they (the Athenians) should try to intervene', exactly as in 100. 1.

μέρος ἀντιπέμπειν . . . τὰς ἐφόδους: 'To send out part of their army as a counter-measure (ἀντι- αὐτοῖς) and themselves occupy ⟨with that part of their army⟩ the approaches ⟨to the proposed counterwall⟩ with their stakes before the Athenians could stop them.' αὐτοῖς is Bekker's necessary emendation for αὐτούς. After φθάνειν, B has αὐτοί, the other MSS. having ἄν; ἄν is not wanted, for we are still concerned with what the Syracusans were deciding to do, and we do not pass over to what they thought the Athenians would do until we come to ἐκείνους δέ. Obviously the Syracusans could not expect to defeat the *whole* Athenian army with *part* of their own army; therefore the function of this 'part' must be to plant and defend a stockade (easily defensible by a small force against much larger forces, if the defenders are vigilant) while the rest of the army pressed on with the building of the counterwall.

τοῖς is very doubtful, since no stakes have been referred to so far, and these stakes were not a permanent feature of the fighting; it may originate in a marginal correction of αὐτούς to αὐτοῖς.

ἐκείνους δέ . . . τρέπεσθαι: More trouble with ἄν, which appears twice in the other MSS. but not at all in B. We need at least one ἄν (and there is no linguistic objection to two), since we are now being told what the Syracusans thought the Athenians *would* do, not what they were deciding to do themselves. ἀναπαυομένους, which B gives us in place of ἄν παυομένους, is, moreover, inappropriate; we want not 'resting from', but 'breaking off'.

3. κάτωθεν τοῦ κύκλου: 'On the seaward side of the Circle', i.e. between the Circle and the harbour, or 'on ground lower than the Circle'; but Thucydides does not explain whether he means between the Circle and the edge of the plateau or between the edge and the harbour. Since the Second Counterwall is described simply as 'across the marsh' (101. 2), and the edge of the plateau is 'above the marsh' (101. 1), we may suspect that Thucydides was unaware of the considerable tract of sloping ground which separated the edge from the marsh. From a tactical point of view, it would have been ideal for the

Syracusans if they could have built this first counterwall *along* the edge of the plateau; this would have given them a wall which could be attacked from one side only. But, as we have seen, they proposed to protect their counterwall by putting stakes on 'the approaches', and a wall built along the edge would have no special 'approaches'; it could have been attacked, during its building, from *any* point on its northern side. It is therefore probable that the Syracusans built the counterwall across the sloping tract between the plateau and the marsh, planting stakes at various points on and immediately below the edge, wherever descent would be easiest for the enemy.

ἐγκάρσιον τεῖχος: 'A wall at right angles', sc. to the Athenian wall.

τοῦ τεμένους: Presumably the sanctuary of (Apollo) Temenites (75. 1 n.).

100. 1. δίχα γιγνομένοις: Perhaps an additional argument for the hypothesis that the counterwall ran below the edge of the plateau; had it been on the plateau, the union of separate parts of the Athenian force would have been quick and easy.

φυλὴν μίαν: Assuming that there were three tribes at Syracuse (as normally in Dorian cities), one third of the army seems a surprisingly large garrison for the counterwall, and the reference may be to a tribal contingent of one age-category only.

τούς τε ὀχετοὺς αὐτῶν . . . διέφθειραν: Thanks to Arethusa, the inexhaustible spring on Ortygia, this deprivation could never be fatal to Syracuse.

ποτοῦ ὕδατος: If we think of this phrase as equivalent to an adjective qualifying ὀχετούς its position, in the relative clause, is a little less surprising.

τῶν ψιλῶν τινὰς ἐκλεκτούς: This shows an interesting absence of rigidity in the Athenian social, economic, and military organization. When speed was all-important (as here) for an operation, and some exceptionally fast runners were to be found among the light-armed troops, there was no hesitation in equipping and using these men as hoplites.

πρὸς τὸ ὑποτείχισμα: Straight down the edge of the plateau, as fast as possible.

πρὸς τὴν πόλιν: on the plateau, between the Circle and the Winter Wall.

εἰ ἐπιβοηθοῖεν: 'in case they (the Syracusans) should try to intervene.'

πρὸς τὸ σταύρωμα: Along the sloping tract below the edge, from the west, having descended from the plateau much further to the west, possibly even at Euryelos.

τὸ παρὰ τὴν πυλίδα: If τό is right (om. B) it does not distinguish one stockade from others, for only one stockade is in question throughout,

but means 'that ⟨part of the stockade which ran⟩ past . . .'. Then BH
have πυραμίδα, of which πυλίδα in the other MSS. seems to be a banal
corruption; there is no more difficulty in a passing reference to 'the
pyramid' than in the reference to 'the figtree' (98. 2).

101–102. The Athenian Southern Wall and the Second Syracusan Counterwall

101. 1. **ἀπὸ τοῦ κύκλου ἐτείχιζον . . . τὸν κρημνόν:** We might infer
from these words by themselves that the Circle was *on* the edge, and
that the Athenians built a wall *along* the edge eastwards and westwards
from it. But § 3 τὸ πρὸς τὸν κρημνόν . . . ἐξείργαστο shows that they did
not. Perhaps, therefore, πρός should be inserted here (so Stahl).
Alternatively, if the 'double wall' (103. 1), i.e. pair of walls, which they
built from below the edge towards the sea was in fact 'double' from
the Circle onwards, the building of *two* walls from the Circle to the
edge might be described in the words 'they fortified the cliff from the
Circle'.

2. **διὰ μέσου τοῦ ἕλους:** One cannot plant a stockade or dig a ditch
through a lake; therefore the area which Thucydides calls 'the marsh'
was not all standing water, but was a low-lying area containing marshy
patches.

3. **περὶ ὄρθρον:** ὄρθρος precedes ἕως; hence 'before first light'.
ᾗ πηλῶδες ἦν κτλ.: If the Athenians needed flat boards to cross the
ground 'where it was firmest', there must have been some very watery
tracts north of the counterwall.

4. **καὶ μάχη ἐγένετο:** With the main Syracusan forces, as the sequel
shows, not simply with the garrison of the stockade and ditch, who
were by now dead or in flight.
παρὰ τὸν ποταμόν: The two wings of the Syracusan army were thus
retreating on divergent courses; the right wing had gone so far back to
the east, towards the city, that the left wing had the Athenian left
between itself and the city. Therefore it tried to get to the Olympieion,
for which it was necessary to cross the river by the bridge. If it is true
that they retreated '*along* the river', the battle must have begun
a good 3 km. from the city, close to the point where the river turns
sharply to the south-east. This argues a surprising length for the
Syracusan stockade, and it becomes impossible to locate the marshy
ground which the Athenians crossed in order to capture the stockade,
considering that the pitched battle did not develop until after the whole
of the stockade was in Athenian hands. It is therefore necessary to
suppose that the Syracusan left wing retreated not *along* the river,
south-eastwards, but *towards* the river, south-westwards. The fault

lies not in the MSS.' text but in Thucydides' visualization of the terrain.

5. **φυλή**: cf. 98. 4 n.

6. **ἀπὸ τοῦ εὐωνύμου**: The Athenian left had been pressing the Syracusan right back towards the east and the city.

ἀπεχώρουν: Over the bridge and to the fortified position at the Olympieion.

102. 2. δεκάπλεθρον προτείχισμα: This advanced fortification lay to the east of the Circle and was probably connected with it by a fortified way. Hdt. ii. 149. 3 reckons six πλέθρα to a stade, and this is consonant with other passages in which πλέθρον or compound adjectives in -πλεθρος are used; but πλέθρον is also the standard unit of *area*—rather as if we used the word 'mile', when we wished, to mean 'square mile'—and Thucydides does not reveal whether he means a fortification which measured ten plethra one way and an unspecified distance the other, or one of which the perimeter was ten plethra long, or one which was ten square plethra in area.

διεκώλυσεν: sc. αὐτοὺς αἱρεῖν.

τὰς γὰρ μηχανάς . . . ἐμπρῆσαι: Close to the wall, so that it could not be scaled. The μηχαναί would be cranes, ramps, and scaffolding; the Athenians had not had any occasion yet to build siege-engines.

ἀδυνάτους ἐσομένους: As the reference is to Nikias himself as well as to the others with him, the nominative plural would be grammatically possible; cf. 49. 2.

ἐρημίᾳ ἀνδρῶν: It sounds as if the Circle was left wholly denuded of soldiers; yet, if this was so, it is hard to see how Nikias' attendants had time to fire the machinery before the enemy was upon them. The wall may therefore have been manned by a skeleton garrison, just enough to make the Syracusans pause to consider at what point they would assault it.

3. **ἐπανῄει**: Straight up the edge, and therefore not in a solid formation. Stronger nerves and quicker reactions on the part of the Syracusans might yet have saved the day for them.

103. 1. τείχει διπλῷ: Unlike the English 'double wall', τεῖχος διπλοῦν can mean a pair of walls which start from the same point and thereafter run a considerable distance apart.

103. 2-4. *Consequences of the Athenian Victory*

103. 2. ἐκ τῆς Ἰταλίας: Thucydides refers to supplies from Italy in general terms in vii. 14. 3 and 25. 1, but tells us nothing precise save that in the early summer of 413 (vii. 25. 2) there was a stock of shipbuilding timber, destined for the Athenians, at Kaulonia.

τῶν Σικελῶν: cf. 88. 4.

ἐκ τῆς Τυρσηνίας: The result of the Athenian approach mentioned in 88. 6. In the narrative of 414–413 we hear of Etruscan troops (e.g. vii. 53. 2) but no more of the Etruscan ships.

πεντηκόντοροι: cf. 43 n.

3. τοὺς δὲ λόγους . . . πρὸς τὸν Νικίαν: The definite article affects the translation; not 'and they discussed an armistice . . .', but lit., 'their talk they made of an armistice . . .', 'they spoke only of an armistice, both among themselves and in negotiation with Nikias'.

4. ἀνθρώπων ἀπορούντων: This at first sight looks highly general, 'when men are in despair', but the following words relate closely to Syracuse, 'and more ⟨closely⟩ besieged than before ⟨they made their plan to avoid this predicament⟩'. Hence lit., 'as is to be expected, they being men in despair . . .', i.e. 'as one would expect of men who were in despair . . .'.

ἢ δυστυχίᾳ ἢ προδοσίᾳ: Bad luck and treachery are not, to our way of thinking, indifferent alternatives; but accusations of treachery and venality were made very freely in Greek states, and a record of good luck was an important qualification in a commander (cf. 17. 1). Incompetence, the usual reason for a commander's failure, does not seem to be taken into account; perhaps having elected their generals themselves the Syracusans were not willing to admit that their judgement of military competence had been wrong.

Ἡρακλείδην καὶ Εὐκλέα καὶ Τελλίαν: This Herakleides is certainly not the son of Lysimachos (73. 1), for that Herakleides was one of the generals now dismissed, and is probably to be identified with Herakleides son of Aristogenes, commander of a Syracusan contingent in the Aegean five years later (X. HG i. 218). Eukles (son of Hippon) was also with that contingent. Nothing is known of Tellias.

104. The Approach of Gylippos

104. 1. καὶ αἱ ἀπὸ τῆς Κορίνθου νῆες: 93. 3.

πρὸς ταῖς σφετέραις δέκα: This number includes the two with Gylippos and Pythen, as becomes clear in vii. 2. 1+7. 1.

Λευκαδίας . . . καὶ Ἀμπρακιώτιδας: Both Leukas and Ambrakia were Corinthian colonies and consistently loyal to Corinth.

2. πρεσβευσάμενος: The middle is used of sending envoys, the active of going on an embassy (in LSJ s.v. πρεσβεύω II. 3b the difficult passage v. 39. 2 is entirely misunderstood).

καὶ τὴν τοῦ πατρὸς ἀνανεωσάμενος πολιτείαν: This is the text of B: 'and having renewed his father's citizenship (sc. of Thurioi)'. But citizenship is not something which one can 'renew', and the text of ACEFHM is far superior: κατὰ τὴν τοῦ πατρός ποτε πολιτείαν 'in accordance with the citizenship which had once been granted to his father'; cf. κατὰ τὸ ξυγγενές, κατὰ τὸ ξυμμαχικόν, and (75. 3) κατὰ τὴν ἐπὶ Λάχητος γενομένην ξυμμαχίαν πρεσβεύεσθαι. Presumably ἀνανεωσάμενος was interpolated after κατά had been corrupted to καί.

Kleandridas, Gylippos' father, became a citizen of Thurioi when he was exiled from Sparta in 446/5, and commanded the Thurians successfully in their local wars.

κατὰ τὸν Τεριναῖον κόλπον: As Thucydides believed that it was a north wind which drove Gylippos out to the open sea, he must have thought that the bay in question was on the east or south coast of the 'toe' of Italy. In that area north-east and offshore winds prevail. However, Terina lay on the *north-west* coast of the 'toe', and the Bay of Terina was the modern Bay of Santa Eufemia, where the prevailing winds are west-south-west. Gylippos is highly unlikely to have gone there, bypassing Sicily, nor would he have gone all the way back from there to Taras. The simplest explanation of this difficulty is that Thucydides had Skylletion in mind but mistakenly thought of it under the name of Terina.

105. Fighting in the Peloponnese

105. 1. αἵπερ τὰς σπονδάς . . . ἔλυσαν: The peace treaty bound 'Athens and her allies' and 'Sparta and her allies' not to attack each other μήτε τέχνῃ μήτε μηχανῇ μηδεμιᾷ. Now Thucydides suggests that the raids based on Pylos, hostile landings in parts of the Peloponnese other than Lakonia, and participation in the Mantinea campaign, did not constitute significant breaches of the treaty, whereas an attack on Lakonian territory did (and, as § 2 shows, would have done so even if the Athenians had only contributed a contingent to an Argive force carrying out such an attack). Certainly the raids from Pylos could be regarded as the work of Helots in revolt, an Athenian attack on Corinthian territory could be excused on the grounds that Corinth had refused to be a party to the peace treaty, and even Athenian assistance to Argos could be overlooked—if one really wanted to overlook it—on the grounds that Argos was not an ally at the time of the treaty. Elsewhere, however, Thucydides implies that the Spartans were forbearing in not treating the activity at Pylos as a breach of the treaty, and in vii. 18. 3 he gives Pylos equal weight with the present attack on Lakonia as a cause of the Spartan decision to renew open hostilities in 414/13. But in the same chapter he explains why the Spartans did not

want to fight until their case was unimpeachable: they had a bad con-
science about their aggressive attitude in 431, and thought that their
setbacks were a divine punishment.

2. ἐς Ἐπίδαυρον τὴν Λιμηρὰν καὶ Πρασιάς: Epidauros Limera, not
to be confused with the better-known Epidauros in the Argolid, is the
modern Monemvasia, on the east coast of the eastern 'prong' of the
Peloponnese; Prasiai lay some 60 km. north of it.

καὶ ὅσα ἄλλα: If this is right—and B's ἄλλα ἅττα looks like a banal
correction to remove the difficulty—the analysis must be: 'landing at
Epidauros . . . and ⟨at⟩ all the other places ⟨at⟩ which ⟨they landed⟩
they ravaged the land'.

εὐπροφάσιστον . . . ἐποίησαν: i.e. made it easier for them to make
their grievance public in a form which could not be rebutted on
technical grounds.

3. ἐς τὴν Φλειασίαν: Phleius remained obstinately loyal to Sparta (or,
more properly, hostile to Argos) and was therefore a constant object of
Argive attack; cf. 95. 1.

INDEXES

(All references are to pages of the Introduction and Commentary)

I. TEXT

II. GREEK WORDS

(ii) Corrections and amplifications of LSJ:

III. LANGUAGE AND STYLE

IV. PEOPLE AND PLACES

V. GENERAL